In the Footsteps o
Wege zum Viktori

Studien zur englischen Literatur

herausgegeben von

Prof. Dr. Dieter Mehl

Englisches Seminar der
Rheinischen Friedrich-Wilhelms-Universität, Bonn

Band 15

LIT

In the Footsteps of Queen Victoria: Wege zum Viktorianischen Zeitalter

herausgegeben von
Christa Jansohn

LIT

Bibliografische Information Der Deutschen Bibliothek
Die Deutsche Bibliothek verzeichnet diese Publikation in der Deutschen
Nationalbibliografie; detaillierte bibliografische Daten sind im Internet
über http://dnb.ddb.de abrufbar.

© LIT VERLAG Münster – Hamburg – London   2003
Grevener Str./Fresnostr. 2   48159 Münster
Tel. 0251–23 50 91   Fax 0251–23 19 72
e-Mail: lit@lit-verlag.de   http://www.lit-verlag.de

INHALT

Illustrationen ix

Danksagung xi

Grußwort
SIR PAUL LEVER, BRITISH AMBASSADOR TO GERMANY

Queen Victoria: Symbol einer Epoche 3
CHRISTA JANSOHN

CULTURAL MEMORIES, OR IMAGES OF QUEEN VICTORIA

Consuming Monarchy: The Changing Public Images
of Queen Victoria 41
RALF SCHNEIDER

Victoria, Shakespeare's Second Queen 67
GEORGIANNA ZIEGLER

The Invention of an Empress: Factions and Fictions of Queen
Victoria's Jubilees of 1887 und 1897 as Acts of Cultural Memory 83
VERA NÜNNING and ANSGAR NÜNNING

Der Tod und die Königin: Viktorianischer Totenkult und
Queen Victoria als Witwe 113
FRANZ MEIER

SCIENCE, SOCIETY AND VICTORIAN CULTURE

Christianity, Science and the Victorians: An Introduction 135
BARBARA KORTE

Nur ein viktorianisches Dilemma? *Flatland* zwischen zwei
Wissenschaftstraditionen..153
JÜRGEN MEYER

The Pleasures of Men and the Subjection of Women.............................177
MICHAEL MEYER

Prince Albert und das universitäre Studium in Bonn
und Cambridge 201
FRANZ BOSBACH

Victorian Christmas: or, "What have the Victorians
ever done for us?" 225
KENNETH WYNNE

READING AND WRITING IN VICTORIAN ENGLAND

The Bourgeois Pleasures of a Queen: Late-Victorian Fiction.................239
JULIA KUEHN

Charles Dickens und Queen Victorias England.....................................261
DIETER MEHL

Alice's Adventures in Wonderland: Eine Kuriosität der
viktorianischen Kinderliteratur 279
INGEBORG BOLTZ

Oscar Wilde and Shakespeare's Secrets 301
RUSSELL JACKSON

Off the Beaten Track: Victorian Culture and
the Refashioning of Late Romantic Travel Writing 315
RALPH PORDZIK

Fish and Fetish: Mary Kingsley in West Africa 331
SILVIA MERGENTHAL

Illustrationen

"The Queen's Jubilee Drawing Room", (unnamed artist),
Illustrated London News, 21 May 1887, n.p. 65

"The 'Louis' Velveteen",
Illustrated London News, 23 April 1887, 15. 66

"Prince Albert 'At Home.' When he will sustain (no end of) different
characters"
Punch, 12 (London, 1847), 225. 202

"H.R.H. Field-Marshall Chancellor Prince Albert Taking the Pons
Asinorum. After the Manner of Napoleon Taking the Bridge of Arcola"
Punch, 15 (London, 1848), 225. 219

Danksagung

Der vorliegende Band ist aus einer Ringvorlesung anläßlich des 100. Todesjahres der Königin Viktoria im Wintersemester 2001/2002 am Bamberger Zentrum für Großbritannienstudien hervorgegangen.

Mein Dank gilt allen Beteiligten für ihr engagiertes Interesse an der Vorlesung sowie ihre unkomplizierte und kollegiale Zusammenarbeit bei der Fertigstellung dieses Bandes.

Besonderer Dank gilt Sir Paul Lever, britischer Botschafter in Deutschland, der die Schirmherrschaft über die Vorlesungsreihe übernahm. Danken möchte ich ferner Rosemary Neberle, die den Studierenden auf einer erlebnisreichen Exkursion nach Coburg die "zweite Heimat" der Königin zeigte, während Kenneth Wynne, Lektor an der Universität Bamberg, auf einer weiteren Exkursion nach London die Studierenden nicht nur in die "Victorian Underworld" führte, sondern ihnen mit Witz und Charme auch die weniger sensationellen viktorianischen Stätten näherbrachte.

Für die kritische Durchsicht der Bibliographie bin ich Dr. Sebastian Köppl von der Universitätsbibliothek Bamberg zu Dank verpflichtet.

Ausdrücklicher Dank gebührt auch meinen Mitarbeitern, Oliver Groß, M.A., Mary Reid und Dr. Anne-Julia Zwierlein, für geduldiges Korrekturlesen; besonders danken möchte ich aber Jürgen Krippner, der neben vielen anderen Arbeiten am Zentrum mit viel Sachkenntnis und Ausdauer das Manuskript für den Druck eingerichtet hat.

Bamberg, im August 2002   C. J.

As patron of the lecture series "In the Footsteps of Queen Victoria", may I congratulate all those involved in setting up a varied and successful programme of events.

The theme of Queen Victoria is a good starting point for those wishing to research more deeply into the history of British-German relations. The Centre for British Studies in Bamberg, not too far from her husband Prince Albert's birthplace in Coburg, was ideally placed to take on this task.

This year Queen Elizabeth II celebrates her Golden Jubilee: 50 years on the throne, one of the longest reigns in our history. Queen Victoria's (with 64 years) was of course the longest. So it's tempting to draw comparisons. In both cases a long period of peace (or relative peace) and growing prosperity. As well as the typical British combination of stability and change. And in both cases a Queen's Consort with strong connections to Germany.

But the differences are of course more striking. To many Britons the Victorian age symbolises, perhaps unfairly, class distinction, prudery, old-fashioned manners and the pursuit of empire. The age of our present Queen stands, we like to think, for a more egalitarian, more classless and more tolerant country.

But British achievements in the age of Queen Victoria were remarkable. So the period is well worth studying. Under the excellent supervision of Professor Christa Jansohn, the Centre for British Studies organised a stimulating programme of lectures, as well as excursions to London and, of course, Coburg. I was delighted that so many came to hear my own talk at the Centre on this subject on 31 October 2001 in Bamberg. I particularly enjoyed talking to a number of students afterwards.

May I once again congratulate the Centre for British Studies for organising such an excellent lecture series and wish staff and students every success for the future.

Sir Paul Lever
British Ambassador to Germany

Queen Victoria: Symbol einer Epoche

Von *Christa Jansohn* (Bamberg)

Nach 81 Jahren, sieben Monaten und 29 Tagen verstarb Queen Victoria am 22. Januar 1901, um 6.30 Uhr, im Osborne House, Isle of Wight. 64 Jahre war sie an der Macht und regierte als Königin des Vereinigten Königreiches Großbritannien, Irland und seiner Kolonien und den Dependencen in Europa, Asien, Afrika, Amerika und Australien; gleichzeitig war sie seit 1876 Kaiserin von Indien. Zeitweilig herrschte sie über mehr als eine halbe Milliarde Menschen, die auf einem Gebiet lebten, das hundertmal so groß war wie das Mutterland. Am 22. Januar 1901 hatte jeder vierte Erdenbürger seine Herrscherin verloren und Europa seine "grandmother".[1]

Als die Nachricht von ihrer schweren Erkrankung bekannt wurde, waren die Tage bis zu ihrem Dahinscheiden geprägt von minutiösen Berichterstattungen über den Zustand der Königin sowie von tiefer und achtungsvoller Anteilnahme. So trafen in kurzen Abständen aus dem Ausland eine Reihe von Sympathiebeweisen ein, die – zusammen mit einer detaillierten Beschreibung des Krankheitsverlaufs[2] –, besonders auch in der deutschen Presse ausführlichst behandelt wurden. Im *Coburger Tageblatt* wird dem Leser zum Beispiel mitgeteilt:

> Der Sultan [verlangte], über den Zustand der Königin fortwährend unterrichtet zu werden. – Der Khedive von Egypten hat einen seiner Leiboffiziere zu Lord Cromer gesandt, um diesem sein Bedauern über die Erkrankung der Königin auszudrücken. – Sämmtliche französische Kanadier drückten, wie aus Toronto berichtet wird, ihr Beileid über den ungünstigen Gesundheitszustand der Königin aus. – Die amerikanische Presse, besonders diejenige von New York, sieht in dem engli-

---

[1] Noch heute gehört Queen Victoria zu den hundert bekanntesten Persönlichkeiten in Großbritannien, von denen nur dreizehn weiblichen Geschlechts sind. Vgl. Matt Wells, "The 100 greatest Britons ... lots of pop, not so much circumstance" und "Heroes ... and zeros", *The Guardian*, 22. August 2002, 3.

[2] Vgl. *Coburger Tageblatt*. Generalanzeiger für Stadt und Land, Nr. 19, 16. Jahrgang, Mittwoch, 23. Januar 1901. [Vor-Ausgabe]. Die genaue Krankheitsbeschreibung wird in der heutigen Forschung eher angezweifelt: "Es verlautet aus guter Quelle, daß der plötzliche Wechsel im Befinden der Königin auf einen Schlaganfall zurückzuführen ist. Eine Seite des Gesichts der Königin sowie ihr Sprechvermögen wurden hierdurch in Mitleidenschaft gezogen, auch die Nahrungsaufnahme ist mit großen Schwierigkeiten verbunden. Kurz bevor der Zustand der Bewußtlosigkeit bei der Königin eintrat, verweilte der Prinz von Wales noch eine Viertelstunde allein bei seiner Mutter." (o.S.)

schen Thronfolger, dem Prinzen von Wales, einen Freund der Vereinigten Staa-
ten, [...] Ein ununterbrochener Depeschenwechsel findet zwischen dem Quirinal
und London statt. Der Minister Sonnino erklärte, Italien verliere in der Königin
eine aufrichtige Freundin. [...] Wie aus Kopenhagen mitgeteilt wird, hat der König
längere Zeit geweint, als er die letzten Nachrichten über den Zustand der Königin
erhielt.[1]

Besondere Anteilnahme ging freilich von Deutschland aus, wo Kaiser Wilhelm II., der Enkel der Königin, sofort nach England aufbrach, um am Bett
Victorias zu wachen. Sein Aufenthalt (19. Januar bis 5. Februar) stieß in
der englischen und deutschen Presse auf großes Interesse. Zwar versuchten
einige der Journalisten, diesen spontanen Besuch Wilhelms als politische
Solidaritätserklärung für das vom Burenkrieg gebeutelte England zu deu-
ten, die meisten aber betonten die familiär-emotionale Komponente, wobei
besonders die Boulevardblätter (z.B. *Daily Mail, Morning Post*), aber auch
seriöse Zeitschriften, wie der *Daily Telegraph*, zunächst die Krankenwache
des Kaisers ebenso pathetisch ausschlachteten wie Tage später dessen Rolle
beim Begräbnis der Königin.

Das Ableben Queen Victorias wurde zum inszenierten Medienereignis,
das mit den technischen Errungenschaften der viktorianischen Epoche aufs
engste verwurzelt war. So häuften sich fotografische und zeichnerische
Dokumentationen, die das bewegende Ereignis und dessen Protagonisten
mystifizierten und stilisierten[2], auch wenn die zahlreichen Verluste aus dem
Burenkrieg den "schwülstigen Ton der Nachrufe [konterkarierten], in denen die Dahingeschiedene als Friedensfürstin gepriesen wurde."[3] Mit
Unbehagen und recht verhalten blickte man deshalb in die Zukunft:

> At the close of the reign we are finding ourselves somewhat less secure of our po-
> sition than we could desire, and somewhat less secure abreast of the problems of
> the age than we ought to be, considering the initial advantages we secured.[4]

Der Lobpreis auf das viktorianische Zeitalter schien ein Ende zu haben,
seine Mystifizierung und (Selbst-)Stilisierung sollte anderen Schlagwörtern
weichen. Vor allem aber die beiden Weltkriege veränderten nicht nur die
europäische Landkarte, sondern sie hinterließen auch tiefe Spuren im Be-

---

[1] Ibid.

[2] Vgl. hierzu die materialreiche Abhandlung von Lothar Reinermann, *Der Kaiser in
England. Wilhelm II. und sein Bild in der britischen Öffentlichkeit* (Paderborn, 2001), S.
212-243, bes. S. 218-225.

[3] Ibid., S. 218.

[4] *The Times*, 23. Januar 1901, LA., S. 4, zitiert nach Lothar Reinermann, *a.a.O.*, S.
218.

wußtsein der Menschen. An die alte Völkerfreundschaft zwischen Engländern und Deutschen sollte erst wieder nach 1945 angeknüpft werden können.

Mit 64 Jahren war die Ära Queen Victorias die längste Regierungszeit, die je ein britischer Herrscher erreicht hat. Ihr Name steht für ein ganzes Zeitalter, das mit zahlreichen Legenden und vielen Vorurteilen behaftet ist. So ist lange Zeit die Königin Sinnbild "einer Matrone von lustfeindlicher, moralinsaurer Schicklichkeit, Zurückhaltung und Abstinenz"[1] gewesen, obgleich besonders ihre persönlichen und politischen Briefe und Tagebücher – ein Gesamtwerk von immerhin 700, vielfach noch nicht publizierten Bänden – sie durchaus als leidenschaftlich empfindende, willensstarke und offenherzige Frau zeigen. Daß diese Korrektur ebenfalls Gefahr läuft, lediglich ein Klischee durch ein anderes auszutauschen, liegt freilich auf der Hand.

Ähnliches gilt für die oft überstrapazierten viktorianischen Werte bzw. Leitbegriffe, die in der Forschung gerne verwendet werden, wobei man sie häufig nach geschlechtsspezifischen und/oder kollektiven Begriffen ordnet, so zum Beispiel nach männlichen Normen, "Paternalism", "Gentlemanliness", "Chivalry", "Muscular Christianity", oder nach weiblichen, wie "Angels in the House", "Fallen Women", "New Women" oder nach allgemeinen Selbstbildern, wie "Liberty", "Empire" oder "The White Man's Burden".[2]

Für die Verwendung stereotyper Normen sind freilich Politiker besonders empfänglich. Ein recht junges Beispiel bietet in diesem Kontext Margaret Thatcher, die während ihrer Amtszeit in den angeblich typisch viktorianischen Werten wie Fleiß, Familienleben, Patriotismus und Sparsamkeit den enormen Erfolg des viktorianischen Zeitalters sah und als Leitbilder für die britische Gesellschaft des 20. Jahrhunderts heranziehen wollte. Auch hier fällt die Kritik nicht schwer:

> To behave as though there were a set of Victorian values, fixed and immutable, commanding common assent is profoundly misleading. To preach a return to them is to counsel the impossible.[3]

---

[1] So Kurt Tetzeli von Rosador, "Victorias Disziplinierung des Herzens", in: *Queen Victoria. Ein biographisches Lesebuch*, ed. Kurt Tetzeli von Rosador und Arndt Mersmann (München, 2001), S. 281-301, S. 289.

[2] So Vera Nünning in *Der englische Roman des 19. Jahrhunderts* (Stuttgart, 2000), S. 19. Die stichwortartige Übersicht wird freilich im Laufe ihrer Einführung differenziert.

[3] Eric M. Sigsworth, "Introduction", in: *In Search of Victorian Values. Aspects of Nineteenth-Century Thought and Society*, ed. Eric M. Sigsworth (Manchester, 1988), S. 1-9, S. 1 und 8.

Wie die angeführten Beispiele belegen, wird man deshalb gut daran tun, eine komplexe und differenzierte Sichtweise der Epoche und ihrer Monarchin anzustreben. Was dabei die Charakterisierung Queen Victorias anbelangt, wird man anhand der überlieferten Quellen das gängige Bild der Königin korrigieren können. Allerdings wurden viele der Aufzeichnungen nach ihrem Tod vernichtet oder von ihrer Tochter neu geschrieben, so daß wiederum eine gewisse Einseitigkeit in der Beurteilung die Folge ist. Dennoch wird sich rasch herauskristallisieren, daß Königin Victoria eine Herrscherin war, die ihr Leben stets zwischen Last und Lust, zwischen Sinnenfreude und Trauerorgie, zwischen Pflichterfüllung und Abenteuertum lebte. Nicht die starre Fixierung auf einen der Pole bringt uns dabei die Persönlichkeit näher, sondern die feinen Nuancierungen zwischen ihnen.

Auch von der ganzen Epoche her läßt sich das 19. Jahrhundert nicht einfach auf ein einheitliches und klar strukturiertes "Victorian World Picture" oder "Victorian Frame of Mind" reduzieren[1], vielmehr wird man hier ebenfalls eine Reihe von Differenzierungen vornehmen müssen, um es nicht bei bloßen Schlagwörtern bewenden zu lassen. Eines dieser Schlagwörter ist sicherlich auch die Bezeichnung der viktorianischen Epoche als "age of transition", ein Begriff, der von Matthew Arnold, Thomas Carlyle oder John Stuart Mill benutzt wurde, vor allem aber recht euphorisch von Prinz Albert bei der Eröffnung der Weltausstellung: "... we are living at a period of most wonderful transition ...". Auch hier ist, wie Kurt Tetzeli überzeugend darlegt, die Frage des Standpunktes entscheidend, und "in einer höchst differenzierten, sich im radikalen Umbruch befindenden Klassengesellschaft wie der viktorianischen gab es viele Standpunkte."[2]

Als kleinster gemeinsamer Nenner bleibt bei einer flüchtigen Charakterisierung des viktorianischen Zeitalters festzuhalten, daß keine Epoche zuvor einen vergleichbaren Wandel in Wirtschaft, Politik, Gesellschaft erfahren hatte. Ihre Beurteilung ist allein eine Frage der Perspektive[3], wie dies besonders eindringlich die diversen Überblicke über die viktorianische Literatur zeigen, die einerseits die schreibenden Frauen fast gänzlich auslassen, andererseits die Literatur von Frauen so in den Mittelpunkt stellen, daß durch den "neuen Blick" eine andere Beurteilung der Epoche möglich

---

[1] Vgl. etwa David Newsome, *The Victorian World Picture. Perceptions and Introspections in an Age of Change* (London, 1997), und Walter Houghton, *The Victorian Frame of Mind* (Berkeley, 1957).

[2] Kurt Tetzeli von Rosador, "Viktorianisches Zeitalter", in: *Die englische Literatur*, ed. Bernhard Fabian. Band 1: Epochen – Formen (München, 1991), S. 154-215, S. 156.

[3] Ibid., S. 154.

wird.[1] Diese neuen Blicke sind aber keinesfalls nur als Korrektiv zu verstehen, vielmehr sind sie eine perspektivische Ergänzung anderer, meist traditionell orientierter Betrachtungen.

Mögen die vorliegenden Beiträge weitere Möglichkeiten bieten, dem Leser die verschiedenen Wege in das Zeitalter zu erleichtern, das bekanntlich schon zu Lebzeiten von Zeitgenossen nach der langen Regierungszeit Königin Victorias benannt wurde. Daß nicht alle Perspektiven gezeigt werden können, hängt mit der Komplexität der Epoche zusammen, die eine extensive Behandlung zwischen zwei Buchdeckeln unmöglich macht. Deshalb möchte die Bibliographie einige Lücken schließen und auf weitere Wege ins viktorianische Zeitalter aufmerksam machen.

Viel ist in der vorliegenden Einleitung gemahnt worden, auf die Komplexität der viktorianischen Epoche zu achten und auch die Königin Victoria nicht ausschließlich als Sinnbild von Prüderie und Pflichterfüllung zu sehen. Daß aber diese in unserem Gedächtnis so fest verwurzelten Klischees dennoch wiederum künstlerisch sehr geschickt verarbeitet werden können, soll abschließend das 1973 entstandene Lied "Queen Victoria" von Leonard Cohen zeigen.

Leonard Cohen (geb. 21. September 1934), neben Bob Dylan wohl der größte Songwriter unserer Zeit und letzter Vertreter der Beat-Generation, befaßt sich in diesem Lied ebenfalls mit der Königin. Der Sänger verbindet die uns bekannten stereotypen Vorstellungen mit einem Lobpreis auf die Königin, um durch die Identifikation des Sängers mit Victoria den Verlust seiner eigenen Geliebten leichter zu verschmerzen. Fragend wendet er sich zunächst an die Königin um Hilfe, die durch Moral und Strenge seine ehemalige Geliebte zurechtweisen bzw. ihn trösten könnte, um dann zusammen mit ihr als "two severe giants" die Welt zu irritieren mit ihrem gemeinsamen unvergleichbaren Gefühl des Verlustes. Durch den Verweis, daß beide im selben Jahrhundert leben, fühlt sich der Sänger in seinem unendlichen Schmerz offensichtlich ganz in der Nähe Victorias. Zumindest was seinen Liebesschmerz und seinen Verlust anbelangt, befindet er sich ganz in den "Footsteps" der Königin:

---

[1] Ein gutes Beispiel bietet der Abschnitt von Hans Ulrich Seeber in seiner von ihm herausgegebenen Literaturgeschichte (*Englische Literaturgeschichte* [1991] [Stuttgart, 1999]) im Vergleich zur genderspezifischen Sichtweise von Ina Schabert, *Englische Literaturgeschichte aus der Sicht der Geschlechterforschung* (Stuttgart, 1997).

Queen Victoria

Queen Victoria,
My father and all his tobacco loved you,
I love you too in all your forms.
The slim and lovely virgin floating among German beer,
The mean governess of the huge pink maps,
The solitary mourner of a prince.

Queen Victoria,
I am cold and rainy,
I am dirty as a glass roof in a train station,
I feel like an empty cast iron exhibition,
I want ornaments on everything,
Because my love, she's gone with other boys.

Queen Victoria,
Do you have a punishment under the white lace,
Will you be short with her, will you make her read those little bibles,
Will you spank her with a mechanical corset.
I want her pure as power, I want her skin slightly musty with petticoats
Will you wash the easy bidet out of her head?

Queen Victoria,
I'm not much nourished by modern love,
Will you come into my life
With your sorrow and your black carriages,
And your perfect
Memories.

Queen Victoria,
The Twentieth Century belongs to you and me.
Let us be two severe giants not less lonely for our partnership,
Who discolour test tubes in the halls of Science,
Who turn up unwelcome at every World's Fair,
Heavy with proverbs and corrections,
Confusing the star-dazed tourists
With our incomparable sense of loss.[1]

---

[1] Christof Graf, *Leonard Cohen. Songs of a Life* (München, 2002), S. 131-132. Vgl. auch: http://www.leonardcohensite.com/songs/queen.htm [Zugriff: 22. Juni 2002]. Copyright © 1973 Leonard Cohen and Sony / ATV Music Publishing Canada Company. Der Song ist auf der CD: Leonard Cohen, *Live Songs* (Sony Music Entertainment, 1973).

Auswahlbibliographie

1.   Queen Victoria: Leben, Werk und Rezeption
2.   Geschichte: 1837-1901
3.   Wirtschafts- und Sozialgeschichte
4.   Weltreich und Außenpolitik
5.   Religions-, Kirchen- und Mentalitätsgeschichte
6.   Bildungsgeschichte
7.   Naturwissenschaften
8.   Viktorianische Literatur und Kultur
8.1. Bibliographien
8.2. Literatur und Kultur
8.3. Architektur, Inneneinrichtung und bildende Künste
8.4. Photographie
8.5. Musik
8.6. Theater
8.7. "Material Culture"
8.8. Anthologien
9.   Zeitschriften
10.   Reihen
11.   Websites
12.   Dokumentar- und Spielfilme

1. Queen Victoria: Leben, Werk und Rezeption

Cecil, Algernon, *Queen Victoria and Her Prime Ministers* (New York, 1953).

Charlot, Monica, *Victoria. The Young Queen* (Oxford, 1991).

Duff, David, *Victoria and Albert* (New York, 1972).

Farwell, Byron, *Queen Victoria's Little Wars* (New York, 1972).

Homans, Margaret, *Royal Representations: Queen Victoria and British Culture, 1837-1876* (Chicago, 1998).

Houston, Gail Turley, *Royalties. The Queen and Victorian Writers* (Charlottesville, 1999).

Jaffé, Deborah, *Victoria: A Celebration* (London, 2000).

Longford, Elizabeth, *Queen Victoria: Born to Succeed* (New York, 1964).

The Private Album of Queen Victoria's German Governess Baroness Lehzen, ed. Michaela Blankart und Siegfried-H. Hirsch (Bamberg, 2001).

Queen Victoria in Her Letters and Journals, ed. Christopher Hibbert (New York, 1985).

Queen Victoria 1819-1901. Zum 100. Todesjahr. Katalog zur Sonderausstellung Schloss Callenberg bei Coburg: 1. Mai - 31. Oktober 2001, ed. Ewald Jeutter und Birgit Cleef-Roth (Coburg, 2001).

Remaking Queen Victoria, ed. Margaret Homans and Adrienne Munich (Cambridge, 1997).

Strachey, Lytton, *Queen Victoria* (New York, 1921).

Victoria, Queen, *Leaves from the Journal of Our Life in the Highlands, from 1848 to 1861*: To which are prefixed and added extracts from the same journal giving an account of earlier visits to Scotland, and tours in England and Ireland, and yachting excursions, ed. Arthur Helps (London, 1868).

---, *More Leaves from the Journal of a Life in the Highlands, from 1862 to 1882*, ed. Arthur Helps (London, 1868).

---, *The Letters of Queen Victoria: A Selection from her Majesty's Correspondence between the Years 1837 and 1861*, ed. Arthur C. Benson and Reginald B. Brett (New York, 1907).

---, *The Letters: A Selection from Her Majesty's Correspondence and Journal between the Years 1886 and 1901*, ed. George Earle Buckle. 3 vols. (New York, 1930).

---, *Dearest Child: Letters Between Queen Victoria and the Princess Royal, 1858-1861. A Selection from the Kronberg Archives*, ed. Roger Fulford (London, 1964).

---, *Dearest Mama: Private Correspondence of Queen Victoria and the Crown Princess of Prussia, 1861-1864*, ed. Roger Fulford [1968] (London, 1981).

Weintraub, Stanley, *Victoria: An Intimate Biography* (New York, 1987).

Woodham-Smith, Cecil, *Queen Victoria: Her Life and Times, 1819-1861* (London, 1972).

2. Geschichte: 1837-1901

Bentley, Michael J., *Politics Without Democracy: Great Britain, 1815-1914: Perception and Preoccupation in British Government* (Oxford, 1985).

Briggs, Asa, *The Age of Improvement 1783-1867* [1959] (London, 1979).

Clark, George Kitson, *The Making of Victorian England* [1975] (London, 1991).

Cook, Chris, *The Longman Companion to Britain in the Nineteenth Century 1815-1914* (London, 1999).

Feuchtwanger, Edgar J., *Democracy and Empire, Britain 1865-1914* [1985] (London, 1994).

Halévy, Elie, *A History of the English People in the Nineteenth Century* (rpt. London, 1987).

Harrison, John F.C., *The Early Victorians, 1832-1851* (London, 1971).

Lee, Stephen J., *Aspects of British Political History 1815-1914* (London, 1994).

The Longman Handbook of Modern British History: 1714-2001, ed. Chris Cook and John Stevenson (Harlow, ⁴2001).

Niedhart, Gottfried, *Geschichte Englands im 19. und 20. Jahrhundert* (München, 1987).

Pugh, Martin, *The Making of Modern British Politics 1867-1939* (Oxford, 1982).

Seaman, Lewis C.B., *Victorian England. Aspects of English and Imperial History* 1837-1901 [1973] (London, 1985).

Viktorianisches England in deutscher Perspektive, ed. Adolf M. Birke und Kurt Kluxen (München, 1983).

Wood, Anthony, *Nineteenth Century Britain: 1815-1914* [1960] (Harlow, 1982).

3. Wirtschafts- und Sozialgeschichte

Bailey, Peter, *Leisure and Class in Victorian England* (London, 1978).

The Cambridge Social History of Britain, 1750-1950, ed. Francis M.L. Thompson (Cambridge, 1990).

Davidoff, Leonore and Catherine Hall, *Family Fortunes: Men and Women of the English Middle Class, 1780-1850* [1987] (London, rev. 2002).

The Development of the British Welfare State 1880-1975, ed. James R. Hay (London, 1978).

Englander, David, *Poverty and Poor Law Reform in Nineteenth-Century Britain: From Chadwick to Booth, 1834-1914* (Harlow, 1998).

Foster, John, *Class Struggle and the Industrial Revolution* (London, 1974).

Fox, Alan, *History and Heritage: The Social Origins of the British Industrial Relations System* (London, 1985).

Fraser, Derek, *The Evolution of the British Welfare State. A History of Social Policy Since the Industrial Revolution* [1973] (Basingstoke, 1998).

Harris, José, *Private Lives, Public Spirit: A Social History of Britain, 1870-1914* (Oxford, 1993).

Hopkins, Eric, *A Social History of the English Working Classes* [1979] (London, 1982).

Hunt, Edward H., *British Labour History, 1815-1914* [1981] (London, 1988).

In Search of Victorian Values. Aspects of Nineteeth-Century Thought and Society, ed. Eric M. Sigsworth (Manchester, 1988).

Joby, R.S., *The Railway Builders: Lives and Works of the Victorian Railway Contractors* (Newton Abbot, 1983).

Jones, Eric L., *The Development of English Agriculture, 1815-73* [1968] (London, 1979).

Joyce, Patrick, *Work, Society and Politics. The Culture of the Factory in Later Victorian England* (Brighton, 1980).

Lee, Clive Howard, *The British Economy since 1700: A Macroeconomic Perspective* (Cambridge, 1986).

Mathias, Peter, *The First Industrial Nation: An Economic History of Britain, 1700-1914* [1969] (London, 1993).

Mayhew, Henry, *London Labour and the London Poor* [1849-1850]. Selections Made and Introduced by Victor Neuburg (London, 1985).

Mintz, Steven, *A Prison of Expectations. The Family in Victorian Culture* (New York, 1983).

Musson, Albert E., *British Trade Unions, 1800-1875* [1972] (London, 1983).

---, *The Growth of British Industry* (London, 1978).

Pelling, Henry, *A History of British Trade Unionism* [1963] (Harmondsworth, 1988).

Ransom, Philip J., *The Victorian Railway and How It Evolved* (London, 1990).

Rubinstein, David, *Before the Suffragettes: Women's Emancipation in the 1890s* (Brighton, 1986).

Rule, John, *The Labouring Classes in Early Industrial England: 1750-1850* [1986] (London, 1993).

Shanley, Mary L., *Feminism, Marriage, and the Law in Victorian England, 1850-1895* (Princeton, 1989).

Simmons, Jack, *The Victorian Railway* (London, 1991).

Smelser, Neil J., *Social Change in the Industrial Revolution: An Application of Theory to the British Cotton Industry* [1959] (Aldershot, 1994).

Stedman Jones, G., *Outcast London: A Study in the Relationships between Classes in Victorian Society* (Oxford, 1971).

Suffer and Be Still: Women in the Victorian Age, ed. Martha Vicinus [1972] (Bloomington, 1982).

Tames, Richard, *Economy and Society in Nineteenth-Century Britain* (London, 1972).

Thompson, Edward P., *The Making of the English Working Class* [1963] (Harmondsworth, 1980).

Tosh, John, *A Man's Place: Masculinity and the Middle-Class Home in Victorian England* (New Haven, 1999).

Tranter, Neil L., *Population and Society, 1750-1940. Contrasts in Population Growth* (London, 1985).

---, *Sport, Economy and Society in Britain* (Cambridge, 1998).

Williams, Karel, *From Pauperism to Poverty* (London, 1981).

Wohl, Anthony S., *The Eternal Slum: Housing and Social Policy in Victorian London* (London, 1977).

Women's History: Britain, 1850-1945, ed. June Purvis [1995] (London, 1997).

4. Weltreich und Außenpolitik

Bodelsen, Carl A., *Studies in Mid-Victorian Imperialism* [1924] (New York, 1968).

Bourne, Kenneth, *The Foreign Policy of Victorian England, 1830-1902* (Oxford, 1970).

Britain Pre-Eminent: Studies of British World Influence in the Nineteenth Century, ed. Christopher J. Bartlett (New York, 1969).

Cain, Peter J. and Antony G. Hopkins, *British Imperialism: Innovation and Expansion, 1688-1914* [1993] (London, 1997).

Cain, Peter J., *Economic Foundations of British Overseas Expansion 1815-1914* [1980] (Basingstoke, 1986).

Chamberlain, Muriel E., *The Longman Companion to the Formation of the European Empires: 1488-1920* (Harlow, 2000).

---, *'Pax Britannica'?: British Foreign Policy, 1789-1914* [1988] (London, 1993).

Cottrell, Philip L., *British Overseas Investment in the Nineteenth Century* (London, 1975).

Davis, Lance E., and Robert A. Huttenback, *Mammon and the Pursuit of Empire: The Political Economy of British Imperialism, 1860-1912* (Cambridge, 1986).

Hayes, Paul, *The Nineteenth Century, 1814-80* (London, 1975).

Hobsbawm, Eric J., *The Age of Empire 1875-1914* (London, 1987).

Hyam, Ronald, *Britain's Imperial Century, 1815-1914: A Study of Empire and Expansion* [1976] (Basingstoke, 1995).

Joll, James, *Britain and Europe: Pitt to Churchill, 1793-1940* (London, 1950).
The Oxford History of the British Empire. The Nineteenth Century, ed. Andrew Porter (Oxford, 1999).
Pakenham, Thomas, *The Boer War* [1979] (London, 1997).
Platt, Desmond C., *Finance, Trade and Politics: British Foreign Policy, 1815-1914* (Oxford, 1968).
Porter, Bernard, *The Lion's Share. A Short History of British Imperialism* 1850-1983 [1975] (London, 1996).
Robinson, Ronald and John Gallagher, *Africa and the Victorians: The Official Mind of Imperialism* (London, 1961).
Semmel, Bernard, *The Rise of Free Trade Imperialism: Classical Political Economy. The Empire of Free Trade and Imperialism, 1750-1850* [1970] (Cambridge, 1978).
Seton-Watson, Robert W., *Britain in Europe, 1789-1914. A Survey of Foreign Policy* [1938] (New York, 1968).
Taylor, Alan J.P., *The Struggle for Mastery in Europe, 1848-1918* [1954] (Oxford, 1977).
Thompson, Andrew S., *Imperial Britain. The Empire in British Politics c. 1880-1932* (Harlow, 2000).

5. Religions-, Kirchen- und Mentalitätsgeschichte

Armstrong, Anthony, *The Church of England, the Methodists and Society, 1700-1850* (London, 1973).
Arnstein, Walter, "Recent Studies in Victorian Religion", *Victorian Studies*, 33 (1989), 149-175.
Bebbington, David W., *Evangelicalism in Modern Britain: A History from the 1730s to the 1980s* [1989] (London, 1995).
---, *The Nonconformist Conscience. Chapel and Politics 1870-1914* (London, 1982).
Best, Geoffrey, *Mid-Victorian Britain, 1851-75* [1971] (London, 1985).
Bowen, Desmond, *The Idea of the Victorian Church: A Study of the Church of England 1833-1889* (Montreal, 1968).
Brown, Stewart Jay, *The National Churches of England, Ireland, and Scotland, 1801-1846* (Oxford, 2001).
Burn, William Laurence, *The Age of Equipoise. A Study of the Mid-Victorian Generation* (London, 1964).
Chadwick, Owen, *The Victorian Church*. 2 vols. (London, 1966 and 1970).

Church and State in Britain since 1820, ed. David Nicholls (London, 1967).

Davies, Horton, *Worship and Theology in England*, 5 vols. (Princeton, 1961-1975), Vol. 3: *From Watts and Wesley to Maurice, 1690-1850.* Vol. 4: *From Newman to Martineau.*

Gilbert, Alan D., *Religion and Society in Industrial England: Church, Chapel and Social Change 1740-1914* [1976] (London, 1984).

Hilton, Boyd, *The Age of Atonement: The Influence of Evangelicalism on Social and Economic Thought* (Oxford, 1988).

Heyck, Thomas W., *The Transformation of Intellectual Life in Victorian England* (New York, 1982).

Houghton, Walter E., *The Victorian Frame of Mind: 1830-1870* (New Haven, 1957).

Inglis, Kenneth S., *Churches and the Working Classes in Victorian England* [1963] (London, 1974).

Jay, Elizabeth, *The Religion of the Heart: Anglican Evangelicalism and the Nineteenth-Century Novel* (Oxford, 1979).

Krueger, Christine, *The Reader's Repentance: Women Preachers, Women Writers, and Nineteenth-Century Social Discourse* (Chicago, 1992).

Larsen, Timothy, *Friends of Religious Equality: Nonconformist Politics in Mid-Victorian England* (Woodbridge, 1999).

Moore, James R., *The Post-Darwinian Controversies* (Cambridge, 1979).

Newsome, David, *The Victorian World Picture: Perceptions and Introspections in an Age of Change* (London, 1997).

Norman, Edward, *The Victorian Christian Socialists* (Cambridge, 1987).

Religion and Irreligion in Victorian Society. Essays in Honour of R.K. Webb, ed. Richard W. Davis and R.J. Helmstadter (London, 1992).

Religion and Revolution in Early Industrial England: The Halévy Thesis and Its Critics, ed. Gerald Wayne Olsen (Lanham, MD, 1990).

Robertson, John M., *A History of Freethought in the Nineteenth Century* (London, 1929).

Royle, Edward, *Victorian Infidels: The Origins of the British Secularist Movement, 1791-1866* (Manchester, 1974).

Tamke, Susan S., *Make a Joyful Noise unto the Lord: Hymns as a Reflection of Victorian Social Attitudes* (Athens, 1978).

Victorian Values. Personalities and Perspectives in an Age of Change, ed. Gordon Marsden (London, 1990).

Walls, Frank H., *Popular Anti-Catholicism in Mid-Victorian Britain* (Lewiston, 1993).

Ward, William R., *Religion and Society in England, 1790-1850* (London, 1972).

Yates, Nigel, *The Oxford Movement and Anglican Ritualism* (London, 1983).

Zemka, Sue, *Victorian Testaments: The Bible, Christology, and Literary Authority in Early-Nineteenth-Century British Culture* (Stanford, 1997).

6. Bildungsgeschichte

Anderson, Robert D., *Education and Opportunity in Victorian Scotland: Schools & Universities* (Oxford, 1983).

---, *Universities and Elites in Britain since 1800* (Basingstoke, 1992).

Bamford, Thomas W., *Rise of the Public Schools: A Study of Boys' Public Schools in England and Wales from 1837 to the Present Day* (London, 1967).

Children, School and Society in Nineteenth Century England, ed. Anne Digby and Peter Searby (London, 1981).

Dent, Harold C., *1870-1970: A Century of Growth in English Education* (London, 1970).

The History of the University of Oxford, ed. T.H. Aston. Vol. 7: *Nineteenth-Century Oxford*, ed. M.G. Brock and M.C. Curthoys (Oxford, 2000).

Kamm, Josephine, *Hope Deferred: Girls' Education in English History* (London, 1965).

Lawson, John and Harold Silver, *A Social History of Education in England* (London, 1978).

Layton, David, *Science for the People: The Origins of the School Science Curriculum in England* (New York, 1979).

Mangan, James A., *Athleticism in the Victorian and Edwardian Public School: The Emergence and Consolidation of an Educational Ideology* [1981] (London, 2000).

Murphy, James, *Church, State and School in Britain, 1800-1970* (London, 1971).

Sanderson, Michael, *Education, Economic Change and Society in England: 1780-1870* (London, 1983).

Searby, Peter, *A History of the University of Cambridge*. Vol. 3: 1750-1870 (Cambridge, 1997).

7. Naturwissenschaften

Barber, Lynn, *The Heyday of Natural History, 1820-1870* (London, 1980).

Buchanan, Robert A., *The Power of the Machine: The Impact of Technology from 1700 to the Present Day* (London, 1994).

Bynum, William F., *Science and the Practice of Medicine in the Nineteenth Century* (Cambridge, 1994).

Cannon, Susan F., *Science in Culture: The Early Victorian Period* (New York, 1978).

Cosslett, Tess, *The "Scientific Movement" and Victorian Literature* (London, 1982).

Digby, Anne, *Making a Medical Living: Doctors and Patients in the English Market for Medicine, 1720-1911* (Cambridge, 1994).

Evangelicals and Science in Historical Perspective, ed. David N. Livingstone, D.G. Hart and Mark Noll (New York, 1999).

Gillispie, Charles Coulston, *Genesis and Geology: A Study in the Relations of Scientific Thought, Natural Theology, and Social Opinion in Great Britain, 1790-1850* [1951] (Harvester, 1996).

Haley, Bruce, *The Healthy Body and Victorian Culture* (Cambridge, 1978).

Hartley, Lucy, *Physiognomy and the Meaning of Expression in Nineteenth-Century Culture* (Cambridge, 2001).

Himmelfarb, Gertrude, *Darwin and the Darwinian Revolution* (New York, 1962).

Irvine, William, *Apes, Angels, and Victorians: Darwin, Huxley, and Evolution* (New York, 1955).

Knight, David, *The Age of Science: The Scientific World-View in the Nineteenth Century* (Oxford, 1986).

Lightman, Bernard, *The Origins of Agnosticism: Victorian Unbelief and the Limits of Knowledge* (Baltimore, 1987).

Literature and Science in the Nineteenth Century. An Anthology, ed. with an Introduction and Notes by Laura Otis (Oxford, 2002).

Loudon, Irvine, *Medical Care and the General Practitioner 1750-1850* (Oxford, 1986).

Mackenzie, Donald, *Statistics in Britain, 1865-1930: The Social Construction of Scientific Knowledge* (Edinburgh, 1981).

Morrell, Jack, *Science, Culture and Politics in Britain: 1750-1870* (Aldershot, 1997).

Morton, Peter, *The Vital Science: Biology and the Literary Imagination, 1860-1900* (London, 1984).

Newman, Charles, *The Evolution of Medical Education in the Nineteenth Century* (London, 1957).

Pelling, Margaret, *Cholera, Fever and English Medicine, 1825-1865* (Oxford, 1978).

Peterson, M. Jeanne, *The Medical Profession in Mid-Victorian London* (London, 1978).

Porter, Roy, *Health for Sale: Quackery in England 1660-1850* (Manchester, 1989).

Porter, Theodore M., *The Rise of Statistical Thinking: 1820-1900* (Princeton, 1986).

Russell, Colin A., *Science and Social Change: 1700-1900* (London, 1983).

Richards, Robert J., *The Meaning of Evolution: The Morphological Construction and Ideological Reconstruction of Darwin's Theory* (Chicago, 1992).

Rylance, Rick, *Victorian Psychology and British Culture: 1850-1880* (Oxford, 2000).

Sass, Louis, *Madness and Modernism* (Cambridge, Mass., 1992).

Science and Religion in the Nineteenth Century, ed. Tess Cosslett (Cambridge, 1984).

Scull, Andrew T., *Madhouses, Mad-Doctors and Madmen: The Social History of Psychiatry in the Victorian Era* (Philadelphia, 1981).

---, *The Most Solitary of Afflictions: Madness and Society in Britain, 1700-1900* (New Haven, 1993).

Turner, Frank Miller, *Between Science and Religion: The Reaction to Scientific Naturalism in Late Victorian England* (New Haven, 1974).

Victorian Science in Context, ed. Bernard Lightman (Chicago, 1997).

Young, Robert, *Darwin's Metaphor: Nature's Place in Victorian Culture* (Cambridge, 1985).

8. Viktorianische Literatur und Kultur

8.1. Bibliographien

Altick, Richard D. and William R. Matthews, *Guide to Doctoral Dissertations in Victorian Literature: 1886-1958* (Westport, 1973).

British Short Fiction Writers: 1880-1914; The Realist Tradition, ed. William B. Thesing (Detroit, 1994).

A Checklist of Women Writers, 1801-1900: Fiction – Verse – Drama. Comp. Robin C. Alston (London, 1990).

Nineteenth Century Short Title Catalogue, series I, phase I, 1801-1815, 6 vols.; series II, phase I, 1816-1870, 55 vols. (Newcastle-upon-Tyne, 1986).

Storey, Richard, *Primary Sources for Victorian Studies: A Guide to the Location and Use of Unpublished Materials* (London, 1977).

---, *Primary Sources for Victorian Studies: An Updating* (Leicester, 1987).

Wolff, Robert Lee, *Nineteenth Century Fiction: A Bibliographical Catalogue Based on the Collection Formed by Robert Lee Wolff* (New York, 1985).

8.2. Literatur und Kultur

Altick, Richard D., *The English Common Reader: A Social History of the Mass Reading Public, 1800-1900* (Chicago, 1957).

---, *The Present of the Present. Topics of the Day in the Victorian Novel* (Columbus, 1991).

---, *'Punch': The Lively Youth of a British Institution, 1841-1851* (Columbus, 1997).

---, *Writers, Readers, and Occasions: Selected Essays on Victorian Literature and Life* (Columbus, 1989).

Antor, Heinz, *Der englische Universitätsroman: Bildungskonzepte und Erziehungsziele* (Heidelberg, 1996).

Archibald, Diana C., *Domesticity, Imperialism, and Emigration in the Victorian Novel* (Columbia, 2002).

Armstrong, Isobel, *Victorian Poetry. Poetry, Poetics and Politics* (London, 1993).

Bailin, Miriam, *The Sickroom in Victorian Fiction. The Art of Being Ill* (Cambridge, 1994).

Beer, Gillian, *Darwin's Plots: Evolutionary Narrative in Darwin, George Eliot and Nineteenth-Century Fiction*. Second Edition [1983] (Cambridge, 2000).

Booth, Michael R. et al., *1750-1880* (1975), vol. 6 in: *The Revels History of Drama in English*, ed. L. Potter et al. (London, 1975-83).

Bown, Nicola, *Fairies in Nineteenth-Century Art and Literature* (Cambridge, 2001).

Briggs, Asa, *Victorian People. A Reassessment of Persons and Themes, 1851-67*. Revised edition [1965] (London, 1990).

Buckley, Jerome Hamilton, *The Victorian Temper. A Study in Literary Culture* (London, 1952).

Byerly, Alison, *Realism, Representation, and the Arts in Nineteenth-Century Literature* (Cambridge, 1997).

A Companion to the Victorian Novel, ed. William Baker (Westport, 2002).

The Cambridge Companion to the Victorian Novel, ed. Deirdre David (Cambridge, 2001).

Childers, Joseph W., *Novel Possibilities. Fiction and the Formation of Early Victorian Culture* (Philadelphia, 1995).

Cockshut, Anthony Oliver J., *The Art of Autobiography in 19th- and 20th-Century England* (New Haven, 1984).

Cohen, Monica F., *Professional Domesticity in the Victorian Novel: Women, Work, and Home* (Cambridge, 1998).

Correa, Delia da Sousa, *George Eliot, Music and Victorian Culture* (Houndmills, 2002).

A Companion to Victorian Poetry, ed. Richard Cronin (Oxford, 2002).

Cronin, Richard, *Romantic Victorians: English Literature, 1824-1840* (Basingstoke, 2002).

Dennis, Barbara, *The Victorian Novel* (Cambridge, 2000).

Dillon, Steven C., *Late Nineteenth-Century English and American Literature* (Austin, Texas, 1990).

Dolin, Kieran, *Fiction and the Law. Legal Discourse in Victorian and Modernist Literature* (Cambridge, 1999).

Douglas-Fairhurst, Robert, *Victorian Afterlives: The Shaping of Influence in Nineteenth-Century Literature* (Oxford, 2002).

The Early and Mid-Victorian Novel, ed. David Skilton (London, 1993).

Englische Literatur zwischen Viktorianismus und Moderne, ed. Paul Goetsch (Darmstadt, 1983).

Feldmann, Doris, *Politik und Fiktion. Die Anfänge des politischen Romans in Großbritannien im 19. Jahrhundert* (München, 1995).

Flint, Kate, *The Woman Reader, 1837-1914* (Oxford, 1993).

---, *The Victorians and the Visual Imagination* (Cambridge, 2000).

Fraser, Hilary and Daniel Brown, *English Prose of the Nineteenth Century* (London, 1996).

Frawley, Maria H., *A Wider Range. Travel Writing by Women in Victorian England* (London, 1994).

Gilbert, Sandra M. and Susan Gubar, *The Madwoman in the Attic: The Woman Writer and the Nineteenth-Century Literary Imagination* (New Haven, 1979).

Gilmour, Robin, *The Novel in the Victorian Age: A Modern Introduction* (London, 1986).

---, *The Victorian Period. The Intellectual and Cultural Context of English Literature: 1830-1890* (London, 1993).

Goetsch, Paul, *Die Romankonzeption in England 1880-1910* (Heidelberg, 1967).

Green, Laura Morgan, *Educating Women: Cultural Conflict and Victorian Literature* (Athens, 2001).

Griest, Guinevere L., *Mudie's Circulating Library and the Victorian Novel* (Bloomington, 1970).

Gutleben, Christian, *Nostalgic Postmodernism: The Victorian Tradition and the Contemporary British Novel* (Amsterdam, 2001).

Guy, Josephine M., *The Victorian Social-Problem Novel. The Market, the Individual and Communal Life* (Houndmills, 1996).

Harrison, Antony H., *Victorian Poets and the Politics of Culture. Discourse and Ideology* (Charlottesville, 1998).

Harvey, John Robert, *Victorian Novelists and Their Illustrators* (London, 1970).

Hewitt, Douglas, *English Fiction of the Early Modern Period. 1890-1940* (London, 1988).

Hönnighausen, Lothar, *Grundprobleme der englischen Literaturtheorie des 19. Jahrhunderts* (Darmstadt, 1977).

---, *The Symbolist Tradition in English Literature. A Study of Pre-Raphaelitism and Fin de Siècle* (Cambridge, 1988).

Horsman, Alan, *The Victorian Novel* (Oxford, 1990).

Huberman, Jeffrey H., *Late Victorian Farce* (Ann Arbor, Mich., 1986).

Hughes, Winifred, *The Maniac in the Cellar: Sensation Novels of the 1860s* (Princeton, 1980).

Keating, Peter John, *The Working Classes in Victorian Fiction* (London, 1971).

Literature in the Marketplace: Nineteenth-Century British Publishing and the Circulation of Books, ed. John O. Jordan and Robert L. Pattern (Cambridge, 1995).

Knowing the Past: Victorian Literature and Culture, ed. Suzy Anger (Ithaca, 2001).

Landow, George P., *Victorian Types, Victorian Shadows: Biblical Typology in Victorian Literature, Art and Thought* (London, 1980).

Langland, Elizabeth, *Telling Tales: Gender and Narrative Form in Victorian Literature and Culture* (Columbus, 2002).

Ledger, Sally, *The New Woman: Fiction and Feminism at the Fin de Siècle* (Manchester, 1997).

Leighton, Angela, *Victorian Women Poets: Writing Against the Heart* (Charlottesville, 1992).

Logan, Thad, *The Victorian Parlour. A Cultural Study* (Cambridge, 2002).

Marchand, Leslie A., *The Athenaeum. A Mirror of Victorian Culture* [1941] (New York, 1971).

McDonald, Peter D., *British Literary Culture and Publishing Practice, 1880-1914* (Cambrige, 1997).

Miller, Andrew H., *Novels Behind Glass. Commodity Culture and Victorian Narrative* (Cambridge, 1995).

Müllenbrock, Heinz-Joachim, *Der historische Roman des 19. Jahrhunderts* (Heidelberg, 1980).

Nachbaur, Uta B., *Mythos als Maskenspiel: Studien zum Frauenbild in der englischen Literatur der 'Nineties'* (Münster, 1994).

The Nineteenth-Century Novel: A Critical Reader, ed. Stephen Regan (London, 2001).

The Nineteenth-Century Novel: Identities, ed. Dennis Walder (London, 2001).

The Nineteenth-Century Novel: Realisms, ed. Delia da Sousa Correa (London, 2000).

Die 'Nineties'. Das Englische Fin de Siècle zwischen Dekadenz und Sozialkritik, ed. Manfred Pfister und Bernd Schulte-Middelich (München, 1983).

Nünning, Vera, *Der englische Roman des 19. Jahrhunderts* (Stuttgart, 2000).

Peterson, Linda H., *Victorian Autobiography. The Tradition of Self-Interpretation* (New Haven, 1986).

Pordzik, Ralph, *Der englische Roman im 19. Jahrhundert* (Berlin, 2001).

Pykett, Lyn, *The "Improper" Feminine. The Women's Sensation Novel and the New Woman Writing* (London, 1992).

A Reader's Guide to the Nineteenth-Century English Novel, ed. Julia Prewitt Brown (New York, 1985).

Rereading Victorian Fiction, ed. Alice Jenkins and Juliet John (Houndmills, 2000).

Richards, Bernard, *English Poetry of the Victorian Period. 1830-1890* [1988] (Harlow, 2001).

Russell, Norman, *The Novelist and the World of Mammon: Literary Responses to the World of Commerce in the Nineteenth Century* (Oxford, 1986).

Schabert, Ina, "Die Viktorianische Epoche", in: Dies., *Englische Literaturgeschichte aus der Sicht der Geschlechterforschung* (Stuttgart, 1997), S. 471-611.

Scheinberg, Cynthia, *Women's Poetry and Religion in Victorian England* (Cambridge, 2002).

Schramm, Jan-Melissa, *Testimony and Advocacy in Victorian Law, Literature and Theology* (Cambridge, 2000).

Silver, Anna Krugovoy, *Victorian Literature and the Anorexic Body* (Cambridge, 2002).

Small, Helen, *Love's Madness: Medicine, the Novel, and Female Insanity, 1800-1865* (Oxford, 1996).

Stang, Richard, *The Theory of the Novel in England 1850-1870* (London, 1959).

Stonyk, Margaret, *Nineteenth Century English Literature* (London, 1983).

Sutherland, John A., *The Longman Companion to Victorian Fiction* (London, 1988).

Tery, Reginald C., *Victorian Popular Fiction, 1860-1880* (London, 1983).

Tetzeli, Kurt von Rosador, "Viktorianisches Zeitalter", in: *Die englische Literatur*. Band 1: Epochen, ed. Bernhard Fabian (München, 1991), S. 154-215.

Trodd, Anthea, *Domestic Crime in the Victorian Novel* (New York, 1989).

Turner, Martha A., *Mechanism and the Novel: Science in the Narrative Process* (Cambridge, 1993).

Turner, Paul, *Victorian Poetry, Drama, and Miscellaneous Prose 1832-1890* (Oxford, 1989).

Victorian Fiction: A Second Guide to Research, ed. George H. Ford (New York, 1978).

Victorian Literature and Society: Essays Presented to Richard D. Altick, ed. James R. Kincaid (Columbus, 1984).

The Victorian Novel, ed. Francis O'Gorman (Oxford, 2002).

The Victorian Novel, ed. Ian Watt (London, 1971).

Victorian Parlour Games. Compiled by Patrick Beaver [1974] (Wigston, 1995).

Victorian Prose: A Guide to Research, ed. David J. DeLaura (New York, 1973).

The Victorian Vision. Inventing New Britain, ed. John M. MacKenzie (London, 2001).

Weliver, Phyllis, *Women Musicians in Victorian Fiction, 1860-1900: Representations of Music, Science and Gender in the Leisured Home* (Hampshire, 2000).

Werlin, Robert J., *The English Novel and the Industrial Revolution: A Study in the Sociology of Literature* (New York, 1990).

Wheeler, Michael, *The Art of Allusion in Victorian Fiction* (London, 1979).

---, *English Fiction of the Victorian Period 1830-1890* (London, 1985).

Wiesenthal, Chris, *Figuring Madness in Nineteenth-Century Fiction* (New York, 1997).

Willey, Basil, *More Nineteenth Century Studies: A Group of Honest Doubters* (New York, 1973).

---, *Nineteenth Century Studies. Coleridge to Matthew Arnold* [1950] (Harmondsworth, 1964).

Williams, Raymond, *Culture and Society 1780-1950* [1958] (New York, 1983).

---, *The English Novel from Dickens to Lawrence* (London, 1970).

Women and Literature in Britain 1800-1900, ed. Joanne Shattock (Cambridge, 2001).

The Women Question: Society and Literature in Britain and America, 1837-1883, ed. Elizabeth K. Helsinger and Robin L. Sheets. 3 vols. (Manchester, 1983).

Wynne, Deborah, *The Sensation Novel and the Victorian Family Magazine* (Basingstoke, 2001).

Young, Arlene, *Culture, Class and Gender in the Victorian Novel* (Basingstoke, 1999).

Young, George M., *Victorian England. Portrait of an Age* [1939] (Oxford, 1983).

---, *Victorian Essays*, ed. William D. Handcock (London, 1962).

8.3. Architektur, Inneneinrichtung und bildende Künste

Amery, Colin, *Victorian Buildings of London 1837-1887* (London, 1980).

Bell, Quentin, *Victorian Artists* (London, 1967).

Bendiner, Kenneth, *An Introduction to Victorian Painting* (New Haven, 1985).

Burton, Anthony, *Vision and Accident: The Story of the Victoria and Albert Museum* (London, 1999).

Cooper, Jeremy, *Victorian and Edwardian Furniture and Interiors. From the Gothic Revival to Art Nouveau* (London, 1990).

Cooper, Nicholas, *The Opulent Eye. Late Victorian and Edwardian Taste in Interior Design* (London, 1976).

Crimson, Mark, *Empire Building. Orientalism and Victorian Architecture* (London, 1996).

Dixon, Roger and Stefan Muthesius, *Victorian Architecture* [1978] (London, 1997).

Eastlake, Charles, *History of the Gothic Revival* [1872] (London, 1978).

Edwards, Clive D., *Victorian Furniture: Technology and Design* (Manchester, 1993).

Exposed. The Victorian Nude, ed. Alison Smith (London, 2001).

Gere, Charlotte, *Nineteenth-Century Decoration. The Art of the Interior* (London, 1989).

Girouard, Mark, *The Victorian Country House* (London, 1979).

Jenkyns, Richard, *Dignity and Decadence: Victorian Art and the Classical Inheritance* (London, 1992).

Lambourne, Lionel, *Victorian Painting* (London, 1999).

Millar, Delia, *Views of Germany from the Royal Collection at Windsor Castle. Queen Victoria and Prince Albert on their Journeys to Coburg and Gotha*. Exhibition catalogue [5. April - 5. Juli 1998, Veste Coburg] (Windsor, 1998).

Muthesius, Stefan, *The High Victorian Movement in Architecture 1850-1870* (London, 1972).

Orbach, Julian, *Blue Guide: Victorian Architecture in Britain* (London, 1987).

The Pre-Raphaelites. Tate Gallery Exhibition. Introduced by Alan Bowness (London, 1984).

Read, Benedict, *Victorian Sculpture* (New Haven, 1982).

Steegman, John, *Victorian Taste. A Study of the Arts and Architecture from 1830 to 1870*. With a Foreword by Nikolaus Pevsner [1950] (Cambridge, 1970).

Strong, Roy, *And When Did You Last See Your Father?: The Victorian Painter and British History* (London, 1978).

Summerson, John Newenham, *Victorian Architecture: Four Studies in Evaluation* (New York, 1970).

Symonds, Robert W. and B.B. Whineray, *Victorian Furniture* [1962] (London, 1987).

8.4. Photographie

British Photography in the Nineteenth Century, ed. Mike Weaver (Cambridge, 1989).

Gernsheim, Helmut, *Masterpieces of Victorian Photography* (London, 1951).

The Golden Age of British Photography: 1839-1900. Photographs from the Victoria and Albert Museum, London, ... [an exhibition ... Victoria and Albert Museum, London, 6 June - 19 August 1984], ed. and introduced by Mark Haworth-Booth (Millerton, 1984).

Smith, Lindsay, *Victorian Photography, Painting and Poetry. The Enigma of Visibility in Ruskin, Morris and the Pre-Raphaelites* (Cambridge, 1995).

Turner, Benjamin Brecknell, *Rural England Through a Victorian Lens*, ed. Martin Barnes, Mark Haworth-Booth, Malcolm Daniel (London, 2001).

Victorian and Edwardian Country-House Life from Old Photographs, ed. Anthony J. Lambert (London, 1981).

Victorian Life in Photographs. Photographic Research by Harold Chapman (London, 1974).

Victorian London Street Life in Historic Photographs, ed. John Thompson. [Nachdruck der Ausgabe von London 1877] (New York, 1994).

A Victorian Portrait: Victorian Life and Values as Seen Through the Work of Studio Photographers, ed. Asa Briggs and Archie Miles (New York, 1989).

8.5. Musik

Bailey, Peter, *Popular Culture and Performance in the Victorian City* (Cambridge, 1998).

Bradley, Ian, *Abide With Me: The World of the Victorian Hymn* (London, 1997).

British Music Hall 1840-1923. A Bibliography and Guide to Sources, with a Supplement on European Music-Hall, ed. Laurence Senelick, David F. Cheshire and Ulrich Schneider (Hamden, 1981).

Busby, Roy, *British Music Hall: An Illustrated Who's Who from 1850 to the Present Day* (London, 1976).

Cheshire, David F., *Music Hall in Britain* (Newton Abbot, 1974).

Disher, Maurice W., *Victorian Song: From Dive to Drawing Room. Decorated with "fronts" from Ballads and Piano Pieces* (London, 1955).

Felstead, S. Theodore, *Stars Who Made the Halls* (London, 1946).

Gatens, William J., *Victorian Cathedral Music in Theory and Practice* (Cambridge, 1986).

Haill, Catherine, *Victorian Illustrated Music Sheets* (London, 1981).

Kift, Dagmar, *Arbeiterkultur im gesellschaftlichen Konflikt: Die englische Music Hall im 19. Jahrhundert* (Essen, 1991).

---, *The Victorian Music Hall: Culture, Class and Conflict* (Cambridge, 1996).

Kilgarriff, Michael, *Grace, Beauty and Banjos: Peculiar Lives and Strange Times of Music Hall and Variety Artists* (London, 1998).

The Last Empires: A Music Hall Companion, ed. Benny Green (London, 1986).

LeRoy, George, *Music Hall Stars of the Nineties* (London, 1952).

MacInnes, Colin, *Sweet Saturday Night. Pop Song 1840-1920* (London, 1967).

Mander, Raymond and Joe Mitchenson, *British Music Hall* (London, 1974).

Mohn, Barbara, *Das englische Oratorium im 19. Jahrhundert: Quellen, Traditionen, Entwicklungen* (Paderborn, 2000).

Music Hall: The Business of Pleasure, ed. Peter Bailey (Milton Keynes, 1986).

Music Hall: Performance & Style, ed. J.S. Bratton (Milton Keynes, 1986).

Read, Jack, *Empires, Hippodromes & Palaces* (London, 1985).

Musical Settings of Early and Mid-Victorian Literature: A Catalogue, ed. Bryan N.S. Gooch and David S. Thatcher (New York, 1979).

Musical Settings of Late Victorian Literature and Modern British Literature: A Catalogue, ed. Bryan N.S. Gooch and David S. Thatcher (New York, 1976).

Schneider, Ulrich, *Die Londoner Music Hall 1850-1920* (Tübingen, 1983).

Tavern Singing in Early Victorian London, ed. Laurence Senelick (London, 1997).

8.6. Theater

Booth, Michael R., *Theatre in the Victorian Age* [1991] (Cambridge, 1999).

---, *Victorian Spectacular Theatre 1850-1910* (Boston, 1981).

British Theatre in the 1890s. Essays on Drama and the Stage, ed. Richard Foulkes (Cambridge, 1992).

The Cambridge Companion to Victorian and Edwardian Theatre, ed. Kerry Powell (Cambridge, 2002).

Jackson, Allan S., *The Standard Theatre of Victorian England* (Rutherford, 1993).

Jenkins, Anthony, *The Making of Victorian Drama* (Cambridge, 1991).

Powell, Kerry, *Women and Victorian Theatre* (Cambridge, 1997).

Rowell, George, *The Victorian Theatre. 1792-1914: A Survey* [1967] (Cambridge, 1978).

Schoch, Richard W., *Shakespeare's Victorian Stage: Performing History in the Theatre of Charles Kean* (Cambridge, 1998).

Taylor, George, *Players and Performances in the Victorian Theatre* (Manchester, 1989).

Victorian Theatre, ed. Russell Jackson (London, 1989).

Vlock, Deborah, *Dickens, Novel Reading, and the Victorian Popular Theatre* (Cambridge, 1998).

8.7. "Material Culture"

Anything Shows: Victorian Material Culture with contributions on gen- dered, classified, and colonized singular and mass-produced objects and their representations, private and public exhibitions, realist and fantasy literature, ed. Kurt Tetzeli von Rosador, *Journal for the Study of British Cultures*, 8:2 (2001), 113-235.

Berriedale-Johnson, Michelle, *The Victorian Cookbook* (London, 1989).

Cocoa & Corsets: A Selection of Late Victorian and Edwardian Posters and Showcards, ed. Michael Jubb (London, 1984).

The Crystal Palace Exhibition. Illustrated Catalogue: London (1851). An unabridged republication of the Art-Journal Special Issue. Over 1500 Illustrations with a new introduction by John Gloag F.S.A. (New York, 1970).

Hughes, George B., *Victorian Pottery and Porcelain* (London, 1959).

Mersmann, Arndt, *'A True Test and a Living Picture'. Repräsentationen der Londoner Weltausstellung von 1851* (Trier, 2001).

Richards, Thomas, *The Commodity Culture of Victorian England: Advert- ising and Spectacle, 1851-1914* (Stanford, 1990).

Wardle, Patricia, *Victorian Silver and Silver-Plate* (London, 1963).

Victorian Jewellery: A Complete Compendium of over four thousand pieces of Jewellery. Introduced by Peter Hinks (London, 1992).

Der Viktorianische Haushaltskatalog. Eine vollständige Sammlung von über fünftausend Artikeln zur Einrichtung und Dekoration des viktoria- nischen Heimes. Eingeleitet von Dorothy Bosomworth [c. 1883] (Hil- desheim, 1992).

8.8. Anthologien

A Companion to the Victorian Novel, ed. Patrick Brantlinger (Oxford, 2002).

A Companion to Victorian Poetry, ed. Richard Cronin, Alison Chapman and Anthony Harrison (Malden, 2002).

English Verse. 1830-1890, ed. Bernard Richards (London, 1980).

Literature and Science in the Nineteenth Century. An Anthology, ed. with an Introduction and Notes by Laura Otis (Oxford, 2002).

Nature and Industrialization. An Anthology, ed. Alasdair Clayre (Oxford, 1977).

The New Oxford Book of Victorian Verse, ed. Christopher Ricks (Oxford, 1987).

Nineteenth Century Literature Criticism: NCLC; Excerpts From Criticism of the Works of Novelists, Poets, Philosophers, and Other Creative Writers Who Died Between 1800 and 1899, From the First Published Critical Appraisals to Current Evaluations, ed. Cherie D. Abbey and Janet Mullane (Detroit, 1981–).

The Nineteenth-Century Novel: A Critical Reader, ed. Stephan Regan (London, 2001).

Nineteenth Century Women Poets. An Oxford Anthology, ed. Isobel Armstrong (Oxford, 1996).

The Penguin Book of Victorian Verse: A Critical Anthology, ed. George MacBeth (Harmondsworth, 1969).

Sexual Heretics: Male Homosexuality in English Literature from 1850 to 1900: An Anthology. Selected by Brian Reade (London, 1970).

Victorian Criticism of the Novel, ed. Edwin M. Eigner and George J. Worth (Cambridge, 1985).

Victorian Ghost Stories: An Oxford Anthology, ed. Michael Cox and R.A. Gilbert (Oxford, 1992).

Victorian Poetry, ed. Duncan Wu (Oxford, 2002). [Based on: *The Victorians: An Anthology of Poetry and Poetics*, ed. Valentine Cunningham (Oxford, 2000)].

Victorian Prose and Poetry, ed. L. Trilling and H. Bloom (1973), in: *The Oxford Anthology of English Literature*, 6 vols., ed. Frank Kermode and J. Hollander (Oxford, 1973).

Victorian Short Stories: An Anthology. Selected by Harold Orel (London, 1987).

Victorian Women Poets: An Anthology, ed. Jennifer Breen (London, 1994).

Viktorianische Lyrik. Englisch/Deutsch, ed. Armin Geraths und Kurt Herget (Stuttgart, 1985).

The White Man's Burdens: An Anthology of British Poetry of the Empire, ed. Chris Brooks and Peter Faulkner (Exeter, 1996).

Women's Poetry. Late Romantic to late Victorian: Gender and Genre, 1830-1900, ed. Isobel Armstrong (Basingstoke, 1999).

9. Zeitschriften

Cahiers victoriens & édouardiens
ELT: English Literature in Transition, 1880-1920
The Journal of Pre-Raphaelite Studies
Journal of Victorian Culture
Nineteenth-Century Art Worldwide

Nineteenth-Century Contexts
Nineteenth-Century Feminisms
Nineteenth-Century Fiction
Nineteenth-Century Literature
Nineteenth-Century Studies
Nineteenth-Century Theatre
Victorian Literature and Culture
Victorian Periodicals Review
Victorian Poetry
Victorian Review
Victorian Studies
SEL: Studies in English Literature 1500-1900
Studies in the Novel

[Zugang zu den meisten Websites der Zeitschriften über: http://www.indiana.edu/~victoria/journals.html; Zugriff: 22. Juni 2002]

10. Reihen

Cambridge Studies in Nineteenth-Century Literature and Culture (Cambridge University Press)
Victorian Literature and Culture (University Press of Virginia)
Victorian Life and Literature (Ohio State University Press)
The Nineteenth Century (Ashgate Publishing)
Studies in Eighteenth and Nineteenth Century Literature (SENL) (Pearson Education)

11. Websites

Victorian British
http://andromeda.rutgers.edu/%7Ejlynch/Lit/victoria.html
Umfangreiche Website in der von Jack Lynch zusammengestellten Website "Literary Resources on the Net" (Rutgers-Newark).[1]

---

[1] Der Zugriff zu den einzelnen Websites in Abschnitt 11 und 12 dieser Bibliographie erfolgte am 22. Juni 2002.

Victoria Research Web (VRW)
http://www.indiana.edu/~victoria/
Initiiert von Patrick Leary, Koordinator der "Victorian Discussion List".

The Victorian Web
http://65.107.211.206/victov.html
Nach Sachgebieten gegliederte und ansprechend gestaltete Website.

Victorian Web Sites
http://www.lang.nagoya-u.ac.jp/~matsuoka/Victorian.html
Bietet eine ausführliche und aktuelle Bibliographie zahlreicher Websites, Konferenzen usw.

12. Dokumentar- und Spielfilme

Eine Reihe von Filmen wird aufgeführt auf der "British Royal History" Website: http://www.royalty.nu/Europe/England/Victoria.html unter "Movies and Documentaries".

Ein sehr empfehlenswerter Dokumentarfilm wurde 2001 gedreht: *Queen Victoria. Geheimnisse einer Königin* (Länge: 62 Minuten). Erhältlich über: VIDICOM, Peter Bardehle, Geffckenstr. 15, 20249 Hamburg.

Die Literatur der "viktorianischen Epoche"

Um einen knappen Überblick über die wichtigsten literarischen Vertreter/innen der viktorianischen Epoche zu geben, sind im folgenden einige Autoren/Autorinnen und ihre Werke in chronologischer Reihenfolge zusammengestellt.[1] Dabei wurden folgende Abkürzungen gewählt:

L   Lyrik
E   Erzählende Literatur
D   Drama
NF   Nichtfiktionale Prosa

---

[1] Es handelt sich hierbei um eine leicht überarbeitete Fassung aus: *Was sollen Anglisten und Amerikanisten lesen?*, ed. Christa Jansohn, Dieter Mehl und Hans Bungert (Berlin, 1995), S. 60-81.

Viele der Texte können in den folgenden Anthologien nachgelesen werden:

NAEL   *The Norton Anthology of English Literature*, 2 vols., ed. Meyer H. Abrams et al. (New York, ⁶1993).

NOBVV   *The New Oxford Book of Victorian Verse*, ed. Christopher Ricks (rpt. Oxford, 1990).

Einige Werke wurden mit einem bzw. zwei Sternchen versehen. Die Einteilung in ** = sehr empfehlenswert und * = empfehlenswert ist dabei sicherlich subjektiv, gibt aber dennoch in den meisten Fällen einen Hinweis auf ihre derzeitige Bedeutung im literarischen Kanon.

Thomas Carlyle (1795-1881)
NF   Sartor Resartus (1833-1834); Auswahl nach NAEL
NF   The French Revolution (1837); Auswahl nach NAEL
NF   Past and Present (1843); Auswahl nach NAEL

William Barnes (1801-1886)
L   Gedichte; Auswahl nach NOBVV

John Henry Newman (1801-1890)
NF   Apologia pro Vita Sua: Being a Reply to a Pamphlet Entitled: "What, Then, Does Dr Newman Mean?" (1864)
NF   The Idea of a University (1873)

Benjamin Disraeli (1804-1881)
E   Sybil: or, The Two Nations (1845)

Elizabeth Barrett Browning (1806-1861)
L   Poems (1840); Auswahl nach NAEL
L*   Poems (1850); Auswahl nach NAEL
E   Aurora Leigh (1856); Auswahl nach NAEL

Charles [Robert] Darwin (1809-1882)
NF*   The Origin of Species by Means of Natural Selection; or, The Preservation of Favoured Races in the Struggle for Life [On the Origin of Species] (1859)

Edward Fitzgerald (1809-1883)
L   Rubáiyát of Omar Khayyám (1859); Auswahl nach NOBVV

Alfred Lord Tennyson (1809-1892)
L*   Poems, Chiefly Lyrical (1830)
L   Poems (1842)
L   The Princess: A Medley (1847)
L*   In Memoriam A. H. H. (1850)
E   The Idylls of the King (1859-1872); Auswahl nach NAEL, NOBVV
L**   Gedichte; Auswahl nach NOBVV, NAEL

Elizabeth [Cleghorn] Gaskell (1810-1865)
E   Mary Barton (1848)
E   Cranford (1851-1853)
E**   North and South (1855)
NF*   The Life of Charlotte Brontë (1857)

William Makepeace Thackeray (1811-1863)
E**   Vanity Fair. A Novel Without a Hero (1847-1848)
E*   The History of Henry Esmond (1852)
E   The Newcomes: Memoirs of a Most Respectable Family (1853-1855)

Robert Browning (1812-1889)
L   Men and Women (1855)
L*   Dramatis Personae (1864)
E*   The Ring and the Book (1868-1869)
L*   Gedichte; Auswahl nach NOBVV

Charles [John Huffham] Dickens (1812-1870)
E   The Posthumous Papers of the Pickwick Club [= The Pickwick Papers] (1836-1837)
E   Oliver Twist (1837-38)
E*   David Copperfield (1849-1850)
E**   Bleak House (1852-1853)
E**   Hard Times (1854)
E*   Little Dorrit (1855-1857)
E*   Great Expectations (1860-1861)
E*   Our Mutual Friend (1864-1865)

Edward Lear (1812-1888)
L   A Book of Nonsense (1845; erweitert 1861, 1863, 1870); Auswahl nach NOBVV

Samuel Smiles (1812-1904)
NF   Self-Help: With Illustrations of Character and Conduct (1859)

Anthony Trollope (1815-1882)
E   The Warden (1855)
E*   Barchester Towers (1857)
E   Can you Forgive Her? (1864)

Charlotte Brontë (1816-1855)
E** Jane Eyre (1847)
E   Shirley (1849)
E*   Villette (1853)

Emily Jane Brontë (1818-1848)
E** Wuthering Heights (1847)
L   Gedichte; Auswahl nach NOBVV

George Eliot [Mary Ann Evans] (1819-1880)
E*   Adam Bede (1859)
E** The Mill on the Floss (1860)
E*   Silas Marner (1861)
E** Middlemarch (1871-1872)
E   Daniel Deronda (1876)

Charles Kingsley (1819-1875)
E   Alton Locke (1850)

John Ruskin (1819-1900)
NF   Modern Painters (1843-56); Auswahl nach NAEL
NF   The Stones of Venice (1851-1853); Auswahl nach NAEL

Anne Brontë (1820-1849)
E   The Tenant of Wildfell Hall (1848)

Matthew Arnold (1822-1888)
L   The Strayed Reveller, and Other Poems (1849)
L   Poems (1853)
L   New Poems (1867)
NF* Essays in Criticism (1865; Second Series 1888); Auswahl nach L
L** Gedichte; Auswahl nach NAEL, NOBVV

Wilkie Collins (1824-1889)
E*   The Moonstone (1868)

Robert Michael Ballantyne (1825-1894)
E   The Coral Island (1857)

George Meredith (1828-1909)
E   The Ordeal of Richard Feverel (1859)
L   Modern Love (1862); Auswahl nach NOBVV
E*   The Egoist (1879)

Dante Gabriel Rossetti (1828-1882)
L   Poems (1870)
L   Ballads and Sonnets (1881)
L*   Gedichte; Auswahl nach NOBVV, NAEL

Christina G[eorgina] Rossetti (1830-1894)
L   Goblin Market and Other Poems (1862)
L*   Gedichte; Auswahl nach NOBVV

Lewis Carroll [Charles Lutwige Dodgson] (1832-1898)
E**   Alice's Adventures in Wonderland (1865)
E   Through the Looking-Glass (1871)
L   Gedichte; Auswahl nach NOBVV

William Morris (1834-1896)
L   The Defence of Guenevere and Other Poems (1858); Auswahl nach
      NAEL, NOBVV
E   News from Nowhere (1890)

James Thomson (1834-1882)
L   The City of Dreadful Night (1874); Auswahl nach NOBVV
L   Gedichte; Auswahl nach NOBVV

Mary Elizabeth Braddon (1835-1915)
E   Lady Audley's Secret (1862)

Samuel Butler (1835-1902)
E   Erewhon (1872)
E*   The Way of All Flesh (1873-1885, 1903)

Algernon Charles Swinburne (1837-1909)
D　　Atalanta in Calydon (1865)
L*　　Poems and Ballads (1866; 1889); Auswahl nach NAEL, NOBVV

Walter [Horatio] Pater (1839-1894)
NF*　"Conclusion" zu Studies in the History of the Renaissance (1873); Auswahl nach NAEL

Thomas Hardy (1840-1928)
E　　Far From the Madding Crowd (1874)
E*　　The Return of the Native (1878)
E　　The Woodlanders (1887)
E**　Tess of the D'Urbervilles (1891)
E**　Jude the Obscure (1896)
L**　Late Lyrics and Earlier (1922); Auswahl nach NAEL, NOBVV, OBTCEV

Henry James (1843-1916)
E*　　Daisy Miller (1878)
E**　The Portrait of a Lady (1881)
E*　　The Turn of the Screw (1898)
E**　The Ambassadors (1903)
E*　　The Wings of the Dove (1902)

Gerard Manley Hopkins (1844-1889)
L**　Poems (1918); Auswahl nach NAEL, NOBVV

Bram [Abraham] Stoker (1847-1912)
E　　Dracula (1897)

Robert Louis [Balfour] Stevenson (1850-1894)
E*　　Treasure Island (1883)
E**　The Strange Case of Dr. Jekyll and Mr. Hyde (1886)
E*　　The Master of Ballantrae (1889)

George [Augustus] Moore (1852-1933)
E　　Esther Waters (1894)

Oscar [Fingal O'Flaherty Wills] Wilde (1854-1900)
E*   The Picture of Dorian Gray (1890)
D   Lady Windermere's Fan (1892)
D** The Importance of Being Earnest (1895)
L   The Ballad of Reading Gaol (1898)

Marie Corelli (1855-1924)
F   A Romance of Two Worlds (1886)
F   The Sorrows of Satan (1895)

Sir Arthur Wing Pinero (1855-1934)
D   The Second Mrs Tanqueray (1893)
D   Trelawny of the 'Wells' (1898)

George Bernard Shaw (1856-1950)
NF   The Quintessence of Ibsenism (1891)
D   Arms and the Man (1894)
D*   Candida (1894)
D*   Mrs. Warren's Profession (1894); NAEL

George Robert Gissing (1857-1903)
E   New Grub Street (1891)

Arthur Conan Doyle (1859-1930)
E   The Adventures of Sherlock Holmes (1892)
E   The Hound of the Baskervilles (1902)

Rudyard Kipling (1865-1936)
E   The Jungle Books (1894-1895)
E*   Kim (1901)

CULTURAL MEMORIES,
OR IMAGES OF QUEEN VICTORIA

Consuming Monarchy:
The Changing Public Images of Queen Victoria

By *Ralf Schneider* (Tübingen)

1. Introduction

When Victoria, Queen of Great Britain and Empress of India, died on 22 January 1901, after almost 64 years of rule, there was a general feeling that an epoch in British history had come to its end. It was partly the longevity of this, the longest reign in British history, which made it inevitable that Victoria's time would also come to be labelled with her name – when she died, there was hardly a person alive who could remember any other monarch than Victoria. She had also stamped her personality on her country at a time in which this country was undergoing major changes in politics, social structure, economics, science and the arts, and in which the institution of the monarchy was affected by these changes itself. Thus, with Victoria's death it also became apparent that something new had lastingly taken hold in British civilisation: the institution of the modern constitutional monarchy.

Victoria's personal development and her political position as a monarch were characterised by a number of contradictory tendencies that have developed fully in the modern, constitutional monarchy as we know it today.[1] First, during Victoria's reign, the British monarchy underwent a

---

[1] The events of Victoria's life are amply documented in a wealth of biographies, which have appeared since her death (and will no doubt keep appearing, especially after the centenary of her death in 2001). They differ mainly in terms of either literary or historiographical aspirations of the biographers and the emphasis placed on either the personal or the political aspects of Victoria's life. I have found immensely readable those of Lytton Strachey, *Queen Victoria* (London, 1912) and Elizabeth Longford [i.e. Elizabeth Packenham, Countess of Longford], *Victoria R.I.* (London, 1964), the first of Victoria's biographers to have had access to the Royal archives; more literary in its recreation of location, atmosphere and thoughts and feelings of persons is Edith Sitwell, *Victoria of England* (London, 1946); Stanley Weintraub's *Victoria: Biography of a Queen* (London and Sydney, 1987) is more matter-of-fact in style than the other biographies, but it has the advantage of being based on material unavailable to the earlier writers. All biographers make extensive use of the thousands of surviving letters of and to Victoria (*Letters of Queen Victoria*; series I: 1837-1861, ed. Arthur Christoph Benson and Viscount Esher [London, 1907]; series II: 1862-1885, ed. George Earle Buckle (London, 1926-28); series III: 1886-1901, ed. George Earle Buckle [London, 1930-32]),

process of de-politicisation, as far as the direct rulership of the country was concerned, but at the same time, the figure of the monarch acquired additional layers of symbolic representation that were also put to good use by politicians; second, the supremacy of the aristocracy survived largely unscathed, but the royals promoted the values of the middle classes; third, although Victoria led a much more secluded life in that pre-paparazzian age than today's royals ever could, she was increasingly exposed to the public's curiosity; fourth, whereas the monarchy responded to the changes in its environment, it nevertheless remained a symbol of stability. The monarchy was able to survive in the face of these tensions precisely because it managed to produce ever new public images of the monarch. The events of the nineteenth century triggered varying responses to and assumptions about the Queen at different times. They produced a continuous flow of eulogic or derogatory representations of Victoria, and they required Victoria herself and her advisers to actively construct images of monarchy ready for public consumption. These public images appeared in multitudinous forms and were circulated by the diverse media in which public opinion was negotiated in the nineteenth century: texts written for the periodical press, broadsheets and ballads, poems and songs, visual images in paintings, engravings (often as caricatures and cartoons) and photographs.[1] The fact that the monarch was a woman in a century famous (or infamous) for its relegation of women to the non-political sphere of the home cuts across most public representations of Victoria, whether created by others or through her own agency.[2]

---

as well as the memoirs of her contemporary statesmen, court officials and relatives. Since the central events and episodes in Victoria's life are uncontroversial, I shall refrain from footnoting each incident and instead refer the reader generally to any of the titles mentioned.

[1] The nineteenth-century volumes of many periodicals contain a host of such images; see, for instance, *Punch* or the *Illustrated London News*, which was begun in 1842 and, selling at one shilling per copy, soon came to dominate the market of metropolitan middle-class weeklies. Selections of images can be found in Dorothy Marshall's *The Life and Times of Victoria* (London, 1972), which provides, besides, another accessible account of Victoria's life, a great number of illustrations; and Helmut and Alison Gernsheim's *Queen Victoria: A Biography in Words and Pictures* (London, 1959) which contains numerous photos. For more cartoons, see Michael Wynn Jones, *A Cartoon History of the Monarchy* (London, 1978), pp. 40-45 and 68-77.

[2] The intricacies of the monarch's gender with respect to her influence and images have attracted historians, cultural critics and feminist scholars alike; see the explorations of the phenomenon in Dorothy Thompson, *Queen Victoria: Gender and Power* (London, 1990), in a number of contributions to *Remaking Queen Victoria*, ed. Margaret Homans and Adrienne Munich (Cambridge, 1997), and in Margaret Homans, *Royal*

2. Accession and the Melbourne Years (1837-1840): Ups and Downs

To fully understand the impact of the public images of Victoria, it is necessary to have a brief look at the public image of the British monarchy at the
time of Victoria's accession to the throne in the late 1830s. In the century
before Victoria, the Crown had lost much of both its influence and acceptance in British society.[1] Victoria was a descendant of the house of Hanover, whose members had added the British throne to their rulership in
Germany in 1714. George I was, although only distantly related to the
British royal family, the only Protestant and therefore the only eligible
candidate for the throne, according to the Act of Settlement, which excluded Catholics from succession. The four Georges partly witnessed the
decline of the powers of the Crown in the eighteenth century, and to some
extent they caused it themselves through their lack of identification with
their British subjects; their refusal or inability to learn the language, as was
the case with George I and George II; their interest in furthering the influence of their German rather than their British affairs and their establishment of the post of Prime Minister, to whom governing power was eventually transferred. The reign of George III, the first of the Hanoverians to be
born in England and more popular than the first two Georges, saw the
French Revolution, which brought in its wake republican, radical and an-
archistic ideas to England to foster anti-monarchist sentiments. He also had
the double misfortune of losing the American colonies and of suffering
from an illness which turned him insane. His son, George IV, had already
ruled the country as Regent in the later years of his father's illness, when
he was still the Prince of Wales. It took George IV only little time to destroy what respect his father had earned for the monarchy. Even before his
ten-year reign, he had acquired a reputation for being pleasure-seeking,
dishonourable and spendthrift – qualities unlikely to endear him to his
subjects.

Due to the lack of legitimate children, George IV was succeeded by one
of his brothers. William IV had served in the Navy and was called the
"Sailor King". He was infamous for an embarrassing lack of manners and

---

Representations: Queen Victoria and British Culture, 1837-1876 (Chicago and London,
1998).

[1] On the political status and social acceptance of the Crown in late eighteenth- and
early nineteenth-century Britain, see John Golby and William Purdue, *The Monarchy
and the British People: 1760 to the Present* (London, 1988), pp. 15-43 and John Cannon
and Ralph Griffiths, *The Oxford Illustrated History of the British Monarchy* (Oxford
and New York, 1988), pp. 530-550.

intellect, which earned him his other nickname, "Silly Billy". What is important about King William in terms of the status of the Crown, is that his reign saw the passing, after much haggling, of the Great Reform Act of 1832, which is held to be one of the most important political events of the nineteenth century. It extended franchise and reformed the system of parliamentary representation in the House of Commons. Certainly, this first Reform Act did not create a full, democratic voting system in any modern sense – it did not even enfranchise the middle classes fully. But one of its effects was that more influence could be exerted by more voters from wider social strata than before, and that the distribution of seats in the House of Commons reflected the geographical and social structure of England more adequately than before the reform. The new legislation did not affect the rights of the sovereign or the House of Lords, nor did it change the power structures much: the land-owning aristocracy still ruled the land, and their loyalty to the monarchy was traditional and not easily undermined.[1]

And yet the very circumstances of the passing of the 1832 Reform Act laid bare changes in constitutional relationships and indicated that the depoliticisation of the Crown that was to develop during Victoria's reign had already begun.[2] Despite much opposition from the King and the House of Lords, both had been forced by the majority of the electorate, by the House of Commons and by public opinion to agree to measures they opposed in principle. Politics had turned out to be more a question of securing the support of an increasingly amorphous and anonymous public rather than of influencing Parliament by granting its members royal favours and privileges. This development was to continue through the second and third Reform Acts in 1867 and 1884, respectively, when franchise was by and by extended even to some parts of the working classes (although only the male population profited from this).

To the relief of some observers, King William died after a reign of only seven years. In Hanover, succession was restricted to male heirs according to Salic Law, which was disregarded in Britain, so that the personal union between the thrones of England and Hanover was split up: William did not

---

[1] On the social structure and influence of the upper classes, see J.V. Beckett, *The Aristocracy in England, 1660-1914* (Oxford, 1986), especially chapter 13.

[2] The question as to whether the decline in powers of the monarchy was only beginning in Victoria's reign or had already been completed at the time of her accession, has been much discussed by historians and biographers. For an early example of such a discussion, see Frank Hardie, *The Political Influence of Queen Victoria, 1861-1901* [1935] (London, 1963), who tends to see already the Reform Bill of 1832 as the culmination of the process.

have children, and so his brother Ernest Augustus became King of Hanover, and his niece Alexandrina Victoria succeeded him to the British throne at the age of eighteen. As the above remarks have shown, young Victoria had one rather unflattering advantage over her predecessors from the start: she could not possibly sink lower in the esteem of her subjects than they, but this also meant that the office of monarch, which she took over, was burdened with mistrust and suspicion. The Prime Minister at the time of Victoria's accession was Lord Melbourne, a good-looking, elderly gentleman of Whiggish orientation. He acted as adviser and mentor to the young Queen, who enjoyed his company as much as she relied on his judgement in matters of politics. Victoria had grown up in rather secluded circumstances and an all-female household, watched over by her over-anxious mother and Baroness Lehzen, her governess until 1830 and companion and confidante after that. Until the day of her accession, Victoria had virtually not been on her own for one single hour in her life: for fear that the line of succession might be endangered by accidents or attempts at assassination, she had always had to share her mother's bedroom and was not even allowed to descend a staircase without someone holding her by the hand. Her education comprised the female accomplishments that were the norm at the time – languages, in which she excelled, drawing, in which she also had a talent, and music and dance, which she liked – but in history and politics her achievements were, at most, satisfactory. She was by no means ideally prepared for the office of the monarch, and so it was not only fortunate but quite necessary that an experienced politician guide her through her first years as the figurehead of the Kingdom.[1]

Victoria's succession and coronation had taken place in an atmosphere of widespread admiration for and relief at the grace, taste and good manners of the new sovereign. The fact that the new monarch was a young woman made her appear "less threatening and more malleable to politicians", and "less vicious and more decorative to the wider public".[2] At the same time, however, her gender and her age gave rise to fears that she might succumb to all sorts of negative influences. Only two years after her coronation, two incidents placed the newly-won public respect in jeopardy. These incidents are indicative of the tension mentioned above, between Victoria's power to exert influence and her being limited to mere representation. They also show the typical entanglement between the private, personal sphere of a

---

[1] Her other male adviser was her uncle Leopold, who had become King of the Belgians in 1831, and with whom she exchanged frequent letters. The more Victoria became used to her new role, however, the more she felt her uncle's letters were patronising and meddling with her affairs – her responses cooled perceptibly.

[2] Dorothy Thompson, *Queen Victoria*, p. 23.

monarch and his or her public roles. In 1839, Lady Flora Hastings, one of the ladies-in-waiting to the Duchess of Kent, Victoria's mother, was suspected of being pregnant when she returned to the court, after a period of absence, with a noticeably changed figure – what was scandalous about this was that she was unmarried, and the danger was that Victoria's court might acquire that reputation of immorality which previous courts had often enough deserved. Although a physical examination testified Lady Flora's virginity, the Queen had not been quick enough in her affirmation of the Lady's innocence – and the examination by a physician was in itself a gross intrusion into a lady's privacy and the most extreme of all measures to be resorted to. The powerful Hastings family, who happened to be Tory, managed to direct public opinion against Victoria by voicing the suspicion that Victoria had been unduly influenced in her distrust of Lady Flora by her Whig Prime Minister. The situation was not helped much by the fact that poor Lady Flora died from a massive tumour of the liver shortly afterwards.

The second incident, which occurred in the same year, has become known as the "Bedchamber Crisis". Lord Melbourne's Cabinet had lost its support in the House of Commons and was forced to resign. The Tory leader, Sir Robert Peel, was the obvious candidate for the post of Prime Minister. To appoint the Prime Minister was the Queen's prerogative, and she disliked Peel as much as she was fond of Melbourne. During the negotiations about the formation of a new government, Peel suggested that the Queen should replace some of her closest female servants, the Ladies-of-the-Bedchamber, in order to demonstrate the Crown's neutrality in matters of party politics, for the bedchamber ladies had been appointed by Melbourne, and most of them were married to members of the Whigs or belonged to traditional Whig families. While Peel's fear that the Queen might be influenced politically by her closest surroundings was probably justified, Victoria was furious at what she considered an infringement of her prerogatives. There was some confusion as to the legal situation, but strictly speaking the Prime Minister had the right to staff the royal household. However, Peel could not be sure of his majority in the Commons, so that his position in the negotiations was rather weak. Ultimately the Queen ordered Melbourne to form a government once again. It was only in 1841, when Melbourne had finally lost support in Parliament, that Peel succeeded him as Prime Minister, much to the regret of the young Queen.

The Bedchamber crisis shows two things: first, although the choice of the Prime Minister was technically the monarch's prerogative, the only thing that made sense was to choose a candidate who would command a comfortable majority in the House of Commons, otherwise the administration of the country would be effectively blocked. During Victoria's reign, premiership changed not less than nineteen times, and ten different persons held the office. Such changes cannot of course be attributed to Victoria's whims of taste or unstable inclinations. Rather, they indicate that the changing party majorities in the House of Commons dictated to her the candidates for the post. The Bedchamber crisis illustrates, secondly, that Victoria kept trying to exert influence wherever and whenever she could. This was particularly easy in the case of elections resulting in insecure majorities and minority governments, as occurred for instance in 1846, 1858 and 1866. In 1851 she secured the dismissal of the foreign secretary, Lord Palmerston, because she disagreed with his policies and, more importantly, with his taking action without previously informing the Queen. Victoria also influenced or vetoed the appointment of particular cabinet ministers, foreign envoys and, in her role as the head of the Church of England, Anglican bishops. Nominally, she retained the right to dissolve Parliament, but the power to do so lay with the Prime Minister. The monarchy was thus situated between a situation of power and active influence on the one hand, and the necessity to adapt to the wishes of the government on the other, who were in turn supposed to represent the wishes of the voters. What the Lady Flora affair and the Bedchamber Crisis also highlight is that in the first years of Victoria's reign public opinion about the monarch was still far from settled on a positive image. The construction of images of Victoria did not yet lie in the hands of Victoria herself, but was subject to manipulation by various groups of partisan views.

3. The Albert Years (1840-1861): Family Rule

The second phase of Victoria's reign began when she married the German Prinz Albert von Sachsen-Coburg-Gotha, her cousin, in 1840. The match had been made by her influential relatives, but turned out to be a love match after all, at least as far as Victoria was concerned. She was very much in love with the young prince, whose beauty she admired as much as his sense of duty and his education. Albert gained a reputation as a patron of the arts, architecture and the sciences, and untiringly made improvements in whatever section of public life he could lay hands on.[1] His official, constitutional position in the ruling of the country was virtually non-existent: he was neither king nor ruler. Parliament slighted him by granting

---

[1] On the Prince Consort, see the biography by Stanley Weintraub, *Albert: Uncrowned King* (London, 1997).

him only £ 30,000 allowance a year instead of the £ 50,000 to be expected and proposed by the government, and he was only officially given the compromise title of Prince Consort as late as 1857 (although it had been in use before). Still, he had his share in the ruling of the country behind the scenes. He is said to have encouraged Victoria to be less stubborn, and he assuaged her temper more than once – his intervention for instance led to a compromise with Peel in the question of the Ladies-of-the-Bedchamber in 1841. Charles Greville, a court official, noted in his diary in 1845:

> ... they are one person, and as he likes and she dislikes business, it is obvious that while she has the title, he is really discharging the functions of the Sovereign. He is King to all intents and purposes.[1]

Albert's idealism and eagerness for grand projects was satisfied in the Great Exhibition of 1851, for which Albert deserves the title of the master-mind.[2] It was natural that in an age of progress, industry and self-help, Albert's industriousness was appreciated by many of his contemporaries. But this esteem was always counterbalanced by many people's dislike of his stiff and awkward manners, and by a deep mistrust of the German prince among politicians and some sections of the nobility. Suspicion that he abused his influence over the Queen for non-English interests never subsided during his life. As far as Victoria was concerned, the alleged malleability of the Queen was still a major aspect of her public image.

In contrast to George IV and William IV, the royal couple led a family life, and they actively sought to fix this notion and transmit it to the public through many paintings and a veritable flood of photographs. The tradition of state portraiture still dictated that the royal family was depicted wearing suitable state attire in many paintings, but the presence of the children shifted the focus away from the political towards the domestic even in paintings of that type.[3] That Victoria was fond of the new medium of photography, which was only as old as her reign, shows how immensely progress-oriented she was. It also gave her an opportunity of appearing in a de-

---

[1] Quoted in Stanley Weintraub, *Victoria*, p. 187.

[2] Asa Briggs, "The Crystal Palace and the Men of 1851", in: *Victorian People: A Reassessment of Persons and Themes 1851-67* (Harmondsworth, 1954), pp. 23-59, remains a good and concise introduction to the Great Exhibition in its political, cultural and social context. For a more recent and more profound analysis, see Jeffrey A. Auerbach's excellent study, *The Great Exhibition of 1851: A Nation on Display* (New Haven and London, 1999).

[3] See, for instance, a family portrait of Victoria and Albert with their first five children, painted in 1846 by Franz Xaver Winterthaler, Victoria's favourite court painter; reproduced in Dorothy Marshall, *The Life and Times of Victoria*, pp. 62-63.

cidedly non-official pose. In the family photos and the photos of Victoria and Albert alone, there is no pomp about the dress or demeanour of the figures.[1] These pictures of Victoria and Albert might just as well show any wealthy upper-middle class couple.[2]

The royal couple had nine children, seven of whom were born in the first ten years of their marriage (which means, by the way, that Albert was forced to do some of the work, for the almost continuous state of pregnancy and the childbirths must have taken up a considerable amount of Victoria's time and energy). The costs of maintaining the ever-growing royal household, or households, were enormous – a fact that elicited much republican criticism and bourgeois lament throughout the second half of the century.[3] But still the royal family's lifestyle came nowhere near the luxuries and extravagances characteristic of the previous kings, especially George IV. Quite the contrary: many guests to the royal family complained about the dullness, frugality and sobriety of an evening with the Queen and the Prince Consort. Victoria and Albert's lifestyle may have disappointed the pleasure-seeking aristocracy, but it certainly pleased the Victorian middle classes, who were in the process of advancing to the dominant position in the social structure of England. The middle classes had developed a particular system of values from a conglomeration of religious, educational and economic factors. These values comprised domesticity, i.e. the importance of the home and the concomitant separation of the public sphere from the private; other components were the focusing of the female role on motherhood and charity, the belief in the ethics of assiduous work

---

[1] On the function of Victoria's portraiture in the promotion of middle-class values, see Ira B. Nadel, "Portraits of the Queen", *Victorian Poetry*, 25 (1987), 169-191 and Margaret Homans, *Royal Representations*, pp. 44-57; on the varying aspects of Victoria's personality and career mediated through paintings and engravings, see Susan P. Casteras, "The Wise Child and Her 'Offspring': Some Changing Faces of Queen Victoria", in: *Remaking Queen Victoria*, ed. Margaret Homans and Adrienne Munich, pp. 183-199.

[2] Margaret Homans points out that in the photos of the couple, some of which were engraved for public circulation, others printed as *cartes de visite*, Victoria and Albert needed to come to terms with ambiguous conventions: as a wife, Victoria would have to be portrayed seated, looking up to her standing husband, whereas the reverse was expected from her as a queen. The poses the royal couple strike in the photos made at the family home, Osborne House, by the photographer Miss Day, in fact enact the two possibilities. See *Royal Representations*, pp. 21 and 46-48.

[3] On criticism of the monarchy such as this, see the views presented to the socially diversified readership of the periodical press – dailies from London and other cities, provincial weeklies, cheap dailies from the 1880s on, and republican newspapers –, which Richard Williams has analysed in *The Contentious Crown: Public Discussion of the British Monarchy in the Reign of Queen Victoria* (Aldershot, 1997).

and in constant, man-made progress – and all these were values which the bourgeoisie shared with the royals.[1] Victoria and Albert came to be seen as a model couple, they and their children as the model family, which perceptibly changed the traditional public image of the monarch: "We have come to regard the Crown as the Head of our *morality*", as Walter Bagehot, author of the influential study *The English Constitution* of 1867, put it.[2] The welfare of the Queen and her offspring became a daily concern for many people, and it was only under Victoria that the first national anthem of the world made its way into the repertoire of songs that a family would play and sing at home, as is indicated for example on the covers of song books on which the royal family would be depicted, or in an engraving by Henrietta Ward, which shows a mother sitting at the piano and teaching her three children to sing "God Save the Queen".[3]

When, on the occasion of the opening of the Great Exhibition in 1851, the royal couple proceeded to their seats under their canopy placed in the Crystal Palace holding their eldest son and daughter by the hand, this ostentatious display of family closeness caused a storm of affection. But it was not only on such extraordinary occasions that Victoria's subjects got glimpses of the royal family. The wider public appeal of the monarchy was ensured by technological developments and the fruits of industrialisation in the second half of the nineteenth century: Victoria liked travelling by train, and the rapidly growing railway network gave the royals the opportunity to see their country and be seen by their subjects.[4] In addition to this, public presence of the royals was secured by the increasing number and availability of newspapers and magazines. The printing machines, the

---

[1] The changing status of the middle classes and the development of middle-class values in the social, political and economic contexts of the Victorian age is explored in detail in F.M.L. Thompsons magisterial study, *The Rise of Respectable Society: A Social History of Victorian Britain, 1830-1900* (London, 1988) and in Leonore Davidoff and Catherine Hall, *Family Fortunes: Men and Women of the English Middle Class 1780-1850* (London, 1987).

[2] Oxford World Classics (Oxford, 2001), p. 53. The book was first published in 1867, and a second, enlarged edition followed in 1872. Bagehot is aware that he can make this statement not because of any constitutional arrangement, but only because of the happy coincidence that Victoria differed from her predecessors in that respect.

[3] A typical song book cover is reproduced in Dorothy Thompson, *Queen Victoria*, p. 45. Ward's engraving is reproduced in Deborah Cherry, *Painting Women: Victorian Women Artists* (London, 1995), plate 14; for a discussion of this picture, which was exhibited in the Royal Academy in 1857, see pp. 127-130.

[4] See, for instance, images of the royals in trains in John Golby and William Purdue, *The Monarchy and the British People*, p. 55 and Dorothy Marshall, *The Life and Times of Victoria*, pp. 136-137.

techniques of producing paper and the possibilities of reproducing en-gravings, drawings, watercolours and, at the end of the century, even pho-tos, were rapidly improving. Illustrated periodicals could be sold cheaply, providing image after image of Victoria for public consumption, catering to the tastes of an ever-growing reading and viewing public eager to be informed about every trivial little detail in the dress and demeanour, the fortunes and misfortunes of the Queen, Prince Albert and their children. Whereas Victoria herself, with her plump figure and her taste for modera-tion, was not a likely candidate for setting trends in female fashion, her daughters and her daughter-in-law, Princess Alexandra, who was widely admired for her beauty, championed many a fashionable style of dress. The images of royalty glimpsed from engravings, photographs or even live ap-pearances, are sure to have been more thrilling than the everyday encoun-ters with the stylised and frozen profiles of the monarch on coins or stamps to which the population had long become accustomed. From our early 21st-century view, the wide availability of likenesses is yet another strik-ing connection between Victoria and contemporary royalty.

Although Victoria liked being photographed, she deemed it unsuitable for a monarch to be photographed smiling, and only a handful of such photos exists.[1] Perhaps this is one reason why a public image of Victoria has persisted that characterises her as stern and Puritan. The attribution is misleading, however. Not only does no proof exist that Victoria ever actu-ally uttered the sentence "We are not amused", attributed to her and thought to characterise her so well, but there are indeed various hints that she actively sought the pleasures of life and was very much amused most of the time: it is well known that she loved food and was already consider-ably obese in her young years; there is absolutely no reason to believe that the conception of her nine children was purely an ordeal for her; and in later years she travelled to the Riviera and enjoyed the sunshine and bath-ing in the sea.[2] We must be aware of the unreliability of public images construed from photos. In a similar vein, we find a large number of por-traits of the royal family, both painted and photographed, in which the family is peacefully united or the children are romping merrily about. One must keep in mind, however, that such incidents did by no means reflect

---

[1] Nor would most of Victoria's contemporaries have posed for the camera smiling or laughing. The roots of portrait photography in portrait painting ensured for a long time that sitters would mostly choose a composed and demure expression, and anyway expo-sure time of two to three minutes in the early days of photography would have prevented snapshots of a person inadvertently caught laughing.

[2] On the last issue, see the recent book by Michael Nelson, *Queen Victoria and the Discovery of the Riviera* (London, 2001).

their everyday life. Both parents would have been occupied most of the time by the multitude of tasks they were obliged to fulfil or had chosen themselves; they would frequently travel without the children; and in spite of giving birth nine times, Victoria was never fond of babies. What we find, therefore, are images of the Queen as a mother, and the royals as a family, that suited the dominant middle-class ideology.

4. Years of Mourning (1861-1870s): Missing Monarchy

The death of Albert in 1861 left Victoria shattered, utterly and inconsolably struck down by grief. So great was the shock inflicted by her loss that she withdrew from public view almost completely – in the 1860s she would stay at Balmoral for up to five months a year. She fashioned a new image for herself, that of the lonely Widow Queen. Although one might argue that the Victorians were generally obsessed with death and the rituals surrounding it, Victoria clearly wanted to outdo her subjects in that respect. Widows would wear the conventional widow's weeds, a style of dress that prescribed black dress (mostly crape or wool fabrics that would not shine) and a black veil for the first year of mourning, and after that allowed milder mourning in more shiny material such as silk and colours such as mauve, lavender or beige, in combination with a white veil.[1] Whereas most widows would stop wearing conspicuous mourning attire in due course, normally after around two and a half years, Victoria continued to wear the widow's weeds until the end of her life, never putting on the royal robes again.[2] She soon became known as "The Widow at Windsor", not only in the famous poem by Rudyard Kipling. At the same time, she

---

[1] On the strict conventions of Victorian mourning dress see, for instance, Jane Ashelford, *The Art of Dress: Clothes and Society 1500-1914* (New York and London, 1996), pp. 237-249 and *passim*; see also the exhibition photos and text in Caroline Goldthorpe, *From Queen To Empress: Victorian Dress 1837-1877* (New York, 1988), pp. 68-77. Peter Robinson, a firm of drapers in London, opened a large shop specialising in articles of mourning in Regent Street in 1865 (and were the first to produce a photographed catalogue of their articles); see Madeleine Ginsburg, *Victorian Dress in Photographs* (London, 1982), pp. 52-54. Robinson's "Court and Family Mourning and Black Goods Warehouse" frequently advertised in the *Illustrated London News*, as did another successful mourning dress provider, Jay's Dressmakers and Milliners, also situated in Regent Street. See also the article by Franz Meier in this volume.

[2] To the dismay of her advisers and family, she did not even wear state robes for her Crown Jubilees, when she preferred instead to add her wedding veil and lace to her black dress, and to wear only the small Imperial crown; see Caroline Chapman and Paul Raben, *Debrett's Queen Victoria's Jubilees 1887 & 1897* (London, 1977).

turned her prolonged mourning into a veritable Albert cult: there exist numerous photographs, obviously heavily posed, which show Victoria and her children in various constellations, and even the servants of the royal household, melodramatically bewailing their loss under the bust of the late Albert. For almost ten years Victoria would only leave her seclusion in order to unveil one of the many statues of Albert which were beginning to appear all over the country. Charles Dickens jokingly wrote in a letter to his illustrator John Leech in 1864:

> If you should meet with an inaccessible cave anywhere to which a hermit could retire from the memory of Prince Albert and testimonials to the same, pray let me know of it. We have nothing solitary and deep enough in this part of England.[1]

Five years after Albert's death, Victoria could only with great difficulty be persuaded to fulfil one of her most important public and political functions: the opening of Parliament;[2] and as late as 1890, thirty years after her Prince Consort's death, she was still unveiling Albert statues, opening Albert memorial buildings, inaugurating Albert memorial institutions, schools, colleges, museums and the like.

Victoria's withdrawal from royal ceremony and public spectacle was criticised by many commentators.[3] Her advisers felt that for the monarchy

---

[1] Quoted in Stanley Weintraub, *Victoria*, p. 234. This trend can be illustrated by David Cannadine's count of free-standing or equestrian commemorative statues of royalty (excluding "reliefs, allegorical, animal, abstract and cemetery sculpture") erected in London alone: from the death of Albert to 1900, 48 such statues were erected, whereas in the three decades before, from Victoria's accession until 1860, the number only reaches 20; see "The Context, Performance, and Meaning of Ritual: The British Monarchy and the 'Invention of Tradition', c. 1820-1977", in: *The Invention of Tradition*, ed. Eric Hobsbawm and Terence Rogers (Cambridge, 1983), pp. 101-164; for the figures quoted, see p. 164.

[2] Margaret Homans interprets Victoria's behaviour on that occasion as a dramatic performance of nothing but her reluctance to perform: "The Lord Chancellor read [the Queen's speech] for her, while she sat crownless, dressed in black, staring rigidly ahead, her royal robes merely draped over the throne behind her." *Royal Representations*, p. 64 (summarising the description of the scene in Elizabeth Longford, *Victoria R.I.*, p. 348). Only in seven other years did Victoria open Parliament in person, and never did she read the opening speech herself; see Frank Hardie, *The Political Influence of Queen Victoria*, p. 248.

[3] Famous cartoons show the deserted British throne, carelessly covered by the royal robes above the caption "Where is Britannia?" (*Tomahawk*, June 1867) and Victoria as "Queen Hermione", addressed by Britannia in the role of Paulina from Shakespeare's *Winter's Tale*: "'Tis time! Descend; be stone no more!" (*Punch*, 23 September 1865), reproduced in Margaret Homans, *Royal Representations*, pp. 65 and 66, respectively.

to summon up respect and support in the population, it must be visible – they had understood the symbolic power of ritual and pomp.[1] But how to put this to the Queen without explicitly interpreting her understandable desolation as selfishness and neglect of duties was a delicate problem, as Prime Minister Gladstone painfully came to realise. In any case, the positive outcome was that by appearing in public only rarely, Victoria managed to attract even greater and more loyal crowds on the few occasions when she did venture out, as is indicated for instance in a watercolour reproduced in the *Illustrated London News* of 2 April 1872, reporting the Queen's visit to the East End of London. Victoria herself provided the eager public with a glimpse of her private life when she published extracts from her diary in 1868. Her *Leaves from the Journal of Our Life in the Highlands* were carefully selected from her original diary to emphasise the domesticity and family flavour of the Queen's life and to tone down her political activities.[2] Selling 20,000 copies immediately, the book was a best-seller to all intents and purposes.

With the hindsight of our 21st-century perspective, the significance of the years of mourning and seclusion can hardly be overestimated, because they resulted in a number of developments which contributed to the shaping of the modern British monarchy. It seems to be a law of contemporary mass-information society that sparing use of public presence demands more respect and interest in a person than his or her frequent public appearances. At the same time, speculation about the private lives of the celebrities thrives whenever hard facts are unavailable. Thus, one effect of Victoria's seclusion was that when she came to develop a close friendship with one of her servants at Balmoral, John Brown, and frequently insisted on taking him with her as a companion, rumour spread that she had secretly married Brown, and some newspapers even suggested she had borne him a child. Accordingly, the nickname "Mrs Brown" came into use. When Brown died in 1883, Victoria mourned him in a way comparable to her behaviour after Albert's death: his room was preserved the way he had last left it, just like the Prince Consort's room in 1861, and she had busts of him made and distributed in all the royal residences. When Victoria published the second volume of diary extracts in 1884, this was as clearly a

---

[1] In his *The English Constitution*, Walter Bagehot shrewdly observes the very fabric of the network of power and representation in nineteenth-century Britain. Of special interest is his differentiation between the "efficient" and the "dignified" aspects of the constitution and his analysis of the "theatrical" elements necessary for popular representation. On Bagehot, see also Margaret Homans, *Royal Representations*, chapter 3.

[2] Victoria, Queen of Great Britain, *Leaves from the Journal of Our Life in the Highlands: From 1848-1861* (London, 1868).

tribute to John Brown as the first volume had been a tribute to Albert, and advisers tried in vain to dissuade her from publishing the book at all.[1] Although one might suppose that a woman who had been a widow for so long had every right to seek out a companion, Brown was after all a servant, and the whole affair revived old fears that the monarch might come under the influence of an ambitious upstart interested more in his personal profit than in the well-being of the country.[2]

Another result of the Queen's continued seclusion was that it had become clear that the public was not worse off if neither she nor the Prince Consort meddled actively in affairs of the state. In spite of Victoria's withdrawal, government ran smoothly. The Queen still went on informing herself about what she needed and wished to be informed about, and she still went on signing those papers she was required to sign. The function of the Queen in the governing of her country was formulated by Bagehot in the following way: "To state the matter shortly, the sovereign has, under a constitutional monarchy such as ours, three rights – the right to be consulted, the right to encourage, the right to warn."[3] Bagehot points out the necessity of a monarch who is above party politics, and who can therefore be used as a symbol for national unity, a simplification of the complex actions of a government consisting of many members with various interests, more often than not heading in different directions. The de-politicisation of the Crown in favour of symbolic representation was a fact her contemporaries, and no doubt Victoria herself, were very much aware of.

Yet another effect of Victoria's widowhood was that it brought the human, emotional appeal of the monarchy to the fore. Events such as Albert's death, the premature deaths of two of Victoria's children – Alice in 1878, Leopold in 1884 – and the many marriages and childbirths in the large royal family made it clear for everyone that the Queen was as much subject to the life-cycles of love, birth, motherhood and bereavement as anybody else in the country. In the evaluation of her prolonged mourning, the monarch's gender certainly played a role: ostentatious display of emotion was more likely to elicit the people's affection in a female ruler than it would have done in a king. On Albert's death, Victoria received thousands of letters of condolence, and Christina Rossetti captured popular sentiments

---

[1] *More Leaves from the Journal of a Life in the Highlands: From 1862-1882* (London, 1884).

[2] In 1997 the film version *Her Majesty Mrs. Brown* with Judi Dench (Queen Victoria) and Billy Connolly (John Brown) became very popular.

[3] Walter Bagehot, *The English Constitution*, p. 75. Although Bagehot probably underestimates Victoria's power to interfere in the daily business of politics, his analysis is overall precise enough for the modern constitutional monarchy.

at a time before the dissatisfaction with the Queen's withdrawal, when she composed the poem "Our Widowed Queen" immediately after Albert's death. Full of emotional appeal and strongly promoting Christian faith, the poem is based upon a notion of Victoria not predominantly as a sovereign, but as a woman, wife and mother:

Our Widowed Queen

The Husband of the Widow care for her,
The Father of the fatherless:
The faithful Friend, the abiding Comforter,
Watch over her to bless.

Full twenty years of blameless married faith,
Of love and honour questioned not,
Joys, griefs imparted: for the first time Death
Sunders the common lot.

Christ help the desolate Queen upon her throne,
Strengthen her hands, confirm her heart:
For she henceforth must bear a load alone
Borne until now in part.

Christ help the desolate Woman in her home,
Broken of heart, indeed bereft:
Shrinking from solitary days to come,
Beggared though much is left.

Rise up, O Sons and Daughters of the Dead,
Weep with your Mother where she weeps:
Yet not as sorrowing without hope be shed
Your tears: he only sleeps.

Rise up, O Sons and Daughters of the realm,
In pale reflected sorrow move:
Revere the widowed hand that holds the helm,
Love her with double love.

In royal patience of her soul possest
May she fulfil her length of days:
Then may her children rise and call her blest,
Then may her Husband praise.[1]

---

[1] In: *The Poetical Works of Christina Rossetti*, ed. William Michael Rossetti (London, 1904), p. 352. I am indebted to Alexandra Riebe for drawing my attention to this poem.

In sum, Victoria's distance from everyday public and political life made the *idea* of 'Victoria' all the more available for the projection of various wishes, hopes, fears and sympathies.

5. Empire and Jubilee Years (1870s-1901): The Queen of Consumerism

The symbolic function of the monarch was exploited from the late 1860s on, when in connection with Britain's foreign affairs and the celebration of Victoria's fiftieth and sixtieth coronation anniversaries the monarchy experienced a new wave of public appreciation. This coincided with a renewed interest in, and professionalisation of, ritual and ceremony after much ineptitude and dullness in these matters which had predominated during the first three quarters of the century.[1] Victoria's wide and complex family relations had long guaranteed her interest and influence in foreign affairs. Later in life, she came to be called the 'Grandmother of Europe', and not only because of her age. Through Victoria's nine children and 41 grandchildren, the monarchs and nobility of many countries – among them some of the most powerful nations in military and economic terms – were directly related to the British Crown: Germany, Russia, Spain, Sweden, Denmark, Greece, Norway, and Romania, to name only some.

The example of Canada shows the extent to which Victoria had become a symbolic presence which was common currency also abroad. In 1867 Canada was the first country to be proclaimed a 'Dominion' of the British Empire (later the Commonwealth), a country which enjoys autonomy in both domestic and foreign affairs, but still regards the Queen as its head of state. The other obvious example of how Victoria came to represent claims of British dominance is India. In 1877, Prime Minister Benjamin Disraeli successfully proposed a bill in Parliament to create Victoria Empress of India.[2] Although Victoria had never been to India herself, she took much pride in that title, and added a touch of the exotic to her residences by placing Indian rugs, bowls and pictures in them, and by employing Indian servants. One of these, Abdul Karim, was the object of much suspicion and mistrust, as had been John Brown. Victoria defended Karim by declaring

---

[1] See David Cannadine's lucid analysis of the poor quality of much royal ceremonial presence up to the 1870s, and the changes thereafter, in: "The Context, Performance, and Meaning of Ritual", in: *The Invention of Tradition*.

[2] In a famous cartoon in *Punch*, Disraeli is depicted as a mixture of haberdasher and Aladdin, offering the Queen the Imperial crown. This cartoon is reproduced in almost all books on Victoria.

his ethnicity irrelevant as stubbornly as she had Brown's social status. For the population, the person of the Queen created a sense of unity for a vast and varied empire and a target for the projection of pride: in Britain alone, she now ruled over almost forty million subjects, and the acquisition of the colonies meant that in the 1890s one person in four in the world was a subject of Queen Victoria. The fact that the monarch was an elderly lady, a widow, a mother and a grandmother gave the whole enterprise of aggressive imperial expansion a much more peaceful aspect than it deserved. It made the metaphor of the family a wonderfully efficient tool in the propagation and justification of imperialist ideology. Britain, with an actual matriarch at its head, could easily be projected as the mother country whose alleged duty and burden was the education of her children, the colonies.

The Empire Years were also crucial years as far as the image of the Crown *in* Britain was concerned, for they coincided with the Golden Crown Jubilee in 1887 and the Diamond Jubilee in 1897, which were in turn embedded in the wider context of renewed interest in ceremony and ritual. Not only did the Jubilees offer another opportunity to display pride in the Imperial possessions, made visible especially in 1897 by the participation in the parades of regiments from the colonies in the uniforms of their countries; these occasions also led to the culmination of one trend that had begun earlier in the century: the commodification of the monarchy.[1] Images of Victoria had long been crafted for public consumption, but with the breakthrough of commodity culture, this gained a new quality altogether. As early as 1847, an observer had complained in *Punch* about the increasing number of advertisements dominating the appearance of the country:

> Advertisements are spreading all over England, – they have crept under the bridges – have planted themselves right in the middle of the Thames – have usurped the greatest thoroughfares – and are now just on the point of invading the omnibuses. Advertising is certainly the great vehicle for the age. [...] We are haunted with advertisements enough in all shapes, tricks, and disguises. [...] Let us be a nation of shopkeepers as much as we please, but there is no necessity that we should become a nation of advertisers.[2]

---

[1] The role of the Crown as a promoter for consumer goods and the image of Victoria as a consumer have been analysed by Thomas Richards, *The Commodity Culture of Victorian England: Advertising and Spectacle, 1851-1914* (London and New York, 1991), pp. 73-118.

[2] Quoted from *The Age of Change: 1770-1870. Documents in Social History*, ed. John T. Ward (London, 1975), p. 44.

The warning was of course fruitless, and advertising became indeed a catalyst for a burgeoning economy of consumer goods, the development of which was fuelled, among other factors, by the Great Exhibition.[1] A 'nation of shopkeepers' can only survive as such, after all, if it is 'a nation of shoppers' as well. Advertising also created a public space for the presentation and negotiation of various values and ideologies, and the image of the Queen was used in advertising in a twofold capacity, as a promoter of commodities and as a commodity itself.[2]

This development can be said to have started partly with the celebration of the Golden Jubilee. In spite of many contemporary reports praising the spontaneous display of loyalty and affection for the Queen, the official Jubilee ceremonies were in fact minutely planned by the Office of Works, and the routes of the Jubilee processions were published weeks in advance to ensure maximum attendance and maximum order.[3] Commemorative plates were produced and children were given Jubilee Mugs as a present, not only at the Children's Jubilee celebrated in Hyde Park with 30,000 children, but throughout the country. The effect of such articles was that the likeness of the Queen was made available on household goods, thus lending commonplace commodities a grandeur they did not in themselves possess – a capital on which later advertisers and manufacturers were able to trade. Today's visitors to Britain will realise that this tradition, which

---

[1] On the role of the Great Exhibition in the shaping of British consumer culture, see the chapter "Commerce and Culture" in: Jeffrey A. Auerbach, *The Great Exhibition of 1851*, pp. 91-127. The changing amount and size of advertisements in pages of the *Illustrated London News* and other periodicals over the years are a good indicator for the growing strength of advertising. Leonard de Vries, *Victorian Advertisements* (London, 1968), reproduces several hundred ads and is probably the most comprehensive collection of such material.

[2] Beside Richards' account in *The Commodity Culture of Victorian England* and the illustrations therein, see the wealth of advertisements, trade cards and show cards, biscuit tins, cigar and cigarette boxes, etc. bearing the crown or the likeness of Victoria (and her offspring) reproduced mostly in colour in: Robert Opie, *Rule Britannia: Trading on the British Image* (Harmondsworth, 1985), pp. 38-50.

[3] On the planning, management (and mismanagement) of the Jubilees, see the detailed account by Jeffrey L. Lant, *Insubstantial Pageant: Ceremony and Confusion at Queen Victoria's Court* (London, 1979). The fact that the Government paid the £ 80,000 devoured by the Diamond celebration, whereas ten years earlier it was Victoria herself who had paid £ 50,000 from her privy purse to meet the costs of the Golden Jubilee (see pp. 216 and 239), indicates that public acceptance of the Queen had considerably increased in the decade between the two dates, and that politicians were able and willing to conceive of Victoria's anniversary as a politically fruitful enterprise which would justify heavy investments.

dates back to the eighteenth century, is still alive in every gift shop.[1] What was apparently not planned about the first Jubilee was that shopkeepers, advertisers and manufacturers of every kind jumped at the notion of the Jubilee and offered special Jubilee products.[2] The mugs and plates as well as commemorative medals were popular *official* Jubilee items, but loyal subjects from all classes could also obtain, sometimes for just a few pennies, objects carrying the Queen's likeness or the regalia, such as miniature portraits and miniature crowns, banners, bookmarks, jump-rope handles, or perfume bottles.[3] The "Jubilee Scent Bottle" carried a stamp-like profile image of Victoria and sported a stopper in the form of the crown. In the ad, the Empire is referred to not merely out of pride in the extent of Victoria's possessions, but also, and importantly, as a vast market: "May be purchased throughout the Empire". There is some irony in the fact that the crown on top of the bottle had to be unscrewed in order to get at the contents: the monarchy, one might say, has been degraded to packaging – what matters is the product it sells.

There were no rules or laws to regulate advertising yet, and royalty had for some time been used for marketing products, as for instance in an advertisement of Cadbury's Cocoa, showing the Queen and Princess of Wales on their way to Windsor.[4] In particular, no law existed that could enforce truth in advertising, so that the use of the phrase "by appointment", when such an appointment had never been made, was of no consequence. The notion of Victoria had turned out to be so universal, familiar and do-

---

[1] On the tradition of commemorative plates, mugs, jugs and the like, see John May and Jennifer May, *Commemorative Pottery, 1780-1900* (London, 1972). This book and John May's *Victoria Remembered: A Royal History 1817-1861* (London, 1983), illustrate that the Jubilee pottery items were nothing special, for not only were such articles produced throughout the century on occasions of varying importance, they also carried the likenesses of other members of the nobility, politicians, military heroes, and sometimes even lesser celebrities, such as prize boxers.

[2] There appears to be a precedent for this: when David Garrick initiated the Shakespeare Jubilee celebrations at Stratford-upon-Avon in 1769, medals and ribbons were produced as souvenirs, as well as memorabilia supposed to have been made from the mulberry tree in Shakespeare's garden. I am indebted to Catherine Alexander for this information.

[3] See the photos in Caroline Chapman and Paul Raben, *Debrett's Queen Victoria's Jubilees* and in William E. Fredeman, "'She Wrought Her People Lasting Good': A Commemorative Exhibition in Color of Artifacts Associated with Queen Victoria", *Victorian Poetry*, 25 (1987), 223-241. The "Jubilee Scent Bottle" advertisement of S. Mordan & Co. is reproduced and discussed in Thomas Richards, *The Commodity Culture of Victorian England*, pp. 93-95.

[4] In *The Queen*, 2 August 1884, reproduced in Leonard de Vries, *Victorian Advertisements*, p. 2 and Dorothy Marshall, *The Life and Times of Victoria*, p. 137.

mestic an image that it would sell almost anything. It seems to have been most strongly associated with common domestic articles, such as pills, food, clothes and soap, in connection with which the advertising industry increasingly portrayed Victoria. A combined Jubilee celebration and product ad of Sunlight Soap places the images of old and young Victoria side by side, which was certainly meant to transfer to the product the notions of stability and vitality associated with the long reign.[1] Perhaps the advertisers were even more presumptuous in this case; perhaps they wanted to suggest that by the use of this product, Victoria had not lost her youthful freshness even under the heavy burden of half a century's reign. A leaflet of 1893, advertising tea, strikes a similar note. It does not shrink from crude montage, showing Victoria handing the Prince of Wales and his newly-wed wife, Princess Alexandra, a package of Mazawattee Ceylon as what appears to be a wedding present. This royal wedding had taken place in 1863, and the ad suggests that the product is able to evoke a taste of the good old days ("Recalls the Delicious Teas of 30 Years Ago"), the passing of time indicated by the presence of the aged Queen.[2] Another leaflet, advertising an oats product in 1897 as "The Latest Development of Jubilee Year", depicts Victoria and a packet of the product next to a caption which puns on the respective value of both: "The two Safeguards of the Constitution".[3] The last years of Victoria's reign also saw the invention of the epithet "The Queen of ..." as an advertising strategy transferring royal superiority to a product, thus setting it off against its competitors, as is indicated for instance in a Beetham's Glycerine and Cucumber skin lotion advertisement in the *Illustrated London News* of 10 April 1897, purporting to sell "The Queen of Toilet Preparations" (p. 503).

In the last two decades of the nineteenth century, the role of women and the idea of domesticity were redefined: the middle-class female was discovered to be the main addressee of advertisements. Women were turned into shoppers, and the woman's sphere was 'widened' to include not only the home, but also the shops and department stores frequented by a largely female clientele.[4] It comes as no surprise, then, that Victoria herself was

---

[1] In *Graphic*, 28 June 1897, reproduced in Thomas Richards, *The Commodity Culture of Victorian England*, p. 117. The juxtaposition of the same two images can be seen in a showcard for Royal Fast Pile Velveteen of 1897, which uncharacteristically does not show the product, but, in a wreath of roses, a view of Windsor castle and the two images of Victoria; reproduced in Robert Opie, *Rule Britannia*, p. 42.

[2] Reproduced ibid., p. 44.

[3] Reproduced ibid., p. 47.

[4] To what extent the development of advertising and consumer culture went hand in hand with the definition and re-definition of femininity can be traced very well through the many women's magazines of the time; see Cynthia L. White, *Women's Magazines*

presented as a consumer. In a number of advertisements she is depicted either wearing or examining, and probably buying, black velvet or artificial velvet for dresses – quite a natural marketing ploy, since her strict adherence to widows weeds had associated her inseparably with that (or a comparable) material in the public mind.[1]

A magazine advertisement for velvet and a watercolour depicting the Queen's reception of debutantes in 1887 demonstrate how easily the transition was made between the realm of social symbols and that of consumer goods, and they highlight, once again, the importance of the Jubilee as a catalyst for both consumer culture and the commodification of Victoria's image. The image entitled "The Queen's Jubilee Drawing Room" (fig. 1) was a free Jubilee supplement to the *Illustrated London News* of 21 May 1887, and the "Louis" velveteen advertisement (fig. 2) had appeared, strangely enough, already in the issue of 23 April of that year. Since it is unlikely that a court journalist would have had to resort to copying motifs from advertisements for his or her reports, the fact that the ad was published *before* the extra page suggests that either the motive must have been seen by whoever drew the ad long before the painting was due to be reproduced, or in fact that the two were executed by the same person.

Victoria was of course a very special consumer, who unlike other female shoppers would not execute the domestic chores herself. The advertising industry thus shrank from depicting her in the act of consumption. Still, in a Sapolio polish ad, a caricatured old queen and king feature in the process of bringing the crown jewels to shine anew in order to maintain their subjects' admiration, as the text points out.[2]

1693-1968 (London, 1970), pp. 41-92, and Margaret Beetham, *A Magazine of Her Own? Domesticity and Desire in the Woman's Magazine, 1800-1914* (London and New York, 1996), esp. pp. 142-154 and 190-209. See also the introductory chapters in Rachel Bowlby, *Just Looking: Consumer Culture in Dreiser, Gissing and Zola* (London and New York, 1985), pp. 1-34. On the importance of fashion in this connection, see Jane Ashelford, *The Art of Dress*, pp. 256-271.

[1] See the "My Queen Vel-Vel ad" from *Graphic*, 20 August 1887, reproduced in Thomas Richards, *The Commodity Culture of Victorian England*, p. 98. Victoria's black dress is turned to good use in an unexpected way on a Crichley's Starch Gloss showcard from 1885, depicting the Queen with her children, two of them playing music (even the long-deceased Prince Consort is there to complete the family circle, in a painting hung on the back wall); the girls are dressed in shining white, and Victoria's white veil and lace collar are highlighted by the darkness of her dress. The showcard is reproduced in Robert Opie, *Rule Britannia*, p. 45.

[2] *Illustrated London News*, 29 January 1887, p. 125. In contrast to Thomas Richards, who sees Victoria herself depicted in this image (in: *The Commodity Culture of Victorian England*, p. 100), I can detect no similarities between stout and portly Queen Victoria and the wizened little old woman in the ad, and the presence of the old king figure

The monarch, who could once boast of being anointed, elected by the grace of God, had thus entered the realm of domestic consumerism – cynics might say that ointment had been replaced by detergent. This connection between the Crown and the Commonplace should not be understood merely as a trivialisation of monarchy. Rather, it was one way of expressing a feeling that many of her subjects in all classes of society shared, namely that Victoria had become a household word. After all, the consumption and use of goods associated with the Queen either by advertisements or by the reproduction of her very image on them, established a close link between the monarch and her subjects in their daily lives. She thus served as a symbol of stability in times of social, demographic, technological, scientific and ideological change in more than a merely official, political sense.

6. Conclusion

The monarchy in the phases of Victoria's reign saw a decrease in immediate political influence. The administration and legislation of a modern industrialised state had to be left to an increasing number of specialists or would-be specialists chosen by the majority of the voters. After the Reform Acts of 1867 and 1884 the electorate had increased to include ever more voters from the lower social strata, and domestic politics had become a more varied and unreliable affair. At the same time, the British Empire reached out to cover territories and cultures so vast and diverse that the very notion of its extent and significance became hard to grasp at all. Thus, a reassuring symbol of unity, a recognisable figurehead – in every sense of the word – of national identity and stability, capable of glossing over the internal and external diversities and changes in Britain, was highly welcome in the public as well as in the private sphere.

The increase in the symbolic significance of the monarch as an image representing national unity and a point of identification for people in all walks of life needs to be seen in connection with the growth of commodity culture and the advertising industry. By widely distributing domestic consumer goods and activities in the public sphere, advertising worked towards bridging the ideological gap that existed between the public and the private. In the framework of a gendered semantics of domesticity, the fact

---

would further seem to forbid the association. For a similar example, see a "Matchless metal polish ad" of 1910 reproduced in Robert Opie, *Rule Britannia*, p. 42, in which, however, the polishing of an oversized crown and sceptre is done by miniature servants in Beefeater costumes.

that the monarch was a woman facilitated the transitions between the two. The monarchy could be presented as closely connected to the daily life of British subjects by producing images of Victoria as a consumer and by aligning her with the goods for consumption. Thus, by a succession of images of 'Victoria', either projected onto the person Victoria or publicised by her, the British monarchy in the nineteenth century mastered the transition to a modern, constitutional monarchy, paving the way for later epochs.

Fig. 1: "The Queen's Jubilee Drawing Room", (unnamed artist), *Illustrated London News*, 21 May 1887, n.p. Copyright: Mary Evans Picture Library. Reproduced by permission.

"LOUIS" VELVETEEN.

THE

The strictest examiner may try every test of touch and sight without discovering that these are other than the Genoa Velvets they so closely resemble, while the peculiar arrangements resulting in the Fast-woven Pile enable them to stand interminable wear that would ruin real velvets at four times the price.

Special attention is drawn to the colours, which for brilliancy, depth of tone, and magnificent appearance are quite perfection.

Note well! The word "Louis" in connection with this Velveteen, is spelled "L-O-U-I-S," and in no other way.

Every yard of the genuine bears the name "Louis," and the wear of every yard, from the cheapest quality to the best, guaranteed.

MAY BE HAD FROM DRAPERS THROUGHOUT THE KINGDOM.

Fig. 2: "The 'Louis' Velveteen", *Illustrated London News*, 23 April 1887, 15.
Courtesy of Wuerttembergische Landesbibliothek Stuttgart.

Victoria, Shakespeare's Second Queen

By *Georgianna Ziegler* (Washington)

Friendship's Offering, the elegant gift-book annual for 1843, includes a frontispiece engraving showing the youthful Queen Victoria and Prince Albert seated on a sofa, she with the baby Prince of Wales in her lap and first-born daughter, Vicky, at her knee.[1] The accompanying poem by Camilla Toulmin looks backward over the ancient rulers of Britain to whom Victoria is heir and imagines that "the best and wisest" of them, "Do greet thee with Banquo's mirror fair," where they "Had traced thyself – thy virtues on its crystal side".[2] Toulmin here refers to Shakespeare's *Macbeth*, where Banquo appears with eight kings in Macbeth's final apparition, the last of whom holds up a mirror which shows "many more" kings to come. While Macbeth views only the doom of his barren crown, Victoria sees her virtuous self as the culmination of an illustrious royal line. The hidden actor in this imagined fantasy is Shakespeare himself, the creator of the ghostly mirror and the presenter of a whole line of English kings through his history plays. Carrying this fantasy one step further, we might even say that Toulmin has written Victoria into Shakespeare's script. The nineteenth century whole-heartedly appropriated Shakespeare and his plays as no previous era had done, and Victoria as queen both facilitated this appropriation and was implicated by it. Through their personal love of the theater, she and Albert provided respectability for a kind of entertainment that was rapidly falling into public disrepute, while as the queenly ruler of an empire and the ideal of womanhood, Victoria represented the English values associated with Shakespeare and his characters and came to be represented herself *as* those characters.

Six years after Toulmin's piece appeared, John Kemble Chapman in 1849 celebrated the first season of commissioned dramatic performances at Windsor Castle by voicing a similar sentiment:

> Enthroned beneath that canopy where an Alfred awakened amongst the inhabitants of this island a taste for literature and the polite arts, none will dispute the title of Queen Victoria to be the chief arbitress of the empire's taste – the guide of the nation's morals. [...] Her Majesty has had the good taste and the courage to

---

[1] *Friendship's Offering*, vol. 20 (London, 1843). The frontispiece is by F.P. Stephanoff.

[2] Ibid., p.2.

come forward and rescue from neglect that department of letters which beholds a Shakspere at its head, and the members of that profession whose chief business it is to interpret and popularise Shakspere ...[1]

Chapman invokes the name of Alfred – the Anglo-Saxon king who cultivated the arts – as Toulmin had invoked Banquo, to represent the honorable ancient past of British royalty, now inherited by a young woman who, because she embodies both taste and morality, has the power to revive English drama, epitomized by Shakespeare.

In reality, Victoria's taste in theater ran more heavily to opera than to Shakespeare, but when the two were combined along with a beautiful leading lady, as in Rossini's *Otello*, her early enthusiasm knew no bounds, as evidenced by the effusions in her diary over the three performances of this opera that she attended when she was fourteen and fifteen.[2] *King John* at Drury Lane in 1833 seems to have been her first Shakespeare play and led her to a notable preference for Macready's acting, but five years later when she was eighteen and newly crowned, she saw *Hamlet* with Charles Kean, and immediately fell under his spell.

> His conception of this very difficult and I may almost say incomprehensible character, is admirable; his delivery of all the fine long speeches quite beautiful [...] the two finest scenes I thought were the *Play-scene*, which he acts, they say, quite differently to any other actor who has performed Hamlet; and the scene with his mother, the Queen.[3]

Victoria's early views on Shakespeare were formed in part through conversations with her mentor, Lord Melbourne, but her marriage to Albert brought her an even closer companion who loved the theater and who helped to guide her interest in that direction.[4]

---

[1] *The Court Theatre, and Royal Dramatic Record; being a complete history of theatrical entertainments at the English Court, from the time of King Henry the Eighth down to the termination of the series of entertainments before Her Most Gracious Majesty Queen Victoria, His Royal Highness Prince Albert, and the Court, at Windsor Castle, Christmas, 1848-9*, ed. John K[emble] Chapman (London, [1849?]).

[2] Victoria wrote on 6 April 1835 that she had seen *Otello* again – "Desdemona, Mdlle. Grisi, who looked beautiful and sung most exquisitely and acted beautifully. She personates the meek and ill-treated Desdemona in a most perfect and touching manner." In: *The Girlhood of Queen Victoria*, ed. R.B.B. Esher (New York and London, 1912), vol.1, p. 111. [Referred to in text as *Diaries*.]

[3] Victoria, *Diaries*, vol.1, pp. 265-266.

[4] Victoria's early reading of Shakespeare came from copies of Lambs' *Tales from Shakespeare*, and Pittman's *School Shakspeare*, given to her respectively in 1826 (when

It was Albert who proposed setting up a stage for the performance of plays at court, thus leading to the first Windsor Castle season commemorated by John Chapman. Victoria chose Charles Kean to manage the court theater, which he did for almost ten years from 1848 to 1857. The first season opened with *The Merchant of Venice* and included *Hamlet*. The royal family frequented other London theaters as well, and in all they saw seventy-six productions of Shakespeare's plays until the early death of Albert in 1861. Their favorites – all of which they saw several times – were *King John, Macbeth, Richard II, Richard III, Henry V, King Lear*, and *The Winter's Tale*.[1] Not surprisingly, it is the plays about British history that most attracted them, but some of this attraction was undoubtedly caused by the wonderful scenic effects, especially what Victoria calls the "striking Tableaux" which she notes in her journal. After their first viewing of *The Winter's Tale* in 1856, she comments:

> Albert was in ecstasies, for really the 'mise-en-scène', the beautiful and numerous changes of scenery, the splendid and strictly correct antique costumes, all taken from the best works and models, the excellent grouping of every scene, the care with which every trifle was attended to, made a unique performance.[2]

Upon looking at her journals and sketchbooks, it becomes evident that Victoria was always drawn to the visual over the verbal; from an early age she described actors' gestures and made sketches of her favorite performers in costume. At the age of thirteen she recorded the charades at Chatsworth where members of the court put on scenes from several plays;[3] later her own children took part in family theatricals; and in the last years of her reign, "tableaux-vivants" were still being enacted at Balmoral and Osborne.

Nevertheless, in spite of these visual preferences, Victoria also enjoyed that other nineteenth-century pastime – reading aloud. In 1844 she invited the elderly Charles Kemble to court for a reading of *Cymbeline*, and years later she was entertained with readings by her actress-friend, Helena Faucit, Lady Martin. Fanny Kemble recorded that her father's usual two-hour reading for audiences who "required that the plays should be compressed into the measure of their intellectual *short*-suffering capacity," had to be cut to forty-five minutes for the court.[4] The popular magazine *Punch* had a

---

she was seven) and 1831 (when she was twelve). (Lynne Vallone, *Becoming Victoria* [New Haven, 2001], p. 47).

[1] Statistics reckoned from "A Calendar of Queen Victoria's Theatregoing" in: George Rowell, *Queen Victoria Goes to the Theatre* (London, 1978), pp. 128-138.

[2] Quoted ibid., p. 56.

[3] Victoria, *Diaries*, vol. 1, p. 56.

[4] Frances Ann Kemble, *Records of Later Life* (New York, 1882), p. 653.

field-day with this attempt to refine the court.[1] It printed a fake letter from Kemble recounting his conversations about Shakespeare with a sampling of courtiers and their subsequent "conversion" to the Bard after hearing the readings. The twenty-three year old "Maid of Honor" comes close to being a parody of the young Victoria herself:

> Had certainly heard of Shakspeare, when a little girl and before she came to court; but had seldom had her attention called to the subject since. [...] Thinks she has heard it said that he was a low man, and wrote very bad English; for that reason was advised never to hear him except in Italian at the opera. Knew an opera called *Otello*; [...] Had certainly heard of the swan of Avon; believes that she once saw it in the Zoological Gardens. [...] such has already been my success with this be-nighted young woman, that [...] every night [she] takes her rest with the Family Shakspeare under her pillow.[2]

The intellectual snobbery about the court that colors this piece lingers today in modern British humor, but by raising the hypothetical question "What do you expect?", the piece implicitly answers that it, in fact, *does* expect a certain level of engagement with the best of English culture on the part of the court.

Punch was a staple of many households from the Queen's down through those of the middle classes. Its aim was to keep the country honest, and like the many bowdlerized editions of Shakespeare designed for reading at home to a mixed audience, *Punch* was touted as a magazine that "may safely be introduced into the family circle, where it will provoke many a hearty laugh, but never can call a blush to the most delicate cheek." Prince Albert himself said, "if you want to know what public men are like, you must study the caricatures of their day," and neither he nor the Queen was exempt from *Punch's* humorous bite.[3] The magazine relied heavily on liter-ary parody "to make a topical point," and no other writer was parodied as frequently as Shakespeare. As Richard Altick has noted, "In doing so, [*Punch*] followed a long tradition based on the assumption that the rank and file of the English people knew enough Shakespeare to appreciate a

---

[1] Queen Victoria herself is known to have read *Punch*; see Richard Altick, *Punch: the Lively Youth of a British Institution* (Columbus, 1997), pp. 17-18. For a survey of the representations of Victoria in *Punch* see William E. Fredeman, "A Charivari for Queen Butterfly: *Punch* on Queen Victoria," in *Victorian Poetry*, 25 (1987), 47-73. Be-sides the few associations with Shakespearean characters, Victoria was also represented as Calypso, Red Riding Hood, and Queen Elizabeth, among others. Neither Altick nor Fredeman deals extensively with any of the Victoria/Shakespeare cartoons.

[2] Quoted in *Littell's Living Age*, 1 (July 22, 1844), 332.

[3] Quoted in Altick, *Punch*, pp. 10, 18.

joke that alluded to one of his plays".[1] With its trademark combination of irreverence and adulation, *Punch* drew on Shakespeare's plays at key moments during Victoria's reign to comment on social weaknesses or political crises. Appropriating the Queen into the Shakespearean text, *Punch* treated Victoria as a kind of Alice who might be made to see what ought to be done only by finding herself in a context at once familiar and strange.

In August of 1845 while on a visit to Bonn, Victoria participated in the dedication of a statue to Beethoven on the seventy-fifth anniversary of his birthday. *Punch* reported that Victoria was inspired by that occasion to propose erecting a commemorative statue to Shakespeare at Dover. The Queen had made no such proposal, but it was the very *absence* of royal interest in supporting the icon of English culture that prompted *Punch* to this further satire. What the piece ironically claims for Victoria is what it wants her to be: a national figurehead who honors herself and her country by honoring its greatest treasure – Shakespeare.

> All glory then to Queen Victoria! who, in honouring [...] God-lighted genius, casts a lustre on herself and reign! All glory to the monarch who, with the quick and delicate sympathies of womanhood, acknowledges the power that makes the true grandeur of her own land – who acknowledges in her native English, as breathed by Shakspeare, a thoughtful muse that softens and refines the world![2]

Two years later, the Queen is still being chided for her apparent unresponsiveness to Shakespeare. A newspaper article from May of 1847 reports Douglas Jerrold's comments from the sixth annual meeting of the Shakspeare Society which honored Mary Cowden Clarke's new *Concordance*. Jerrold notes:

> In consequence of a Queen presiding over us, as in Shakespeare's time, Mrs. Cowden Clarke intended to dedicate the work to her present Majesty; and so, as we think, to bestow a compliment, but it was refused. It would surely not have been so by the Queen who delighted in the 'Merry Wives of Windsor'.[3]

The greatest sting in this remark may be the implication that Elizabeth was the better queen, taken in the context of the generally ambivalent attitudes towards the earlier queen during Victoria's reign.[4] Elizabeth was often seen

---

[1] Altick, *Punch*, p. 93.

[2] *Punch*, 9 (1845), 118.

[3] Apparently the Queen declined "'in consequence of the *very numerous* applications ...'" (Richard Altick, *The Cowden Clarkes* [London, 1948], p. 121).

[4] On the conflicted attitudes towards Queen Elizabeth as a model for Queen Victoria, see Nicola J. Watson, "Gloriana Victoriana: Victoria and the Cultural Memory of Eliza-

as coarse, vulgar, and unladylike. An article in the *Spectator*, for example, in 1844, commenting on the young Victoria's visit to the chapel in Burghley House where Elizabeth had been, remarks unfavorably on Elizabeth's low taste, her spinsterhood and childlessness. It concludes, "Shakspeare graced Elizabeth's day, but Victoria's day is more worthy of Shakspeare."[1] Elizabeth was seen as a queen who compromised her femininity in order to rule. Victoria, with her marriage, motherhood, and good manners, epitomized the female ruler. All that was lacking, according to the satirists, was that Victoria herself be more appreciative of and thus worthy of Shakespeare. The institution of theatrical seasons at Windsor beginning in 1848 helped to rehabilitate her image with a public that was more insistently adopting Shakespeare as its national icon.

In his conclusion to *The Court Theatre*, John Chapman summarized the cultural importance of Victoria's act:

> In the stately hall of her ancient palace she witnessed the ever-enduring creations of Nature's master-mind presented in living reality before her, and afforded a proof of her estimation of the morality and dignity of the drama that should never be forgotten by those who love it ...[2]

The "stately hall" and "ancient palace" remind us that Victoria may be bringing Shakespeare into the home, but it is the home of the nation, that place that ties her to the ancient lineage of British kings. The conception of Shakespeare as "Nature's master-mind" and his work as "ever-enduring" raises him also to a place of timeless honor in the history of this nation. Shakespeare thus graces Victoria by the lustre of his genius and his ties to the culture of the past, while Victoria graces Shakespeare by accepting him into her home – making his work "a domestic entertainment" – that ensures its propriety for her people.[3]

---

beth I", in: *Remaking Queen Victoria*, ed. Margaret Homans and Adrienne Munich (Cambridge, 1997), pp. 79-104; and Margaret Homans, *Royal Representations: Queen Victoria and British Culture, 1837-1876* (Chicago, 1998), pp. xxxii-xxxiii, 11-12, etc.

[1] *Spectator*, Nov. 16, 1844 in *Littell's*, 3 (1844), 490.

[2] Chapman, *Court Theatre*, p. 78.

[3] During an 1857 Kean production of *Richard II* at Windsor, the Queen was startled to find the last scene "set in St. George's Hall, the very room in which the performance itself was taking place." Writing about this incident, Richard Schoch comments that "the reincarnation of Victoria's ancestral figures within her own home [...] exemplifies what the performance attempted to provide for its entire audience: an opportunity to review the personages and places of the nation's history and, more crucially, to identify with that history at a personal level." (Richard Schoch, *Shakespeare's Victorian Stage* [Cambridge, 1998], p. 123).

Many of these associations are illustrated emblematically on the title page to the 1860 edition of Shakespeare's *Works* published in London and New York by John Tallis. The title itself appears superimposed on a globe, showing the half of the world in which England had its empire – Africa, India, and Australia. Six small surrounding vignettes depict five nineteenth-century London theaters and Shakespeare's birthplace. At the top and bottom of the globe are larger vignettes depicting, respectively, the production of *The Merchant of Venice* before the court at Windsor and a production of what may be *Julius Caesar* before Queen Elizabeth in one of her palaces. Crowning the top vignette is the royal coat-of-arms with lion and unicorn rampant. The whole design says clearly that Britain is proud of its theater; that it respects its greatest playwright (whose birthplace is shown) by performing his works at court; that he is appreciated now, perhaps more than he was in his own time (there are many more people watching the production at Victoria's court than at Elizabeth's, and there are more theaters); that Britain has built its current culture upon the past (the pictures of the Globe, Shakespeare's birthplace, and Elizabeth at court are all at the bottom of the page); and that the works of Shakespeare now extend English civilization over the globe, as do the words of the title *The Works of William Shakspere* spread over the map beneath.

In 1858 Victoria officially became Queen of India, but already in the 1840s it was Carlyle who gave expression to Shakespeare as the national poet-hero and his implication in the grand scheme of empire-building. "Consider now, if they asked us, Will you give-up your Indian Empire or your Shakspeare, you English [...] should not we be forced to answer: Indian Empire or no Indian Empire; we cannot do without Shakspeare!" Carlyle goes on to imagine what the 1860 title page illustrates; that soon

> this Island of ours, will hold but a small fraction of the English: in America, in New Holland, east and west to the very Antipodes, there will be a Saxondom covering great spaces of the Globe. And now, what is it that can keep all these together into virtually one Nation?

– his answer, of course is Shakespeare, or as he calls him, "King Shakspeare" who shines "in crowned sovereignty, over us all, as the noblest, gentlest, yet strongest of rallying-signs".[1]

Victoria herself certainly shared this position with Shakespeare; as queen she was the noblest and "strongest of rallying signs," and as a woman she was the "gentlest." The American, Sarah Hale, described Victoria's ap-

---

[1] Carlyle's comments appear in "The Hero as Poet", from *On Heroes, Hero-Worship and the Heroic in History* (London, 1897), pp. 135, 136.

pearance before men of many nations at the opening of the great Crystal Palace Exposition in 1851, "as one who had the 'monarch power,' yet sweetly modified by the character of wife and mother."[1] All of these public images coalesce in a full-page political cartoon, published in *Punch* on October 10, 1857 during the siege of Lucknow and following news of the massacre of Cawnpore in July, when hundreds of English women and children were brutally murdered, after three weeks under siege in unspeakable conditions. Upon hearing the news, the Queen wrote to her uncle, King Leopold, "'the horrors committed on the poor ladies – women and children – are unknown in these ages and make one's blood run cold.'"[2] The cartoon shows her kneeling in a plain dress, her head circled by a small crown, and her eyes raised to heaven. In one arm she holds an infant to her breast, while her other hand reaches protectively for three small children who stand in front of her. A small boy kneels at her side in prayer, and around her kneel children, and women veiled in mourning, representing both those who have died and those at home who mourn for them. Under the cartoon are simply the words, "O God of battles! steel my soldier's [sic] hearts!" No source was needed, for much of the public would have recognized the words of Henry V from Shakespeare's play, before the battle of Agincourt. Carlyle in 1840 had called the battle "one of the most perfect things" in Shakespeare; "there is a noble Patriotism in it [...] a true English heart breathes, calm and strong, through the whole business".[3]

In her discussion of the depiction of women as part of the artistic response to the Indian Mutiny, Pamela Gerrish Nunn points out that the actual occurrence of women and children as victims allowed Victorian society to re-assert the roles of "female distress and male valor," countering "the discomfiting image of the strong-minded, would-be independent woman of recent times" stemming from "reform in divorce law and married women's economic rights" in the early 1850s.[4] Nunn reads this *Punch* cartoon as showing the Queen aligned with her suffering female subjects, "a solidarity amongst 'good' women, in contrast with the distance Victoria

---

[1] Sarah J. Hale, *Woman's Record; or, Sketches of all distinguished women, from "the beginning" till A.D. 1850* (New York, 1853), p. 809.

[2] Cecil Woodham-Smith, *Queen Victoria* (New York, 1972), p. 385. "The Queen was haunted '*day* and night' by the horror of the massacre, and asked Lady Canning [wife of the Governor-General of India] to let those 'who have *lost* dear ones in so dreadful a manner *know* of my sympathy. A woman and above all a wife and mother can only *too well* enter into the agonies' of the bereaved" (Giles St. Aubyn, *Queen Victoria: A Portrait* [New York, 1992], p. 306).

[3] Carlyle, "Hero as Poet", p. 131.

[4] Pamela Gerrish Nunn, *Problem Pictures: Men and Women in Victorian Painting* (Aldershot, 1995), pp. 73-74.

put between herself and strong-minded women such as those who had been campaigning for social change".[1] I would like to complicate this argument by suggesting that the association of Victoria with Henry V in this cartoon reminds the audience of her sameness *and* difference with the great British hero-king. Like Henry, she is the ruler of Britain, responsible for her troops and her people. Because she is a woman, however, she can fill only part of his duties; she cannot take command in the field, but she can pray for the divine support of her armies. Victoria is represented in the attitude of the saintly woman, popular at the time, hands clasped and eyes raised to heaven;[2] nevertheless, she wears the crown of her political office. This image, however, is double-edged, for while associating Victoria with the heroic and popular Henry V, it implies a contrast with his well-trained army, outnumbered but sustaining low casualties at Agincourt, against the outnumbered troops in India with the enormous casualties of British soldiers and civilians.

As a result of the Sepoy Mutiny, Victoria took over the governance of India from the East India Company in 1858, changing the wording of the proclamation so that it "'should breathe feelings of generosity, benevolence, and religious toleration,'" as coming from a female sovereign who wished to be conciliatory.[3] This time the *Punch* cartoon shows Victoria standing in her regal robes, and holding up her scepter while she looks down at an Indian woman kneeling at her feet, who raises her hand to touch the scepter in submission.[4] The woman's dark skin, baggy trousers, and nose ring signify her as "other" – a woman who is as different from Victoria as it is possible to be, submitting herself to the epitomy of English womanhood. Nunn explicates this image as the mother with the prodigal daughter, but it might also be seen as the domesticated, civilized woman bringing the uncivilized into her fold.[5] In another way, however, one is again reminded of Shakespeare's Henry V, who "generously" offers not to

---

[1] Ibid., p. 77.

[2] This iconographic type may be traced to Titian's "Penitent Magdalen" and reappears in many paintings, including Johnson's "Cordelia" for Charles Heath's *Heroines of Shakspeare*, 1848. On the type, see Susan Haskins, *Mary Magdalen* (New York, 1993), pp. 242-243.

[3] Woodham-Smith, *Queen Victoria*, p. 386.

[4] *Punch*, September 11, 1857.

[5] Nunn, *Problem Pictures*, p. 90. Nunn quotes from the introductory material to this volume of *Punch* which sexualizes the female figure at Victoria's feet, seeing in her the other side of womanhood, sensual desire, as opposed to Victoria's comfortable motherhood. "And behold a maiden, dusky, but lovely as the summer night [...]. Her form, modestly but lightly attired, was graceful as is that of the gazelle [...]. Her name was India."

rape and pillage the citizens of Harfleur if they will give up their town peacefully, and who then seals his bargain with the French by forcing Katherine to an agreement of marriage. In both cases – Henry in France and Victoria in India – there may be toleration but it comes as part of the project for conquest or colonization. Shakespeare is implicated in the grand hegemonic scheme of Victorian Britain.[1]

Lending authority to this scheme were the large, elegant volumes of the "Imperial Shakspere," edited by the ubiquitous Charles Knight and published by Virtue in 1875, the year before Victoria was created Empress of India. Designed for book shelves or "drawing-room table," this edition saw itself as a successor to the earlier Boydell Shakespeare by including engravings of paintings from the modern English school – many of them exhibited at the Royal Academy – forming "a lasting record of the present state of High Art." The plays with accompanying images were sold in parts which could then be bound at the discretion of the purchaser. The size and cost of the volumes directed them to upper middle-class households with the leisure to sit in their drawing rooms and look at illustrated books. The nationalistic agenda behind this edition is made clear in the rhetoric of its advertisement on the back cover of the first installment, combining pride in the English school of painting with "the national love for the poet, the reverence for his genius, and the patriotic pride in his writings." The term "Imperial" from the series title suggests at once the size of the volumes (imperial is a standard large-sized paper), the exalted quality of the literature and art presented therein, and the British Empire itself. Here Shakespeare and the English artists inspired by him are packaged in a format that proclaims British cultural superiority at home and abroad. Underscoring this view are the advertisements on three of the parts for a similar handsome publishing enterprise: Virtue's *History of India and of the British Empire in the East*, illustrated with steel engravings and maps.

Henry V was not the only one of Shakespeare's characters through whom Victoria was represented. Just a short time before the mutiny in India, England had extricated itself from a disastrous and botched campaign in the

---

[1] A copy of Shakespeare's *Plays* (London, 1842) at the Folger Library contains a handwritten note on the flyleaf saying that the book was used by various men of the Sterling family in the Crimea, the Indian Mutiny, the Egyptian Campaign, and the Soudan. By the time it went off to the last of these campaigns, it must have been felt to carry talismanic properties, but it was literally a piece of English culture carried into strange and dangerous places.

On Kean's attempt to stage *Henry V* shortly after the Crimean War, see Schoch, *Shakespeare's Victorian Stage*, pp. 138-139. "Kean wanted simultaneously to bask in a 'glow of patriotic enthusiasm' and yet to disown the violence out of which that very patriotism blazed forth."

Crimea. After suffering defeat in battle, low troop morale, insufficient supplies and much disease, the British spent months negotiating with the other involved powers – Russia, France, Austria, and Germany – before a peace treaty was signed at the end of March 1856. Reflecting the general frustration leading up to the treaty, a cartoon in *Punch* for February 23, 1856 is entitled "Scene from A Midsummer Night's Dream (As Performed at Windsor Castle)". It shows Victoria as Titania, putting flowers in a wreath around the ass's head of a general seated on the ground, who is labeled "Bottom [...] By General Mismanagement." The accompanying text on the facing page cleverly rewrites the Shakespearean scene. Announcing that he has just come from the Crimea, Bottom says,

> Why I was sent thither I know not, being but an ass; but, marry, they were greater asses that sent me. I went to feed and to lead lions, and truly I have fed and led them, and that in such sort that they need feeding and leading no more. Now for my reward, for I humbly hope a worshipful ass may be rewarded for his good service.

Bottom represents the English officers sent with little preparation or support into a terrible campaign in which they lost many of their men, those who "need feeding and leading no more." The Queen as Titania says, "I know thy deeds," everyone around me on whom I rely has said "that thou hast done / That which should be rewarded. Therefore take / Orders, and rank, and pay, with our Court favour." The Queen is shown here being as misled by her advisors as the English officers were by their superiors. *Tita*nia here wears the dress of *Brit*annia, but she has laid her shield aside, while she plays with flowers, suggesting that she has laid off some of her responsibilities to shield the country and its military. The figure of Oberon hovering in the background is not identified, but he would seem to represent the lately-deceased Wellington, on whose death Victoria noted in her journal, "'He seems to have gone out like a lamp.'"[1] Oberon holds a wand with a sparkling star at its tip, suggesting that if Wellington had been present, he might have made everything about the Crimean morass come out smoothly in the end.[2] About twenty years later, Victoria would again be styled as "Queen Titania," this time by her Prime Minister, Disraeli, to whom she sent primroses with her dispatches. He described her in his letters as a Titania "'who had been gathering flowers with her Court in a soft and sea-girt isle, and had sent me some blossoms which, according to the

---

[1] Quoted in Elizabeth Longford, *Victoria R.I.* (London, 1964; rpt. 1998), p. 231.

[2] The actual 1856 season of plays at Windsor did not include a performance of *A Midsummer Night's Dream*.

legend, had deprived the recipient of his senses.'"[1] Disraeli's flattery of the
fifty-six-year-old Queen, worthy of an Elizabethan courtier, continued the
following year when he facilitated the passage of the Royal Titles Act in
Parliament, thus working a kind of magic himself to make her Empress of
India.

The imperial title was one Victoria almost missed by withdrawing herself
entirely from any public expression of her queenly duties in the years following the death of Prince Albert in 1861. Two years of mourning would
have been considered acceptable under Victorian protocol, but when year
followed year and the Queen still withdrew from all public ceremonies except those dedicating memorials to Albert, members of her government
were frustrated, the people were anxious, and there was even talk of her
abdication.[2] Four years into this bleak period, on September 23, 1865,
Punch published another cartoon using Shakespearean associations to
comment on the problem of a queen who refused her royal duties. Here
Victoria is Hermione; dressed in white with her full regalia – robes of state,
crown, orb and scepter – she is revealed on a pedestal as Paulina/Britannia
draws the curtains from in front of her. The caption reads: "'Tis time! Descend; be stone no more."

In her study, *Royal Representations*, Margaret Homans points out that the
power of the monarchy in the nineteenth century, though reduced, "was
understood to remain theatrical, as it had been in Elizabethan times".[3] She
argues convincingly that during these years following Albert's death, "the
monarch's chief representational form [was] her invisibility," and furthermore, that Victoria consciously "represented" her absence in a variety of
ways, including the dedication of innumerable memorials to Albert and the
publication of books about him and about her life in the Highlands.[4] Her
few public appearances were carefully staged, notably her presence in
widow's weeds, watching the Prince of Wales's wedding from a gallery
overlooking St. George's Chapel – which Victoria herself described as "'a
scene in a play'" – and her first appearance in 1866 at an opening of Parliament since her husband's death.[5] On the latter occasion she remained
silent, a small figure in black, sitting on the throne over which were draped
the robes of state she refused to wear, listening to her speech being read by

---

[1] Quoted in Stanley Weintraub, *Victoria: An Intimate Biography* (New York, 1988),
p. 414.

[2] See Homans, *Royal Representations*, p. 59 and Weintraub, *Victoria*, p. 321.

[3] Ibid., p. 59.

[4] Ibid.

[5] Homans, *Royal Representations*, pp. 60, 64.

the Lord Chancellor.[1] She described herself, again using theatrical imagery, as having been "dragged in deep mourning, alone in State as a Show".[2]

In his editorial comments on *The Winter's Tale*, Stephen Orgel notes that while seeing and hearing are both explored as ways of knowing in the play, neither is deemed more important than the other: "it makes no difference whether [...] knowledge is constituted by what we observe or what we are told."[3] For the Victorians, seeing was eminently important. A society that distributed and collected thousands of objects and images through manufacture and the printed media needed to see the queen's person as a validation of the monarchy it was supporting.[4] The *Punch* cartoon plays on this need and on the popularity of the statue scene in the theater of the time. It is, in fact, very close to the drawing of this scene recording the famous Charles Kean production of *The Winter's Tale* in 1856, which Queen Victoria had attended four times, commenting on the splendidness of its costumes and scenery in her journal.[5] The drawing, reproduced in the *Illustrated London News*, shows Hermione in classical white robes, standing on a pedestal of steps and looking out to her left, while Paulina stands just to her right, pointing at the "statue" she has revealed to the court. The stage design is made to give the impression of hundreds of people waiting for the revelation. The *Punch* cartoon shows Victoria/Hermione in the white of her coronation robes, also standing atop a stepped pedestal and looking to her left. Instead of pointing, the Britannia/Paulina figure also on her right, holds the curtain while she looks in on the "statue." The crowds at court are metaphorically replaced by the thousands of readers of *Punch* and the general citizenry of Victoria's realm.

In the play, when Leontes sees the statue he comments, "Hermione was not so much wrinkled, nothing / So aged as this seems" (V.iii.28-29). The "statue" has aged because it is not art, but life. The image of Victoria produced by *Punch* is based on her youthful appearance during the years when Albert was alive; the actual Queen who will return to her people will show the signs of grief and the blackness of her mourning garb; like the statue in the play, she will be the same but different. During Hermione's absence, Paulina keeps her memory alive and then reveals the woman she has hidden for so many years. The helmeted figure of Britannia, associated during

[1] Weintraub, *Victoria*, p. 335.
[2] Quoted in Homans, *Royal Representations*, p. 64.
[3] Orgel, Introduction to *The Winter's Tale* (Oxford, 1996), p. 58.
[4] On the proliferation of images and things during the Victorian period, see Asa Briggs, *Victorian Things* (London, 1990) and Thomas Richards, *The Commodity Culture of Victorian England* (Stanford, 1990).
[5] Rowe, *Queen Victoria Goes to the Theatre*, p. 56.

Victoria's reign most strongly with the might of Britain, draws the curtain to reveal the Queen who is the rightful human figurehead behind the allegorical representation of her nation.[1] Victoria's world, however, is not the world of the play where it seems impossibilities can occur. While Leontes rejoices in the return of his wife from a supposed death, Victoria still mourned the real death of her beloved Albert; none of the many statues of him raised in response to her grief would bring back the living man.

It is the aged, widowed figure of the Queen, shrouded in black mourning weeds, grandmother to half the houses of Europe and an empire as well, who dominates the last forty years of her reign. Gone are the performances of Shakespeare at Windsor Castle; indeed, only during the last twenty years of the reign, beginning in 1881, did Victoria reinstitute command theatrical performances at court. Most of these consisted of opera and popular plays, with the exception of an invitation to Henry Irving and Ellen Terry to perform the trial scene from *The Merchant of Venice* at Sandringham in April 1889.[2] But Shakespeare no longer needed support from the court; he had achieved full respectability on the English stage, where his plays were represented with both the epitome of spectacular theater under Herbert Beerbohm-Tree, and the newer experimental staging of William Poel and of Frank Benson at the Shakespeare Memorial Theatre in Stratford. Meanwhile, Victoria continued to have Shakespeare read to her at home by the actresses Caroline Heath and Isabella Glyn (both of whom had worked for Charles Kean) and who successively held the post of "Reader to the Queen." In the 1880s Victoria read with interest Helena Faucit Martin's essays on Ophelia and Desdemona, leading to her invitation for Martin's book *Letters on Shakespeare's Women* to be dedicated to the Queen.[3] As Shakespeare was thus domesticated at court, so in the homes of Victoria's subjects was he made available through hundreds of popular and scholarly editions, and confirmed as a Literary Figure through integration into the

---

[1] Marina Warner notes, "In the course of the nineteenth century, Britannia, the personification of the constitution, fades before Britannia as the might of Britain. Not surprisingly the dissemination of the figure increases during the reign of Queen Victoria." The helmet of Athena was added to the figure in 1821, giving a military aspect that was only subdued in 1971 by the addition of an olive branch (Marina Warner, *Monuments and Maidens: the Allegory of the Female Form* [London, 1985; rpt. 1995], p. 48).

[2] See the list of command performances in Rowell, *Queen Victoria Goes to the Theatre*, p. 138.

[3] On the Queen's Readers, see *The Private Life of the Queen* (London, 1897); rpt. (Old Working, Eng., 1979), pp. 122-123; on the Queen and Lady Martin, see Theodore Martin, *Helena Faucit, Lady Martin* (Edinburgh and London, 1900), pp. 369 and 383.

schools' curriculum.[1] No doubt Shakespeare would have succeeded on his own merits, but his serious revival on the mid-nineteenth-century stage and his reification as the cultural icon of the British Empire were surely enhanced by the commentaries of the age linking his name with that of his second queen – Victoria.

---

[1] On Shakespeare in the schools, see Linda Rozmovits, *Shakespeare and the Politics of Culture in Late Victorian England* (Baltimore, 1998), esp. chapter 2.

The Invention of an Empress:
Factions and Fictions of Queen Victoria's Jubilees
of 1887 and 1897 as Acts of Cultural Memory*

By *Vera Nünning* (Heidelberg) and *Ansgar Nünning* (Giessen)

Prologue: On Building Empires and Inventing Empresses

Though Great Britain may have acquired its world-empire and "conquered and peopled half the world in a fit of absence of mind"[1], as John Seeley's memorable words put it, politicians and writers were anything but absent-minded when they were faced with the manifold problems of organising the member-units, maintaining the unity of the British Empire, and enhancing its cultural and political significance. A host of Victorian writers – poets, politicians, and journalists alike – took great pains to rhetorically conjure up the unity of the empire by conceptualizing the relationship between Great Britain and her colonies in terms of vivid fictions and suggestive metaphors. It was the ideologically charged metaphor of the empire as a big, happy and harmonious family that served as the foremost unifying device. To view the empire as a family, with Great Britain as the mother country and her offspring scattered around the world, was one way of transforming heterogeneous facts into a homely image, of domesticating England's imperial mission.[2]

And this is where Queen Victoria, *Regina and Imperatrix* since 1876 when she was proclaimed 'Empress of India', comes in. At first glance, "this most bourgeois of queens"[3] was the most unlikely empress that anyone could have imagined. Having scarcely been seen by her subjects for 15

---

* We should like to thank our assistants Dagmar Sims and Annegret Stegmann for their valuable help in tracking down relevant sources, and Astrid Erll and Rose Lawson for their careful proof-reading of an earlier version of this paper.

[1] John Robert Seeley, *The Expansion of England* [1883] (London, 1900), p. 10.

[2] For a more detailed analysis, see Ansgar Nünning, "Metaphors of Empire: Victorian Literature and Culture, and the Making of Imperialist Mentalities", in: *Anglistentag 1997 Gießen. Proceedings of the Conference of the German Association of University Teachers of English: Volume XIX*, ed. Raimund Borgmeier, Herbert Grabes and Andreas H. Jucker (Trier, 1998), pp. 347-367.

[3] Alison Booth, "Illustrious company: Victoria among other women in Anglo-American role model anthologies", in: *Remaking Queen Victoria*, ed. Margaret Homans and Adrienne Munich (Cambridge, 1997), pp. 59-78, p. 60.

years after the death of her beloved husband Albert, the Prince consort, in 1861, the Queen who was to become Empress had become conspicuous by her absence and famous for her invisibility. The Royal Titles Bill of 1876, which bestowed the title of 'Empress of India' on the English Queen, served to bring her out into the limelight again, but the real turning-point that changed her public image came a decade later. Queen Victoria's long reign abounded in great state occasions, culminating as it did in the Indian and Colonial Exhibition of 1886, the Golden Jubilee of 1887, and the Diamond Jubilee of 1897. Most people, then and now, agree that the 1897 Jubilee was the most brilliant, perhaps second only to Queen Elizabeth II's recent Golden Jubilee, but they were both equally efficient in memorializing the Queen's imperial reign, thus reinventing Queen Victoria as Empress.

What these state occasions have in common is that they arguably constitute popular acts of cultural memory, constructing rather than merely reflecting what they sought to represent, viz. the Queen of Great Britain and Empress of India at the peak of her career and as a symbol for the unity of the British Empire. The urgency and insistence with which Victorian writers harped on the same rhetorical and metaphorical line, eulogizing the English Queen and emphasizing the unity and harmony of both her reign and the empire, indicates that great efforts were made to *represent* the state of the empire as healthy. Elizabeth Ermarth's shrewd observation about the representation of social order in nineteenth-century narratives applies equally well to the language of popular imperialism: The role of Queen Victoria as 'Empress of India', just like the contested unity of the empire, was not so much "a reality to be reflected but a problem to be solved".[1] By looking at the fictions, myths and metaphors that appear in the textual representations surrounding the two magnificent jubilees with their pompous celebrations, it is possible to throw light on the varying ways in which both the Queen of Great Britain and the British Empire were given form, on how the monarch and empire were perceived and conceptualized at the time.

From the point of view of the literary and cultural historian interested in the forms and functionings of cultural memory, it is the representations of Queen Victoria which originated from these gigantic official parties which are of particular interest. Our project in this paper will be to reconstruct the main stages and discursive strategies which contributed to what we have called 'the invention of an empress'. Though one would be hard pressed to separate fact(ion)s from fictions in many cases, an analysis of some of the representations of the two jubilees can arguably shed light on the position

---

[1] Elizabeth Deeds Ermarth, *The English Novel in History 1840-1895* (London, New York, 1997), p. 125.

Queen Victoria occupied in "the ideological and cultural signifying systems of her age"[1], "in the British cultural imaginary"[2] at the time. Though limitations on space preclude the possibility of tracing all the stages, events, texts, and other media involved in what we have called 'the invention of an empress' in the detail which this fascinating cultural process merits, we hope to be able to throw new light on some of those representations by which she became known and which served to change her image by forging a new link between the formerly so domestic Queen and Great Britain's empire.

1. The Invention of an Empress, Act I: The Royal Titles Act of 1876

In order to be able to fully appreciate what a tall order it was to transform "England's Domestic Queen"[3] into an empress, one must briefly recall the predominant images of Queen Victoria prior to the time when the title of 'Empress of India' was conferred on her in 1876. Being both a devoted wife and a dedicated mother, she represented many of the features and virtues that the age cherished and Coventry Patmore immortalized in the image of the passive domestic angel in the house. On the other hand, however, she happened to be the ruler of a powerful country, and her image was shaped by "the culture of a rapidly changing Britain and its increasingly colonized domain".[4] As Elizabeth Langland has shown in her excellent monograph *Nobody's Angels*, Victoria, being renowned for both her devotion as a wife and her imperiousness, embodied "the contradictory roles of self-reliant monarch and dependent wife":

> In her reliance on Albert, in her professed inaptitude for public rule, Victoria constructed herself through emergent middle-class values; she presented herself

---

[1] Margaret Homans and Adrienne Munich, "Introduction", in: *Remaking Queen Victoria*, pp. 1-10, p. 2. Homans' and Munich's wide-ranging and first-rate collection of articles provides by far the best account of "the varieties of representation by which she [Victoria] became known" (p. 3), but none of the articles deals primarily with the representations of the two jubilees and their role in the (largely retrospective) construction of her as Empress; for brief and illuminating discussions of the two jubilees, see however, ibid., pp. 49, p. 51-2, p. 97, p. 142-44, p. 195, p. 235.

[2] Maria Jerinic, "How We Lost the Empire: Retelling the Stories of the Rani of Jhansi and Queen Victoria", in: *Remaking Queen Victoria*, pp. 123-139, p. 124.

[3] Cf. the title of ch. 3 of Elizabeth Langland's *Nobody's Angels: Middle-Class Women and Domestic Ideology in Victorian Culture* (Ithaca, London, 1995), p. 62.

[4] Homans and Munich, "Introduction", in: *Remaking Queen Victoria*, p. 2.

through a scrim of domestic virtues emphasizing home, hearth, and heart. That she should, nonetheless, without disabling or disqualifying self-contradiction, take her place as head of the most powerful country in the world bespeaks her own signal role in the construction of a new feminine ideal that endorsed active public management behind a facade of private retirement.[1]

Whereas Victoria's role in the construction of a new feminine ideal and in shaping the domestic image of the Angel in the House has recently been explored in some detail, the question of how the domestic virtues she stood for fitted in with her role as the head of the state and later on as an empress has hardly been assessed.[2] At first glance, one may be inclined to think that her being the embodiment of middle-class familial values and virtues was not exactly conducive to the attempt to turn the English monarch into an empress. As we will try to show, the "complex accommodations of the public and private woman that allowed the fact of female power to exist as long as it was mystified by appropriate rhetorics of home, hearth, and heart"[3] fulfilled important ideological and propagandistic functions in that they served to forge a link between the idealised domestic sphere and the empire, thus imperializing the monarch and domesticating England's imperial mission.

It is the questions of how this link was forged, of what were the most important stages in the invention of Victoria as an empress, and of which discursive and metaphorical strategies were involved in this process which we should like to pursue in our following investigations. At the risk of great oversimplification, one can argue that there are three key events involved in shaping the image of the monarch as 'Empress of India', act one, of course, being the Royal Titles Bill of 1876 (scene 1, as it were) and the Imperial Assemblage of 1877 (scene 2), and acts two and three being the carefully planned Golden Jubilee of 1887 and the Diamond Jubilee of 1897, both of which received such a wide coverage in the media that they may well be described as 'media events' in the modern sense of the term. It was the textual and visual representations of these media events, more than anything else, that served to familiarize the British populace with both the emergent image of Queen Victoria as 'Empress of India' and with the empire and the imperial idea as well, albeit with a domesticated version of the empire, as we will attempt to show.

---

[1] Langland, *Nobody's Angels*, p. 62, p. 63.

[2] Cf. however Adrienne Auslander Munich, "Queen Victoria, Empire, and Excess", *Tulsa Studies in Women's Literature*, 6,2 (1987), 265-281.

[3] Langland, *Nobody's Angels*, p. 65.

But let us first of all briefly recapitulate the historical facts which constituted act one, or rather the rhetorical and legal fictions which constituted the historical facts in the first place. The double meaning of the term 'fiction' "as literary, nonreferential narrative and [...] (often [...] in its plural form) as theoretical construct"[1] is essential for the questions that the article tries to answer in that we are concerned with the interplay between works of fiction and poetry and the cultural construction of the (essentially fictive) notion of the English queen being the 'Empress of India' as well as other theoretical and ideological constructs which constituted the imperial idea.[2] As Said has observed, such "fictions have their own logic and their own dialectic of growth or decline".[3]

If one wants to chart the dialectic of growth and decline that the fiction of the 'Empress of India' had, one might as well begin in the year 1876.[4] Instigated by the Queen herself, the Prime Minister Benjamin Disraeli, who was a well-known champion of expansionism, conferred on the Queen the newly invented and prestigious title of 'Empress of India' in 1876. This was anything but an innocent act, designed merely to add another jewel to her crown or to provide another bit of what David Cannadine has felicitously called 'ornamentalism'.[5] What Disraeli in fact did was perform an

---

[1] Dorrit Cohn, "Optics and Power in the Novel", *New Literary History*, 26 (1995), 3-20, p. 18.

[2] As the *Oxford English Dictionary* shows, the word 'fiction' has quite different meanings. On the one hand, the word can designate "[t]hat which, or something that, is imaginatively invented" or, more specifically, "[t]he species of literature which is concerned with the narration of imaginary events and the portraiture of imaginary characters", viz. "[a] work of fiction; a novel or tale" (*Oxford English Dictionary*, s.v. "fiction"). On the other hand, 'fiction' refers to any "supposition known to be at variance with fact, but conventionally accepted for some reason of practical convenience, conformity with traditional usage, decorum, or the like" (ibid.). In this latter sense, fictions are used in Law, for instance, with the fiction that a corporation is a person separate from its members being a case in point. Such legal fictions are theoretical constructs or rules that assume something as true that is clearly false or at variance with fact.

[3] Edward Said, *Orientalism. Western Conceptions of the Orient* [1978] (Harmondsworth, 1995), p. 62, p. 328.

[4] As Bernard S. Cohn has shown in his excellent article "Representing Authority in Victorian India", in: *The Invention of Tradition*, ed. Eric Hobsbawm and Terence Ranger [1983] (London, 1992), pp. 165-210, one would actually have to go back at least as far as the end of the so-called 'Indian Mutiny' and to the discussions of 1858 concerning the declaration of Victoria as Empress of India. We will be very brief here, because Cohn has given a detailed account of the events leading up to the Royal Titles Act and the events surrounding the Imperial Assemblage; see ibid., pp. 183-207.

[5] See David Cannadine, *Ornamentalism. How the British Saw their Empire* (London, 2001).

important christening ceremony, thereby doing Queen Victoria a great favour by fulfilling her a long-cherished dream. Moreover, he also initiated
the invention of a new tradition which turned out to be of great importance
for the representation of authority in Victorian India. The Royal Titles Bill,
which bestowed the title of 'Empress of India' on the English Queen,
served to affirm both the principle of colonial sovereignty and the – imaginary – unity of the British Empire. The Imperial Assemblage of 1877, an
imposing ceremony designed to officially proclaim the Queen Empress of
India, marked "the completion of the symbolic-cultural constitution of
British India".[1]

It might be noted in passing that both the Royal Titles Bill and the rationale of the Imperial Assemblage were fostered by, and in their turn reflected,
that "system of ideological fictions" which Edward Said in his seminal
work has called *Orientalism*.[2] They were both largely based on "the idea
that Indians were a different kind of people from the British", that "Indians
were more susceptible to high-sounding phrases, and would be better ruled
by appeal to their Oriental imagination".[3] Moreover it was hoped that the
Royal Titles Act, which received the royal assent on 27 April 1876, and the
Imperial Assemblage would conspicuously "'place the Queen's authority
upon the ancient throne of the Moguls, with which the imagination of [our]
Indian subjects associate the splendour of supreme power!'", as Lord
Lytton, the newly appointed viceroy and governor general of India, pointed
out in one of his letters to Queen Victoria:[4]

> And so, thanks largely to Disraeli, the British monarchy was refurbished and rein-
> vented as an imperial crown of unprecedented reach, importance and grandeur.
> One indication of this was that from 1876, successive sovereigns were empresses

---

[1] B. Cohn, "Representing Authority in Victorian India", p. 179, who provides a brilliant account of this complex process, by sophistically delineating the construction of "a
ritual idiom through and by which British authority was to be represented to Indians"
(ibid., p. 176).

[2] Said, *Orientalism*, p. 321. Cf. Lawrence James, *Raj: The Making and Unmaking of
British India* (London, 1997), p. 316: Disraeli's "Jewishness and his former wanderings
in the Middle East had convinced him that he possessed a special insight into that mysterious creation of Western imagination, the Oriental mind".

[3] B. Cohn, "Representing Authority in Victorian India", p. 184. Cf. also Bernard
Cohn, *Colonialism and its Form of Knowledge: The British in India* (Princeton, 1996),
who also talks about "'Orientalizing' India" (p. 121).

[4] Lytton to Queen Victoria, 21 April 1876; quoted from B. Cohn, "Representing Authority in Victorian India", p. 187-88. Another Orientalist stereotype shines through in
Lytton's observation that the Indian aristocracy were "'easily affected by sentiment and
susceptible to the influence of symbols to which facts inadequately correspond'" (ibid.,
p. 192).

or emperors of India as well as queens or kings of the United Kingdom of Great Britain and (Northern) Ireland. [...] More substantively, this meant that from Victoria to George VI, British sovereigns unified an imperial dominion of ever greater dimensions, and ordered an imperial hierarchy of ever greater complexity.[1]

Given its alleged appeal to the 'Oriental' imagination, it does not come as a surprise that the title of 'Empress' was thought to be 'un-English' by some observers in England. There had been quite a bit of opposition to the idea of conferring the title of 'Empress' on the English Queen when it was first broached in 1858, and when Disraeli brought the Queen's pet project up again in 1876 it was not unanimously applauded either. The reasons for this public adversity are worth noting, for even in 1876 the terms 'empire' and 'empress' had negative connotations, implying despotism, military conquest and tyranny, which were held to be irreconcilable with English institutions and English national identity.[2] Commenting on the Royal Titles Bill, *The Spectator* put these reservations into the following words:

> It is not easy to realize that such a policy as that of the 'Imperialists' as they are called on the Continent, should have, we will not say any root, but even any possibility of root, in these islands.[3]

What made the Royal Titles Bill acceptable – albeit only just acceptable – to the English was the belief that the despotic implications of the term 'empress' appealed to the mentalities of the Indians and the "Oriental' imagination. In view of the ambivalent public response to the Bill championed by Disraeli, Victoria desisted from pursing her original wish to become 'Empress of Great Britain, Ireland and India'. Notwithstanding whatever opposition there had been to the idea of conferring the new title of 'Empress' onto the Queen of England, the Royal Titles Act and the Imperial Assemblage served "to create a new function, purpose and justification for monarchy, at a time when it was in need of all these things, by connecting it with, and lending its historic lustre to, the recently and rapidly expanding empire":

---

[1] Cannadine, *Ornamentalism*, p. 101.

[2] The same ambivalence can be observed with regard to the term 'empire'. In his influential book *The Expansion of England* [1883] (London, 1900), the English historian John Robert Seeley opined that the word 'empire' was an inadequate designation for the relationship between England and her colonies: "The word Empire seems too military and despotic to suit the relation of a mother-country to colonies." (p. 44) Cf. also *Imperialism: The Story and Significance of a Political Word, 1840-1960*, ed. Richard Koebner and Helmut Dan Schmidt (Cambridge, 1964).

[3] *The Spectator*, 8 April 1876.

For as British monarchs were themselves becoming much more imperial, so the British Empire was itself becoming much more royal. This two-way process, whereby an imperialized monarchy merged with and moulded a monarchicalized empire, was exceptionally complicated [...] the British Empire was a *royal* empire, presided over and unified by a sovereign of global amplitude and semi-divine fullness, and suffused with the symbols and signifiers of kingship, which reinforced, legitimated, unified and completed the empire as a realm bound together by order, hierarchy, tradition and subordination.[1]

The Royal Titles Act and the Imperial Assemblage thus serve to show that the rituals and images held to be representative of a nation or an empire since time immemorial are quite often of surprisingly recent origin. More often than not they are invented to begin with, thus reflecting the present-day needs and concerns of a community trying to establish continuity with a suitable historical past. In a groundbreaking work Eric Hobsbawm and Terence Granger coined the phrase *The Invention of Tradition* to describe such processes. From the point of view of the cultural historian trying to explore cultural icons and national identities, "the use of ancient materials to construct invented traditions of a novel type for quite novel purposes"[2] can indeed be most revealing, as the Royal Titles Bill and the controversies surrounding it demonstrate. It is thus neither the administrative details nor the planning of the Imperial Assemblage nor the immediate political significance of the Royal Titles Bill that we are mainly concerned with but the textual representations of Victoria as 'Empress of India' that were disseminated on both this occasion and later on when England celebrated her two jubilees. As Margaret Homans has pointed out,

[t]he mid-1870s mark a turning-point in her reign, both because the public, the press, and politicians ceased to complain so much of her lack of visibility and because Victoria became Empress of India in 1876. After 1876, empire and imperialism must become the focus of attention for any study of the Queen's representations.[3]

As far as we know, no one has as yet heeded Homans' advice that "after 1876, empire and imperialism must become the focus of attention for any study of the Queen's representations": "As woman, mother, wife, and widow, Empress of India, and Queen of England, Victoria becomes a site for the concept's [i.e. Englishness] simultaneous consolidation and contra-

---

[1] Cannadine, *Ornamentalism*, pp. 101-102.

[2] Eric Hobsbawm, "Introduction: Inventing Traditions", in: *The Invention of Tradition*, ed. Eric Hobsbawm and Terence Ranger [1983] (London, 1992), pp. 1-14, p. 6.

[3] Margaret Homans, *Royal Representations: Queen Victoria and British Culture, 1837-1876* (Chicago, London, 1998), p. 229.

dictions."[1] How was the paradox that "Victoria was and is widely understood to be a domestic monarch who modeled ordinary middle-class womanhood even while she presided as empress over one quarter of the planet's territories"[2] resolved? How were the private sphere of domesticity that the matrimonially devoted monarch stood for and the public sphere of politics and empire which she also represented linked?

The most powerful link between her domestic and imperial images and identities which was found tended to take the form of kinship metaphors. It was the emotionally loaded metaphor of the queen as the mother of the nation that served as the most important unifying device, performing "the ideological task of amalgamating Victoria's work as queen of England to the ideal of motherhood".[3] The ubiquitous metaphor of the empire as a family, for instance, invokes the parent-child image to describe the imperial relationship. In other words, the boundary between the domestic sphere and the public sphere was gradually dissolved, with the languages of family life and politics becoming more and more blurred.

The implications of kinship metaphors are not very difficult to determine. What is involved in the metaphors of the queen as the mother of the nation and of the British Empire as a family is a mapping of the structure of the family onto the domain of politics in such a way as to set up the appropriate correspondences between the slots of the source domain and those of the target domain. Moreover, the relations in the source domain also get mapped onto relations in the target domain. What is arguably much more important than any analysis of the structural correspondences between the slots and relations of the source domain and the target domain is an investigation of the properties and cultural connotations associated with any given source domain. That is why the metaphors of popular imperialism should rather be explored as a cultural phenomenon and why cognitive metaphor theory is in dire need of being historicized.[4]

---

[1] Elizabeth Langland, "Nation and nationality: Queen Victoria in the developing narrative of Englishness", in: *Remaking Queen Victoria*, pp. 13-32, p. 13-14. Langland provides an excellent account of how "women, and the domestic sphere they 'governed', were amalgamated to England's imperialist mission": "In this development, England itself emerges as a feminine Britannia, the fertile soil of her English sons' achievements, and Englishness takes on an increasingly masculine construction" (p. 14), but she hardly looks at the representations of the two jubilees that we are mainly interested in.

[2] Homans and Munich, "Introduction", in: *Remaking Queen Victoria*, p. 6.

[3] Langland, *Nobody's Angels*, p. 67.

[4] For a detailed proposal and examination, see Ansgar Nünning, "Metaphors the British Thought, Felt and Ruled By, or: Modest Proposals for Historicizing Cognitive Metaphor Theory and for Exploring Metaphors of Empire as a Cultural Phenomenon",

One of the reasons that the metaphors of the queen as the mother of both the nation and the empire, and of the empire as a family were so powerful is that they make use not only of general knowledge about kinship and genealogy but also of the specific cultural connotations that the Victorians associated with the domain of the family. Even though the Victorian idealization of the home and of family life is too well-known to require any lengthy rehearsal, it may be worth recalling just how idealized this domain actually was.[1] According to the ideological views put forth in such widely read works as Coventry Patmore's famous poem *The Angel in the House* (1854) and John Ruskin's enormously popular lecture *Of Queens' Gardens* (1864), the Victorian family was thought to be "a school of sympathy, tenderness, and loving forgetfulness of self".[2] Frederic Harrison's 1893 lecture on "Family Life" is worth pausing over for the light it throws on the ways in which Victorian bourgeois culture sang the praises of both the home and family life: "The Home is the primeval and eternal school where we learn to practise the balance of our instincts, to restrain appetite, to cultivate affection, to pass out of our lower selves – to *Live for Humanity*".[3] Harrison sums up what else there was to be learned in the school that the Victorian home and family and – by the implications of the metaphors of popular imperialism – the British Empire were thought to be:[4]

> sentiment (1) of *attachment*, comradeship, fellowship, (2) of *reverence* for those who can teach us, guide us, and elevate us, of *love* which urges us to protect, help, and cherish those to whom we owe our lives and better natures.[5]

It is only against the backdrop of what Houghton (1957, 341) has aptly called "the exaltation of family life"[6] that the normative power of the meta-

---

in: *Literature and Linguistics: Approaches, Models, and Applications. Studies in Honour of Jon Erickson*, ed. Marion Gymnich, Ansgar Nünning and Vera Nünning (Trier, 2002), pp. 101-127.

[1] In addition to the works mentioned and quoted from below, cf. e.g. James Anthony Froude, *Oceana, or England and her Colonies* (London, 1886), p. 385, p. 395.

[2] John Stuart Mill, *The Subjection of Women* [1869] (London, 1974), p. 253.

[3] Frederic Harrison, "Lecture II: Family Life", in: F. Harrison, *On Society* [1893] (New York, 1918), pp. 32-55, p. 42.

[4] Cf. Zohreh T. Sullivan, *Narratives of Empire: The Fictions of Rudyard Kipling* (Cambridge, 1993), p. 3, who points out that the metaphor of the empire as family established a conceptual framework that saw "the empire as drawing room – a refined and civilized space where appropriate rules of conduct would ensure permanent occupancy".

[5] Harrison, "Lecture II", in: *On Society*, p. 33.

[6] Walter E. Houghton, *The Victorian Frame of Mind 1830-1870* (New Haven, London, 1957), p. 341.

phor of the imperial family of "Greater Britain"[1] can be properly gauged. Metaphors of empire not only import entities and structural relations from the various source domains into the target domain of the empire, they also imply how the entities in the target domain are to be evaluated.[2] The metaphor of the empire as a family maps the feelings, norms, and values of the private sphere of the family onto the relationship between England and her colonies. It turns the relation between colonizer and colonized into an intimate and mutually profitable arrangement based on emotional ties, "transforming the empire into a Victorian domestic idyl".[3] Moreover, kinship metaphors suggest that the colonial children have lots to gain and learn in the imperial school of sympathy, tenderness, and civilization: discipline, duty, chastisement, and love of both their queenly mother and their mother(-country).

By encoding both the queen's public role and the empire in kinship metaphors, Victorian poetry served to map the middle-class familial values and virtues embodied by the queen onto the public sphere, thus constructing a homely image of the monarch and empress, while at the same time domesticating England's imperial mission. With regard to how family metaphors served to forge links between the domestic sphere represented by Queen Victoria prior to her being turned into the Empress of India and the public sphere of politics and empire, Tennyson's famous poem "Opening of the Indian and Colonial Exhibition by the Queen" (1886) is a case in point. In the first stanza, the lyrical I, or rather the lyrical we, the royal plural representing both England and the monarch, welcomes the sons and brothers from the colonies.

> Welcome, welcome with one voice!
> In your welfare we rejoice,
> Sons and brothers that have sent,
> From isle and cape and continent
> Produce of your field and flood,
> Mount and mine, and primal wood;
> Works of subtle brain and hand,

---

[1] Charles Wentworth Dilke, *Greater Britain: A Record of Travel in English-Speaking Countries during 1866 and 1867* (New York, 1868).

[2] Cf. George Lakoff and Mark Turner, *More than Cool Reason: A Field Guide to Poetic Metaphor* (Chicago, London, 1989), p. 65.

[3] Jyotsna G. Singh, *Colonial Narratives / Cultural Dialogues: "Discoveries" of India in the Language of Colonialism* (London, New York, 1996), p. 91.

> And splendours of the morning land,
> Gifts from every British zone;
> Britons, hold your own![1]

Tennyson's ideologically charged use of kinship metaphors serves as a kind of double filter through which both the queen, and later the empress, and the empire were perceived. Such a double filter is permeable only to the salient features of the source and target domains, i.e. to those elements that are relevant in the present context. On the one hand, the filter lets through only those features of the source domain of the family that can reasonably be mapped onto the public sphere and the empire. On the other hand, only those aspects of the empire come into focus which are covered by kinship terms. The sons coming back from the colonies dutifully bring back to their mother(-country) a host of presents, making their mother even more happy to see them. Moreover, the appropriation of the vocabulary of family life also mutes the cultural conflicts and contradictions inherent in the relationship between colonizer and colonized. The second stanza of Tennyson's poem "Opening of the Indian and Colonial Exhibition by the Queen" is a case in point. The royal voice expresses the hope that the colonial children would take after their imperial mother:

> May we find, as ages run,
> The mother featured in the son;
> And may yours for ever be
> That old strength and constancy
> Which has made your fathers great
> In our ancient island State,
> And wherever her flag fly,
> Glorying between sea and sky,
> Makes the might of Britain known;
> Britons, hold your own![2]

As Tennyson's poem underscores, kinship metaphors imply notions of order, succession, and lineage. Moreover, it suggests that the colonial sons, descending as they do from their mother-country, have inherited all of the splendid salient characteristics of their British mother and father, especially, "that old strength and constancy / Which has made your fathers great". It was the emotionally charged parent-child image that largely determined the Victorian perception of the relationship between both their

---

[1] Alfred Lord Tennyson, *The Poems of Tennyson*, ed. Christopher Ricks (London, 1969), pp. 1357-8.

[2] Ibid., p. 1358.

monarch and the English nation and between Great Britain and her colonies. Conjuring up what Froude called "the invisible bonds of relationship"[1], Tennyson's use of kinship metaphors not only created "the bond which holds the Empire together"[2], but also prepared the ground for the next stage in the cultural invention of an empress, viz. Queen Victoria's Golden Jubilee.

2. The Invention of an Empress, Act II: Representations of the Golden Jubilee of 1887

Though Queen Victoria continued to be associated with the domestic sphere throughout her long life, her long and spectacular reign became more and more imperial during the last two decades of the nineteenth century. Like the texts depicting the opening of the Indian and Colonial Exhibition by the Queen, the representations of her Golden Jubilee of 1887 played an important role in this context in that they served to disseminate an imperial image of the English monarch. The celebrations of her two Royal Jubilees were in fact "designed to celebrate Great Britain's empire in a grand manner": "In addition to the booms in print culture and literary genres, the Jubilee celebrations also made evident the growing power and visibility of commodity culture".[3]

Though limitations of space make it possible to look at more than a fraction of the texts that this boom in print culture, literary genres, commodity culture occasioned, a brief glance at some of the poetical representations of the first of the two jubilees may serve to show how the link between the domestic sphere and the familial values Victoria embodied and her public role as the ruler of a great nation was forged. The poet laureate, Alfred Lord Tennyson, once again did an excellent job on this occasion, as on so many other occasions before. In his well-known ode "On the Jubilee of Queen Victoria" he not only praised the English monarch, but he also sang the praises of the British Empire, celebrating its great achievements:

> Fifty times the rose has flowered and faded,
> Fifty times the golden harvest fallen,
> Since our Queen assumed the globe, the sceptre.

---

[1] Froude, *Oceana*, p. 393.

[2] Ibid., p. 391.

[3] *Imperialism and Orientalism: A Documentary Sourcebook*, ed. Barbara Harlow and Mia Carter (Oxford, 1999), p. 388, p. 390.

> She beloved for a kindliness
> Rare in Fable or History,
> Queen, and Empress of India,
> Crowned so long long with a diadem
> Never worn by a worthier,
> Now with prosperous auguries
> Comes at last to the bounteous
> Crowning year of her Jubilee.[1]

Tennyson significantly refrains from telling a coherent story of the imperial reign. What he provides instead is a mere series of disjointed metaphors, images, and glimpses of the monarch, her virtues, and her reign. Though the Queen is duly eulogized, the focus is still on her domestic and 'womanly' virtues rather than on her role as a ruler of a great nation, on her being "gracious, gentle, great and Queenly" (ibid.), whatever the last epithet is meant to signify in this context. In the fifth stanza, the link between the domestic sphere and the public sphere, between "womanhood" and "Queenhood", is not only explicitly thematized but also underscored by emphasizing her 'womanly' capacity for sorrow and sympathy:

> Queen, as true of womanhood as Queenhood,
> Glorying in the glories of her people,
> Sorrowing with the sorrows of the lowest![2]

Nonetheless, the British Empire is anything but absent from this poem. It is not so much the "Queen, and Empress of India" mentioned in the second stanza herself, however, who seems to either represent the empire or to get the credit for British achievements but the nameless (presumably male) "You", the "Patriot Architect" and empire-builder, addressed no fewer than nine times in the fourth, sixth, eighth, and tenth stanza who is called upon to rejoice, to celebrate, and to "Raise a stately memorial" or "Some Imperial Institute" as sites of memory of "this year of her Jubilee":

> You, the Patriot Architect,
> You that shape for Eternity,
> Raise a stately memorial,
> Make it regally gorgeous.
> Some Imperial Institute,
> Rich in symbol, in ornament,
> Which may speak to the centuries,
> All the centuries after us,

---

[1] Tennyson, *The Poems of Tennyson*, p. 1370.
[2] Ibid.

> Of this great Ceremonial,
> And this year of her Jubilee.[1]

In the ninth and tenth stanza the empire even acquires pride of place. Tennyson's poem thus leaves the reader in no doubt about who or what is to be remembered by the "stately memorial" he asks the textual addressee to raise:

> Fifty years of ever-broadening Commerce!
> Fifty years of ever-brightening Science!
> Fifty years of ever-widening Empire![2]

In the second but last stanza of Tennyson's poem, the patriotic speaker addresses Britain's colonial sons and brothers directly, appealing to them to rejoice "in harmony" and to sing "in unison". In this stanza the rhetoric of unity reaches its climax, when the (factually highly questionable) unity of the British Empire is finally affirmed in a unanimous and imperial chorus in which all the "patient children of Albion" chime in:

> You, the hardy, laborious,
> Patient children of Albion,
> You, Canadian, Indian,
> Australasian, African,
> All your hearts be in harmony,
> All your voices in unison,
> Singing 'Hail to the glorious
> Golden Year of her Jubilee!'[3]

In short, Tennyson's poem "On the Jubilee of Queen Victoria" manages to forge a subtle link between both "womanhood" and "Queenhood", and the "Queen, and Empress of India" and her empire. The poem is in fact an effective exercise in cultural memory in that it is primarily conceived as an appeal to the present not only to celebrate, but also to memorialize both the Queen's imperial reign, or rather a highly idealized version of it, and "Fifty years of ever-widening Empire!". Tennyson had already dealt with the same theme in his poem "To the Queen" (1873), which shares nothing but the title with the poem that was his first publication as Poet Laureate in 1851, in which Victoria is praised "as Mother, Wife, and Queen", while

---

[1] Ibid., p. 1371.
[2] Ibid., p. 1371.
[3] Ibid., p. 1372.

"the care / That yokes with empire" is only briefly mentioned in passing.[1] If one compares Tennyson's poem with Elizabeth Barrett Browning's "The Young Queen" (1838), one can appreciate the sea change that both Queen Victoria's image and the prevailing attitudes towards the British Empire underwent during her long reign.[2] Whereas Barrett Browning's poem underscores "the queen's passive role in her queenship" and her "spiritual incapacity for the weight of rulership"[3] Tennyson's "To the Queen" despite its somewhat misleading title, published in 1873 deals primarily with the empire, thundering against the possibility of Canada severing her connection with Great Britain and singing once again the popular imperial(ist) tune of loyalty, love, and harmony:

> ... The loyal to their crown
> Are loyal to their own far sons, who love
> Our ocean-empire with her boundless homes
> For ever-broadening England, and her throne
> In our vast Orient, and one isle, one isle,
> That knows not her own greatness: if she knows
> And dreads it we are fallen. ...[4]

The "flurry of Jubilee articles in the religious press of the day"[5] harps essentially on the same tune, not only celebrating her jubilee and calling upon the British public to cheer their beloved Queen, but also intensifying the process of myth making. No less a man than John Henry Newman even called her "a being of poetry".[6] Being both the mother of her nation and the embodiment of the mother-country England, Queen Victoria was gradually projected into the imperial script, while the imperial mission and relationship continued to be metaphorically familiarized and domesticated.

---

[1] Cf. ibid., pp. 990-92, p. 991.

[2] Cf. Vera Nünning, "Where the Discourses of Nationalism and Religion Meet: The Forging of an Empire of the Mind in Nineteenth-Century Debates about the British Empire", in: *Religious Thinking and National Identity / Religiöses Denken und nationale Identität*, ed. Hans-Dieter Metzger (Berlin, Wien, 2000), pp. 149-176.

[3] Cf. Langland, *Nobody's Angels*, p. 66.

[4] Tennyson, *The Poems of Tennyson*, p. 1755.

[5] Mark S. Looker, "'God Save the Queen': Victoria's Jubilees and the Religious Press", *Victorian Periodicals Review*, 21,3 (1988), 115-119, p. 115.

[6] Quoted from Looker, "'God Save the Queen'", p. 115.

3. The Invention of an Empress, Act III: Representations of the Diamond Jubilee of 1897

The Diamond Jubilee of 1897 was not only one of the most brilliant and glittering national celebrations that Britain had seen till then, it was also a remarkably effective act of imperial self-fashioning and cultural memory. Though there were some dissenting voices[1], the spirit that prevailed on the occasion of the Diamond Jubilee was characterized by national rejoicing, unabashed patriotism and pride in the achievements associated with the British Empire. Being even more spectacular and sensational than the Golden Jubilee, it was planned and staged in such an effective way that it was turned into an outstanding media event which would be "for ever memorable":

> The Diamond Jubilee of 1897 stands as probably the most glittering national celebration of modern British times. [...] It marked a solid national pride in 60 years of peace and progress in every field of human activity.[2]

When one compares the representations of Queen Victoria's Golden Jubilee of 1887 with those of her Diamond Jubilee of 1897, what is perhaps most striking is that the empire seems to have secured pride of place at the end of the century. It is the empire rather than the Queen herself that occupies centre stage in most of the representations surrounding the Diamond Jubilee. Moreover, the Queen is no longer primarily represented as the symbol of domesticity or epitome of womanhood but rather as the head of the "Imperial family" of Greater Britain. The gap between the 'Domestic Queen' and the 'Empress of India' was effectively closed by the well-planned Royal Procession:

> Joseph Chamberlain was the first to suggest that the sixtieth year of the Queen's accession should celebrate the Imperial family under the British Crown and the Queen endorsed the plan. [...] in wave after wave of glittering ranks came the living evidence of the vast Empire: Giant Maoris, New Zealand Mounted Troups,

---

[1] As far as dissenting voices were concerned, cf. e.g. George Gissing's sombre novel *In the Year of the Jubilee* (1894), Rudyard Kipling's ambivalent poem "Recessional" (1897), published on the morning of Diamond Jubilee, and the pamphlet written by Keir Hardie ("The Diamond Jubilee – Monarchy or Republic?") attacking the Jubilee (reprinted in Caroline Chapman and Paul Raben, *Debrett's Queen Victoria's Jubilees 1887 & 1897* (London, 1977), no page numbers.

[2] Caroline Chapman and Paul Raben, *Debrett's Queen Victoria's Jubilees 1887 & 1897*, no page numbers (p. 40, p. 43). Chapman and Raben provide a brief summary of the festivities.

The Jamaica Artillery, The Royal Nigerian Constabulary, Negroes from the West Indies, British Guiana and Sierra Leone, the Cape Mounted Rifles, New South Wales Lancers, the Trinidad Light Horse and Zaptiehs from Cyprus, the Borneo Dyak Police, 'upstanding Sikhs, tiny little Malays, Chinese with a white basin turned upside down on their heads', grinning Houssa's from the Gold Coast and perhaps best of all, the turbanned and bearded Lancers of the Indian Empire 'terrible and beautiful to behold'.[1]

It comes as no surprise, therefore, that Victorian commentators stressed the imperial dimension of the event and the extravagant celebrations devoted to commemorate it. It was not England, but the British Empire which celebrated both a rare event, the sixtieth anniversary of Victoria's accession to the throne, and itself.[2] *The Times*, for instance, was in no doubt that the jubilee was an event not just of utmost national importance, but one that was widely taken notice of throughout the empire. Celebrating the event as "a moment of patriotic excitement" and "'heightened national consciousness'", the writer takes great pains to emphasize what the Queen stands for and to insert her in a narrative of material and imperial progress. Though the focus at first seems to be on the Queen, it quickly shifts to what she represents, viz. "rational progress", culminating in visions of harmony and unity that the writer conjures up to idealize the relationship between the colonies and the English mother-country:

To-day the eyes of the whole Empire, and of millions of men beyond its pale, will be fixed upon London, and upon the great and inspiring ceremony in which we celebrate the sixty years of the Queen's reign. They will be fixed on the revered and beloved figure of the woman who for two full generations has represented, to so large a fraction of the human race, the principles of order, of civilization and of rational progress. They will be fixed upon one who, in a period of all-embracing change, has offered during all these years an extraordinary instance of political and moral stability. [...]

[...] Since the Queen first made a like State progress, as she passed to her coronation in 1838, what transformations! These Colonies, who form perhaps the most applauded section of her escort, have travelled thousands of miles to be here. [...] They have come representing not a few small, scattered communities, but millions of men, brave, intelligent, wealthy, and loyal. These Indians, too, children of "the unchanging East", are changed. They are proud Princes tracing their descent back for many centuries; and yet they have become faithful vassals of the Queen. They are a sign and symbol of the British Peace which now, after many a struggle and one heroic episode, prevails from Ceylon to the Himalayas.[3]

---

[1] Ibid., p. 44.

[2] Cf. ibid., pp. 47-68.

[3] *The Times*, 22 June 1897. Quoted from Chapman and Raben, *Debrett's Queen Victoria's Jubilees 1887 & 1897* (p. 40).

Leaving aside for the moment the Orientalist stereotypes that were ubiquitous in the imperial discourse, what is perhaps most striking in this patriotic
emanation is the self-conscious reflection on the symbolic dimension of
this well-planned media event. It is the values and national achievements
which the queen represents rather than the monarch or her jubilee itself
which provide the real focus of this news story. The real protagonist of this
story of success is the empire rather than the Queen herself, whose jubilee
merely marks the occasion for commemorating both the success story of
national progress and the rise of the British Empire. As in many similar
representations of the Diamond Jubilee, the writer resorts to a rhetoric of
'then-and-now' in order to highlight the spectacular improvements that
have been achieved. What comes first and foremost, is, of course, the empire.

The long and cumbersome ode that Sir Lewis Morris composed in celebration of Queen Victoria's Diamond Jubilee in June 1897 provides another case in point. The poem may not be one of the great poetic accomplishments of the nineteenth century, but from the point of view of the
history of mentalities it is quite revealing in that it tells the cultural historian quite a lot about how the empire and the Empress were perceived by
the contemporaries, what imperialism was as a cultural phenomenon, as a
habit of mind or a structure of ideas and attitudes. The first two stanzas
therefore deserve to be quoted at some length:

> Rejoice! give thanks for all the centuries
> Since first our little island's crescent story,
> A feeble radiance, woke the waning skies
> To rise in full-orbed glory.
> Twelve centuries ago our Britain rose,
> Girt round by watchful foes,
> And did prevail at last – such power in valour lies,
> Such force the brain, the arm of Freedom fires.
> Such lofty thought her soul inspires.
> Hers were the faults, the virtues of the Strong,
> The passionate love of Right, the burning hate of Wrong.
> [...]
>
> Oh, gracious Island-Queen,
> Mother of freemen! over all the earth
> Thy Empire-children come to birth.
> Vast continents are thine, or spring from thee,
> Brave island-fortress of the storm-vext sea!
> The giant commonwealths which sway the West
> Were nourished at thy breast;
> The fair-grown sisters of the Austral main

That hold the South in fee
Are thine, and love thy laws and speak thy tongue;
The dusky millions of thy fabulous East –
Dim empires older than the dawn of Time –
Thy crescent realm on Afric's peopled shore,
The white man's grave no more,
Ruled by just laws, and learning to grow free,
Rejoice, by thy Britannic Peace increased.
Thy praise is by a myriad voices sung;
Thou tread'st alone thy onward path sublime;
Thou hast not been in vain![1]

Though the last stanza does indeed focus on the queen, passing in quick review her long reign, what we have here is not so much an ode to the queen on the occasion of her Diamond Jubilee as an ode to Great Britain as the owner of an empire 'on which the sun never sets'. The first two stanzas of this somewhat embarrassing jingoistic ode celebrate a long period of continuous progress, economic growth, political stability, and territorial expansion. What the poem also amounts to is an unabashed eulogy of Britishness (rather than Englishness)[2], celebrating as it does British virtues like valour, strength, energy, freedom, liberty, and justice. Nowadays we of course know that Britishness, like Englishness, "is necessarily a construct, an artifice. Whoever defines or identifies it is at best selecting, sifting, suppressing, in the search for what is taken to be representative".[3] It is because of the constructed nature of such notions as Englishness and Britishness that texts like this ode can tell us which aspects of national life struck Victorians as characteristic.

Moreover, kinship metaphors once again feature prominently in this poetic evocation of the Queen's Jubilee, which is actually a patriotic representation of the empire. The ubiquitous metaphor of the empire as a family implies that Great Britain was the mother country and the colonies were her children. Another reason why kinship metaphors were instrumental in forging the unity of the empire is that they suggest that the colonies were England's progeny ("Were nourished at thy breast"). The ode explicitly

---

[1] *The Times*, 22 June 1897. Cf. also Max Beloff, *Britain's Liberal Empire 1897-1921* (London, 1970), p. 21.

[2] Cf. Vera Nünning, "Where Literature, Culture, and the History of Mentalities Meet: Changes in British National Identity as a Paradigm for a New Kind of Literary / Cultural History", in: *REAL – Yearbook of Research in English and American Literature* 16 (2000): *Literary History / Cultural History*, ed. Herbert Grabes (Tübingen, 2001), pp. 211-238.

[3] Paul Langford, *Englishness Identified. Manners and Character, 1650-1850* (Oxford, 2000), p. 14.

suggests that at least the settler colonies actually descend from the English mother-country, that England's colonies are the children or "daughter-countries".[1] Second, kinship metaphors imply that colonies are far from independent from the parent community. Third, they evoke a feeling of fellowship, "a sense of kindred".[2] So far as the metaphor of the imperial family is concerned, England's rule over her colonies is interpreted not just within the logic of kinship relations but also in terms of the norms and values associated by the Victorian public with family life.

By creating analogies between the private domain of the family and the public sphere of international relations, kinship metaphors profoundly affected the way in which the British Empire was perceived and understood. They suggest, then, "that the essential character of the Empire was to be that of the family. It would be characterized by relationships, entered into willingly out of mutual respect, and with benefits for all concerned".[3] Kinship metaphors imply that the relationships between England and her colonies and between Queen Victoria and her colonial children were based on unity, love and harmony:

> Great Empire! those who come to-day from far,
> Seeking some symbol of our common love,
> Know through their souls Imperial pulses move,
> Following, as did the Magi once, the Star
> Of this new birth of Time, this happy reign.[4]

What is important in this context is the extent to which authors like Sir Lewis Morris were employing familiar images and metaphors available in their culture at large. By adopting these images they not only acceded to the collective idea of the empire as an harmonious family held together by nothing but "our common love", they simultaneously managed to bridge the gap between the domestic and the public sphere. What is completely occluded, not only in this jubilee ode and in its use of kinship metaphors, but also in Tennyson's poem written on the occasions of the Colonial Exhibition of 1886 and the Golden Jubilee of 1887, are the political, economic, and military aspects of imperialism. It is quite obvious that the attempt to domesticate the imperial relationship was meant to nip in the bud

---

[1] Charles Wentworth Dilke, *Problems of Greater Britain* (London, New York, 1890), 2 vols., vol. I, p. 5.

[2] Seeley, *The Expansion of England*, p. 45.

[3] Ann Parry, *The Poetry of Rudyard Kipling: Rousing the Nation* (Buckingham, 1992), p. 85.

[4] *The Times*, 22 June 1897. Quoted from Chapman and Raben, *Debrett's Queen Victoria's Jubilees 1887 & 1897*, p. 42.

whatever problems or conflicts might arise. The ways in which kinship terms were used demonstrate that the "whole imperial struggle collapsed into a family squabble", as the historian Gordon S. Wood aptly put it.[1]

The power of such metaphorical representations of Queen Victoria's Jubilees rested largely on the way they linked the private sphere with the collective and public domain. What is perhaps the most impressive of the many functional advantages of kinship metaphors is their power to represent complex political and historical issues in a simplified, familiar, and emotionally and ideologically charged language. Kinship metaphors assimilated both the role of the 'Empress of India' and the political problems of the empire to the vocabularies of everyday life, translating the imperial relationship between Queen Victoria as the mother of the nation and the empire and her colonial offspring into the language, norms, and values of the private sphere of family life. By framing abstract phenomena that defied direct experience in the language of home and family, they familiarized large sections of the British public with both the imperial ideology, i.e. with a set of ingrained and largely unconscious beliefs, ideas, feelings, and values, and with the idea of their monarch being the 'Empress of India'. By doing so, such representations of Queen Victoria and the empire "brought home to the understanding of the most parochial of Little Englanders the sense and knowledge of what the British empire means".[2]

4. Inventing an Empress, Domesticating an Empire: Representations of Queen Victoria's Jubilees from a Functionalist Point of View

Rather than just taking the imperialist rhetoric of unity, order, and harmony implied in both the invention of Queen Victoria as an empress and the kinship metaphors of the empire as a family at face value, or even mistaking such tropes for a simple reflection of historical relations, one might look more closely at the functions that such discursive 'inventions of traditions' and rhetorical strategies served to fulfill. An analysis of their functions can arguably shed light on the "representational politics"[3] of popular imperialism. In contrast to models, which *represent* structural relations, conceptual

---

[1] Gordon S. Wood, *The Radicalism of the American Revolution* (New York, 1992), p. 165.

[2] Sir Walter Besant, "Is it the Voice of the Hooligan", *Contemporary Review*, LXXVII (Jan. 1900), pp. 27-39; quoted from *Kipling: The Critical Heritage*, ed. Roger L. Green (London, 1971), p. 256.

[3] Ermarth, *The English Novel in History*, p. 125.

fictions and metaphors *impose* structures and sense onto the target domain; they "often do creative work".[1] There are at least seven functions that can be identified, although many of them are syncretized in specific texts.[2]

In the first place, by reducing the complexity and elusiveness of the imperial relation, the Royal Titles Bill and the idealized representations of the queen as 'Empress of India' symbolically established artificial cohesion, clear cut hierarchies, and a corporate sense of the superiority of the British. Their most obvious function was to symbolize both a new order and submission to authority in British India and to serve as sense-making devices, eliminating "some of the contradictions and lacunae in the cultural-symbolic constitution"[3] of India. Despite their inevitably reductive and fictive character, such representations fostered one of the dominating fictions of British imperialism that the Victorian age lived by[4], viz. the ingrained belief in English superiority and the concomitant conviction that the native peoples in India as well as in the various other colonies were in dire need of elevation and civilization. Said even goes so far as to locate "the essence of Orientalism" in "the ineradicable distinction between Western superiority and Oriental inferiority", which was itself based on the "binary typology of advanced and backward (or subject) races".[5] Because of what Said has called "the structures of attitude and reference" that constituted the imperial world-view, the fiction of the 'Empress of India' went hand in hand with, and enhanced, another assumption fostered by Social Darwinism, viz. the ingrained belief "that subject races should be ruled, that they *are* subject races, that one race deserves and has consistently earned the right to be

---

[1] Mark Turner, *Death is the Mother of Beauty: Mind, Metaphor, Criticism* (Chicago, London, 1987), p. 19; cognitive theories agree that metaphors *create* their analogies and correspondences.

[2] The following discussions of the functions that the invention of an empress fulfilled is indebted to Hobsbawm, "Introduction", pp. 9-12, and to Nünning, "Metaphors of Empire", pp. 355-361.

[3] B. Cohn, "Representing Authority in Victorian India", p. 174.

[4] This phrase is, of course, an allusion to an influential book on the theory of metaphor, viz. to George Lakoff and Mark Johnson's *Metaphors We Live By* (Chicago, London, 1980).

[5] Said, *Orientalism*, p. 42, p. 206. For a detailed account of the most important fictions of British imperialism, see Vera Nünning and Ansgar Nünning, "Fictions of Empire and the Making of Imperialist Mentalities: Colonial Discourse and Post-Colonial Theory as a Paradigm for Intercultural Studies", *Anglistik und Englischunterricht* 58: *Intercultural Studies: Fictions of Empire*, ed. Vera Nünning and Ansgar Nünning (Heidelberg, 1996), pp. 7-31.

considered the race whose main mission is to expand beyond its own do-main".[1]

Second, both the Royal Titles Bill and the representations of Queen Victoria's jubilees served as an important means of fostering and maintaining loyalty: "loyalty had to be symbolized to be effective in the eyes of subordinates and followers".[2] This emotional function is particularly obvious in the case of kinship metaphors because they imply a feeling of fellowship and a sense of togetherness. According to Turner, the "dominant component in kinship metaphors is Feeling".[3] Kinship metaphors emphasize the unity of the empire, as Tennyson's poem "Hands All Round" shows, which is explicitly addressed to "all the loyal hearts who long / To keep our English Empire whole!"[4] Metaphorical representations of the Queen as the mother of the nation and the colonial children not only served as rhetorical assertion about the unity of the empire, they also paid constant lip service to a wide range of emotional values and moral obligations by casting the imperial relationship in a very benevolent light.

A third function of both the invention of Queen Victoria as the 'Empress of India' and of kinship metaphors consisted in providing contemporaries with simplified, but more or less coherent frameworks for reinterpreting historical developments.[5] Such discursive and metaphoric fictions proved to be powerful tools for making sense of the imperial experience. By actually commenting upon the events and relations they purported merely to reflect or to report, the representations discussed above served as a means for explaining complex historical processes and constellations. The structure and logic inherent in the metaphor of the imperial family, for instance, reduces the complexity of the imperial relationships and transforms a chaotic series of historical events into simple stories. The invention of an empress was arguably instrumental in fostering the notion that "authority once achieved must have a secure and usable past".[6] It provided a codified repre-

---

[1] Edward Said, *Culture and Imperialism* (London, 1993), p. 62. For the key phrase "structures of attitude and reference", cf. ibid., pp. 61ff., p. 73, p. 89, p. 114, p. 134, p. 157 and *passim*.

[2] B. Cohn, "Representing Authority in Victorian India", p. 171.

[3] Turner, *Death is the Mother of Beauty*, p. 41.

[4] Tennyson, *The Poems of Tennyson*, p. 1311.

[5] Tennyson's famous poem "Opening of the Indian and Colonial Exhibition by the Queen" (1886) is a case in point. For an analysis of the ideological implications of the kinship metaphors used in that poem, see A. Nünning, "Metaphors of Empire", pp. 356-358.

[6] John H. Plumb, *The Death of the Past* (Boston, 1971), p. 41. See also B. Cohn, "Representing Authority in Victorian India", pp. 167-8, to whom we owe the reference to Plumb.

sentation of the imperial past, the effectiveness of which was not diminished by the fact that it was based on a largely fictive or mythic account of the history of both India and the empire:

> The hyperbolic historical fantasy voiced by Disraeli was part of the myth later acted out in the Imperial Assemblage. India was diversity – it had no coherent communality except that given by British rule under the integrating system of the imperial crown.[1]

Fourth, the dissemination of the image of the domestic queen and the motherly empress fulfilled important normative and socializing functions because such representations served to inculcate value systems, beliefs, and conventions of behaviour. In doing so, they authorized and propagated ideologically charged views of the relationship between the mother-country and her colonial children. They projected the norms of behaviour associated with Victorian family life onto the relationship between England and her colonies. Although as a rule one cannot extract a very sophisticated political philosophy from any of these metaphors, they tend to leave no doubt as to what the desirable form of the imperial relationship was. With its ties to the patriarchal and paternalist discourse, the metaphor of the queen as the mother of the nation and the empire implies that the colonial children were in need of parental control and guidance. Such metaphorical representations thus determined the way in which both the queen and the British Empire were conceptualized, in fact domesticating the imperial relationship and mission.

Fifth, the invention of 'the Empress of India', just like kinship metaphors of empire, fulfilled legitimizing functions because it provided rationalizations of the imperial experience and justifications of the empire. Forging emotional and functional links between the colonizers (read conquerors) and the colonized, the Royal Titles Act was an important means of legitimizing the institutions of the empire, Queen Victoria's status and imperial relations of authority. Representations of Victoria's ascension to the imperial throne on 1 January 1877 and of the queen as empress and mother of the colonial children underscored the need for British imperial rule.

Sixth, representations of Queen Victoria as Empress of India were an important propagandistic and ideological means of nurturing the culture's dominant fictions, because they served "to announce, enhance and glorify British authority as represented by the person of their monarch".[2] They arguably served as subtle ideological handmaidens of imperialism, because

---

[1] B. Cohn, "Representing Authority in Victorian India", p. 184.
[2] Ibid., p. 193.

they glorified the imperial relationship by disseminating highly advantageous images of the empire and of the sovereign. They helped to create that culturally sanctioned system of ideas, beliefs, presuppositions, and convictions which constitutes imperialist mentalities.[1] Establishing British dominance symbolically and rhetorically, the images of the Queen as Empress which were disseminated on the occasions of the two magnificent jubilees thus fulfilled an overtly propagandistic function, contributing to what Mangan has felicitously called "making imperial mentalities".[2]

Lastly, and arguably most importantly, poetic, metaphorical and journalistic representations of Queen Victoria as 'Empress of India' were central to the formation and maintenance of collective identities. The images and stories projected by the texts examined above were instrumental in what one might call the imaginative forging of the British Empire, because not only a nation but "any imagined community, is held together in part by the stories it generates about itself".[3] The 'invention of an empress' served as an important means of maintaining an advantageous British self-image and of forging Britain's national identity, something which was neither natural nor stable, but discursively constructed.[4] Enhancing Britain's self-pride in its achievements or emphasizing the unity of the empire was thus not an end in itself, but part of that complex political and cultural process that Linda Colley has felicitously called "Forging the Nation".[5]

---

[1] Cf. Said, *Orientalism*, p. 321, who calls Orientalism a "system of ideological fictions" and who equates that phrase with such terms as "a body of ideas, beliefs, clichés, or learning" (p. 205), "systems of thought", "discourses of power", and with Blake's famous "mind-forg'd manacles" (p. 328).

[2] James A. Mangan, "Introduction: Making Imperial Mentalities", in: *Making Imperial Mentalities: Socialisation and British Imperialism*, ed. J.A. Mangan (Manchester, New York 1990), pp. 1-22.

[3] Stephen Arata, *Fictions of Loss in the Victorian Fin de Siècle* (Cambridge, 1996), p. 1; for the concept of imagined communities, see Benedict Anderson, *Imagined Communities: Reflections on the Origins and Spread of Nationalism* (London, 1983).

[4] Cf. Said, *Culture and Imperialism*, p. 60: "In an important sense, we are dealing with the formation of cultural identities understood not as essentializations [...] but as contrapuntal ensembles, for it is the case that no identity can ever exist by itself and without an array of opposites, negatives, oppositions".

[5] Cf. Linda Colley, *Britons: Forging the Nation 1707-1837* (New Haven, London, 1992). In this respect, as V. Nünning has shown, the so-called 'Indian Mutiny' was one of the most significant ideological and moral turning-points because this key event of imperial history transformed both the reputation of the army and the conception Britain had of itself, of its national characteristics, and of its role in the world. For a detailed analysis, see Vera Nünning, "'Daß Jeder seine Pflicht thue'. Die Bedeutung der *Indian Mutiny* für das nationale britische Selbstverständnis", *Archiv für Kulturgeschichte*, 78 (1996), 363-391.

5. Epilogue: Queen Victoria's Jubilees as a Paradigm for the Study of the History of Mentalities and Cultural Memories

Of necessity, what we have presented is a limited and simplified account of a broad and complex subject, and it has been impossible to pursue all the themes and ramifications in the detail which they actually merit.[1] What we hope to have shown, however, is that the representations of Queen Victoria's Jubilees significantly altered her public image, turning the 'Domestic Queen' into a familiar and idealized icon of the British Empire, while at the same time domesticating the imperial mission and the imperial relationship: "With this iconic image proliferating in the colonized territories and within the British Isles, Victoria seemed to validate imperialism and render it harmless, even comforting."[2] By the time of her Diamond Jubilee she was still hailed as "a grand example of humility, of patience, of long suffering – in a word, of Womanliness", but the cultural 'invention of an empress' seems to have been largely completed by then. The article published in *Vanity Fair* on 24 June 1897 epitomizes the new image that a host of writers had managed to create for Queen Victoria, an image amalgamating not only Victoria's work as Queen of England to the ideal of motherhood but also her role as a mother of her people and of "Empress of every country over which the British flag waves":

> Queen Victoria is Empress of India only by name; in spirit she is Empress of every country over which the British flag waves; and of each of the millions who knows her sway. [...] Our Ruler is a Queen who has been a mother to her people.[3]

---

[1] There are, of course, a host of literary and historical sources dealing with the Queen's contradictory relation to imperialism (including portraiture, illustrations, stamps, colonial coins, mugs, and a wide range of other manifestations of material culture) which we have not been able to discuss. Kipling's ambivalent poems (e.g. "Recessional", "The Widow's Party", and "The Widow at Windsor"), the Queen's *Journal*, and the cartoons published in *Punch* (see e.g. 1 April 1876, p. 124; 15 April 1876, p. 146; 28 August 1876, p. 82) would be three important cases in point. For a bemused American perspective, see Mark Twain's essay "Queen Victoria's Jubilee", in: *The Complete Essays of Mark Twain*, ed. and with an introduction by Charles Neider (Garden City, N.Y., 1963), pp. 189-199. As the title of the article is meant to indicate, we are also aware of the fact that we have imposed one particular 'plot' on a complex story and on polyvalent material which could be approached from other angles as well.

[2] Homans and Munich, "Introduction", in: *Remaking Queen Victoria*, p. 3.

[3] Chapman and Raben, *Debrett's Queen Victoria's Jubilees 1887 & 1897*, p. 76.

In conclusion we would like to provide a brief assessment of the value that an analysis of the representations of Queen Victoria's jubilees may have for the study of the history of mentalities and cultural history, arguing that they can be seen as a paradigm example for the study of cultural memories.[1] While purporting merely to represent these important state occasions, the literary and journalistic texts examined above arguably shaped the prevailing view of both Queen Victoria as empress and of the relationship between England and her colonies. They not only popularized certain values, biases, and epistemological habits, they also provided agreed-upon codes of understanding and cultural traditions of looking at both the Queen as Empress and the British Empire.

As the above analysis of some of a selection of poetic, metaphorical and journalistic representations of Queen Victoria's Jubilees may have shown, it is not only poets who think in terms of myths and metaphors, but also whole cultures.[2] The suggestive and familiar notions that the metaphors of the Queen as a mother to her people and of the empire as family evoked served to create and support the perceptual and ideological fictions that formed the conceptual matrix of imperialism. The plethora and ubiquity of such metaphors support the hypothesis that such metaphors embody what Elizabeth Ermarth in a different context has called "the collective awareness of a culture".[3] By giving shape and meaning to the British Empire, they constructed an important "article of collective cultural faith"[4], namely the imperial idea, Victorian England's imperialist view of the world.

Working simultaneously on different cognitive, emotional, normative, and ideological levels, the patriotic representations of Queen Victoria's Jubilees should be seen as a productive medium that played a creative role in the generation of the ideological fictions that provided the conceptual and emotional backbone of British imperialism. Shaping habits of thought, popular feeling, and people's views of the present and the imperial past, these representations were instrumental in creating what Said has called "imperialism's consolidating vision" because they "nurtured the sentiment, rationale, and above all the imagination of empire".[5] The myths, metaphors,

---

[1] Cf. also Nicola J. Watson, "Gloriana Victoriana: Victoria and the cultural memory of Elizabeth I", in: *Remaking Queen Victoria*, pp. 79-104.

[2] Cf. Jürgen Link and Wulf Wülfing, "Einleitung", in: *Bewegung und Stillstand in Metaphern und Mythen*, ed. J. Link and W. Wülfing (Stuttgart, 1984), pp. 7-14, who argue that metaphors to a great extent pre-structure mentalities and who emphasize the collective nature of this process: "Nicht nur Dichter [...] 'denken in Bildern', auch 'Kulturen' insgesamt" (p. 14).

[3] Ermarth, *The English Novel in History*, p. 89.

[4] Ibid., p. 122.

[5] Said, *Culture and Imperialism*, p. 288, p. 12.

and narrative fictions that these texts disseminated played an important part in shaping imperialist mentalities because they organised the conceptual and emotional realities and conditioned the way in which the Victorian public perceived, experienced, and thought of both their monarch and empress. They not only established a world view and a configuration of values that was conducive to maintaining and advancing the imperial cause, they also initiated new ways of commemorating the Queen's imperial reign and the British Empire:

> A whole range of public ceremonials was evolved and elaborated, invented and inaugurated, to commemorate the rites of passage of imperial British monarchs in ways that were both far-reaching and of unprecedented extravagance. [...] And they all stressed history and hierarchy, unity and order, crown and empire. ...[1]

The ideological fictions which these public ceremonials and their textual representations helped to create served as a filter through which the 'Empress of India' and the British Empire came into the English public consciousness. The limited imagery and rhetoric of popular imperialism provided a conceptual, emotional, and normative framework which functioned as a more or less distorting lens through which the alleged unity of the empire was perceived and understood. It is arguably the ideologically charged metaphorical representations disseminated by Tennyson, Morris, Alfred Austin, and a host of other authors of commemorative verse rather than any political event which helped to popularize the image of the 'Empress of India' and which secured the unity of the British Empire for so long.

Rather than being merely a passive vehicle that reproduced either the prevailing image of Queen Victoria or the imperial ideology of their time, the texts written on the occasion of Queen Victoria's Jubilees should be conceptualized as playing a creative role in the construction of the ideological fictions that provided the mental framework of imperialism. Instead of regarding them as mere ornamental devices of poetry, political rhetoric, and patriotic journalism it is more rewarding to conceptualize these representations as an active force in their own right which was involved in the actual generation of ways of thinking and of attitudes and, thus, of something that stands behind historical developments.[2] What Edward Dowden said about the enormous influence of Kipling's poetry, is equally true of the effect that the representations of the two jubilees exerted: "They have served to evoke or guide the feelings of nations, and to determine action in

---

[1] Cannadine, *Ornamentalism*, p. 106.

[2] Cf. Said, *Orientalism*, p. 94: "Most important, such texts can *create* not only knowledge but also the very reality they appear to describe."

great affairs."[1] The representations of these public ceremonials, many of which were disseminated world-wide, served to turn these anniversaries into great imperial events which were, in fact, early instances of what are now called transnational 'media events':

> From Victoria's Golden and Diamond Jubilees, to the Silver Jubilee of George V and the coronation of George VI, every great *royal* event was also projected as an *imperial* event: marked in London by carefully orchestrated processions, with everyone in their properly assigned place. Thus was the British Empire presented as an ordered, unified hierarchy, with a semi-divine sovereign at its apex.[2]

The representations of these glittering media events not only significantly altered the way the British Empire was understood by its contemporaries, they also served to create a new imperial image of the no longer merely domestic English Queen. What we have called 'the invention of an empress' was therefore much more than just the ingenious idea of Disraeli. It should be conceptualized as the emergent result of a very complex cultural process in which any number of writers of commemorative verse, journalists, and administrators was involved. Whatever their actual intentions may have been at the time, between themselves they managed to reframe Queen Victoria's public image, refashioning the Domestic Queen not only as 'Empress of India', but even as "Empress of every country over which the British flag waves".

---

[1] Dowden, "The Poetry of Mr. Kipling", *New Liberal Review*, XXXVIII (Febr. 1901), 53-61; quoted from Green, *Kipling: The Critical Heritage*, p. 259.

[2] Cannadine, *Ornamentalism*, p. 109.

Der Tod und die Königin: Viktorianischer Totenkult und Queen Victoria als Witwe

Von *Franz Meier* (Regensburg)

1. Der Tod als Konstrukt

Nicht nur die Theorien des sogenannten 'Radikalen Konstruktivismus'[1], sondern auch verschiedene Ansätze im Rahmen der *gender studies* und der *queer theory* haben in den letzten Jahrzehnten zunehmend unseren Blick dafür geschärft, in wie hohem Maße selbst die vermeintlich 'natürlichsten' Kategorien unserer menschlichen Erfahrung kulturell bestimmt, wo nicht geschaffen sind. Dass 'Geschlechtlichkeit' und 'Sexualität' letztlich keine biologischen *facta bruta* sondern diskursive Konstrukte sind, gehört nach Michel Foucault und Judith Butler nachgerade zum Credo zeitgenössischer Kulturtheorie.[2] Die der Sexualität (scheinbar) diametral entgegengesetzte Kategorie des Todes hingegen erscheint oft noch als letztes Refugium einer ontologischen Weltsicht. Vor der 'Realität des Todes', so scheint es, verblassen alle konstruktivistischen Sophistereien; er allein scheint dem poststrukturalistischen Verdikt Widerstand zu leisten, das besagt, es gebe 'nichts außerhalb des Textes'.[3]

---

[1] Zum "Diskurs des Radikalen Konstruktivismus" als interdisziplinärem Wissenschaftsparadigma vgl. etwa die beiden Sammelbände *Der Diskurs des Radikalen Konstruktivismus*, ed. Siegfried J. Schmidt (Frankfurt am Main, 1987) und *Kognition und Gesellschaft: Der Diskurs des Radikalen Konstruktivismus 2*, ed. Siegfried J. Schmidt (Frankfurt am Main, 1992); aber auch etwa Gebhard Rusch, *Erkenntnis, Wissenschaft, Geschichte: Von einem konstruktivistischen Standpunkt* (Frankfurt am Main, 1987); *Einführung in den Konstruktivismus*, ed. Heinz Gumin und Heinrich Meier (München, 1997); oder *Die erfundene Wirklichkeit*, ed. Paul Watzlawick (München, 1981).

[2] Vgl. insbesondere Michel Foucault, *Der Wille zum Wissen* [=*Sexualität und Wahrheit*, vol. 1] (Frankfurt am Main, 1983); sowie Judith Butler, *Gender Trouble: Feminism and the Subversion of Identity* (New York, 1990); Dies., *Bodies that Matter: On the Discursive Limits of "Sex"* (New York, 1993). Genannt seien darüber hinaus – stellvertretend für eine ganze Reihe weiterer Autoren – die folgenden Werke von Geoffrey Weeks, *Sexuality and Its Discontents: Meanings, Myths and Modern Sexualities* (London, 1985); Ders., *Sex, Politics and Society: The Regulations of Sexuality Since 1800* (London, 1993); Ders., *Making Sexual History* (Cambridge, 2000).

[3] Vgl. Jaques Derrida, *Of Grammatology* [1967], übers. Gayatri C. Spivak (Baltimore, 1976), S. 158.

Und doch: Ein genauerer Blick auf die Kulturgeschichte des Todes, wie er uns etwa durch die mentalitätsgeschichtlichen Untersuchungen von Ariès und Vovelle gewährt wird[1], lässt sehr bald erahnen, dass, wenn schon nicht die ohnehin unerkennbare 'Realität' des Todes, so doch seine uns zugängliche 'Wirklichkeit'[2], sich letztlich ebenso als konstruierte entpuppt wie die der Sexualität. Auch die Bestimmungen und Bedeutungen des Todes sind von einer historischen und regionalen Variabilität, die ihn als "transzendentales Signifikat"[3] ungeeignet erscheinen lässt.[4] "Death is the constructed Other", schreiben daher Bronfen und Goodwin in der Einleitung zu ihrem Sammelband *Death and Representation.*[5] Und Baudrillard bezeichnet den Tod als letztlich "nichts anderes als die *gesellschaftliche* Abgrenzungslinie, welche die 'Toten' von den 'Lebenden' trennt".[6] Wohl gemerkt: Das alles will nicht sagen, dass es 'den Tod nicht gebe', oder dass er uns, wie Epikur meinte, 'nichts anginge'.[7] Es heißt, dass das, was wir von ihm wissen können, wie wir ihn (am anderen) 'erleben', Teil unseres kulturellen und damit historischen Bedeutungsfeldes ist.

Nichts macht das deutlicher als der Wandel zwischen den beiden zuletzt vergangenen kulturgeschichtlichen Epistemen in England – Viktorianismus und Moderne – hinsichtlich ihres Umgangs mit dem Tod. Der britische Soziologe Geoffrey Gorer hat darauf bereits 1965 in einem denkwürdigen

---

[1] Vgl. etwa Philippe Ariès, *Studien zur Geschichte des Todes im Abendland* (München, 1976); Ders., *Bilder zur Geschichte des Todes* (München, 1984); Ders., *Geschichte des Todes* (München, 1993); Michel Vovelle, *Mourir autrefois: attitudes collectives devant la mort aux XVIIe et XVIIIe siécles* (Paris, 1974); Ders., *La mort et l'occident: de 1300 à nous jours* (Paris, 1983).

[2] Nach Siegfried J. Schmidt, "Medien, Kultur: Medienkultur: Ein konstruktivistisches Gesprächsangebot", in: *Kognition und Gesellschaft*, ed. Ders., S. 425-450, ist es sinnvoll, "zwischen ontologischer (aber unerkennbarer) Realität auf der einen Seite und kognitiver (von unserem Wissen gebildeter) Wirklichkeit auf der anderen Seite" zu unterscheiden (S. 431).

[3] Vgl. etwa Jacques Derrida, "Semiologie und Grammatologie: Gespräch mit Julia Kristeva", in: *Postmoderne und Dekonstruktion: Texte französischer Philosophen der Gegenwart*, ed. Peter Engelmann (Stuttgart, 1990), S. 140-164, S. 143.

[4] Vgl. die "Introduction" der Herausgeberinnen, in: *Death and Representation*, ed. Elisabeth Bronfen und Sarah Webster (Baltimore, 1993), S. 3-25, S. 4.

[5] Ibid., S. 20.

[6] Jean Baudrillard, *Der symbolische Tausch und der Tod* (München, 1982), S. 200.

[7] Vgl. Epikur, "Brief an Meneikeus", in: Ders., *Briefe, Sprüche, Werkfragmente: Griechisch/Deutsch*, ed. u. übers. Wolfgang Krautz (Stuttgart, 1980), S. 41-51, S. 45: "Das Schauererregendste aller Übel, der Tod, betrifft uns überhaupt nicht; wenn 'wir' sind, ist der Tod nicht da; wenn der Tod da ist, sind 'wir' nicht. Er betrifft also weder die Lebenden noch die Gestorbenen, da er ja für die einen nicht da ist, die anderen aber nicht mehr für ihn da sind."

Aufsatz mit dem provokativen Titel "The Pornography of Death" verwiesen. "The natural processes of corruption and decay have become disgusting", schreibt er darin über das 20. Jahrhundert,

> as disgusting as the natural processes of birth and copulation were a century ago; preoccupation about such processes is (or was) morbid and unhealthy, to be discouraged in all and punished in the young. Our great-grandparents were told that babies were found under gooseberry bushes or cabbages; our children are likely to be told that those who have passed on (Fie! on the gross Anglo-Saxon monosyllable) are changed into flowers, or lie at rest in lonely gardens. The ugly facts are relentlessly hidden ...[1]

In der Tat scheint der Tod seit Ende des 19. Jahrhunderts (nicht nur) in England zunehmend jene Position des kulturellen Anderen einzunehmen, welche zuvor die Sexualität besetzte. Ob man für die dabei gebrauchten Strategien den traditionelleren Begriff der Tabuisierung oder den modischeren der Diskursivierung (Foucault) benutzt, ist hier vielleicht weniger wichtig, als die diesen Strategien gemeinsame Problematisierung und Reglementierung eines existentiellen Teils menschlicher Lebenswirklichkeit. Die von Gorer selbst maßgeblich angestoßene Entwicklung der Thanatologie, der 'Wissenschaft vom Tode', kann in diesem Zusammenhang als paradigmatischer Beleg für die janusköpfige Natur dieser Strategien gelesen werden. Zwar hat die neue Forschungsdisziplin seit den 60er Jahren zweifellos zu einer verstärkten Diskussion über den Tod angeregt[2], doch fand diese fast ausschließlich in Spezialdiskursen statt. Alltäglich ist im 20. und 21. Jahrhundert paradoxerweise der überraschende, gewaltsame, der 'unnatürliche' Tod, der 'eigentlich' nicht zu unserem Alltag gehört. Der Tod als selbstverständliche Gegebenheit jedoch, als zu erwartendes Ereignis, als

---

[1] Geoffrey Gorer, "The Pornography of Death", *Encounter*, 5.4 (1955), 49-52; rpt. in: Ders., *Death, Grief, and Mourning in Contemporary Britain* (London, 1965), S. 169-175 ["Appendix Four"], S. 172.

[2] Vgl. etwa die folgenden Bibliographien: Robert Fulton, *Death, Grief and Bereavement: A Bibliograpy 1845-1975* (New York, 1977); Ders. et al., *A Bibliography of Death, Grief and Bereavement 1975-1980* (New York, 1981); M.L. Kutscher, *A Bibliography of Books on Death, Bereavement, Loss and Grief Since 1935*, 2 vols. (New York, 1974); Ders. et al., *A Comprehensive Bibliography of the Thanatology Literature* (New York, 1975); Larry A Platt, *Death and Dying: A Research Bibliography Series*, 2 vols. (Statesboro, 1986); G.H. Poteet, *Death and Dying: A Bibliography 1950-1974*, 2 vols. (Troy, NY, 1976); Michael A. Simpson, *Dying, Death and Grief: A Critically Annotated Bibliography and Source Book of Thanatology and Terminal Care* (New York, 1979); Ders., *Dying, Death, and Grief: A Critical Bibliography* (Berkeley, 1987).

'Normalität' wurde (zumindest bis vor kurzem)[1] fast nur im Rahmen der selben eng begrenzten (und kontrollierenden) Diskurse thematisiert, die im 19. Jahrhundert angetreten waren, die Sexualität zu 'bändigen': im Rahmen von Medizin, Psychologie und Soziologie.

2. Der Viktorianische Kult des Todes und der Trauer[2]

Wie anders waren da die Viktorianer! Sie, die aus lauter Prüderie angeblich die Beine ihrer Pianos verkleideten[3] und die Bücher männlicher und weiblicher AutorInnen in getrennten Regalen unterbrachten ("unless they happen to be married")[4], kultivierten Tod, Sterben und Trauer als öffentliches Thema und Spektakel.[5] Der Tod, zumal jener im Bürgertum, diente nicht zuletzt der Repräsentation. Doch die öffentliche Inszenierung war stets auch (mehr oder weniger 'authentischer') Ausdruck einer privaten Affektivität – vor allem im Rahmen der zum Ideal verklärten Familie. Für die Viktorianer war der Tod ein repräsentatives Ereignis, aber auch Gelegen-

---

[1] Ob jüngere Entwicklungen wie die Hospizbewegung oder die zunehmende Diskussion über sogenannte Sterbehilfe diesbezüglich einen erneuten Paradigmenwechsel ankündigen, kann noch nicht endgültig entschieden werden.

[2] Zu den in diesem Abschnitt geschilderten Zusammenhängen vgl. auch das Kapitel 3.1.2 in meiner Monographie *Sexualität und Tod: Eine Themenverknüpfung in der englischen Schauer- und Sensationsliteratur und ihrem soziokulturellen Kontext (1764-1897)* (Tübingen, 2002) [im Druck].

[3] Vgl. etwa Peter Fryer, *Mrs. Grundy: Studies in English Prudery* (London, 1965), S. 197-198, *passim*; Peter Gay, *The Bourgeois Experience: Victoria To Freud*, 2 vols., vol. 1 [*Education of the Senses*] (Oxford, 1984), S. 346 und 495; Derek Pearsall, *The Worm in the Bud: The World of Victorian Sexuality* (London, 1969), S. xiii und 423.

[4] Vgl. Barry F. Smith, "Sexuality in Britain, 1800-1900: Some Suggested Reviews", in: *The Widening Sphere: Changing Roles of Victorian Women*, ed. Martha Vicinus (Bloomington, 1977), S. 182-198, das Zitat von Lady Gough, S. 182.

[5] Seit den 60er Jahren entstand eine Fülle von Literatur zum viktorianischen Totenkult. Als wichtigste Werke seien genannt: Robert Cecil, *The Masks of Death: Changing Attitudes in the Nineteenth Century* (Lewes, 1991); James Stevens Curl, *The Victorian Celebration of Death* (Newton Abbot, 1972), sowie seine identisch betitelte, neuere Studie (Phoenix Mill, 2000); Pat Jalland, *Death in the Victorian Family* (New York, 1996); John Morley, *Death, Heaven and the Victorians* (Pittsburgh, 1971); oder Michael Wheeler, *Death and the Future Life in Victorian Literature and Theology* (Cambridge, 1990), *sowie* eine ganze Reihe von Aufsätzen in *Death, Ritual, and Bereavement*, ed. Ralph Houlbrooke (London, 1989).

heit zur Kultivierung einer spätromantischen Sentimentalität und eines bürgerlichen Familiengefühls.[1]

Schon das Sterben selbst, die letzten Tage und Stunden eines dahinschei-
denden Menschen, hatte kommunalen Charakter, war weit entfernt von der
einsamen Anonymität des heutigen Tods im Krankenhaus. Am Bett, im
Haus des/r Moribunden versammelten sich Familienmitglieder und
Freunde, um dem/r Sterbenden[2] Beistand zu leisten, aber auch um selbst
Trost zu erfahren. Wie selbstverständlich waren auch Kinder in diese Sterbebettszenen einbezogen.[3] Religiöse Aspekte spielten zweifellos eine
bedeutsame Rolle[4], aber mindestens ebenso wichtig war die Erfahrung
gegenseitiger affektiver Verbundenheit.[5] Im Zuge von Positivismus, Darwinismus und Säkularisierung mögen viele Viktorianer von religiösen Zweifeln angefochten worden sein; die Existenz eines Jenseits jedoch, in dem
sich einst – wie jetzt am Sterbebett – die liebend einander zugetane Familie
wieder vereint sehen würde, wurde selbst von den größten Skeptikern kaum
je ernsthaft in Frage gestellt.[6] Die Jenseitsvorstellung der Viktorianer glich

---

[1] Zur Verbindung von Öffentlichkeitsbedürfnis und "makabre[r] Affektivität" (Ariès,
Studien, S. 46) im Trauerverhalten des 19. Jahrhunderts allgemein vgl. Ariès, *Geschichte*, S. 653; sowie Ders., *Studien*, S. 45, 49.

[2] Aus stilistischen Gründen wird im weiteren Verlauf dieses Aufsatzes auf
Genusdoppelungen verzichtet.

[3] Zur Konvention der viktorianischen Sterbebettszene vgl. etwa Cecil, *Masks of
Death*, S. 52-61, *passim*; oder Wheeler, *Death and the Future Life*, S. 28-47. Die nach
heutigem Empfinden ungewöhnliche Vertrautheit von Kindern mit der Realität des Todes (vgl. dazu etwa Cecil, *Masks of Death*, S. 76-83; Curl, *Victorian Celebration of
Death* (2000), S. 202) ist ein Beleg für die mangelnde Tabuisierung des Todes im Viktorianismus. Vgl. als Beispiele dafür etwa das als Lithographie weit verbreitete Bild
"The Last Moments of HRH The Prince Consort" (siehe unten S. 124, Anm. 5); aber
auch das unbeschwerte Treiben von Kindern auf dem Friedhof in Charles Dickens, *The
Adventures of Oliver Twist; or: The Parish Boy's Progress*, Ders., *The Centenary
Edition of the Works of Charles Dickens*, 36 vols. (London, 1910-1911), vol. 3, S. 46;
in: Ders., *The Old Curiosity Shop, Centenary Edition*, vols. 10 und 11, vol. 11, S. 166;
oder in George Eliot, "Amos Barton", in: Dies., *Scenes of Clerical Life* [=*The Writings
of George Eliot: Together With The Life By J.W. Cross*, vol. 1] (New York, 1970), S. 1-
113, S. 103-104.

[4] Vgl. dazu grundlegend Wheeler, *Death and the Future Life*.

[5] Philippe Ariès bezeichnet diese schon im 18. Jahrhundert einsetzende, aber erst im
19. Jahrhundert kulminierende, affektiv-privatisierte Auffassung vom Tod als "Tod des
Anderen". Vgl. Ariès, *Geschichte*, S. 645, 783, *passim*; Ders., *Studien*, S. 43, 49, *passim*.

[6] Ariès, *Bilder*, S. 183, spricht vom "naive[n] Glaube[n] an ein Jenseits des
Wiedersehens"; und Jalland, *Death in the Victorian Family*, S. 271-276, widmet den
"Family Reunions in the Heavenly Home" ein eigenes Kapitel.

stark dem idealen bürgerlichen *living room*.[1] Von der Nähe zum Sterbenden erhoffte man sich in der frühkapitalistischen, industrialisierten und
arbeitsteiligen Gesellschaft des 19. Jahrhunderts vielleicht gar einen flüchtigen Vorschein dieser utopischen Harmonie. Die Darstellung von Toten in
dieser Zeit betont daher häufig die Schönheit des Leichnams und den Ausdruck tiefen Glücks auf seinem Gesicht.[2] Auch die letzten Worte des
Sterbenden hatten diesbezüglich große Bedeutung und sollten möglichst
diese Utopie bestätigen.[3]

War der als mystisch erlebte Augenblick des Todes vorbei, trat der reprä-
sentative Aspekt in den Vordergrund. Dies geschah nicht nur im Aufbahren
des Toten, das nun auch einem breiteren Kreis von Freunden und Bekannten die Gelegenheit zum letzten Kontakt mit der 'schönen Leiche' ermöglichen sollte (und im übrigen der verbreiteten Angst vor dem Scheintod entgegen wirkte):[4] Vor allem das viktorianische Begräbnis war repräsentativer
Ausdruck der affektiven Zuneigung zum Verstorbenen *und* Präsentation
von ökonomischem wie kulturellem Kapital. Bestattungsinstitute organi-
sierten Leichenwagen, Bestattungsbegleiter (*mutes*) und Grabmonumente
verschiedenster Art; Ausstattungsläden verdienten an Straußenfedern,
Trauerkrepp und Federbuschen für die Pferde. Viktorianische Begräbnisse
kosteten Unsummen[5] und erforderten genaueste Kenntnis der ungeschrie-
benen Gesetze dieses Rituals. Jedes Detail hatte kulturelle Bedeutung im
Rahmen eines ausdifferenzierten semantischen Systems der Trauer. Durch
die Beherrschung dieses (an aristokratische Bräuche angelehnten)[6] *Code*

---

[1] Vgl. Ariès, *Geschichte*, S. 555, 562, 785, *passim*; Wheeler, *Death and the Future
Life*, S. 6; oder Dietrich Schwanitz, *Englische Kulturgeschichte*, 2 vols. (Tübingen,
1995), vol. 2, S. 20, der diese Tendenz schon im 18. Jahrhundert angelegt sieht.

[2] Ariès überschreibt das entsprechende Kapitels seiner Geschichte des Todes, S. 521,
"Die Zeit der schönen Tode"; und Elisabeth Bronfen, *Over Her Dead Body: Death Femininity and the Aesthetic* (Manchester, 1992), S. 87, schreibt: "Visiting a house of
mourning became comparable to visiting a picture gallery. [...] In this period morgues
were visited like picture galleries ...".

[3] "The last words of the dying [...] had a special significance for the Victorians, and
became something of a literary convention in their own right", schreibt Wheeler, *Death
and the Future Life*, S. 30.

[4] Diese Angst setzte massiv im 18. Jahrhundert ein und wird von Ariès, *Geschichte*,
S. 782, als "erste Form der großen Angst vor dem Tode" bezeichnet. Julian Litten, *The
English Way of Death: The Common Funeral Since 1450* (London, 1991), S. 166-167,
sieht hingegen den Schwerpunkt dieser Angst im 19. Jahrhundert. Für spezifisch engli-
sche Beispiele vgl. auch Clare Gittings, *Death, Burial and the Individual in Early
Modern England* (London, 1988), S. 205.

[5] Vgl. Curl, *Victorian Celebration of Death* (2000), S. 206-208, mit einer
zeitgenössischen Kostenaufstellung.

[6] Vgl. Curl, *Victorian Celebration of Death* (2000), S. 197.

legitimierte v.a. das Bürgertum seinen Anspruch auf gesellschaftliche Füh-
rungsposition. Aber auch Staatsbegräbnisse waren Demonstrationen politischer Macht. Das eindrucksvollste Beispiel hierfür war zweifelsohne das
pompöse Begräbnis des Duke of Wellington[1], dessen Leichenwagen allein
£11.000 kostete.[2]

Der viktorianische Kult des Todes endete aber nicht mit dem Begräbnis.
Auch, ja gerade die Phase der Trauer war bis ins kleinste Detail mit Bedeutung aufgeladen. Es existierten genaueste Kleidervorschriften und
Trauerfristen, die je nach Status des Verstorbenen und Verwandtschafts-
grad der Trauernden variierten. Zwischen den Graden der Teilnahme am
öffentlichen Leben während des *full mourning* und *half mourning* existierten ebenso unzählige, feinste Nuancierungen wie zwischen den Schwarz-
und Grautönen der Stoffe – einige von ihnen (*crepe*) ausschließlich für
Trauerzwecke hergestellt.[3] Dabei reichte das Spektrum von repräsentativer
Trauer über unziemliche Eitelkeit[4] bis zur Geschmacklosigkeit – wie Thomas Hardys satirisches Gedicht "At the Drapers" zeigt, in dem ein todkran-
ker Mann seine künftige Witwe beim Aussuchen eines 'tod-schicken'
Trauerkleides beobachtet.[5] Es gab übrigens sogar Trauerunterwäsche, und
manchmal trugen auch Kleinkinder *full mourning*: deutliches Zeichen für
den repräsentativen Aspekt viktorianischer Trauer.

Das Moment privater Affektivität hingegen betont der persönliche Erinnerungskult, der geradezu makabre Züge annehmen konnte. Nicht nur die
heute noch üblichen Memorabilia wie Accessoires oder Portraits des Verstorbenen wurden verehrt, sondern auch aus den Haaren der geliebten Person angefertigte Schmuckstücke (Ringe, Armreife etc.) erfreuten sich
großer Beliebtheit.[6] Und das neue Medium der Photographie ersetzte oder

---

[1] Vgl. Curl, *Victorian Celebration of Death* (1972), S. 3-5; Ders., *Victorian Celebration of Death* (2000), S. 211-218; oder Morley, *Death, Heaven and the Victorians*, S.
80-90; aber auch Jalland, *Death in the Victorian Family*, S. 194-197, der freilich derar-
tig pompöse Staatsbegräbnisse für kulturell wenig repräsentativ hält.

[2] Vgl. Morley, *Death, Heaven and the Victorians*, S. 83.

[3] Zur viktorianischen Trauerkleidung und -mode vgl. etwa Curl, *Victorian Celebration of Death* (2000), S. 199-202; oder Jalland, *Death in the Victorian Family*, S. 300-
307.

[4] Vgl. hierzu die zeitgenössische Satire (in *Hoods Magazine*) auf die Trauermode, zit.
in Morley, *Death, Heaven and the Victorians*, S. 74-75.

[5] Thomas Hardy, "At the Drapers", in: Ders., *The Variorum Edition of the Complete
Poems of Thomas Hardy*, ed. James Gibson (London, 1979), S. 421-422.

[6] Derartiger Schmuck war schon im 18. Jahrhundert sehr verbreitet gewesen. Vgl.
dazu Ariès, *Geschichte*, S. 495; Curl, *Victorian Celebration of Death* (2000), S. 201;
Jalland, *Death in the Victorian Family*, S. 298-299; und Morley, *Death, Heaven and the
Victorians*, S. 14, 66-67. Eine beeindruckende Sammlung solcher Schmuckstücke be-

ergänzte die Totenmaske[1], wobei besonders die Gattung der Kindertoten-
fotos heutige Betrachter erschaudern läßt, weil darauf die kleinen Leich-
name in 'lebensnahen' Posen und oft mit geöffneten Augen abgelichtet
wurden.[2] Hier, aber auch in der Renaissance der Balsamierungskunst[3] und
der Ablehnung der Kremation bis ins späte 19. Jahrhundert hinein[4], zeigt
sich eine erstaunliche Gelassenheit gegenüber den körperlichen Aspekten
des Todes, ja, geradezu eine Faszination durch den toten Körper, die selt-
sam quer steht zu der angeblich sonst so ausgeprägten Körperfeindlichkeit
der Zeit. Vielen freilich war die körperliche Nähe zu den Toten, die auch
beim nun üblichen sonntäglichen Ausflug zum Vorstadtfriedhof[5] eine
Rolle spielte, nicht genug, und sie suchten in spiritistischen Séancen die
direkte Kommunikation mit dem Jenseits und ihren Verstorbenen.[6]

Die viktorianische Faszination des Todes manifestierte sich aber nicht
nur in Gegenständen und Verhaltensweisen des Alltags, sie fand ihren Niederschlag auch auf künstlerischem und literarischem Gebiet. Die Elegie,
eine der ältesten englischen Gattungen, erlebte im Viktorianismus eine
neue Blütezeit und einen Höhepunkt mit Alfred Tennysons (von Queen

---

findet sich in der 'Jewellery Gallery' des Londoner "Victoria and Albert Museum",
Case 27. Vgl. dazu Shirley Bury, *Jewellery Gallery: Summary Catalogue* (London,
1982), S. 155-161.

[1] Vgl. Baumann, "Bilder des Todes: Die Geschichte der Totenphotographie", in: *Tod
und Gesellschaft – Tod im Wandel*, ed. Christoph Daxelmüller (Regensburg, 1996), S.
121-123; Dies., "Gedenket in Liebe und im Gebet ...", in: ibid., S. 103-105, S. 103; sowie Jalland, *Death in the Victorian Family*, S. 289-290. Als Bildbeispiel vgl. etwa die
Abb. 256 in Ariès, *Bilder*, S. 257.

[2] Vgl. Ariès, *Bilder*, S. 258-264, sowie die dortigen Abb. 358-360.

[3] Vgl. Ariès, *Geschichte*, S. 647-648.

[4] Vgl. dazu Morley, *Death, Heaven and the Victorians*, S. 91-101; aber auch Curl,
Victorian Celebration of Death (1972), S. 182; und Ders., *Victorian Celebration of
Death* (2000), S. 182, 184, 186.

[5] Vgl. Ariès, *Geschichte*, S. 668-678; Jalland, *Death in the Victorian Family*, S. 291-
295. Zur Geschichte des viktorianischen Vorstadtfriedhofs (*cemetery*) vgl. grundlegend
Chris Brooks, *Mortal Remains: The History and Present State of the Victorian and Edwardian Cemetery* (Exeter, 1989); aber auch die beiden Bücher von Curl (*Victorian
Celebration of Death*, 1972 und 2000). Zur zunehmenden Bedeutung der Familie in der
Ikonographie der Grabmonumente seit der Wende vom 18. zum 19. Jahrhundert vgl.
etwa David Irwin, "Sentiment and Antiquity: European Tombs, 1750-1830", in: *Mirrors
of Mortality: Studies in the Social History of Death*, ed. Joachim Whaley (London,
1981), S. 131-153, S. 144-147.

[6] Zum Spiritismus im 19. Jahrhundert vgl. etwa Cecil, *Masks of Death*, S. 200-204;
Morley, *Death, Heaven and the Victorians*, S. 102-111.

Victoria geliebtem)[1] Langgedicht *In Memoriam*[2], das aus persönlicher Trauer um Arthur Hallam erwuchs. In anderen, nostalgisch mediaevalisierenden Gedichten wie "Mariana" oder "The Lady of Shalott" zeigt uns der viktorianische Hofdichter allerdings vorwiegend *weibliche* Protagonistinnen als mindestens "half in love with easeful Death"[3], lieber noch als "schöne Leiche".[4] Literarisch inspirierte Maler, v.a. im Umkreis der Präraffaeliten, nahmen diese Motive dankbar auf.[5]

Die Themenverknüpfung 'Weiblichkeit und Tod' erwies sich hier und anderswo im Viktorianismus als besonders fruchtbar, nicht nur weil, wie Poe formuliert hatte, der Tod einer schönen Frau 'das poetischste Thema der Welt' wäre[6], sondern auch weil, wie etwa Bronfen zeigt, männliche künstlerische Kreativität in patriarchalen Kulturen maßgeblich aus dem Versuch der Tilgung des weiblichen 'Anderen' (der 'natürlichen' Kreativität) erwächst.[7] Die 'symbolische Ordnung' (Lacan) des viktorianischen Diskurses immunisiert sich im Tod der schönen Frau (scheinbar) gegen den Einbruch der von ihr repräsentierten 'semiotischen Chora' (Kristeva). Wo Künstler und Dichter Weiblichkeit und Tod in anderer, nicht spätromantisch gebändigter Form zusammenbringen (etwa in Swinburnes "The Leper"), da ist ihnen gesellschaftliche Ächtung sicher. Wo sie jedoch das Sterben ästhetisch verklären, den Tod als sanft und schön erscheinen lassen, da treffen sie den Nerv der Zeit.

---

[1] Vgl. etwa Elizabeth Darby und Nicola Smith, *The Cult of the Prince Consort* (New Haven, 1983), S. 4; sowie Stanley Weintraub, *Queen Victoria: An Intimate Biography* (New York, 1987), S. 310ff.

[2] Vgl. etwa Peter M. Sacks, *The English Elegy: Studies in the Genre from Spencer to Yeats* (London, 1985), S. 166-203; oder Wheeler, *Death and the Future Life*, S. 221-264.

[3] John Keats, "Ode to a Nightingale", VI, 2.

[4] Elisabeth Bronfen, "Die schöne Leiche: Weiblicher Tod als motivische Konstante von der Mitte des 18. Jahrhunderts bis in die Moderne", in: *Weiblichkeit und Tod in der Literatur*, ed. Renate Berger und Inge Stephan (Köln, 1987), S. 87-115. Zur Motivverknüpfung 'Tod und Frau' bei Tennyson vgl. etwa Sylvia Manning, "Death and Sex from Tennyson's Early Poetry to *In Memoriam*", in: *Sex and Death in Victorian Literature*, ed. Regina Barreca (London, 1990), S. 194-210.

[5] Vgl. etwa John William Waterhouse, *The Lady of Shalott* (1888); John Everett Millais, *Ophelia* (1851-52), oder Dante Gabriel Rossettis *The Blessed Damozel* (1878) und *Proserpina* (1874), um nur einige der berühmtesten Gemälde zu nennen.

[6] Vgl. Edgar Allan Poe, "The Philosophy of Composition" [1946], in: *The Portable Poe*, ed. Philip van Doren Stern (Harmondsworth, 1983), S. 549-565, S. 557.

[7] Vgl. etwa Bronfen, "Die Schöne Leiche"; oder Dies., *Over Her Dead Body*.

Am deutlichsten wird das wohl in der geradezu topischen Vorliebe viktorianischer Kunst und Literatur für sentimentale Sterbebettszenen.[1] Deren berühmteste, Charles Dickens' Schilderung des Tods von Little Nell in *The Old Curiosity Shop*, rührte die gesamte Nation (den Autor eingeschlossen) zu Tränen.[2] In dieser Szene vereinigten sich die erwähnten Themen von Weiblichkeit und Tod mit einer weiteren Lieblingsutopie der Viktorianer, der Unschuld des Kindes:

> For she was dead. There, upon her little bed, she lay at rest. The solemn stillness was no marvel now.
> She was dead. No sleep so beautitiful and calm, so free from trace of pain, so fair to look upon. She seemed a creature fresh from the hand of God, and waiting for the breath of life; not one who had lived and suffered death.
> Her couch was dressed here and there with some winter berries and green leaves, gathered in a spot she had been used to favour. "When I die, put near me something that has loved the light, and had the sky above it always." Those were her words.
> She was dead. Dear, gentle, patient, noble Nell was dead. Her little bird – a poor slight thing the pressure of a finger would have crushed – was stirring nimbly in its cage; and the strong heart of its child mistress was mute and motionless for ever.
> Where were the traces of her early cares, her sufferings, and fatigues? All gone. Sorrow was dead indeed in her, but peace and perfect happiness were born; imaged in her tranquil beauty and profound repose.[3]

Das Beispiel zeigt nur allzu deutlich den performativen und inszenatorischen Aspekt des Todes und der Trauer im Viktorianismus. 'Typische' Viktorianer (falls eine solche Pauschalierung in dieser Epoche der Widersprüche sinnvoll ist) empfinden den Tod nicht nur als – in Ariès' Worten – "Tod des Anderen"[4] (also als Verlust eines geliebten Mitmenschen), sondern auch als 'Tod für den Anderen', als repräsentativen und bedeutungs-

---

[1] Zum Motiv der Sterbettszene in der Literatur vgl. v.a. Margarete Holubetz, "Death-Bed Scenes in Victorian Fiction", *English Studies*, 667 (1986), 14-34; John R. Reed, *Victorian Conventions* (Athens, 1975), S. 156-161; oder Wheeler, *Death and the Future Life*, S. 25, *passim*; und für die bildende Kunst: Darby/Smith, *Cult of the Prince Consort*, S. 95.

[2] Vgl. etwa Peter Ackroyd, *Dickens* (London, 1990), S. 317-22; Nina Auerbach, *Woman and the Demon: The Life of a Victorian Myth* (Cambridge, MA, 1982), S. 86-87; Morley, *Death, Heaven and the Victorians*, S. 18.

[3] Charles Dickens, *The Old Curiosity Shop*, vol. 11, S. 374. Der Ästhet und Dandy Oscar Wilde bemerkte am Ende der Epoche vielleicht nicht zu Unrecht: "One must have a heart of stone to read the death of Little Nell without laughing". Zit. nach Richard Ellmann, *Oscar Wilde* (Harmondsworth, 1988), S. 441.

[4] Siehe oben S. 117, Anm. 5.

vollen, somit als kommunikativen Akt. Der eigene Tod und mehr noch der des Anderen wird damit zum Zeichen für das Leben dessen, der verstorben ist und für die Identität jener, die um ihn trauern. Es ist diese semantische Aufladung des Todes und der Trauer im Dienste einer Definition des Selbst, auf der das hochkomplexe Zeichensystem des viktorianischen Totenkultes basiert. Foucault ergänzend könnte man die Formulierung wagen: So wie wir uns heute unserer Identität über die Kategorie der Sexualität zu versichern glauben[1], so versuchten die Viktorianer ähnliches über die Kategorie des Todes.

3. Queen Victoria und die Trauer um Prince Albert

Das gilt auch für jene Figur, die der Epoche ihren Namen gab und sie in vieler Hinsicht repräsentierte, für Queen Victoria selbst. Die weltlichen Genüssen und Vergnügungen durchaus nicht abgeneigte Königin hatte stets ein ausgesprochenes Interesse an der Thematik und dem Kult des Todes.[2] Wie viele Viktorianer besaß sie eine Sammlung von Haarsträhnen Verstorbener[3] und achtete stets auf peinliche Einhaltung der gebotenen Trauer-Etikette.[4] Auf ihrem Landsitz Osborne House soll sie sogar spiritistische Sitzungen abgehalten haben.[5] Der Tod von Freunden und Verwandten wurde ihr zum Anlass exzessiver Trauer, in der sie beinahe zu schwelgen schien.[6] Der Verlust ihrer Mutter im März 1861 stürzte sie in monatelange Konvulsionen des Kummers.[7] "You are right, dear child," gestand sie gegenüber ihrer Tochter Vicky nach dem schweren Verlust, "I do not wish to feel better".[8] Stärkster Ausdruck dieser Neigung aber war zweifellos ihre beispiellose Trauer und ihr Erinnerungskult um ihren Gatten.

Prince Albert, der von Geburt an nicht mit starker physischer Konstitution gesegnet war, starb neun Monate nach Victorias Mutter, am 14. De-

---

[1] Vgl. etwa Michel Foucault, "Das Abendland und die Wahrheit des Sexes," in: Ders., *Dispositive der Macht: Über Sexualität, Wissen und Wahrheit* (Berlin, 1978), S. 96-103, S. 99.

[2] Vgl. Giles St. Aubyn, *Queen Victoria: A Portrait* (New York, 1991), S. 332; Christopher Hibbert, *Queen Victoria: A Personal History* (London, 2000), S. 286, Anm.

[3] Vgl. Hibbert, *Queen Victoria*, S. 497, Anm.

[4] Vgl. Hibbert, *Queen Victoria*, S. 286, Anm.

[5] Ibid., S. 294.

[6] Ibid., S. 265ff.

[7] Vgl. St. Aubyn, *Queen Victoria*, S. 318-319; Hibbert, *Queen Victoria*, S. 266-267; Weintraub, *Queen Victoria*, S. 289-290.

[8] Zitiert nach St. Aubyn, *Queen Victoria*, S. 318.

zember 1861.[1] Er hatte (auch das ein Topos der viktorianischen Zeit) sein kommendes Ende bereits lange vorausgeahnt;[2] und Tage vor seinem Hinscheiden hatte er sich ins sogenannte 'Blaue Zimmer' umbetten lassen, in dem auch George IV und William IV gestorben waren.[3] Die Totenbettszene wurde für die Nachwelt in einem Gemälde, das 1862 als Lithographie weite Verbreitung fand[4], festgehalten (oder besser: hergestellt, denn die dort dargestellte Versammlung entsprach vermutlich nicht genau dem tatsächlichen Kreis der Anwesenden).[5]

Auffällig ist dort erneut der soziale Aspekt des Ereignisses, sowie die selbstverständliche Anwesenheit von Kindern im Sterbezimmer.[6] Die eigene Verfassung im Augenblick von Alberts Tod beschreibt die Queen als "mute distracted despair, unable to utter a word or shed a tear";[7] doch später, als sie die Herzogin von Atholl allein in das 'Blaue Zimmer' führte, soll sie sich plötzlich über den Leichnam geworfen haben.[8] Auch hier zeigt sich wieder die viktorianische Spannung zwischen öffentlicher Repräsentation und privater Affektivität.

Das Staatsbegräbnis am 23. Dezember war nicht ganz so prunkvoll wie das Wellingtons, nicht zuletzt aufgrund mangelnder Vorbereitungszeit[9], denn die Bestattung sollte nicht mit dem Weihnachtsfest kollidieren.[10] Der Leichnam wurde zunächst in der traditionellen 'St. George's Chapel' in

---

[1] Als offizielle Todesursache nannten die Ärzte Typhus, doch vieles deutet auf Magenkrebs hin. Vgl. St. Aubyn, *Queen Victoria*, S. 328; Hibbert, *Queen Victoria*, S. 278; Weintraub, *Queen Victoria*, S. 296-300.

[2] Vgl. St. Aubyn, *Queen Victoria*, S. 322, 326; Hibbert, *Queen Victoria*, S. 279-280; Weintraub, *Queen Victoria*, S. 282, 298.

[3] Vgl. St. Aubyn, *Queen Victoria*, S. 326 und Hibbert, *Queen Victoria*, S. 278-279.

[4] La Port [pseud.], "The last Moments of HRH The Prince Consort" (in Darby/Smith, *Cult of the Prince Consort*, S. 95, Abb. 97; die Lithographie von W.I. Walton in Morley, *Death, Heaven and the Victorians*, S. 141, Abb. 25; oder Wheeler, *Death and the Future Life*, S. 18/19, Abb. 2).

[5] Vgl. Darby/Smith, *Cult of the Prince Consort*, S. 95.

[6] Die Anwesenheit der erst vierjährigen Prinzessin Beatrice ist allerdings nicht durch andere Quellen bezeugt und könnte eine bloße malerische Fiktion darstellen (vgl. Darby/Smith, *Cult of the Prince Consort*, S. 95). Immerhin scheint sie dem Maler aber als solche plausibel erschienen zu sein.

[7] Zitiert in St. Aubyn, *Queen Victoria*, S. 327 und Hibbert, *Queen Victoria*, S. 281.

[8] Vgl. St. Aubyn, *Queen Victoria*, S. 327-328. Weintraub und Hibbert hingegen berichten, die Königin hätte sich an die Anweisung der Ärzte gehalten, den Leichnam wegen Ansteckungsgefahr mit Typhus nicht zu berühren; eine unsinnige Anweisung, denn Victoria hatte den Gatten in den Tagen zuvor wiederholt umarmt und geküsst (vgl. Weintraub, *Queen Victoria*, S. 305; Hibbert, *Queen Victoria*, S. 286).

[9] Vgl. Weintraub, *Queen Victoria*, S. 306.

[10] Ibid., S. 304.

Windsor beigesetzt; doch seine letzte Ruhestätte fand Albert auf Wunsch der Queen ein Jahr darauf in einem eigens für £200.000 errichteten, licht-durchfluteten Mausoleum in 'Frogmore Gardens', in dem auch sie bald ne-ben ihrem Gatten zu ruhen hoffte.[1] Die Anweisungen für die aufwändige Ausgestaltung der Staatstrauer führten dazu, dass in kürzester Zeit alle schwarzen Stoffe ausverkauft waren.[2]

Victoria, die Albert 1840, drei Jahre nach ihrer jugendlichen Thronbe-steigung, geheiratet hatte, war nun erstmals als Herrscherin ganz auf sich gestellt – aber auch als Frau, die sich gemäß viktorianischer Rollenmuster stets als Dienerin des geliebten Mannes definierte. Das Leben als Königin hatte sie daher stets als "a reversal of the right order of things" empfunden.[3] Nun fühlte sie sich "changed from a powerful sovereign [...] into a weak and desolate woman".[4] Ihre Reaktion auf diese Situation und auf den persönlichen Verlust ihrer nächsten Bezugsperson war ein privater Trauer-kult, der teilweise skurrile Formen annahm. Die Königin verfügte nicht nur, dass das Sterbezimmer Alberts praktisch unverändert in dem Zustand blieb, indem es bei seinem Tode gewesen war[5], sie ordnete darüber hinaus an, dass dort täglich neue Kleidung ausgelegt, das Waschzeug gewechselt und heißes Rasierwasser bereitgestellt würde, ganz so als ob Albert noch am Leben sei.[6] Sogar sein Nachtgeschirr wurde jeden Tag gereinigt.[7]

Victoria selbst schlief stets mit einem Nachthemd des Verstorbenen im Arm und einem Abguss seiner Hand in Reichweite.[8] Vierzig Jahre lang trug sie unverändert schlichte schwarze Trauerkleidung[9], in der sie Alberts Schlüssel, Uhr und Taschentuch bei sich trug.[10] Ihre Trauer überschattete lange auch den Alltag am Hof. Alle Mitglieder des Hofes hatten im ersten Jahr *full mourning*, danach immer noch Halbtrauer zu tragen.[11] Die Hochzeit ihrer Tochter Alice mit Prinz Friedrich Willhelm Louis von Hes-sen, sechs Monate nach Alberts Tod, war in Victorias eigenen Worten

---

[1] Vgl. Hibbert, *Queen Victoria*, S. 288-289.
[2] Vgl. Weintraub, *Queen Victoria*, S. 306.
[3] Zitiert in Weintraub, *Queen Victoria*, S. 263.
[4] Zitiert in St. Aubyn, *Queen Victoria*, S. 329.
[5] Eine in England und Schottland damals durchaus übliche Sitte (vgl. Weintraub, *Queen Victoria*, S. 308).
[6] Vgl. St. Aubyn, *Queen Victoria*, S. 348-349, Hibbert, *Queen Victoria*, S. 286-287, Weintraub, *Queen Victoria*, S. 305-306, 316.
[7] Vgl. St. Aubyn, *Queen Victoria*, S. 348-349, Weintraub, *Queen Victoria*, S. 306.
[8] Vgl. Hibbert, *Queen Victoria*, S. 287, Weintraub, *Queen Victoria*, S. 305.
[9] Vgl. St. Aubyn, *Queen Victoria*, S. 335.
[10] Vgl. St. Aubyn, *Queen Victoria*, S. 329.
[11] Vgl. Weintraub, *Queen Victoria*, S. 309; Hibbert, *Queen Victoria*, S. 285.

"more like a funeral than a wedding":[1] "The bride (in mourning for her father) was even required to secure a black trousseau".[2] Im Jahr darauf führte die Queen den Prince of Wales mit seiner Verlobten Alexandra ins Mausoleum in Frogmore, um am Vortag ihrer Heirat den Segen Alberts einzuholen.[3] Bei der (recht bescheidenen) Hochzeit trug sie wie immer Schwarz und war kaum zugegen.[4] Der siebzehnjährigen Prinzessin Louise wurde noch 1865 mit Hinweis auf die Trauerpflicht der Debütantinnenball verweigert.[5] Alle königlichen Bediensteten hatten bis 1869 schwarze Armbinden zu tragen.[6]

Albert war inmitten dieser allgemein verfügten Trauer für Victoria offenbar eine spirituelle Präsenz, mit der sie stetig in Verbindung stand. Ihre politischen Entscheidungen, so gab sie jedenfalls vor[7], waren jene, die Albert getroffen hätte.[8] Vor dem Unterzeichnen wichtiger Dokumente soll sie oft in 'stillem Gespräch' den Rat ihres "blessed Oracle"[9] eingeholt haben.[10] Wie viele Viktorianer, glaubte die Queen nicht nur, dass sie im Jenseits ganz konkret wieder mit dem Verstorbenen vereint sein würde;[11] sie war auch, in den Worten des Duke of Argyll, überzeugt von der "*Life Presence of the dead*" und dass sie von Albert "only *outwardly* separated" sei.[12]

Konsequenz dieses Trauerkults der Königin war ihr beinahe vollständiger Rückzug aus der Öffentlichkeit, den sie zunehmend mit ihrem vorgeblich schlechten Gesundheitszustand zu entschuldigen suchte.[13] General Gray nannte sie deshalb wenig respektvoll "the royal malingerer".[14] Sie nahm nicht mehr an öffentlichen Zeremonien teil; und sie weigerte sich immer

---

[1] Zitiert in St. Aubyn, *Queen Victoria*, Hibbert, *Queen Victoria*, S. 286.

[2] Weintraub, *Queen Victoria*, S. 318; vgl. auch Hibbert, *Queen Victoria*, S. 286.

[3] Vgl. Weintraub, *Queen Victoria*, S. 321; Hibbert, *Queen Victoria*, S. 303.

[4] Vgl. Weintraub, *Queen Victoria*, S. 321-322; Hibbert, *Queen Victoria*, S. 303-305.

[5] Vgl. St. Aubyn, *Queen Victoria*, S. 346, 413.

[6] Vgl. Weintraub, *Queen Victoria*, S. 309.

[7] Vgl. St. Aubyn, *Queen Victoria*, S. 348.

[8] Ibid., S. 347, Weintraub, *Queen Victoria*, S. 304.

[9] St. Aubyn, *Queen Victoria*, S. 347.

[10] Vgl. Hibbert, *Queen Victoria*, S. 291.

[11] Ibid., S. 293-394.

[12] Zitiert in St. Aubyn, *Queen Victoria*, S. 351 und Weintraub, *Queen Victoria*, S. 307. "When Lord Clarendon saw her at Osborne a few months after her loss, she told him she felt sure that the Prince was constantly watching her, and that she had never ceased 'to be in communion with his spirit ... '" (St. Aubyn, *Queen Victoria*, S. 351, vgl. auch S. 352; Hibbert, *Queen Victoria*, S. 291).

[13] Vgl. St. Aubyn, *Queen Victoria*, S. 337-339.

[14] Ibid., S. 337; Weintraub, *Queen Victoria*, S. 354.

wieder, Staatsakte wie die Eröffnung des Parlaments zu vollziehen.[1] Sogar Sitzungen des Geheimen Staatsrates (*Privy Council*) wohnte sie nur von einem angrenzenden Nebenraum aus bei.[2] Die Queen war überhaupt kaum noch in Windsor oder London anzutreffen und weilte zumeist in Osborne House auf der Isle of Wight oder auf Balmoral in Schottland.

Victorias Rückzug ins Private komplementär war ihr Versuch, die Erinnerung an Prince Albert in der Öffentlichkeit zu fördern. Sie tat dies einerseits durch ständige Verweise auf ihn in Gesprächen, durch Publikation seiner Briefe und Reden, von Biographien und von Erinnerungen aus eigener Hand (*Leaves from Our Life in the Highlands*)[3], vorwiegend aber (und in flagranter Missachtung von Alberts eigenen Wünschen)[4] durch eine Unzahl an Gedenkstätten, die sie in ganz Großbritannien für ihn errichten ließ[5] und deren Einweihungen fast die einzigen Gelegenheiten waren, bei denen sie noch öffentlich auftrat.[6] Als sie 1871 zur Eröffnung der Royal Albert Hall fuhr, war die sie grüßende Menschenmenge wohl bereits mehr durch Neugierde auf die "Invisible Queen"[7] denn durch loyale Ergebenheit motiviert.[8] Es schien, als wollte Victoria sich selbst zum Verschwinden

---

[1] Vgl. St. Aubyn, *Queen Victoria*, S. 369-371. Als sie sich 1866 zum ersten Mal wieder (wie immer in *full mourning*) zur Eröffnungszeremonie begab, tat sie das vor allem, um dadurch das Parlament in Bezug auf die Genehmigung der Mitgift Prinzessin Helenas und der Leibrente Prinz Alfreds günstig zu stimmen (vgl. St. Aubyn, *Queen Victoria*, S. 370-371; Hibbert, *Queen Victoria*, S. 311-312; Weintraub, *Queen Victoria*, S. 339-340).

[2] Vgl. St. Aubyn, *Queen Victoria*, S. 331; Weintraub, *Queen Victoria*, S. 312.

[3] Vgl. St. Aubyn, *Queen Victoria*, S. 350; Weintraub, *Queen Victoria*, S. 312 und 336-337.

[4] "If I should die before you," hatte er gebeten, "do not raise even a single marble image in my name" (zitiert in St. Aubyn, *Queen Victoria*, S. 349; vgl. auch Weintraub, *Queen Victoria*, S. 307).

[5] Vgl. Hibbert, *Queen Victoria*, S. 287-288. Zum Erinnerungskult um Albert vgl. ausführlich und mit vielen Illustrationen Darby/Smith, *Cult of the Prince Consort*; zu den Albert-Gedenkstätten auch Curl, *Victorian Celebration of Death* (2000), S. 230-244.

[6] Vgl. Weintraub, *Queen Victoria*, S. 324. Die künstlerische Qualität dieser Denkmäler war nie über jeden Zweifel erhaben: "Lord Clarendon apprehended the appearance not only of many [...] statues of 'the late Consort in robes of the Garter upon some curious and non-descript animal that will be called a horse', but also of numerous 'Albert Baths and Washhouses'. The Queen would not object to such memorials, Clarendon added, since she had 'no more notion of what is right and pure in art than she had of Chinese grammar'" (Hibbert, *Queen Victoria*, S. 288; vgl. auch Weintraub, *Queen Victoria*, S. 314).

[7] St. Aubyn, *Queen Victoria*, S. 353.

[8] Vgl. Weintraub, *Queen Victoria*, S. 362.

bringen, um Albert weiter existieren zu lassen.[1] Hatte während seines Lebens sie in der Öffentlichkeit gestanden, aber Albert viele der Entscheidungen bestimmt[2], so wechselten nun gewissermaßen beide ihre Rollen: Victoria ging ihren Amtsgeschäften nur noch im Verborgenen nach, während der öffentliche Kult um den Prince Consort diesen posthum zur öffentlichen Figur machen sollte.

Dadurch aber hatte die Königin immer weniger Kontakt mit dem Volk und neueren Entwicklungen[3] – und wurde dafür zunehmend kritisiert.[4] Presse und Parlament begannen sie der Pflichtvergessenheit zu bezichtigen, und der Hof fürchtete um das Ansehen der Monarchie.[5] Bereits im März des Jahres 1864 hingen Spott-Plakate am Gitter des Buckingham Palace: "These commanding premises to be let or sold, in consequence of the late occupant's declining business".[6]

Die Kritik erreichte ihren Höhepunkt, als Victorias inniges Verhältnis zu ihrem schottischen Bediensteten John Brown ruchbar wurde, den sie 1865 zu "The Queen's Highland Servant" beförderte.[7] In der Tat pflegten die Queen und ihr persönlicher Diener offenbar einen sehr vertrauten Umgang, und Victoria machte auch nie ein Hehl daraus:[8] "I told him no one loved him more than I did or had a better friend than me"[9], gestand die Königin unverblümt und sah dem *ghillie* (der ihr mindestens einmal das Leben rettete[10]) auch dessen Whisky-Konsum[11] und ruppige Bemerkungen ("What's this ye've got on today, wumman?"[12]) nach. Entgegen bösartiger Spekulationen[13] – bis hin zu Gerüchten über eine heimliche Hochzeit und

---

[1] Dies war wohl auch einer der Gründe, warum sie nicht im entferntesten daran dachte, den Thron vorzeitig an den Prince of Wales abzugeben.

[2] Vgl. Weintraub, *Queen Victoria*, S. 264.

[3] Vgl. Weintraub, *Queen Victoria*, S. 308-309.

[4] Vgl. St. Aubyn, *Queen Victoria*, S. 344-345.

[5] Vgl. Hibbert, *Queen Victoria*, S. 309-310, 331-337; Weintraub, *Queen Victoria*, S. 326, 328-330.

[6] Zitiert in St. Aubyn, *Queen Victoria*, S. 343-344, Hibbert, *Queen Victoria*, S. 310; mit leicht differierendem Wortlaut in Weintraub, *Queen Victoria*, S. 330.

[7] Vgl. St. Aubyn, *Queen Victoria*, S. 356, Hibbert, *Queen Victoria*, S. 324, Weintraub, *Queen Victoria*, S. 373. Zu dieser Beziehung vgl. auch den Film von John Madden, *Her Majesty Mrs. Brown* (1997), mit Judi Dench als Queen Victoria und Billy Connolly als John Brown.

[8] Vgl. Hibbert, *Queen Victoria*, S. 332.

[9] Zitiert in St. Aubyn, *Queen Victoria*, S. 359; Weintraub, *Queen Victoria*, S. 375.

[10] Vgl. Weintraub, *Queen Victoria*, S. 386.

[11] Vgl. St. Aubyn, *Queen Victoria*, S. 359; Weintraub, *Queen Victoria*, S. 382.

[12] Zitiert in St. Aubyn, *Queen Victoria*, S. 357, Hibbert, *Queen Victoria*, S. 324, Weintraub, *Queen Victoria*, S. 382.

[13] Vgl. Hibbert, *Queen Victoria*, S. 321-322, Weintraub, *Queen Victoria*, S. 385-386.

Schwangerschaft[1] – scheint die Beziehung Victorias zu Brown jedoch alles andere als ein 'Verrat' am 'Prince Consort' gewesen zu sein. Vielmehr hatte diese Freundschaft gerade in Victorias enger Bindung an Albert ihre Basis. Denn Brown war offenbar einer der wenigen Menschen, welche die Königin in ihrer exzessiven Trauer zu verstehen suchten (und ihr gerade dadurch diese Trauer überwinden halfen). In seiner ruppig-direkten, aber aufrichtigen Art bot er ihr jene starke, schützende und führende Hand, nach der sie sich in ihrem viktorianischen Selbstverständnis als Frau seit Alberts Tod so sehr sehnte:[2] "God knows," sagte sie zu ihrer Tochter Vicky, "how I want so much to be taken care of".[3] Ihren okkultistischen Neigungen folgend, spekulierte sie vielleicht sogar über eine mögliche Seelenwanderung Alberts in den Körper Browns oder hielt ihn für ein spiritistisches Medium.[4] (Und sollten die Gerüchte über eine mehr als nur freundschaftliche Zuneigung zu Brown einen Funken Wahrheit enthalten[5], so läge wohl am ehesten darin ihre Basis.) Edwin Landseers berühmtes Gemälde *Sorrow* (1865/6)[6] das die trauernde Witwe zu Pferde und John Brown als Diener zeigt – und deshalb (zusammen mit dem Klatsch des Malers über seine beiden Modelle) Anlass zu öffentlichen Spekulationen bot –[7], macht eigentlich gerade diesen Aspekt deutlich: Die schwarze Kleidung beider, und ihr gemeinsam trauervoll gesenkter Blick, mithin die Erinnerung an Albert, bilden das *tertium comparationis*, das sie miteinander verbindet und zugleich auch von der Umwelt isoliert.

---

[1] Vgl. St. Aubyn, *Queen Victoria*, S. 361, Weintraub, *Queen Victoria*, S. 380, 384.

[2] Vgl. Hibbert, *Queen Victoria*, S. 328.

[3] Zitiert in St. Aubyn, *Queen Victoria*, S. 358; Weintraub, *Queen Victoria*, S. 374. Parallelen zwischen Victorias Beziehungen zu Albert und Brown sind trotz deren Gegensätzlichkeit nicht von der Hand zu weisen: Von beiden bekam sie körperlichen Schutz und loyalen, aufrichtigen Rat; der zweite Band ihrer *Leaves* war Brown gewidmet wie der erste Albert (vgl. St. Aubyn, *Queen Victoria*, S. 361; Weintraub, *Queen Victoria*, S. 394); ihre Beschreibung von Browns Ende gegenüber ihrer Tochter Vicky war "full of ironic echoes of Albert's last days" (Weintraub, *Queen Victoria*, S. 391); und an ihren Enkel, Prince George of Wales, schrieb sie: "I have lost my *dearest best* friend who no one in *this* world can ever replace" (zitiert in St. Aubyn, *Queen Victoria*, S. 362; Weintraub, *Queen Victoria*, S. 390). Wie bei Alberts Tod ließ sie Statuen anfertigen und das Sterbezimmer konservieren (vgl. Weintraub, *Queen Victoria*, S. 392-393). Zu den von ihr bestimmten Beigaben für den eigenen Sarg gehörten Photos von Prince Albert *und* John Brown (vgl. St. Aubyn, *Queen Victoria*, S. 598).

[4] Vgl. St. Aubyn, *Queen Victoria*, S. 361; Hibbert, *Queen Victoria*, S. 322, Anm.; Weintraub, *Queen Victoria*, S. 372.

[5] Vgl. dazu die längere Anmerkung in Hibbert, *Queen Victoria*, S. 322-323.

[6] Abgebildet u.a. in St. Aubyn, *Queen Victoria*, S. 558-559, Abb. 23a; oder im Farbbild-Teil von Hibbert, *Queen Victoria*, S. 318/319.

[7] Vgl. St. Aubyn, *Queen Victoria*, S. 361; Weintraub, *Queen Victoria*, S. 374.

4. Viktorianische Diskurse und die Königin als Witwe

Kultur- und diskursgeschichtlich ist Queen Victorias Witwenschaft in mindestens zweierlei Aspekten interessant, die beide bereits angedeutet wurden. Einerseits verbinden sich in Ihrem Trauerkult die viktorianischen Ideologeme der sentimentalen Affektivität innerhalb der Familie und der öffentlichen Repräsentation des Todes, andererseits werden beide vom *Gender*-Diskurs des 19. Jahrhunderts durchkreuzt. In ihm verbinden sich die zunächst getrennt erscheinenden individual-psychologischen und soziokulturellen Bedeutungsfelder von Affektivität und Repräsentation.

Victorias privater wie der öffentliche Kult der Trauer um Albert entsprachen zunächst ganz dem allgemeineren Umgang mit dem Tod im Viktorianismus. Nicht nur die glorifizierende Repräsentation des Toten durch öffentliche Inszenierung und Erinnerung deckt sich mit kulturellen Rastern der viktorianischen Kultur. Auch jener heute als 'morbid' empfundene, private Totenkult um Albert hat seine Basis in einem der Zeit entsprungenen Ideal: dem der affektiven Bindung innerhalb der Familie über den Tod hinaus. Die darin erkennbare Ambivalenz entsprach einer Spannung zwischen öffentlicher und privater Sphäre, welche die gesamte Kultur der Zeit durchzieht. Insofern repräsentierte und prägte Queen Victoria auch in dieser Hinsicht die nach ihr benannte Epoche.[1]

Die Personalunion von Ehefrau und Monarchin aber musste im 19. Jahrhundert wegen des herrschenden *Gender*-Diskurses zwangsläufig in Aporien führen. So lange Albert am Leben war, wurden diese Widerspruche (in ebenfalls typisch viktorianischer Weise) durch die Komplementarität von privater und öffentlicher Sphäre harmonisiert. Zwar war die *public sphere* bezüglich ihrer Geschlechterspezifik sozusagen 'falsch' besetzt, dafür stilisierten Victoria und Albert quasi zum Ausgleich ihr privates Glück um so pointierter im Sinne viktorianischer Erwartungen an die ideale Familie und deren Geschlechterhierarchie. Mit Alberts Tod aber fiel diese kompensatorische Größe fort (und Brown konnte sie höchstens für Victoria selbst, keinesfalls für die Nation ersetzen). Victoria befand sich nun, als alleinstehende Frau an der Spitze eines Weltreichs, in einer Position, die (ihr) aus der Sicht viktorianischer *Gender*-Ideologie geradezu obszön erscheinen

---

[1] Natürlich kann man einwenden, die Königin könne nicht als 'paradigmatische' Vertreterin ihrer Kultur gelten (vgl. Curl, *Victorian Celebration of Death* (2000), S. 230), aber auch sie steht nicht außerhalb der herrschenden Diskurse. Die Strategien die ihr zur Verfügung stehen, um ihre ganz persönlichen Erfahrungen zu strukturieren, ihnen Bedeutung zu verleihen, sind im wesentlichen jene, welche die Kultur der Zeit ihr zur Verfügung stellt. Nur kann sie sie aufgrund ihrer gesellschaftlichen Macht weit radikaler (mit)gestalten als ihre 'durchschnittlichen' Zeitgenossen.

musste. Sie weigerte sich daher, diese Position – zumindest öffentlich – auszufüllen. Legitimiert hat sie das unter Rückgriff auf das kulturell sanktionierte Recht der Ehefrau zur Kultivierung ihrer Trauer. Und sie versuchte ihre Weigerung zu kompensieren durch die Installierung eines öffentlichen Kultes um den verstorbenen 'Prince Consort'.[1]

Diese ohnehin prekäre Balance zwischen privater und öffentlicher Trauer und die damit verbundene Delegation der politischen Repräsentationspflicht an einen Toten war freilich nicht sehr lange aufrechtzuerhalten, denn die sentimentale Bindung an den Toten und dessen öffentliche Repräsentation gerieten zunehmend in Widerspruch zu einem weiteren Prinzip der viktorianischen Gesellschaft: dem Utilitarismus und einer letztlich säkularisiert-puritanischen Arbeitsethik. Gerade unter dem Eindruck der politischen und ökonomischen Krisen im England der zweiten Jahrhunderthälfte musste der idealistisch-nostalgische Totenkult zunehmend als gefährlicher Eskapismus erscheinen, wenn er von der Herrscherin betrieben wurde.[2]

Die sich daran zunehmend entzündende Kritik mag darüber hinaus aber auch ein erstes Indiz sein für die allgemein abnehmende kulturelle Wirkkraft des viktorianischen Totenkultes zur Jahrhundertwende.[3] Als Victoria am 22. Januar 1901 nach 40 Jahren Witwenschaft verstarb, wusste man kaum noch, wie eine offizielle Totenwache auszusehen hatte, und Reginald Brett, später 2nd Viscount of Esher, beklagte die diesbezügliche "historical ignorance, of everyone from top to bottom".[4] Für die Begräbniszeremonie hatte glücklicherweise die Queen selbst noch detaillierteste Anweisungen

---

[1] An dieser Stelle eine Warnung vor Missverständnissen: Die Rede von Diskursen, Strategien, Rollen und Funktionen im Rahmen dieses Aufsatzes impliziert selbstredend nicht, dass Queen Victoria lediglich ein Produkt allmächtiger kultureller Strukturen war; viel weniger noch, dass der Verlust Alberts sie nicht zutiefst erschüttert hätte. Sicherlich entsprangen ihre exzessive Trauer und ihr Wunsch nach Alberts öffentlicher Verehrung ihrer zweifellos tief empfundenen Liebe zu ihm. Die Art, jedoch, wie diese Trauer ausgedrückt, verarbeitet, wohl auch wie sie erlebt wurde, ist bestimmt vom diskursiven Repertoire ihrer Kultur, die sie umgekehrt durch ihr Verhalten mitgestalten half und als deren Repräsentantin sie nicht umsonst gilt. Die Witwe Queen Victoria wird damit in ihrer Zeit zum Schnittpunkt kultureller und psychologischer Faktoren, deren erstere immer individuell manifest werden und deren letztere stets bereits kulturell überformte sind.

[2] Die oben erwähnte, anwachsende Kritik von Regierung, Volk und Presse richtete sich nicht so sehr gegen Victoria, die Ehefrau, als gegen 'Queen Victoria', die Königin, die sich (scheinbar) ihrer Pflicht verweigerte.

[3] Vgl. etwa Curl, *Victorian Celebration of Death* (2000), S. 208-209; Litten, *English Way of Death*, S. 171.

[4] Zitiert in Weintraub, *Queen Victoria*, S. 636.

hinterlassen.[1] Dem Charakter einer Wiedervermählung mit dem Gatten entsprechend, hatte sie sich ein Begräbnis ganz in Weiß gewünscht[2], und dieser Wunsch wurde erfüllt: Über dem Gesicht der Königin lag ihr weißer
Hochzeitsschleier[3], acht weiße Pferde zogen den Leichenwagen[4] – und auf
den Straßen lag frischer Schnee.[5]

---

[1] Vgl. St. Aubyn, *Queen Victoria*, S. 597-598.
[2] Ibid., S. 598-599.
[3] Ibid., S. 598; Weintraub, *Queen Victoria*, S. 638.
[4] Vgl. St. Aubyn, *Queen Victoria*, S. 599.
[5] Ibid., S. 600.

SCIENCE, SOCIETY AND VICTORIAN CULTURE

Christianity, Science and the Victorians: An Introduction

By *Barbara Korte* (Freiburg)

> *Mankind have outgrown old institutions and old doctrines.*
> (John Stuart Mill, "The Spirit of the Age", 1831)

The renowned Victorianist Asa Briggs has pointed out how deeply Victorian society was – or at least appeared to be – still rooted in Christianity:

> The mid-Victorians still called God into the reckoning whenever they needed Him. It was not only the family which was a 'sacred institution'. Thousands of sermons of every denomination proclaimed that the whole English social system rested not only on divine sanction but on the particular operations of Providence. Sunday school scholars were told to thank God for the 'goodness and the grace' bestowed upon them when He made them 'happy English children'.[1]

The Bible continued to function as a master text of British culture, dispersed not only in church but also studied in school and in the secular 'sanctum' of Victorian society, the private home:

> An appreciation of the extent of lay people's Bible literacy is key to understanding Victorian culture. The Bible was preached from pulpits, read daily by heads of households to family members and servants and by Bible readers in the homes of the poor, dispensed through domestic and foreign mission societies, studied in Church-sponsored and non-conforming study groups, as well as by clerical biblical scholars. Victorian printing technologies enabled the realization of evangelical dreams of mass Bible distribution: for example, John Cassell's *Illustrated Family Bible* (1836-8) sold 300,000 copies a week in one-penny numbers.[2]

Martin F. Tupper was a versifier, highly popular (but also ridiculed) at the time for his rhymed, rather commonplace opinions published as *Proverbial Philosophy*. The fourth series of this collection (1869) included a long praise "Of the Bible", culminating in the following closing lines (which are as characteristic of the ideological gist as of the metrical shortcomings of Tupper's output):

---

[1] Asa Briggs, *Victorian People: A Reassessment of Persons and Themes 1851-67* [first published 1954] (Harmondsworth, 1990), p. 20.

[2] Christine L. Krueger, "Clerical", in: *A Companion to Victorian Literature and Culture*, ed. Herbert F. Tucker (Oxford, 1999), pp. 141-154, p. 142.

It is the voice of God to man, encouraging and warning,
It is the speech of man to God, in sampled prayer and praise;
It is the golden thread of life, and strung with precious pearls,
Hung on each Christian infant's neck, its best baptismal birthright,
The amulet and anodyne and jewel of our race,
To soothe us in this vale of tears, and cheer our path to heaven.[1]

Contemporary paintings visualised scenes of Christian life inside and outside church buildings. One of the most popular and frequently reproduced
paintings of Victorian times is William Holman Hunt's *The Light of the
World* (1853; City Art Galleries, Manchester).[2] It depicts an allegorical
scene of Christ knocking at the door to the soul. When first shown, the
painting was misunderstood,

> but Ruskin wrote a letter to *The Times* explaining its symbolism, and it eventually
> became one of the best-known religious pictures of all time, its fame spread by a
> national tour, by countless reproductions, and by the large replica painted with the
> help of an assistant (1900-04), which toured the colonies and was then presented
> to St Paul's Cathedral.[3]

A less famous but culturally as significant painting by Thomas Jones
Barker (c. 1863; National Portrait Gallery, London) shows *'The Secret of
England's Greatness'*, also known as *Queen Victoria Presenting a Bible in
the Audience Chamber at Windsor*. The Bible is presented to one of the
Queen's colonial subjects.[4] Christianity was one of the C's – along with
Commerce and Civilisation – on which, according to David Livingstone,
the project of imperialism rested[5], and Barker's painting signals unmistak-

---

[1] Quoted from *The Victorians: An Anthology of Poetry and Poetics*, ed. Valentine
Cunningham (Oxford, 2000), pp. 302-306, pp. 305f.

[2] Like most other paintings referred to in this essay, it is reproduced in Timothy Hilton, *The Pre-Raphaelites* (London, 1970), n.p.

[3] Julian Treuherz, *Victorian Painting* (London, 1993), pp. 95f.

[4] The National Portrait Gallery's website (www.npg.org.uk), where the painting can
also be seen, gives the following description: "This group epitomises the Victorian concept of the British Empire, which was seen as conferring the benefits of European civilisation, and Christianity in particular, on the peoples over whom it ruled. Prince Albert
stands to the left of Queen Victoria, while on the right in the background are the statesmen Lord Palmerston and Lord John Russell. In the foreground Victoria presents a
Bible to a man wearing African dress. [...] It was engraved under the title *The Bible:
The Secret of England's Greatness* in 1864, suggesting that it was conceived, in part at
least, as an allegory of Empire."

[5] See Eckhard Breitinger, "Travels into the Interior of Africa: The 'Discovery' of a
Continent", *Komparatistische Hefte*, 3 (1981), 11-27, p. 20: "Livingstone's comprehen-

ably that the Bible in Victorian England was a cornerstone of society and culture not only at home, but also in the colonies abroad.

At the same time, however, extensive evidence points to a Victorian crisis of faith, or at least a deep uncertainty about established Christian belief and its institutions.[1] During Victoria's entire reign, therefore, religion was a matter of public debate that occupied not only the leaders of religious organisations, but also the politicians and intellectuals. This debate is one of the cultural areas which make us aware of the cracks in the façade of an apparently self-confident society and highlight the fact that 'Victorian culture' was a composite of many, in part contradictory, discursive formations. The discourse about religion was closely interwoven with other preoccupations of Queen Victoria's Britain: the restructured social situation of the world's leading industrial nation, especially the problems posed by the urban working classes; a political climate of liberalism and reform; a secular materialism evident in a blooming commodity culture enjoyed by the more affluent social ranks; and developments in the sciences, above all some branches of the natural sciences, notably geology and the theory of evolution, which challenged traditional faith with new theories and hard empirical evidence.[2] Applied science, i.e. technology, was the basis for Victorian prosperity and an unprecedented growth of its cities, whose appearance was changed by engineering projects both above and below ground. Techno-

---

sive conception of the missionising task is at once more realistic and more honest than that of the purely religious missionaries. Livingstone admits that the three C's, 'Christianity, Commerce and Civilisation', are irrevocably bound up with each other, and for this reason Livingstone does not even try to degree an order of importance of these three basics." Breitinger specifically refers to passages in Livingstone's *Missionary Travels and Researches in South Africa* (London, 1857).

[1] For short introductory and more detailed surveys of Victorian religious life see W.O. Chadwick, *The Victorian Church* (London, Part I 1966, Part II 1970); J.W. Burrow, "Faith, Doubt and Unbelief", in: *The Context of English Literature: The Victorians*, ed. Laurence Lerner (London, 1978), pp. 153-173; Bernard M.G. Reardon, *Religious Thought in the Victorian Age: A Survey from Coleridge to Gore* (London, 1980); Elizabeth Jay, *Faith and Doubt in Victorian Britain* (London, 1986); *Religion in Victorian Britain*, ed. Gerald Parsons, 4 vols. (Manchester, 1988); Hugh McLeod, *Religion and Irreligion in Victorian England: How Secular Was the Working Class* (Bangor, 1993); *A History of Religion in Britain: Practice and Belief from Pre-Roman Times to the Present*, ed. Sheridan Gilley and W.J. Sheils (Oxford, 1994), Part III: "Industrialization, Empire and Identity", pp. 275-422.

[2] For a collection of influential texts in this debate see *Science and Religion in the Nineteenth Century*, ed. Tess Cosslett (Cambridge, 1984); for a general discussion of the relationship between religion and the natural sciences, see Alister McGrath, *Science and Religion: An Introduction* (Oxford, 1999).

logical progress enabled the Victorians to expand and control an Empire on which the sun never set, and it was generally the basis for an accelerating process of modernisation which affected not only Britain's status in the world but also the everyday life and perceptions of the individual Victorian subject.[1] Science and technology played an increasing role in the educational system and were popularised for a wider readership.[2] With scientific precision, the Victorians investigated not only their colonial others, but also their own society, where the urban poor in particular became the subject of ethnographic scrutiny and meticulous statistics.[3] To an extent far exceeding that of former periods, even the age of Newton, science became an epistemological model, a way of interpreting the world that competed seriously with established explications offered by religion. The Victorians continued to build churches and chapels – but they also erected new secular cathedrals in the new materials of the technological age: the huge glass-and-steel conservatory of the Crystal Palace covered four times the ground area of St Peter's in Rome; it housed the Great Exhibition of 1851, Prince Albert's tribute to the nation's progress and wealth. The equally vast railway terminals, with their arched roofs, were also more than functional: they signified and celebrated the achievements of the transport revolution. And temples were also dedicated to science: the Oxford University Museum, which houses the university's extensive natural history collection, was erected as a centre for the sciences between 1855 and 1860; the London Museum of Natural History moved into its South Kensington building in 1881; and a science and technology collection formed part of what is now known as the Victoria and Albert Museum (founded in 1852); it became independent as the Science Museum in 1909.

Despite such impressive displays, however, the process of modernisation, in which science played so significant a role, also caused anxieties and a heightened awareness of tensions between the ancient and the new in which religion was particularly implicated. While it could be an anchor in a changing world to some, it was at the same time undermined by the very forces to which it seemed an antidote. Scientific thinking, especially find-

---

[1] See, for instance, Wolfgang Schivelbusch's illustrative study of the impact of the railways: *The Railroad Journey: The Industrialization of Time and Space in the 19th Century* (Leamington Spa, 1986) [first published in German under the title *Geschichte der Eisenbahnreise* (Munich and Vienna, 1977)].

[2] See, for example, Bernard Lightman, "Marketing Knowledge for the General Reader: Victorian Popularizers of Science", *Endeavour*, 24 (2000), 100-106.

[3] See, above all, the famous surveys by Henry Mayhew, *London Labour and the London Poor* (1851; reprinted New York, 1968), and Charles Booth, *Life and Labour of the People in London* (1889; reprinted New York, 1969).

ings related to natural history, was essential in undermining Christian orthodoxies and an important motivation for the growing number of agnostics and atheists, even during the early decades of the Queen's reign.

These doubters and unbelievers included George Eliot, Matthew Arnold, Arthur Hugh Clough, Algernon Charles Swinburne and Thomas Hardy, to name only a few representatives from the literary scene. Even men and women of letters who did not wish to abandon Christianity entirely, found themselves in a state of uncertainty which has been recorded in some of the best-known literary documents of the time. Alfred Lord Tennyson's long autobiographical poem *In Memoriam* (written 1833-50 and first published 1850) traces an anguishing spiritual dilemma that could eventually be reconciled with, "That God, which ever lives and loves".[1] Matthew Arnold's poem "Dover Beach" (written c. 1851), however, offers no metaphysical alternative to the "melancholy, long withdrawing roar" of a retreating "sea of faith".[2] Arnold was also an important figure in the contemporary debate on education and suggested in "The Study of Poetry" (1880) that poetry would have to take the place of religion in the interpretation and moral foundation of a culture in which "[t]here is not a creed which is not shaken, not an accredited dogma which is not shown to be questionable, not a received tradition which does not threaten to dissolve."[3] One can also follow the religious debates of the Victorians by reading their novels: James Anthony Froude's *The Nemesis of Faith* (1849); Anthony Trollope's 'Barsetshire novels' (1855-67), which chronicle clerical politics within the Church of England; George Eliot's critical *Scenes of Clerical Life* (1858), and her more favourable portrait of a Methodist in *Adam Bede* (1859); Elizabeth Gaskell's *North and South* (1855), where a parson's religious doubts force him to resign his living in the rural South and move with his family up to the industrial North; William Hale White's story of a 'dissenting minister' in *The Autobiography of Mark Rutherford* (1881); Mary Augusta [Mrs Humphry] Ward's best-selling *Robert Elsmere* (1888), set in the varied religious scene of Oxford; or Samuel Butler's *The Way of All Flesh* (completed in the 1880s but not published until 1901), which portrays a man's painful emancipation from the influence of a tyrannical clergyman father.

---

[1] Quoted from the first published version reprinted in *The Victorians*, ed. Cunningham, pp. 219-252, p. 252, l. 2865.

[2] Quoted from *The Victorians*, ed. Cunningham, pp. 532f.

[3] Matthew Arnold, "Introduction" ["The Study of Poetry"] to *The English Poets: Selections with Critical Introductions*, ed. Thomas Humphry Ward (London, 1880), vol. I, pp. xvii-xlvii, pp. xviif.

The religious discussion, which literary and other documents trace so poignantly, is deeply intertwined with new scientific thinking – but it would be far too simple to hold geology and evolutionary biology alone responsible for the retreat of the sea of faith. Charles Darwin himself had begun to develop doubts about Christianity during the 1830s, long before his famous theories were fully formulated. As he records in his *Autobiography* (c. 1880):

> Thus disbelief crept over me at a very low rate, but was at last complete. The rate was so slow that I felt no distress, and have never since doubted even for a single second that my conclusion was correct. I can indeed hardly see how anyone ought to wish Christianity to be true; for if so, the plain language of the text seems to show that the men who do not believe, and this would include my Father, Brother and almost all my best friends, will be everlastingly punished.
>
> And this is a damnable doctrine.[1]

Darwin's disbelief was fostered in the early decades of Victoria's reign when it emerged that institutionalised religion rested on increasingly debated ground. The Church of England, nominally headed by the British monarch herself, was perceived to bear "everywhere upon it the signs of human imperfection", as Lytton Strachey phrased it in his ironically entitled *Eminent Victorians*.[2] Entering the Church was one of the four professional areas proper to be chosen by English gentlemen (along with the military, law and medicine), but it was frequently not chosen by inclination and therefore executed with little zeal. As Richard Altick summarises in *Victorian People and Ideas*:

> Anglicanism was a gentleman's religion, administered by clergy of worldly tastes and ambitions largely unaffected by the spirit of Christianity. The bishops, nearly all of whom were connected with the aristocracy by blood, marriage, or patronage – several had tutored their noble patrons in their youth – functioned mainly as a powerful bloc in the House of Lords.[3]

The attempts at reforming this church, however, resulted in complicating a religious scene that had been complicated in the first place. Distinguishing Anglicanism from Roman Catholicism, and the strength or 'purity' of Protestant conviction within Anglicanism, had been prime issues in the English religious discourse since the days of Henry VIII. Protestant Non-Conform-

---

[1] Quoted from the excerpt in *Culture and Society in Britain 1850-1890: A Source Book of Contemporary Writings*, ed. J.M. Golby (Oxford, 1986), pp. 58-60, p. 59.

[2] Lytton Strachey, *Eminent Victorians* [first published 1918] (London, 1932), p. 14.

[3] Richard D. Altick, *Victorian People and Ideas* (London, 1974), p. 204.

ists or Dissenters resented the orthodoxy of the Church of England; they included Puritan groups such as the Presbyterians and Congregationalists, but also Quakers, Baptists, Unitarians and, since the late 18th century, Methodists. When Victoria ascended the throne, more liberal attitudes towards Non-Anglicans had already been instituted: the repeal of the Test Act (1828) and Catholic Emancipation (1829) removed the most serious discrimination against Non-Anglicans who were now eligible for Parliament and could obtain university degrees. But the Church of England itself had long encompassed two extremes: the High Church party which emphasised the authority of bishops and maintained traditional 'Catholic' ritual, and Low Church Anglicanism, which was more closely related to the purer Protestantism of the Nonconformists. This division was complicated by three major attempts to reform the Church during the 1830s and 40s: the Evangelical Movement within the Church (which was inspired by the earlier dissenting Evangelicalism), the Broad Church Movement and the Oxford Movement.

Church Evangelicalism maintained that grace was available to those who directed their life strictly according to the Bible and established a strong personal relationship with God[1], who himself called the believer to a life of Bible reading, prayer and seriously pious habits. As John Burrow notes, the Evangelical mission to re-Christianise the country had "enduring effects" on Victorian social and intellectual life, apparent, for instance, "in a prudish literature and a sober clergy; above all in an intense, even strained, religious scrupulousness and self-awareness".[2]

The Broad Church section, by contrast, interpreted the creeds in a liberal, 'latitudinarian' manner; it also intended to make the Church a mediator between capital and labour, a programme later known as Christian Socialism. An influential figure in the movement, who carried its ideas into public-school education, was Dr Thomas Arnold, the revered headmaster of Rugby school[3] and father of Matthew Arnold. Other important members were the Rev. F.D. Maurice and the Rev. Charles Kingsley, the novelist, whose *Alton Locke* (1850) portrays the conversion of its protagonist, a tailor and working-class poet, from the political activism of Chartism to Christian Socialism.

---

[1] For an expression of this relationship see, for instance, a highly popular evangelist hymn by Charlotte Elliott, "Just as I am" (1836); reprinted in: *The Victorians*, ed. Cunningham, p. 24.

[2] Burrow, "Faith, Doubt and Unbelief", p. 158.

[3] He is portrayed with great respect, for instance, in Thomas Hughes's novel about the education of a young Christian gentleman, *Tom Brown's Schooldays* (1857).

The Oxford Movement or Tractarianism was particularly controversial since it seemed to bring the Church of England closer again to pre-Reformation Catholicism and thus nourished old fears of a Roman revival. A reemphasis on ritual and doctrinal authority was a keynote of its programme for reinvigorating the Church in an age of doubt. In the arts, the Oxford Movement inspired, among others, the deeply pious poet Christina Rossetti[1], as well as the painters of the Pre-Raphaelite school. They devoted several of their religious paintings to the Madonna, the cult around which was a matter of debate within Anglicanism; an example is Dante Gabriel Rossetti's "The Girlhood of Mary Virgin" (1848-49; Tate Britain). A painting by John Everett Millais, *Christ in the House of His Parents* (1849; Tate Britain), enjoyed a notorious popularity; its representation of the young Jesus in his worldly father's carpenter's shop was widely abused for its seeming profanity, but also its hint of Roman Catholicism:

> It was 'revolting', it was a 'nameless atrocity', and Charles Dickens wrote a particularly vitriolic attack in which suspicion of Roman Catholicism, aroused by the Tractarian symbolism of the sacrifice of Christ's blood, was mixed with shock at the realistic rather than divine character given by the artist to his Holy Family, with their wrinkled garments, dirty finger nails and unidealized, portrait-like faces, painted from friends and neighbours.[2]

The Oxford Movement is alternatively known as Tractarianism because its chief thinkers, John Henry Newman, Richard Hurrell Froude, John Keble and Edward Pusey, published their ideas in a series of *Tracts for the Times*, beginning in 1833 and for a course of eight years. Suspicion of Roman Catholicism is owed in particular to Tract XC, which discusses the compatibility of the Thirty-Nine Articles (i.e. the doctrine to which Anglican clergy has to assent and the central statement of belief in Anglicanism) with Roman Catholic theology. This tract roused great opposition; it even brought the Tractarians under official ban. The controversy around Anglo-Catholicism intensified when Newman actually converted to Roman Catholicism in 1845. He explained his motives for initiating the Oxford Movement, and later for his conversion, in his *Apologia pro Vita Sua* (1864).[3] Conversions of Anglicans to Roman Catholicism – another prominent case was Henry Manning, who like Newman was later to become a Roman cardinal – were usually met with much hostility:

---

[1] For a selection of her poetry, see *The Victorians*, ed. Cunningham, pp. 662-674.

[2] Treuherz, *Victorian Painting*, p. 80.

[3] Newman's novel, *Loss and Gain* (1848), also uses the material of his conversion.

The new converts to Rome were popularly called 'perverts' rather than converts, and anti-Catholic feeling ran high in the 1850s. Gladstone, himself a High Churchman, whose sister Helen was one such convert, referred to the newspaper report of the event as 'the record of our shame' and urged his father to expel Helen from the family home.[1]

Fears of a Roman revival were further nourished by an act of reorganising Roman Catholicism in England after a heavy influx of immigrants from Ireland. In 1850, Pope Pius IX reestablished dioceses in England and named Nicholas Wiseman Archbishop of Westminster. Alarm among British Protestants was so strong that the (Liberal) Prime Minister, Lord John Russell, felt obliged to calm spirits in a letter addressed to the Anglican Bishop of Durham and published in *The Times*:

> My dear Lord,
>
> I agree with you in considering 'the late aggression of the Pope upon our Protestantism' as 'insolent and insidious', and I therefore feel as indignant as you can do upon the subject. [...]
>
> I confess, however, that my alarm is not equal to my indignation.
>
> Even if it shall appear that the ministers and servants of the Pope in this country have not transgressed the law, I feel persuaded that we are strong enough to repel any outward attacks. The liberty of Protestantism has been enjoyed too long in England to allow of any successful attempt to impose a foreign yoke upon our minds and consciences.[2]

As a result of the various reforms and their consequences, mid-Victorians were confronted with an organisation of religious life that offered a wide spectrum of alternatives to the practising Christian. Nevertheless, organised Christianity lost its attraction for wide parts of the population. The Census of 1851 – the very year in which the Great Exhibition celebrated the secular nation – made it painfully clear to clergymen and politicians that not only intellectuals were abandoning Christianity. On Sunday, March 30, 1851 attendants in Anglican churches and nonconformist chapels in England and Wales were counted. The overall result was that only about a third of the English population went to Sunday service. Most alarming for those in power, however, was that the highest rate of non-attenders was found

---

[1] Burrow, "Faith, Doubt and Unbelief", p. 154. See also Gladstone's reaction to Manning's conversion, as reported in Asa Briggs's *Victorian People*, p. 33: "Gladstone himself told a friend much later in his life that, when the news of Manning's conversion reached him, it seemed like an act of personal injury. 'I felt,' Gladstone said, 'as if Manning had murdered my mother by mistake.'"

[2] Reprinted in *Culture and Society in Britain 1850-1890*, ed. Golby, pp. 38-39, p. 38.

among the working classes. Horace Mann noted in his official "Report on the Religious Census" (1851):

> [W]hile the *labouring* myriads of our country have been multiplying with our multiplied material prosperity, it cannot, it is feared, be stated that a corresponding increase has occurred in the attendance of this class in our religious edifices. [...] it is sadly certain that this vast, intelligent, and growingly important section of our countrymen is thoroughly estranged from our religious institutions in their present aspect.[1]

The spectre of social unrest among the proletarian masses had haunted the upper and middle classes for some decades (during the 'hungry forties' in particular), and it was not eclipsed by the dawning of more prosperous times. What was to become of the nation if these masses could no longer be held in check by a system of Christian values shared with those in the higher ranks of society? In *The British Churches in Relation to the British People* (1849), Edward Miall, a most outspoken critic of the established Church, depicted a dark scenario:

> Out of this slimy bed of physical destitution rises perpetually a pestiferous moral exhalation dangerous to all other classes of society ... Swarms of thieves [...] and of prostitutes [...] carry with them the taint of demoralization into all other sections of the social body.[2]

Retrieving the working classes into the web of institutionalised Christianity, thus to re-expose them to a shared system of values, became a major social concern. However, of all denominations, the Church of England, despite its efforts at reform, was still found to be the least attractive for the urban and rural poor. Horace Mann noted in his official report on the Census:

> Working men, it is contended, cannot enter our religious structures without having pressed upon their notice some memento of inferiority. The existence of pews and the position of the free seats are, it is said, alone sufficient to deter them from our churches: and religion has thus come to be regarded as a purely middle-class propriety or luxury.[3]

---

[1] Quoted from the excerpt in *Culture and Society in Britain 1850-1890*, ed. Golby, pp. 39-45, p. 40.

[2] Ibid., pp. 33-38, p. 35.

[3] Ibid., p. 41.

A remedy which Mann and others suggested was a missionising campaign directed at the proletariat:

> The people who refuse to hear the gospel in the church must have it brought to them in their own haunts. [...] The myriads of our labouring population, really as ignorant of Christianity as were the heathen Saxons at Augustine's landing, are as much in need of missionary enterprise to bring them into practical acquaintance with its doctrines ...[1]

Towards the end of the 19th century, this idea that the labouring classes at home had to be missionised just like the 'heathens' in the colonies, found a prominent expression in the foundation of the Salvation Army. Indeed, General William Booth, in his book *In Darkest England and the Way Out* (1890) – whose title is a deliberate allusion to the many contemporary publications about the 'dark continent' and in particular Henry Morton Stanley's *In Darkest Africa*, which had appeared in the same year – proposed that colonies might be a remedy to the social dilemma: The City Colony, The Farm Colony, and The Over-Seas Colony might help people to "commence at once a course of regeneration by moral and religious influences".[2]

It was thus a highly complex discursive formation within theology and the system of denominations with which new discourses in the sciences[3]

---

[1] Ibid., p. 44.

[2] Ibid., pp. 304-306, p. 305.

[3] Of course, impact of the sciences on Victorian culture went far beyond the matter of faith and doubt. For the wider picture, see, among many others, the following studies and more basic introductions: David Knight, *The Age of Science: The Scientific World-View of the Nineteenth Century* (Oxford, 1986); *Energy and Entropy: Science and Culture in Victorian Britain*, ed. Patrick Brantlinger (Bloomington, 1989); Peter Allan Dale, *In Pursuit of a Scientific Culture: Science, Art, and Society in the Victorian Age* (Madison, 1989); Roy M. MacLeod, *The 'Creed of Science' in Victorian England* (Aldershot, 2000); David Newton, *Science, Technology and Society of the Nineteenth Century* (Detroit, 2001). See also the following titles which make specific reference to literature: Douglas Bush, *Science and English Poetry: A Historical Sketch, 1590-1950* (New York and Oxford, 1950); Arthur Lionel Stevenson, *Darwin among the Poets* (Chicago, 1932); *Victorian Science and Victorian Values: Literary Perspectives*, ed. James Paradis and Thomas Postlewait (New York, 1981); Tess Cosslett, *The 'Scientific Movement' and Victorian Literature* (Brighton, 1982); Gillian Beer, *Darwin's Plots: Evolutionary Narrative in Darwin, George Eliot and Nineteenth-Century Fiction* (London, 1983); John Alfred Victor Chapple, *Science and Literature in the Nineteenth Century* (London, 1986); George Levine, *Darwin and the Novelists: Patterns of Science in Victorian Fiction* (Cambridge, MA and London, 1988); Hermann Josef Schnackertz,

coalesced to further increase the dilemma of faith. One of the first branches of the sciences to shake the foundations of Christian belief was geology, in particular the study of earth history. Of the eminent Victorians, the art critic John Ruskin was a most enthusiastic student of geology, and a great admirer of the Alps. In 1853, he had his portrait painted by John Everett Millais, with a meticulously painted background of rocks and waterfalls as a manifesto to his interest in geology and nature (Sir John Everett Millais, "John Ruskin", private collection). Under Ruskin's influence, which was particularly strong among the Pre-Raphaelites, striking geological detail marks many topographical paintings of the period, such as John Brett's "The Glacier of Rosenlaui" (1856; Tate Britain). William Dyce's "Pegwell Bay, Kent, a Recollection of October 5th, 1858" (1859-60; Tate Britain) has often been noted for its reflection of the contemporary concern with earth history. In the beach scene which this painting depicts, the human figures are virtually dwarfed by cliffs in the background. Such chalk cliffs contain fossils, objects of scientific interest that excited the Victorians just as much as did geology. In his postmodern pastiche of the Victorian novel, *The French Lieutenant's Woman* (1969), John Fowles makes his male protagonist a fossil hunter, as Thomas Hardy had done in *A Pair of Blue Eyes* (1873).

Geology demonstrated that the earth was much older than people had generally assumed until then – especially if they were still willing to believe in a Biblical age of creation calculated at about 6,000 years. Palaeontology revealed that life, too, was ages older than that and, even more disconcertingly, that there were traces of life on earth that had long become extinct. Deborah Cadbury's *The Dinosaur Hunters* (2000)[1] gives a fascinating account of the careers of the scholars who first devoted their attention to giant reptile fossils found in England. The most prominent representative of this new branch of science, Robert Owen, still found it inconceivable to believe that God had not planned every single step in the development of life on earth. But a number of questions now had to be asked and answered. Both geology and palaeontology, then, provided visible evidence that the Biblical account of creation could not be read literally; that the earth was clearly not created in a week, and that God seemed to have created species only to have them vanish again from the surface of the earth. So did God play with his creatures? Or was his creation less perfect than people had

---

Darwinismus und literarischer Diskurs: Der Dialog mit der Evolutionsbiologie in der englischen und amerikanischen Literatur (München, 1992).

[1] Deborah Cadbury, *The Dinosaur Hunters: A Story of Scientific Rivalry and the Discovery of the Prehistoric World* (London, 2000).

believed for times immemorial? "[A]nxious Victorians began to wonder what further unexpected, even loathsome, revelations of divine neglect geology would next bring forth."[1] John Ruskin, commenting on his increasingly weakening faith in 1851, must have spoken for many of his contemporaries when he wrote: "If only the Geologists would let me alone, I could do very well, but those dreadful Hammers! I hear the clink of them at the end of every cadence of the Bible verses ...".[2]

The disconcerting effects of geology and palaeontology were even surpassed by the claims of the theory of evolution, i.e. the notion that species are not specially and distinctly created but evolve from earlier, more primitive life forms. Such ideas had been developed decades before Darwin (for instance in the work of his grandfather, Erasmus Darwin), but it was the Victorian publications which received wide attention and launched a heated debate. British landmark publications before Darwin were Charles Lyell's *Principles of Geology* (1830-33) and Robert Chambers' *Vestiges of the Natural History of Creation* (1844). Lyell's book was one of the factors responsible for Tennyson's crisis of faith; its influence is most obvious in stanzas 54 and 55 of *In Memoriam*, where an inherently cruel natural force and God are presented as dissociated, "at strife" (l. 1045), and where human life appears frail and futile when confronted with Nature who is "red in tooth and claw" (l. 1075) and as "careless of the single life" (l. 1048) as of entire species: "She cries, 'A thousand types are gone: / I care for nothing, all shall go.'" (ll. 1063-64) Man's trusting belief that "God was love in deed / And love Creation's final law" (ll. 1073-74) is invalidated by the findings about natural history.[3]

Darwin's *The Origin of Species* appeared in 1859; it was followed in 1871 by *The Descent of Man*, which elaborated ideas from the earlier work. It was Darwin's evidence of man's descent from more primitive forms of life ("Man still bears in his bodily frame the indelible stamp of his lowly origin"[4]), which caused scientists, men of the Church, and the wider public to take sides in a vehement debate. Darwin's suggestion that man and ape had the same ancestor ("a hairy quadruped, furnished with a tail and pointed ears, probably arboreal in its habits, and an inhabitant of the Old

---

[1] Dennis R. Dean, "'Through Science to Despair': Geology and the Victorians", in: *Victorian Science and Victorian Values*, ed. Paradis and Postlewait, pp. 111-136, 111.

[2] Ruskin in a letter to Henry Auckland, 24 May 1851. Quoted from *The Letters of John Ruskin: Volume I 1827-1869*. Library Edition of The Works of John Ruskin, ed. E.T. Cook and Alexander Wedderburn (London, 1909), p. 115.

[3] Quoted from *The Victorians*, ed. Cunningham, p. 231.

[4] *The Descent of Man*, quoted from the excerpt in *Science and Religion in the Nineteenth Century*, ed. Cosslett, pp. 156-171, p. 171.

World"[1]) – was the key issue in a famous debate between Thomas Henry Huxley, Darwin's most committed defender, and the Anglican Bishop Samuel Wilberforce, at a meeting of the British Association for the Advancement of Science in Oxford in 1860.

Unfortunately, the exchange was not recorded verbatim; Huxley's son Leonard included a selection of accounts of the famous encounter in his *Life and Letters of Thomas Henry Huxley* (1903), including that of the Rev. W.H. Freemantle:

> The Bishop of Oxford attacked Darwin, at first playfully, but at last in grim earnest. [...] 'I should like to ask Professor Huxley [...] as to his belief in being descended from an ape. Is it from his grandfather's or his grandmother's side that the ape ancestry comes in?' And then taking a graver tone, he asserted, in a solemn peroration, that Darwin's views were contrary to the revelation of God in the Scriptures. Professor Huxley was unwilling to respond; but he was called for, and spoke with his usual incisiveness and with some scorn: [...] 'I should feel it no shame to have risen from such an origin; but I should feel it a shame to have sprung from one who prostituted the gifts of culture and eloquence to the service of prejudice and of falsehood.'[2]

That Darwinism was attacked by a representative of a Christian church is understandable. If each species develops gradually, and if man has an ape-like ancestor: how are such ideas compatible with the account of creation in the Book of Genesis, especially the idea that God created man in his own image? And how did man receive his immortal soul, i.e. the quality which, according to Christian belief, distinguishes man from all other creatures? If evolution worked by natural selection, there was also no room any more for the idea of divine guidance or benevolence.

However, not all reactions to the theory of evolution, in Darwinian or pre-Darwinian form, were negative. Charles Kingsley's novel *Alton Locke*, written by a believing Broad Church clergyman, contains an evolutionary dream of its protagonist (chapter 36) in which he advances from the most primitive and unconscious form of life to humanity. The chapter suggests that man has the positive capacity to develop, also in moral terms. On the other hand, the late 19th-century novels of Thomas Hardy suggest a pessimistic view of evolution: man and the world do not make progress, but are degenerating. In *Tess of the d'Urbervilles* (1891), the female protagonist stems from a family's exhausted line, and nature is presented as cruel

---

[1] Ibid., p. 161.

[2] Quoted from the excerpt in *Science and Religion in the Nineteenth Century*, ed. Cosslett, pp. 145-155, p. 153.

and unfeeling. In the earlier *A Pair of Blue Eyes*, a character hangs on the face of a cliff overlooking the English Channel because he has been searching for fossils. As a result of this scientific interest, he is now confronted with the idea of his own death amid the remnants of entire species which died out in much earlier times, and he becomes aware of the insignificance of man in the vast time-scheme of natural history:

> Separated by millions of years in their lives, Knight and this underling [a fossil] seemed to have met in their place of death. [...] The creature represented but a low type of animal existence, for never in their vernal years had the plains indicated by those numberless slaty layers been traversed by an intelligence worthy of the name. Zoophytes, mollusca, shell-fish, were the highest developments of those ancient dates. The immense lapses of time each formation represented had known nothing of the dignity of man. They were grand times, but they were mean times too, and mean were their relics. He was to be with the small in his death. [...] Time closed up like a fan before him.[1]

Hardy's view of man's insignificance in the cosmic plan was also nourished by astronomy which, in the course of the 19th century, extended the knowledge of stellar distances to dizzying expanses. In his novel *Two on a Tower* (1882), the protagonist is an astronomer who despairs of life because the universe is too big for him to comprehend:

> At night, when human discords and harmonies are hushed, in a general sense, for the greater part of twelve hours, there is nothing to moderate the blow with which the infinitely great, the stellar universe, strikes down upon the infinitely little, the mind of the beholder; and this was the case now. Having got closer to immensity than their fellow-creatures, they saw at once its beauty and its frightfulness. They more and more felt the contrast between their own tiny magnitudes and those among which they had recklessly plunged, till they were oppressed with the presence of a vastness they could not cope with even as an idea, and which hung about them like a nightmare.[2]

A law of physics that stirred the Victorian public and increased anxieties about the aims of creation, was the Second Law of Thermodynamics, formulated by William Thomson, later Lord Kelvin, in 1852. According to the first law of thermodynamics, no energy ever gets lost in a closed system. However, the second law was generally understood to mean that even though the energy in a closed system remains the same, the system becomes less and less able to *work* as it becomes more and more disorgan-

---

[1] Thomas Hardy, *A Pair of Blue Eyes* (Oxford, 1985), p. 209.
[2] Thomas Hardy, *Two on a Tower* (London, 1923), p. 70.

ised. The result of this law for life on earth means certain termination in the far future; it will come to a definite and absolute end since the energy system of the sun, too, will one day cease to be productive and to emanate light or heat. In the words of Lord Kelvin:

> Within a finite period of time past the earth must have been, and within a finite period of time to come the earth must again be, unfit for the habitation of man as at present constituted ...[1]

This apocalyptic vision found one of its most impressive literary expressions in chapter 11 of H.G. Wells's *The Time Machine*. His machine gives the time traveller an opportunity to actually witness the final stage of life on a darkening earth:

> A bitter cold assailed me. Rare white flakes ever and again came eddying down. [...] There were fringes of ice along the sea margin, with drifting masses further out; but the main expanse of that salt ocean, all bloody under the eternal sunset, was still unfrozen. [...] The green slime on the rocks alone testified that life was not extinct.[2]

Scientific ideas here inspire a vision of Genesis in reverse, so to speak; the light which God commanded to be at the beginning of the Book of Genesis, will soon go out forever. The purpose of creation, in which Christians had believed for centuries, could not have been questioned – even staged – more effectively.

But it was not only the natural sciences which questioned the literal truth of the stories in the Scriptures. The Bible was now also picked over with the instruments of a newly scientific *textual* criticism. The word of God no longer seemed sacrosanct and authoritative; the master text on which Victorian culture was still officially built, was demythologised, and material evidence for the existence of Biblical sites which archaeologists were bringing to light in Mesopotamia and Egypt was received gratefully by a disconcerted public.[3]

---

[1] William Thomson (later Lord Kelvin), "On a Universal Tendency in Nature to the Dissipation of Mechanical Energy", *Philosophical Magazine*, October 1852, quoted in Chapple, *Science and Literature in the Nineteenth Century*, p. 45.

[2] H.G. Wells, *The Time Machine: An Invention*. A Critical Text of the 1895 London First Edition, ed. Leon Stover (Jefferson, NC and London, 1996), pp. 161f.

[3] See, for example, a book directed at the general public by Joseph Bonomi, *Nineveh and Its Palaces: The Discoveries of Botta and Layard Applied to the Elucidation of Holy Writ*. Illustrated London Library (London, 1852).

The scientific way of reading and interpreting the Bible, the 'Higher Criticism', was developed in Germany in particular. It examined the Bible as a mere text of history and myth rather than a document of 'facts' or even the product of divine inspiration. A particularly influential text, *Das Leben Jesu, kritisch bearbeitet*, was published in 1835-36 by the Tübingen scholar David Friedrich Strauss, and translated into English in 1846 by George Eliot (*The Life of Jesus, Critically Examined*). But it was the publication in 1860 of *Essays and Reviews*, edited by the Rev. H.B. Wilson and written by him and five other Broad Church clergymen as well as one layman, which started a widely-observed discussion in Britain. One of the essays was Benjamin Jowett's "On the Interpretation of Scripture", which defended the new Biblical criticism but also maintained that the true importance of the Bible for the Christian faith would actually be intensified when it was no longer read literally:

> When interpreted like any other book, by the same rules of evidence and the same canons of criticism, the Bible will still remain unlike any other book; its beauty will be freshly seen, as of a picture which is restored after many ages to its original state; it will create a new interest and make for itself a new kind of authority by the life which is in it. It will be a spirit and not a letter; as it was in the beginning, having an influence like that of the spoken word, or the book newly found.[1]

Despite such convictions, however, a meeting of the Anglican bishops in 1861, led by Samuel Wilberforce – the attacker of Darwin – denounced the book for its liberalism and prosecuted two of the contributors for heresy; the *Essays* were synodically condemned in 1864. In a response to *Essays and Reviews* published in the *Quarterly Review* in January 1861, Wilberforce claimed, among other reproaches, that the scientific reading of the Bible would drive believers into the abyss of atheism or the arms of the Pope:

> It is not indeed a 'neo-Christianity', but it is a new religion, which our Essayist would introduce; and they would act more rationally, more philosophically, and, we believe, less injuriously to religion, if they did as their brother unbelievers invite them to do, renounce the hopeless attempt at preserving Christianity without Christ, without the Holy Ghost, without a Bible, and without a Church [...]. In Germany the same attempt has been made; and what has been its issue? The attempt to rationalise Christianity; to remove the supernatural from that which is either a system of supernaturalism or a falsehood [...]. It has issued as its direct result in a wide-spread pantheistic atheism; it has sent souls, wearied out with per-

---

[1] Quoted from J.T. Ward, *The Age of Change: 1770-1870: Documents in Social History* (London, 1975), p. 197.

petual speculations, torn by distracting doubts, and feeling that they must have something certain upon which to rest the burden of their being, into the deep delusions of the Roman system ...[1]

The scientific approach to the Bible, according to one of the Bishops who were part of the Victorian establishment, raised not only two spectres of orthodox Anglicanism – the Scylla of atheism and the Charybdis of Roman Catholicism – but was undermining, in a more fundamental sense, long-assumed certainties: Christ, the Holy Ghost, the Bible, the Church. It is this alleged threat to certainties which may help to explain why the discussion about religion and science and their importance as systems for interpreting the world, became so acute in Victorian culture. An age of unprecedented rapid change, of an accelerated process of modernisation in most areas of life, went hand in hand with an increasing desire for remaining stabilities. Where the apparent certainties of Christianity were challenged, whether by natural history or scientific philology, science became not a blessing, but a threat. The vitality with which Victorian writers and visual artists responded to the issues of religion and science is evidence of the urgency which they had in their culture, and the attention which they accordingly deserve in our attempts to interpret this culture.

---

[1] Quoted from the excerpt in *Culture and Society in Britain 1850-1890*, ed. Golby, pp. 50-54, p. 51.

Nur ein viktorianisches Dilemma?
Flatland zwischen zwei Wissenschaftstraditionen

Von *Jürgen Meyer* (Halle)

1. Zweifel als viktorianische Größe

Der Zweifel (der gedankliche 'Zwie-Fall') und das oft daraus erwachsende Dilemma waren eine verbreitete Erfahrung im 19. Jahrhundert: Zwar wurden die rationalitätsfeindlichen und antibürgerlichen Tendenzen aus der kurzen Epoche der Romantik domestiziert, doch ließen sich die zuvor in eruptiver Expressivität offenbarten Spaltungen zwischen Subjekt/Objekt, Natur/Kultur, Wahrheit/Schönheit, Empirismus/Idealismus usw. nicht zuschütten, sondern gewannen an argumentativer Schärfe und diskursiver Form. Die Risse verliefen dabei nicht nur fein säuberlich entlang den traditionellen Grenzen dieser Entitäten, sondern durchzogen sie selbst – die Einheit des Subjekts wurde ebenso fraglich wie die Ganzheit des Objekts. Daher wurden moralische Kategorien trotz eines äußerlichen Wertkonservativismus zunehmend problematisch.[1] Die noch ungewohnte Erfahrung eines um sich greifenden Glaubensverlustes trotz des raschen Anwachsens materiellen Wohlstands auch in ehedem minderbemittelten Gesellschaftsschichten, ermöglicht durch das gelingende Zusammenwirken von Bildung, Wissenschaft, Technologie und Industrialisierung, und wegen der Verbreitung der sozialen Schattenseiten dieser positiven Entwicklungen, wurde während der langen Regentschaft Queen Victorias als wachsendes Sinndefizit empfunden.

Dieses Defizit ließ die Bedingungen für das menschliche Dasein an sich in physischer wie auch ethischer Hinsicht problematisch werden: Die Ausdifferenzierung der Naturphilosophie des 18. Jahrhunderts in Disziplinen wie Anthropologie, Biologie, Geologie und Paläontologie, Kosmologie und selbst die Philologie mit ihrem Suchen nach zeitlich weit zurückreichenden Ursprachen bzw. Urtexten ließ den Zeitpunkt für den göttlichen Schöp-

---

[1] Daß es sich hier um ein gesamteuropäisches Phänomen handelt, muß nicht ausgeführt werden; gesellschaftlich-weltanschauliche Umbrüche durchzogen ganz West- und Mitteleuropa und fanden namentlich in der zweiten Hälfte des 19. Jahrhundert ihren philosophischen Ausdruck (z.B. Nietzsche, *Also sprach Zarathustra*; Kierkegaard, *Entweder/Oder*) und wurden ob ihrer Radikalität aus mehreren Richtungen stark angefochten.

fungsakt unwahrscheinlich werden. Die Historiographie wurde, wie Michel Foucault und andere es gezeigt haben, zum beherrschenden Diskurs des 19. Jahrhunderts. Hatte im 17. Jahrhundert der Erzbischof Usher mit Hilfe von biblischen Zeitangaben und Genealogien den Beginn der Welt noch auf das Jahr 4004 v.Chr. datiert, so wurde dieses Datum schon aufgrund von Georges Buffons zwischen 1749 und 1804 erschienenen *Allgemeinen und speziellen Naturgeschichte* in Frage gestellt; Forschungsreisende des 19. Jahrhunderts (namentlich Charles Lyell und Charles Darwin) ergänzten die vielfältigen Funde und Beweise aus früheren Dekaden; die schiere Masse und ihre Qualität zwangen die Theologen schließlich, den Schöpfungsakt um Jahrhunderttausende vorzuverlegen (oder gar um "sixty times six sextillions", wie es Edwin A. Abbott, die Hauptfigur der vorliegenden Untersuchung, im programmatisch gegen Walter Paters *Marius*-Roman betitelten *Silanus the Christian* [1906] ausdrückte[1]). Die Vorstellung einer göttlichen Schöpfung stand in Konkurrenz zur natürlichen Evolution; letztere wiederum wurde vor allem im mechanistischen Sinne auf das Konzept des Fortschritts reduziert. Gestattete die Geschichtswissenschaft den Blick zurück in die Vergangenheit, so schien ihre Verbindung mit einer mathematisch-exakten Auswertung von bestehenden Datenkompilationen sogar die Projektion auf die Zukunft zu ermöglichen – was, je nach Wissensdisziplin, zu gleichermaßen optimistischen wie pessimistischen Voraussagen über die Entwicklung des Universums führte (in der Biologie zu evolutionärer Perfektion oder Degeneration, in der Kosmologie zu sublimer Ordnung oder thermodynamischem Chaos).[2]

In diesem Klima intellektueller Zerrissenheit gab es neben den eher spekulativen Überwindungsanstrengungen in Okkultismus und Spiritismus eine nicht unbedeutende Anzahl von um Ausgleich bemühten Persönlichkeiten, die die epistemologisch und weltanschaulich aufgeladenen Schismen zu beseitigen suchten.[3] Frank Miller Turner zählt eine Gruppe von sa-

---

[1] Vgl. Edwin A. Abbott, *Silanus the Christian* (London, 1906), S. 8; zitiert nach Elliot L. Gilbert, "'Upwards, Not Northwards': *Flatland* and the Quest for the New", *English Literature in Transition*, 34:4 (1991), S. 391-404, hier S. 394.

[2] Vgl. Gillian Beer, "'The Death of the Sun': Victorian Solar Physics and Solar Myth", in: Dies., *Open Fields: Science in Cultural Encounter* (Oxford, 1996), S. 219-241.

[3] George Levine, "Scientific Discourse as an Alternative to Faith", in: *Victorian Faith in Crisis: Essays on Continuity and Change in Nineteenth Century Religious Belief*, ed. Richard J. Helmstadter/Bernard Lightman (Houndmills, 1990), S. 225-261, hält dafür, daß die Bemühungen um Ausgleich schon bei den Protagonisten jenes frühen Stadiums im fortwährenden Streit um die später so genannten "zwei Kulturen", Matthew Arnold und T.H. Huxley, ablesbar waren. Sie polemisierten zwar öffentlich gegeneinander, gestanden aber im privaten Kreis den jeweils anderen Wissensbereichen

ges unterschiedlichster Provenienz auf, die sich vom christlichen Glauben und seinen Dogmen abgewandt hatten, aber doch eine geistig-immaterielle Wirklichkeit neben der dinglichen Welt annahmen:

> [Henry] Sidgwick, [Frederic W.H.] Myers and [Alfred Russel] Wallace thought psychical occurences might provide objective empirical evidence of a spiritual realm and of the existence of a mind or personality in dissociation from a physical body. [Georges John] Romanes, [Samuel] Butler, and [James] Ward believed a thorough introspective examination of the human mind provided evidence that mechanistic nature was only an appearance or a mode of an underlying nonmechanical reality.[1]

In verschiedenen renommierten Organisationen wie der *Royal Society* und der *British Association for the Advancement of Science* (*BAAS*) bzw. in halb-institutionellen Zusammenkünften des *X-Club* oder der *Metaphysical Society* trafen sich hochkarätige Intellektuelle, um aktuelle weltanschauliche und erkenntnistheoretische Probleme vorzutragen und zu erörtern.[2] Dabei gab es zwischen diesen Zusammenkünften, Clubs und Gesellschaften auch weitgehende personelle Überschneidungen; herausragende Mitglieder der *Royal Society* wie ihr Präsident, ihr Sekretär und ihr Schatzmeister, John Tyndall, T.H. Huxley und William Spottiswoode, waren beispielsweise im *X-Club* vertreten (unter den Epitheta "the Xcentric", "the Xalted" und "the Xcellent") bzw. in der *Metaphysical Society* aktiv, und sie standen zu verschiedenen Zeiten der *BAAS* vor. Der *X-Club*, dem auch der Sozialdarwinist Herbert Spencer (als "the Xhaustive") angehörte, lud während seiner Blütejahre zwischen 1865 und 1880 renommierte in- und ausländische Wissenschaftler unterschiedlicher Fachrichtungen ein (darunter Charles Darwin und Hermann v. Helmholtz) und wurde wie andere Zirkel zu einem öffentlichkeitswirksamen transdisziplinären Forum.[3] Die dort geführten sachlichen Diskussionen bahnten sich oftmals, begleitet von Zeitungsberichten, ihren Weg in öffentlich ausgetragene *events*, wo sie zur Polarisierung des Publikums führten – es sei der Streit um die Abstam-

---

ein hohes Maß an kultureller und wissenschaftlicher Eigenbedeutung zu (vgl. ibid., S. 248).

[1] Frank Miller Turner, *Between Science and Religion: The Reaction to Scientific Naturalism in Late Victorian England* (New Haven/London, 1974), S. 6.

[2] Vgl. dazu die Studie von Alan Willard Brown, *The Metaphysical Society: Victorian Mind in Crisis, 1869-1880* (New York, 1947).

[3] Vgl. hierzu Roy M. MacLeod, "The X-Club: A Social Network of Science in Late-Victorian England", *Notes and Records of the Royal Society of London*, 24 (1970), S. 305-322, bes. S. 311.

mungslehre erwähnt, den Bishop Samuel Wilberforce nach einem Vortrag von T.H. Huxley im Jahr 1860 verursachte.[1]

Zu den anti-szientifistischen, pro-religiösen Persönlichkeiten wie den genannten wäre wohl auch der Leiter der London City School, der eingangs zitierte Philologe und Theologe Edwin Abbott Abbott (1836-1926)[2] zu zählen, der 1884 *Flatland* unter dem ironisch sprechenden Pseudonym "A. Square" veröffentlichte. Seine Erzählung ist in einem geometrischen Kosmos angesiedelt, in dem Punkte, Linien, Flächen und Körper wie selbstverständlich als lebendige, mit allen menschlichen Schwächen ausgestattete Figuren agieren. Abbott greift eine Anzahl von wissenschaftsgeschichtlich wichtigen Forschungsdebatten, namentlich aus Biologie und Mathematik, auf und setzt sie in Kontext mit den aktuellen Streitfragen um Empirie und Transzendenz. *Flatland* erschien noch 1884 in zweiter Auflage (erst die zweite war mit dem Vorwort des 'Herausgebers' ausgestattet) und wurde danach immer wieder gedruckt. Im Laufe des 20. Jahrhunderts kam es fast in jedem Jahrzehnt zu neuen Auflagen und Erklärungsansätzen, und zwar vor allem im Kontext der Physik und Mathematik. Banesh Hoffmann, einst Assistent bei Albert Einstein und später dessen erster Biograph, läßt in sei-

---

[1] Vgl. das hierzu relevante Zitat im Artikel von Barbara Korte in diesem Band, S. 148. – James A. Secord betrachtet diesen Eklat zwischen T.H. Huxley und Bishop Wilberforce als einen künstlich aufgeblähten Zwischenfall, denn auch diverse Kirchenvertreter hätten sich schon bald nach der Publikation von Darwins *The Origin of Species* der evolutionären Blickweise angeschlossen: "Bishop Wilberforce spoke only for a minority". Vgl. J.A.S., *Victorian Sensation: The Extraordinary Publication, Reception, and Secret Authorship of "Vestiges of the Natural History of Creation"* (Chicago, 2000), S. 513 f.

[2] Zur Biographie Abbotts vgl. *Flatland: A Romance of Many Dimensions, Told by A. Square (Edwin A. Abbott)*. With Illustrations by the Author and a New Introduction by Thomas Banchoff (Princeton, 1991), S. xxi f., sowie die kommentierte Ausgabe von Ian Stewart, Ed., *Edwin A. Abbott: The Annotated Flatland: A Romance of Many Dimensions.* (Cambridge, MA, 2002), S. xiii-xxvii. Trotz einiger Mängel ist dies die bislang am sorgfältigsten aufbereitete und besticht durch eine Vielzahl hilfreicher Erläuterungen, wenngleich sie die unten aufgeführten Kontexte "Kontinuität" und "Unendlichkeit" ebenso unberücksichtigt läßt wie die hier nachgezeichneten biologischen Referenzsysteme. Durch den Akzent auf Mathematik und Physik in der Editionsgeschichte werden zwar diverse Dimensionen des Textes erläutert, andere Bedeutungsschichten (z.B. auch die soziale politische Situation während des Viktorianismus) bleiben weitgehend vernachlässigt – ebenso wie das Fehlen einer Gesamt-Bibliographie mit Studien zu *Flatland* auffällt. Zur Editions- und Wirkungsgeschichte vgl. *F* xix und 33 ff. (Anm. 1) und Gilbert, der 25 Editionen ausfindig gemacht hat ("'Upwards, not Northwards'", S. 392). Die folgenden Zitate im Text beziehen sich auf Stewarts Ausgabe (*F*).

ner erstmals 1952 publizierten Edition von *Flatland*[1] – ebenso wie 25 Jahre zuvor William Garnett – vor allen anderen Dingen ein Vorecho der Relativitätstheorien anklingen, die Einstein 1905 und 1916 formulierte. Hoffmann konzediert, daß das Raum-Zeit-Kontinuum, das Hermann Minkowski für Einsteins Theorie modellierte, in Abbotts *Flatland* keine signifikante Rolle spielt, doch ist es Abbott darum zu tun, die Existenz einer größeren Zahl von Dimensionen als der wahrnehmbaren vorstellbar zu machen. Damit stimmt auch Thomas Banchoff vor dem Hintergrund computergestützter Visualisierungen von höheren Dimensionen überein.

Der Kulturwissenschaftler Elliot L. Gilbert zählt weitere Themen auf und erkennt an:

> It is remarkable to note how many [...] concerns the author is able to touch on in a brief hundred pages: the relative merits of tradition and intuition as sources of knowledge, the burden of history, the appeal of novelty, the deceptiveness of progress, the limitations of hierarchy, the class struggle, the fear of women (often expressed as the threat of the female), the dangers of solipsism, the mysteries of creativity.[2]

Seitens der Literaturwissenschaft wird *Flatland* als kulturgeschichtliches Dokument jedoch eher selten betrachtet – im Gegensatz zu den großen viktorianischen Werken wie denen von Mary Ann Evans (George Eliot), Alfred Lord Tennyson oder Thomas Hardy, die sich wie Abbott vom Thema der Evolution und des Fortschritts (bzw. seiner pessimistisch-regressiven Variante, der *dissolution*) inspirieren ließen. Ob diese Vernachlässigung aus mangelndem Mut zum Dialog mit der 'anderen Dimension' resultiert oder aus der epigonalen Qualität des Textes, sei dahin gestellt.[3] In mancher Hinsicht gehen die Meinungen über seine Ziele auch auseinander. Im Gegensatz zu Banchoff, der in *Flatland* eine Satire auf die patriarchalische, frauenfeindliche Gesellschaftsordnung der viktorianischen Zeit zu finden vermeint[4], vertritt Gilbert die Ansicht, daß Abbott gerade das "woman's suffrage movement"[5] parodiere. Smith, Berkove und Baker schließlich wenden sich nicht jenen Motiven zu, die in Naturwissenschaften und in

---

[1] *Flatland: A Romance of Many Dimensions, Told by A. Square (Edwin A. Abbott)* (Harmondsworth, [1952] repr. 1987), S. 10.

[2] Gilbert, "'Upwards, Not Northwards'", S. 402.

[3] Dietrich Schwanitz verwendet *Flatland* gar als Illustration des systemtheoretischen Gedankens, daß man nur durch den Sprung aus dem System sich Klarheit darüber verschaffen kann. Vgl. D.S., *Systemtheorie und Literatur: Ein neues Paradigma* (Opladen, 1990), S. 27-31.

[4] Banchoff, "A New Introduction", S. xvii f.

[5] Gilbert, "'Upwards, not Northwards'", S. 399.

Science Fiction interessieren, sondern jenen mit theologischer Implikation. Abbott fechte die grundlegenden Denkformen an, die Cardinal Newman vertritt:

> The centerpiece of his [Abbott's] theology, evident long before the attack on Newman's Essay [on Ecclesiastical Miracles], was a rejection of miracles as a basis for Christian belief. [...] Accounts of miracles, even New Testament claims about the virgin birth and the resurrection of Christ, should be subject to "historical and scientific tests".[1]

Flatland ist eine Partitur der (wissenschafts-)kulturellen Fragen jener Zeit, die höchst widerstreitende Stimmen ins Konzert viktorianischer Zweifel treten läßt, nämlich "the totally rationalistic" und "the totally intuitive"[2], die "materialist science" und die "fundamentalist religion"[3], "mathematical and metaphysical quests"[4]. Einig ist sich die Forschung darin, daß "Abbott actually protected the spiritual against the claims of the material".[5] Vor welchem Hintergrund und mit welchen Folgerungen er dies aber tut, ist bislang nicht gezeigt worden: Abbott spielt zwei unterschiedliche Wissenschaftstraditionen, die im Viktorianismus in zuvor ungekannter Härte konkurrierten, gegeneinander aus – nämlich die (wie Abbott in seiner Bacon-Studie 1885 explizit darzulegen bemüht ist[6]) "falsche" utilitaristisch-materialistische Interpretation von Bacons Empirismus, und die "wahre" Empirie, die auch idealistische und spirituelle Elemente zuläßt.

Interessant ist *Flatland* nicht nur wegen seiner Aussage, sondern auch aufgrund der Tatsache, daß es zunächst unter einem Pseudonym erschienen ist, das erst mit der von dem Physiker William Garnett bestellten Neuausgabe von 1926 gelüftet wurde. Abbott inszeniert durch diesen falschen Namen sowie durch die Ereignisse, die A. Square in seiner scheiternden Mission widerfahren, ein Versteckspiel, wie es bis just 1884 um einen sehr einflußreichen, mittlerweile aber weitgehend vernachlässigten populärwissenschaftlichen Text über vier Jahrzehnte hinweg gespielt wurde: Denn der Autor von *The Vestiges of the Natural History of Creation*, Robert Cham-

---

[1] Jonathan Smith, Lawrence I. Berkove und Gerald A. Baker, "A Grammar of Dissent: *Flatland*, Newman, and the Theology of Probability", *Victorian Studies*, 39:2 (1996), S. 129-150, hier S. 131.

[2] Banchoff, "A New Introduction", S. xix.

[3] Rosemary Jann, "Abbott's *Flatland*: Scientific Imagination and 'Natural Christianity'", *Victorian Studies*, 28 (1985), S. 473-490.

[4] Gilbert, "'Upwards, Not Northwards'", S. 400.

[5] Jann, "Abbott's *Flatland*", S. 481.

[6] In: Edwin A. Abbott, *Francis Bacon: An Account of his Life and Works* (London, 1885).

bers, war hauptberuflich als Buchhändler, (Literatur-) Historiker und Verleger tätig (er verfaßte auch eine – ebenfalls evolutiv gedachte – englische Literaturgeschichte[1]) und in den naturwissenschaftlichen Disziplinen ein Laie. In scharfem Gegensatz zu dem "natural law", wie es die Naturwissenschaftler jener Zeit verstanden wissen wollten, bekannte Chambers sich zu einer göttlichen Autorschaft, deren Wirken er in der kosmischen Ordnung manifestiert sah: So stellt er zunächst die Frage: "To what authorship are we to ascribe the whole [universe]?"[2] und beantwortet sie schon wenige Seiten später, noch im ersten Kapitel seines Buches, in der Diskussion der Gesetzmäßigkeiten des Kosmos:

> What, in the science of nature, is a law? It is merely the term applicable where any series of phenomena is seen invariably to occur in certain given circumstances, or in certain given conditions. Such phenomena are said to obey a law, because they appear to be under a rule or ordinance of constant operation. In the case of these physical laws, we can bring the idea to mathematical elements, and see that *numbers*, in the expression of space or of time, form, as it were, its basis. We thus trace in law, Intelligence – often we can see that it has a beneficial object, still more strongly speaking of *mind* as concerned in it. There cannot, however, be an *inherent intelligence* in these laws. The intelligence appears *external to the laws*; something of which the laws are but as the expressions of the Will and the Power. If this be admitted, the laws cannot be regarded as primary or independent causes of the phenomena of the physical world. We come, in short, to a Being beyond nature – its author, its God; ...[3]

Und Chambers fährt unmißverständlich fort:

> Let it then be understood – and this is for the reader's special attention – that when natural law is spoken of here, reference is only made to the mode in which the Divine Power is exercise. It is but another phrase for the action of the ever-present and sustaining God.[4]

Die anschließende Darstellung, die kosmische, geologische, biologische und anthropologische Dimensionen der Welt umfaßt, bemüht sich um die Vereinigung der neuesten Erkenntnisse der Naturwissenschaften mit dem

---

[1] Robert Chambers war der Verfasser der *History of English Language and Literature* sowie der *Cyclopaedia of English Literature* (1843/44). – Vgl. dazu Klaus Stierstorfer, *Die englische Literaturgeschichte von Warton bis Courthope und Ward* (Heidelberg, 2001), bes. S. 165-199.

[2] [Robert Chambers:] *Vestiges of the Natural History of Creation* (London, [11]1860), S. 5.

[3] Ibid., S. 9 (kursiv im Original).

[4] Ibid., vgl. dort im Anhang die S. xlviii u. li.

theologischen Weltbild. Daß dagegen auch kirchlicherseits starke Vorbehalte geäußert wurden, versteht sich fast von selbst. Um sich gegen den Vorwurf von Unwissenschaftlichkeit und Häresie zu wehren, fügte Chambers seiner 1844 erstmals erschienenen Schrift nach 1853 einen Anhang bei, in dem er sich beispielsweise mit den Attacken des Rev. Adam Sedgwick auseinandersetzte. Sedgwick hatte eine mehr als dreihundert Seiten umfassende Auseinandersetzung mit Chambers' Werk vorgelegt und darin Stellung gegen seinen "natürlichen Gottesbeweis" bezogen. Nicht zuletzt wegen dieser zwei Fronten, die Chambers mit seiner Publikation eröffnete, war er darum bestrebt, seine Anonymität möglichst lange zu wahren. Trotz aller Kontroverse und trotz des anhaltenden Skandals aber bereitete Chambers' *Vestiges* den Weg für die Publikation von Darwins *Origin of Species.*[1]

Es wird sich an den Ergebnissen der folgenden Textanalyse zeigen, daß der Theologe Abbott durchaus mit dem Verständnis eines transzendentalen, göttlich induzierten Naturgesetzes sympathisierte und dieses Konzept auf Bacon zurückführte. Der Verweis auf diese wissenschaftsgeschichtliche Tradition allein reicht für eine gattungsgeschichtliche Situierung noch nicht. *Flatland* muß darüber hinaus als negative Zeitutopie gelesen werden, denn angesiedelt ist es im Jahre 2007. In seiner Zweiteilung entspricht der Text mit seiner Schilderung einer gesellschaftlichen Realität im ersten Abschnitt und dem "Erfahrungsbericht" mit Einsichten in fremde Welten an Thomas Mores *Utopia*. Der Ton ist jedoch pessimistisch, und im Gegensatz zu Mores Modelltext endet *Flatland* nicht fragmentarisch-offen mit der Aussicht auf eine zukünftige Diskussion um die Übertragbarkeit jener idealen Zustände der Insel Utopia auf reale britische Verhältnisse, sondern als abgeschlossener Konvertiten-Bericht aus einer Gefängniszelle: A. Square, der Ich-Erzähler, sitzt hier seit sieben Jahren ein und beschreibt seine zweidimensionale Welt sowie seine mystische Begegnung mit der dritten Dimension, deren Evangelium zu verkündigen er ausgezogen war.

---

[1] Eine umfangreiche Darstellung der Umstände, in denen Chambers Darstellung einer spontanen, natürlichen Entstehungsgeschichte der Welt diskutiert wurde, findet sich in Secord, *Victorian Sensation*. Secord wendet sich in seiner Produktions-, Publikations- und Rezeptionsgeschichte der *Vestiges* gegen die Stellung von Darwins *Origin of Species* und dessen Einfluß auf die zeitgenössische Literatur, wie sie von Gillian Beer und George Levine bestätigt wurde (vgl. ibid., S. 489). Secord baut Darwins erhabene Position ab und dagegen Chambers' auf, da seinen Befunden nach die *Vestiges* – auch aufgrund des leichteren Stils – sehr viel breiter und kontroverser als Darwins *Origin* aufgenommen wurden. Secord betrachtet Darwin nicht einmal mehr als *primus inter pares*, denn er mißt Chambers die gedankliche Originalität zu und räumt zugleich Alfred Russel Wallace denselben Rang wie Darwin ein: Unabhängig von diesem gelangte Wallace aufgrund eigener Forschungsreisen und Befunde zu denselben Schlußfolgerungen, machte ihm aber die Ehre nicht streitig (vgl. ibid., S. 507).

Die Aufzeichnungen Squares werden von einem Bewohner aus *Space-land* herausgegeben – dieser will Squares tristes Schicksal als mahnendes *exemplum* aus einer Welt des Vermessen-Seins verstanden wissen und mit dessen Geschichte für Offenheit gegenüber der Intuition, der Imagination und der daraus gewonnen Erkenntnis werben. Ebenso wie in den simulierten editorischen Episteln zu Mores *Utopia* oder zu Jonathan Swifts *Gulliver's Travels* werden im Kommentar des Herausgebers diverse fiktionsentblößende Merkmale gesetzt (es wird u.a. auf die Geistesverfassung des Langzeitinsassen und auf Unstimmigkeiten in der Textgestalt – Tippfehler etc. – hingewiesen).

Teil I, "This World", liefert wie Mores *Utopia* ein Bild der gegenwärtigen Gesellschaft mit all ihren Schwächen und Nachteilen. Wir erfahren darin von unterschiedlichen sozialen Klassen, deren Status sich aus der Anzahl der Seiten des Wesens ergibt: Die Anzahl der Seiten repräsentiert Ansehen und Macht; das Winkelmaß gibt Auskunft über Intellekt und moralische Integrität. Erworbene Eigenschaften vererben sich an nachfolgende Generationen und gehen durch degeneratives Verhalten verloren. Es folgt eine Beschreibung der diskursiven Ordnungen innerhalb dieser Gesellschaft, d.h. eine der Regulative, die das Leben und Überleben bestimmen, sowie ein Aufriß der konfliktreichen Sozialgeschichte.

Teil II, "Other Worlds", liefert den Grund für die langjährige Haftstrafe, zu der Square verurteilt ist: Nicht etwa ein Gewaltverbrechen, sondern eine ungeteilte, begrifflich wie diskursiv schlechthin unmitteilbare Erfahrung, und demzufolge das Aussprechen einer nicht akzeptierten Wirklichkeitsauffassung bildet den Hintergrund für die Einkerkerung Squares. Zu Beginn jedes neuen (nach christlichen Maßstäben gezählten) Millenniums wird die Flächenwelt von Körpern aus der dritten Dimension besucht. Square wurde in der Neujahrsnacht des Jahres 2000 von Mr Sphere in die Geheimnisse der dritten Dimension eingeführt und sollte nach einem Erweckungserlebnis als Apostel der neuen Wahrheit dienen – doch endete er wegen seiner Mission im Gefängnis; immer in der Angst gehalten, dem Martyrium nicht ausweichen zu können: Subjektiv-intuitive Erkenntnis ist in einem Gesellschaftsklima mit Akzent auf Gebrauchswert und Anwendbarkeit von Wissen weder politisch noch existentiell opportun.

Charakterisiert man beide Teile nach dem jeweils zugrunde liegenden Bildvorrat und seinen thematischen Systemreferenzen, so zeigt sich, daß Teil I auf dem Fundament von Soziologie und Biologie errichtet ist, während Teil II primär auf abstrakter Erkenntnis und idealer Wahrheit, veranschaulicht in der Mathematik, beruhen. Zusammengehalten werden sie durch die übergreifende Fiktion einer zweidimensionalen Welt innerhalb eines Multiversums. Abbott beschreibt mit *Flatland* einen imaginären

Nichtort, dessen Komplexität sich durch Anschauung und Vorstellung vervielfacht. Nicht nur hat Square vor seiner Begegnung mit Mr Sphere einen antizipatorischen Traum von einer eindimensionalen Welt, "Lineland", sondern er wird später in einer Vision von Mr Sphere ermuntert, gar in die Singularität von "Pointland" ("the Abyss of No dimensions", *F* 182) hinabzusteigen. Square hebt bei seiner Diskussion mit Sphere um die Beschaffenheit der dritten Dimension ab – und stößt gedanklich weit über "Spaceland" hinaus ins Imaginäre vor. Indem Abbott seinen geometrischen Figuren jeweils die Vorstellungskraft für die Existenz einer höheren Dimension fehlen läßt, versetzt er sie in eine kognitiv analoge Situation zu jener, in der sich der Mensch befindet: Dieser bewegt sich durch drei Dimensionen, doch schon die Vorstellung eines vierdimensionalen Raum-Zeit-Kontinuums ist ihm verschlossen, und auch die Anschauung von mehr als vier Raumdimensionen ist geradezu unmöglich.

Nach der vorangestellten Situierung des Textes im Rahmen einer knappen Wiedergabe bisheriger Forschungsstandpunkte und formaler Aspekte soll nun den vernachlässigten intertextuellen Referenzsystemen, die mit mehr oder minder transparenten Markierungen angelegt sind, nachgegangen werden. Entgegen der Struktur des Textes erfolgt ein Aufriß des fiktionalen Universums und ein Blick auf den (mathematischen) Teil II, bevor die (soziobiologische) Gesellschaft Flatlands anhand von Teil I betrachtet wird.

2. Zwei Mathematiker aus Deutschland und die viktorianische Geometrie

Liest man *Flatland* gegen den zeitgenössischen Hintergrund in der Mathematik und betrachtet dabei die Diskussionen um Geometrie und Zahlentheorie, so ergibt sich ein vielschichtigeres Bild, als es von verschiedenen Herausgebern und Kommentatoren gezeichnet worden ist. Bezüglich der mathematischen Situation sei vorausgeschickt, daß das 19. Jahrhundert europaweit durch eine Grundlagenkrise der Mathematik geprägt war. Sie wurde in Form des Zweifels an der gut zweitausend Jahre lang gültigen euklidischen Geometrie verursacht.[1] Dabei stellt Joan Richards heraus: "It is almost a truism in the history of mathematics that in the nineteenth century most interesting developments in pure mathematics took place outside

---

[1] Während es bei den meisten Axiomen, die Euklid seinerzeit aufgrund logischer Überlegungen gestellt hatte, keine Anfechtungen gab, taten sich Euklid selbst wie auch seine Nachfolger allein mit dem fünften oder Parallelaxiom schwer, das eher auf den Sichtraum zurückzuführen war denn auf eine logische Grundlage.

England: in France, Germany or Italy."[1] Nach Carl Friedrich Gauß' zu Lebzeiten unveröffentlichten Überlegungen entwickelten in den 1830er Jahren
unabhängig voneinander der Russe Nikolai I. Lobatschowskij und der Un-
gar Janos Bolyai unterschiedliche Möglichkeiten einer nicht-euklidischen
Geometrie.[2] Während diese beiden Versuche von der Fachwelt kaum rezipiert wurden, sorgte Bernhard Riemann 1854 mit seinem Göttinger Habili-
tationsvortrag für ein nachhaltiges Echo. Diese Schrift wurde 1873 von
William K. Clifford in *Nature* übersetzt – als die Diskussion um die logische Plausibilität nichteuklidischer oder höherdimensionierter euklidischer
Geometrien längst entfacht war.[3] Riemann übte großen Einfluß auf den
Physiker, Physiologen und Mathematiker Hermann von Helmholtz aus, der
die sphärische Geometrie in anschaulichen Bildern zu verbreiten suchte:

> Denken wir uns – darin liegt keine logische Unmöglichkeit – verstandbegabte
> Wesen von nur zwei Dimensionen, die an der Oberfläche irgendeines unserer
> festen Körper leben und sich bewegen. Wir nehmen an, daß sie nicht die Fähigkeit
> haben, irgend etwas außerhalb dieser Oberfläche wahrzunehmen, wohl aber
> Wahrnehmungen zu machen, ähnlich den unserigen, innerhalb der Ausdehnung
> der Fläche, in der sie sich bewegen. Wenn sich solche Wesen ihre Geometrie aus-
> bilden, so würden sie ihrem Raume natürlich nur zwei Dimensionen zuschreiben.[4]

Helmholtz benutzt hier eine von Carl Friedrich Gauß verwendete und vom
Psychologen Gustav Theodor Fechner entwickelte heuristische Fiktion, mit
deren Hilfe er erläutert, vor welche kognitiven Schwierigkeiten sich ein
Wesen gestellt sieht, das keine praktische Anschauung von der dimensio-
nalen Beschaffenheit seiner Umwelt hat. Schon bevor Helmholtz' Artikel
in englischer Übersetzung ("The Axioms of Geometry") in der Zeitschrift
The Academy (1870) abgedruckt war,[5] kam diese Fiktion mit ihren

---

[1] Joan L. Richards, *Mathematical Visions: The Pursuit of Geometry in Victorian
England* (Boston, NJ, 1988), S. 7.
[2] Vgl. Chr. Houzel, "The Birth of Non-Euclidean Geometry", in: *1830-1930: A Century of Geometry. Epistemology, History and Mathematics*, ed. L. Boi, D. Flament und
J.-M. Salanskis (Berlin, 1992), S. 3-21, sowie E. Scholz, "Riemann's Vision of a New
Approach to Geometry", in: ibid., S. 22-34.
[3] Vgl. Richards, *Mathematical Visions*, S. 74.
[4] Hermann von Helmholtz, "Über den Ursprung und die Bedeutung der geometrischen Axiome" (1869), in: *Raum und Kraft: Aus der Werkstatt genialer Naturforscher*.
Eine Auswahl aus den gemeinverständlichen Vorträgen von H. Helmholtz und H. Hertz,
eingel. und erläutert von Dr. E. Wildhagen (Berlin, s.d. [1932]), S. 202-231, hier S. 207.
[5] Zur weiteren Publikationsgeschichte dieses einflußreichen Artikels vgl. Linda
Darymple Henderson, *The Fourth Dimension and Non-Euclidean Geometry in Modern
Art* (Princeton, NJ, 1983), S. 12: "First given as a speech in Heidelberg in 1870 and
published in *Academy* in London that year, Helmholtz's text was augmented for publi-

epistemologischen Konsequenzen – der Möglichkeit einer logischen, aber unanschaulichen Herleitung der 'wahren' Beschaffenheit der Welt – auf der Insel in Umlauf: Schon 1865 hatte Charles Lutwidge Dodgson (Lewis Carroll) eine Romanze zwischen zwei Linien auf einer von romantischem Abendlicht überfluteten Ebene ersonnen;[1] James Joseph Sylvester entwarf noch vor der Übersetzung von Helmholtz' Artikel 1870 eine zweidimensionale Welt, und insbesondere Charles Howard Hinton ersann 1880 eine mit *Flatland* vergleichbare Fiktion.[2] Helmholtz' Popularisierungen jedoch stellten den wohl wichtigsten Impuls für die anschließende epistemologische Debatte dar. Prominente Mathematiker übten zunächst Zweifel an dieser neuen Geometrie, so William Stanley Jevons: Ihm ging es bei der Kritik an einer Analogisierung von realer und flachen Welt um deren Aussagekraft für den objektiven Wahrheitsgehalt mathematischer Modelle.[3] Richards bilanziert:

> For Helmholtz [...] the first variety of truth, experiential truth, was of primary interest. Purely subjective mathematical truth held no ontological implications, and hence did not interest him.
> Jevon's approach was markedly different. [...] he focused on a third kind of truth, a transcendental or necessary truth, of which geometry was the exemplar. This was a truth in which experience and intellect were joined. It was not bounded by experience, however; it was recognized rather than learned.[4]

Richards führt plastisch vor Augen, wie heftig zwischen 1870 und 1876 in den Zeitschriften *Nature*, *Academy* und *Mind* um diese Fragen gestritten wurde, und resümiert: "By the mid-1870s non-Euclidean ideas were readily available in England"[5] – auch für diejenigen, die keine Spezialisten waren.

Abbott konstruiert in *Flatland* eine euklidische Welt, die von Wesen bevölkert wird,[6] die eigentlich zur Kenntnis nehmen müßten, daß das Univer-

---

cation in *Mind* (London) in 1876. This final version [unter dem Titel "On the Origin and Significance of Geometrical Axioms"] was later incorporated in the second volume of Helmholtz's *Popular Lectures on Scientific Subjects* of 1881." – Vgl. dazu auch Gillian Beer, "Helmholtz, Tyndall, Gerard Manley Hopkins: Leaps of the Prepared Imagination", in: Dies, *Open Fields*, S. 242-272, hier S. 245 f. (Anm. 8).

[1] Zur literarischen Tradition dieses Motivs vgl. Henderson, *The Fourth Dimension*, S. 21 f., sowie Elmar Schenkel, "Geometrie und Phantastik: Die vierte Dimension in der Literatur", *Inklings-Jahrbuch*, 12 (1994), S. 163-184.

[2] Vgl. Stewart, "Introduction", S. xxiii ff. sowie *F* 26 ff. (Anm. 34).

[3] Vgl. Joan Richards, *Mathematical Visions*, S. 86-89.

[4] Ibid., S. 90.

[5] Ibid., S. 74.

[6] Stewart rekonstruiert den Weg dieser Fiktion von Gauß und Fechner über Helmholtz, John Tyndall und George Eliot zu Abbott. Vgl. dazu *F* 171 ff. (Anm. 5).

sum anders ist als das Bild, das sie sich davon machen (nur daß sie sich wie die platonischen Höhlenmenschen willentlich und diskurs-polizeilich dagegen sperren[1]). Nachdem Square wegen seiner mentalen Widerspenstigkeit gewaltsam in die Höhe entführt worden ist und somit die zweite Dimension im Grundriß aus der Vogelperspektive (also der empirisch erfahrenen dritten) kennengelernt hat, führt er seinerseits seinen 'Meister' zur intellektuellen Akzeptanz einer höheren als der dritten Dimension. Verweigert Sphere sich auch zunächst dieser "utterly inconceivable [idea]" (*F* 169), so konzediert er kurz darauf deren Möglichkeit: "... he had received fresh insight, and he was not too proud to acknowledge his error to a Pupil" (*F* 185).

Vordergründig erscheint *Flatland* als Begegnung der Dimensionen: Bevor A. Square in Kontakt zur dritten Dimension tritt, hat er einen Traum in der Nacht vom 30. auf den 31. Dezember 1999. Dieser Traum Squares nimmt allegorisch jene Situation vorweg, die wenige Stunden später Sphere bei seinem 'Advent' in der 'realen' zweiten Dimension erlebt: Er trifft auf einen Bewohner der niedergradigen Dimension, der unter keinen Umständen den Gedanken zuläßt, daß es andere Welten gibt als jene, in der man selbst lebt. Die Frage, die sich angesichts dieser Begegnungen stellt, lautet, welche Idee hinter dem Einfall steht, nach der Beschreibung einer zweidimensionalen Welt und ihrer Gesellschaft in Teil I überhaupt einen zweiten folgen zu lassen? Handelt es sich lediglich um ein dynamisierendes Funktionselement, das dem sperrigen Text mit all seiner inhaltlichen Stasis, die Teil I aufweist, eine heroische Dynamisierung der Handlung erlaubt?

Diese Fragen führen uns zu einem weiteren Mathematiker aus Deutschland, der sein Hauptforschungsgebiet in der (ungelösten) Problematik der Unendlichkeit hatte und versuchte, seine Annahmen arithmetisch und anschaulich-geometrisch zu begründen. Im Zentrum dieser Problematik standen drei Probleme antiker Mathematik – erstens die Frage nach dem Begriff der "Unendlichkeit" selbst (und damit die Unterscheidung der aristotelischen Dichotomie von potentieller vs. aktualer Unendlichkeit, *apeiron* vs. *aphorismenon*), zweitens jene nach dem Wesen der Dimensionalität, schließlich die nach der Kontinuität von Zeit und Raum. Es handelt sich bei dem angesprochenen Mathematiker um Georg Cantor (1845-1918), der allerdings z.B. in Bernard Bolzano einen Vorläufer hatte.[2] Bolzano arbeitete

---

[1] So wird in Kapitel 18 beschrieben, wie Sphere in eine Parlamentsversammlung eindringt und wie dort dieses Ereignis nicht nur negiert, sondern geradezu unter Beseitigung aller zufälligen Zeugen aus dem öffentlichen Gedächtnis gelöscht wird.

[2] Stewart geht auf Bolzano gar nicht, auf Cantor nur *en passant* ein (vgl. *F* 169). Auch das Thema der mathematischen Unendlichkeit spielt für Stewart keine zentrale Rolle. Ein direkter Wirkungszusammenhang zwischen Bolzano, Cantor und Abbott ist

sich an dem Problem der Unendlichkeitskonzepte ab; seine *Paradoxien des Unendlichen* erschienen posthum 1851, das Buch wurde sogleich ins Englische übersetzt und erblickte sogar noch vor der deutschen Herausgabe das Licht der Öffentlichkeit. Der seit 1872 in Halle wirkende Cantor schloß mittelbar daran an und wurde zum Begründer der sehr kontrovers behandelten Mengenlehre. Er wurde dabei vor allem von Richard Dedekind begleitet, der ihn über weite Strecken ermutigte, auf argumentative Probleme hinwies und Beweise gegenlas bzw. sie vereinfachte. Cantors ehemaliger Lehrer Leopold Kronecker, eine einflußreiche Fachpersönlichkeit, hingegen attackierte die Mengenlehre mit viel Polemik als "irrational". Daß Cantor, selbst des Englischen nicht mächtig, sich in den 1890er Jahren auch an der Shakespeare-Bacon-Debatte beteiligte, birgt aus anglistischer Sicht eine tragikomische Fußnote zu seinen Interessen.[1]

Bolzano und Cantor beschäftigten sich intensiv mit den epistemologischen Implikationen ihrer Theorien und unternahmen den Versuch, der rein mathematischen Abstraktion auch eine weltanschauliche, gar theologische und damit letztlich existentielle Dimension abzuringen. Die Geometrie kann dabei als wichtige Wegmarke für Cantors Entwicklung der Mengenlehre gelten. Cantor sah sich vor die Frage gestellt, ob es möglich wäre, eine höhere Dimension auf eine niedrigere abzubilden, z.B. ein Quadrat auf eine Linie. Wäre dies möglich, so wäre damit der Begriff "Dimension" neu zu fassen. Denn dann könnte man nicht mehr zwischen ganzzahligen Dimensionen unterscheiden, sondern es wären auch Zwischengrößen vorstellbar – später so bezeichnete "Fraktale".[2] Eine ähnliche Fragestellung ergab sich im Hinblick auf die Definition einer Linie – wäre sie aus einzelnen, diskreten Punkten zusammengesetzt, oder bildete auch sie ein Kontinuum?

---

auch gar nicht annehmbar, es geht aber um den Kontext, der hier erörtert wird. Georg Cantor wurde erst zu Beginn des 20. Jahrhundert außerhalb seines unmittelbaren regionalen und intellektuellen Umfelds wahrgenommen. In England wurde er um die Jahrhundertwende rezipiert (erst 1906 erschien die erste zusammenfassende englische Übersetzung der späteren Arbeiten Cantors zur Mengentheorie).

[1] Vgl. dazu v.a. Walter Purkert u. Hans Joachim Ilgauds, *Georg Cantor 1845-1918* (Basel, 1987), S. 79-92. Die Verfasser zeigen, daß Cantor sich zwischen 1884 und 1899 einer *idée fixe* hingab, die ihn einen Bacon konstruieren ließ, der, von 1561 bis 1668 lebend, 107 Jahre alt geworden und überdies mit mehreren anderen literarischen Figuren außer Shakespeare identisch gewesen wäre. Wegen solch abstruser Gedanken vermuten die Verfasser, daß Cantor auch aus der Deutschen Shakespeare-Gesellschaft, der er seit 1889 angehört hatte, ausgeschlossen worden sei. Vgl. ibid., S. 90 f.

[2] Vgl. Benoît B. Mandelbrot, *Die fraktale Geometrie der Natur*. Aus dem Englischen übersetzt von Reinhilt u. Ulrich Zähle ([1982] Basel, 1991), S. 16 f.

Die intuitive Antwort gerade auf die erste dieser Fragen verheißt nun, daß die Abbildbarkeit von Quadrat auf Linie nicht gegeben wäre. Cantor ließ übrigens seine 'Entdeckung' in einem Brief vom Juni 1877 an seinen Freund Dedekind nicht unkommentiert: "Je le vois, mais je ne le crois pas" und verkündete noch 1878 eher *nolens-volens* das Gegenteil:

> Wie gesagt gehörte ich selbst zu denen, welche es für das Wahrscheinlichste hielten, daß jene Frage mit einem Nein zu beantworten sei, – bis ich vor ganz kurzer Zeit durch ziemlich verwickelte Gedankenreihen zu der Überzeugung gelangte, daß jene Frage ohne alle Einschränkungen zu bejahen ist. Bald darauf fand ich den Beweis, welchen sie heute vor sich sehen.[1]

Im Gegensatz zu Stewart, der die Relevanz dieser Probleme für die Anlage und Struktur von *Flatland* nicht wahrnimmt[2], kann man das Argument vorbringen, daß Teil II der Romanze aus nichts anderem besteht als einer Beschäftigung mit diesen Fragen: Dazu gehört schon die ("Traum-") Begegnung Squares mit einer Linie bzw. später einem Punkt, sowie vor allem sein "reales" Aufeinandertreffen mit einer Kugel, Mr Sphere. Es ist kaum Zufall, daß Abbott den Traum vom Lineland als 'Verschiebung' seiner Beschäftigung mit einem "unsolved problem" (*F* 113) markiert – dieses 1884 noch ungelöste Problem mag unmittelbar den Hintergrund der oben erörterten Dimensionalitätsfrage und der damit verbundenen Kontinuitätsproblematik in Geometrie und Arithmetik gegeben haben.

Nachdem Square dem Linienkönig vorgeführt hat, wie einfach es ihm ist, sich rechtwinklig zur gewohnten Dimension auf und ab zu bewegen (und im 'Sich-Herablassen' sämtliche Flächenpunkte auf der Linie 'abzubilden'), ruft dieser in geradezu Kroneckerscher Ungeduld aus: "Can anything be more irrational or audacious?" (*F* 127) Sphere bemüht sich zuerst, die rein kognitive Leistung mit einem Gedankenexperiment zu gestalten und somit seinem Schüler die dritte Dimension analytisch, d.h. ohne empirische

---

[1] Georg Cantor in einem Brief an Dedekind, zitiert nach Herbert Meschkowski, *Probleme des Unendlichen* (Braunschweig, 1967), S. 40.

[2] Stewart weist zwar auf "Fraktale" hin (in *F* 36 [Anm. 3] und 130 ff. [Anm. 3]), doch geht er auf das Kontinuitätsproblem nicht ein. Er stellt die Peano-Kurve oder den Hilbert-Raum vor, die in *Flatland* keine Rolle spielen: "Abbott is saying that three-dimensional figures cannot exist inside a two-dimensional plane" (vgl. *F* 36, [Anm. 3]). – Square vertritt anfänglich einen intuitiven Standpunkt: "In such a country, you will perceive at once that it is impossible that there should be anything of what you call a 'solid' kind" (*F* 33). Ihn pflegt er bis zu seinem Erweckungserlebnis, das ihm Mr Sphere im zweiten Teil der Romanze verschafft. Abbott aber führt gerade im kontuierlichen Durchdringen der Linie durch das Quadrat (vgl. Kap. 13) und der Planebene durch die Kugel die Beschaffenheit der Dimensionen vor (vgl. Kap. 15 sowie die Abb. *F* 143).

Anschauung, nahezubringen. Sowohl der König von Lineland als auch Square wollen in ihren Reaktionen auf die Eindringlinge ihren Augen nicht trauen, zumal sie in ihrer niedergradigen Dimension nicht in der Lage sind, das höherdimensionierte Wesen in seiner Gesamtheit, sondern immer nur als kontinuierlich sich in seiner Form verändernden Querschnitt wahrzunehmen. Daher vermuten sie irgend eine Illusion hinter dem Gesehenen ("you merely exercise some magic art" [*F* 127], so der König von Lineland) oder beschimpfen ihre Gegenüber als "monster" (*F* 147).

In seinen Erklärungen fordert Meister Sphere seinen Schüler Square auf, sich einen Punkt vorzustellen und diesen beliebig zu erweitern – heraus kommt eine Strecke mit zwei Endpunkten. Im zweiten Schritt wird diese rechtwinklig um sich selbst erweitert und "quadriert". Anschließend kann Square sich die nächste rechtwinklige Erweiterung in die Höhe nicht mehr vorstellen ("upwards, not northwards", muß Sphere ihn ermahnen). Beide sind sich aber einig, es handle sich dabei um eine arithmetische Progression {0; 2; 4 ...} und auf die Frage nach der Anzahl der Seiten des Würfels findet Square die Lösung: Gefordert ist die Zahl 6. Was für die Seiten einer geometrischen Figur gilt, hat allerdings keinen Bestand für ihre Eck- und Endpunkte, denn sie vermehren sich nicht in arithmetischer (linearer), sondern geometrischer (exponentieller) Progression. Square erkennt bald – und fordert auf diese Weise seinen Lehrmeister heraus –, daß die Linie durch zwei, die rechtwinklige Fläche durch vier, der rechtwinklige Körper durch acht Punkte begrenzt ist {2; 4; 8 ...}; er schließt daraus, daß sich dies mit der zunehmenden Anzahl der Dimensionen *ad infinitum* fortsetzen ließe, und zwar "strictly according to Analogy" (*F* 171). Dagegen sperrt Sphere sich zwar zunächst, denn er sieht die Zahlenreihen nur, hierin in seiner Auffassung ganz traditionell, als *potentiell* unendliche an. Square hingegen argumentiert durchaus im Sinne von Cantors "aktualen Unendlichkeiten". Cantor entwickelte nämlich dafür Abzählweisen und wies nach, daß es tatsächlich verschiedene Arten von Unendlichkeiten gibt, die er mit dem Symbol ω bezeichnet und denen er den Rang von Ordinalzahlen zumißt. So ist Cantors Notation für die arithmetische Progression ω_1 = {1; 3; 5; 7; ... ω+2}, für die geometrische hingegen: ω_2 = {1; 2; 4; 8; 16; 32; ... ω×2}.

Paradox daran scheint, daß jede Zahlenfolge aus ebenso vielen Elementen besteht wie das Unendliche selbst; d.h. die "Mächtigkeiten" (oder "Mannigfaltigkeiten", bzw. in heutiger Terminologie "Mengen") sind ebenso groß wie ihre Summe. Sie werden durch den hebräischen Buchstaben ℵ gekennzeichnet und bilden die Kardinalzahlen.[1] Der Protestant Cantor, der

---

[1] Die Theorie der Kardinalzahlen entwickelte Cantor erst nach dem *terminus post quem* (1884), um den es in dieser Studie geht. Daher kann sie hier vernachlässigt werden.

später mit hochrangigen katholischen Theologen über seine Lehre im Sinne des christlichen Dogmas korrespondierte,[1] kalkulierte die Konnotationen der Symbole ℵ und ω ein. In diesem Sinne bildet die Mengenlehre mit ihrer spirituellen Fundamentierung ein Korrektiv für die materialistische Interpretation der Wissenschaftssprache – und gewinnt für unsere Betrachtungen an Bedeutung.

Abbott stellt die Kontinuumsproblematik in einen weiten gedanklichen Horizont, indem er Squares Besuch beim König von Lineland als Traum, Spheres Ankunft in Flatland als "facts" (*F* 129), die Vorstellung von Pointland schließlich als gemeinsame Vision von Sphere und Square schildert. Es gibt also nicht die kategorial definierbare Dichotomie von materieller Dinglichkeit und immaterieller Imagination (letztere ist in Flatland verpönt), sondern das Sein an sich ist selbst als Kontinuum zu begreifen – spontane Einsichten und imaginäre Erlebnisse spielen daher beim Erkenntnisgewinn eine ähnliche Rolle wie die positivistische Empirie.

3. Spencer und Galton als Herrscher über *Flatland*

War im vorangehenden Abschnitt das Problem der geometrischen und arithmetischen Kontinuität Gegenstand der Betrachtung, so wenden wir uns mit den folgenden Ausführungen dem sozio-biologischen Referenzsystem des Textes zu, das in Teil I nachweisbar ist. Auch dem Gedanke der Evolution, d.h. der schrittweisen Entwicklung von neuen Lebensformen aus bestehenden "alten" liegt der alte Gedanke einer zusammenhängenden "chain of beings" zugrunde, und also einer Natur, die keine Sprünge macht (*natura non facit saltus*). Diese Annahme aber wird in den diskursiven Praktiken der zweidimensionalen Gesellschaft in Teil I von *Flatland* durchkreuzt. Wie sich zeigen wird, umgeht man in dem Moment, da man das biologische "natürliche" Gesetz kennt, dieses durch künstliche Einflußnahme – mit verheerenden Folgen. Insofern sind beide Teile trotz der ihnen zugrundeliegenden unterschiedlichen Denkformen motivisch miteinander durch den Kontinuitätsgedanken verknüpft.

Oberflächlich betrachtet, ist die soziale Ordnung in der Zweidimensionalität von *Flatland* recht einfach strukturiert und dabei durch unüberwindbare Trennungen charakterisiert: Frauen erscheinen, von Natur aus minderdimensioniert, als Striche (vgl. *F* 15). In der sozialen Hierarchie folgen danach die Soldaten und die Arbeiterklasse als gleichschenklige Dreiecke; die

---

[1] Vgl. Meschkowski, *Probleme des Unendlichen*, S. 122-129, und Dauben, *Georg Cantor*, S. 140-148.

middle class besteht aus gleichseitigen Dreiecken. Die *upper middle class* setzt sich aus Intellektuellen und Gentlemen (Vierecke und Fünfecke) zusammen, danach beginnt schon die Klasse des Adels mit seinen Binnendifferenzierungen. Die Kreise sind – ganz in platonischer Idealität – die hierarchisch höchsten, mächtigsten und intelligentesten Mitglieder an der Spitze dieser Gesellschaft (vgl. *F* 43 f.). Es wird an dieser Stratifikation deutlich, daß zunächst vor allem Äußerlichkeiten den sozialen Rang zu bestimmen scheinen. Von sozialer Mobilität können die aufstiegswilligen Individuen angesichts dieser Verhältnisse nicht einmal träumen. Die Gesellschaft in Flatland, so wird hieran deutlich, zerfällt in unterschiedlich komplexe Lebens-"Formen"; es handelt sich dabei um eine Hierarchie, die jede Irregularität verbietet und stigmatisiert. Die zunächst allein nach sozialen Kriterien begründete Stratifikation hat auch ihre biologische Seite.[1] Denn die Nachkommenschaft ist durchaus privilegiert, weil es neben dem sozialen einen starken biologischen Determinismus gibt:

> It is a Law of Nature with us that a male child shall have one more side than his father, so that each generation shall rise (as a rule) one step in the scale of development and nobility. Thus the son of a Square is a Pentagon; the son of a Pentagon, a Hexagon; and so on. (*F* 44)

Interessant ist, daß Abbott sich die natürliche Evolution weniger in darwinistischer als in lamarckistischer Weise vorstellt. Denn es ist nicht allein die genetische Variation (wie sie in Darwins Gedanken der *natural selection* angenommen wird), sondern auch die vererbbare Anpassung von Umwelteinflüssen – wogegen Darwin sich heftig wandte. Selbst im Falle der Soldaten, Händler und Arbeiter, die von allen Aufstiegsmöglichkeiten ausgeschlossen sind, gilt noch, daß die Nachkommen eines Gleichschenkligen

> … may ultimately rise above his degraded condition. For, after a long series of military successes, or diligent and skilful labours, it is generally found that the more intelligent among the Artisan and Soldier classes manifest a slight increase of their third side or base, and a shrinkage of the two other sides. (*F* 44)

Kommt es zu dem erhofften Seiten-Sprung, d.h. zu einem qualitativen biosozialen Aufstieg, so wird der Sprößling sogleich den natürlichen Eltern entrissen und zur Adoption in der höheren Schicht freigegeben, um dadurch zu verhindern, daß er sich in dem für ihn unangemessenen Milieu zurück-

---

[1] Stewart geht verschiedenen auch hier im folgenden angesprochenen Themenkomplexe Darwinismus und Lamarckismus (vgl. *F* 44 ff.) nach, im Verweis auf die Phrenologie (vgl. *F* 47) läßt er aber die Bedeutung von Francis Galton außer Acht.

entwickle (vgl. *F* 45f.). Generell erscheint es vor diesem Hintergrund, als strebe die Gesellschaft der Flatlander einer totalen Perfektion entgegen.

Doch ist dies durch mehrere natürliche Faktoren eingeschränkt, würde doch sonst innerhalb weniger Generationen die Kluft zwischen den niederen Klassen (Dreiecken) und den höheren Schichten (Vierecke bis Kreise) ins Extreme geführt. Dies jedoch verhindert die Natur selbst:

> ... Nature's law prescribes two antagonistic decrees affecting Circular propagation; first, that as the race climbs higher in the scale of development, so development shall proceed at an accelerated pace; second, that in the same proportion, the race shall become less fertile. Consequently in the home of a Polygon of four or five hundred sides it is rare to find a son; more than one is never seen. (*F* 99 f.)

Der demographische Faktor einer umgekehrt zur Seitenzahl abnehmenden Fortpflanzungsaktivität läßt somit die Evolution innerhalb der 'höheren Kreise' sich verlangsamen bzw. geradezu die Gefahr eines Rückschritts aufkommen: An diese Furcht appelliert auch Charles Darwins Vetter, Francis Galton, in seinen Publikationen, in denen er statistische Methoden anwendete und sie mit phrenologischen Studien in Verbindung brachte. So weist er in seiner Studie *English Men of Science* auf einen suggestiven Zusammenhang von relativer Gesundheit und Fortpflanzungsverhalten hin, für den er nicht seine Umfrage-Daten auswertet, sondern die subjektive Erfahrung seiner Leser aus den höheren Kreisen mit einbezieht:

> I think that ordinary observation corroborates this conclusion ["that there are no children at all in one out of every three" scientific families], and that those of my readers who happen to have mixed much in what is called intellectual society will be able to recall numerous instances of persons of both sexes, but especially of women, possessed of high gifts of every kind, including health and energy, but of less solid vigour than their parents, and who have no children.[1]

Besteht in Abbotts *Flatland* eine relationale Abhängigkeit zwischen Vielseitigkeit und Intellekt, so kann sich das Winkelmaß (und damit der IQ bzw. das soziale Ansehen) unter bestimmten Voraussetzungen auch reduzieren – gleich ob infolge von willentlichem oder unwillentlichem individuellem Versagen: So berichtet Square von einem seiner noch triangulären Vorfahren, der sich aufgrund eines Mißgeschicks von 59°30' auf 58° degradiert sah; ein Qualitätsverlust, der erst nach fünf Generationen egalisiert war (vgl. *F* 61). Die progressive Evolution wird in Flatland folglich von *dissolution* konterkariert; eine Haltung, die auch in der zeitgenössischen

---

[1] Francis Galton, *English Men of Science: Their Nature and Nurture* (London 1874, repr. Bristol/Tokyo, 1998), S. 38.

Biologie und Soziologie, besonders in den Schriften Herbert Spencers,[1] vertreten wurde und in die Degenerationshysterie der Nineties mündete.

Auch bei der Vorstellung einer meßbaren Abhängigkeit von Moral und Intellekt handelt es sich keineswegs um einen merkwürdigen Einfall Abbotts, sondern um den Bezug auf die zeitgenössische Phrenologie, die im Zuge der aufkommenden Psychiatrie und einer angenommenen Korrelation von Gehirnvolumen, Intelligenz und moralischer Kompetenz seit den 1820er Jahren erstmals von Franz Joseph Gall und anderen Forschern in Europa entwickelt worden waren. Mit Hilfe einer 'systematischen' Vermessung des Schädels und seiner Proportionalität zum Körpermaß, aber auch in Abstimmung zu Geschlecht und Rasse bzw. (außerhalb des menschlichen Bereichs) der Gattung wurden Rückschlüsse auf die psychischen und intellektuellen Fähigkeiten des Individuums gezogen. Während Alfred Russel Wallace zwischen Hirn und Bewußtsein, also zwischen Organ und mentaler Fähigkeit unterschied,[2] war Francis Galton, der Begründer der im Dritten Reich so verheerend angewendeten "wissenschaftlichen" Eugenik, um einige Grade forscher. 1883 erhob er die Forderung nach einem anthropometrischen Labor, das ein Jahr später im Londoner South Kensington Museum eingerichtet wurde. Dort suchte er u.a. die "natürliche" intellektuelle Unterlegenheit von Frauen gegenüber Männern nachzuweisen (womit er innerhalb der *scientific community* der Zeit nicht allein stand).[3] Er bestand auf

> ... elaborate state action involving a biographical index and the provision of 'eugenic certificates' to encourage the breeding habits of the intelligent at the expense of those of the feckless and poor.[4]

Im Jahr nach Galtons Vorschlag und im selben Jahr der Ausführung weist Abbott in *Flatland* auf ein solches Labor hin bzw. auf die Existenz eines

---

[1] Vgl. K. Theodore Hoppen: "... evolution did not refer only to the development of species towards 'higher forms', but that the prevalence of unhelpful conditions could and did produce 'dissolution' or a regression towards more primitive species". Siehe K.T.H., *The Mid-Victorian Generation 1846-1886* (Oxford, 1998), S. 477 f.

[2] Vgl. Turner, *Between Science and Religion*, S. 78.

[3] Hoppen, *The Mid-Victorian Generation*, S. 492. – Vgl. dazu Abbott: "For as they [women] have no pretensions to an angle, being inferior in this respect to the very lowest of the Isosceles, they are consequently wholly devoid of brain-power, and have neither reflection, judgement nor forethought, and hardly any memory" (*F* 15). In Wahrheit aber sind Frauen auf Linienstärke gefaltete Parallelogramme (vgl. *F* 140) – und als solche den unregelmäßigen, ebenfalls stigmatisierten Formen zugehörig.

[4] Ibid., S. 486. Vgl. dazu Wolfgang Walter, *Der Geist der Eugenik: Francis Galtons Wissenschaftsreligion in kultursoziologischer Perspektive* (Bielefeld, 1983), S. 116 ff.

biographischen Index (oder Herkunftsnachweis), denn Square erwähnt nicht nur ein "Sanitary and Social Board", sondern erörtert auch der genetische Herkunftsnachweis:

"What need of a certificate"? a Spaceland critic may ask: "Is not the procreation of a Square Son a certificate from Nature herself, proving the Equalsidedness of the Father?" I reply that no Lady of any position will marry an uncertified Triangle. (*F* 45, Fußnote)

Der Evolution wird durch Eingriffe in die Gestaltung der Nachkommenschaft 'nachgeholfen' – nicht nur im Sinne einer therapeutischen Anwendung zur Beseitigung 'natürlicher' Unregelmäßigkeiten. Systematisch betriebene Eugenik findet in *Flatland* weiteren Ausdruck darin, daß Mesalliancen zwischen Angehörigen unterschiedlicher Klassen verhindert werden, und daß vor allem in den höheren Schichten auch riskante physische – und oft tödliche – Manipulationen vorgenommen werden:

Art also [beside Natural progress] steps in to help the process of the higher Evolution. Our physicians have discovered that the small and tender sides of an infant Polygon of the higher class can be fractured, and his whole frame reset, with such exactness that a Polygon of two or three hundred sides sometimes [...] overleaps two or three hundred generations, and as it were doubles at a stroke, the number of his progenitors and the nobility of his descent. (*F* 100)

Der soziale Ehrgeiz, der die Eltern diese (physischen) Eingriffe vornehmen läßt, führt zu einer ethischen Verrohung, die in ihrer Rationalität die Dialektik der Aufklärung deutlich macht: Das Prinzip *natura non facit saltus* ist in Flatland durch künstliche Eingriffe in die Natur außer Kraft gesetzt. Zynisch über die Ungeheuerlichkeit dieser Dinge hinweggehend, fügt Square lakonisch hinzu: "Many a promising child is sacrificed in this way. Scarcely one out of ten survives", sie werden auf der "Neo-Therapeutic Cemetery" verscharrt (vgl. *F* 100). Von diesem Stadium der legislativ abgesicherten, künstlichen Lebens-Formung ist es bis zur pragmatisch kalkulierten, staatlich legitimierten Euthanasie nicht mehr weit:

Not that I should be disposed to recommend (at present) the extreme measures adopted in some States, where an infant whose angles deviates by half a degree from the correct angularity is summarily destroyed at birth. [...] The art of healing also has achieved some of its most glorious triumphs in the compressions, extensions, trepannings, colligations, and other surgical and diaetetic operations by which Irregularities has been partly or wholly cured. Advocating therefore a *Via Media*, I would lay down no fixed or absolute line of demarcation; but at the period when the frame is just beginning to set, and when the Medical Board has reported that recovery is improbable, I would suggest that the Irregular offspring be painlessly and mercifully consumed. (*F* 77 f.)

4. Materialismus oder Idealismus?

Abbott übt in Teil I von *Flatland* harte Kritik an der gesellschaftlichen Struktur und an der einseitig materiellen Wissenschaftsgläubigkeit seiner Zeit. Wegen der in den unterschiedlichen Disziplinen verfügbaren wissenschaftlichen Daten gerieten immaterielle Qualitäten, die das menschliche Zusammenleben gestalten, die philosophisch-religiösen, ethisch-moralischen und existentiellen Grundsätze der viktorianischen Kultur in zunehmende Erklärungsnot. Abbott richtet sich allerdings weniger gegen die materialen Befunde in Biologie und Evolutionslehre als viel mehr gegen ihre materialistische Ausbeutung und technologische Anwendung. Abbott scheint sich insbesondere gegen Autoritäten wie Galton zu wenden, die in ihrem positivistischen, geradezu 'vermessenen' Eifer alle Achtung vor der geistigen Dimension des Individuums verlieren. Einer auf psycho-physische Perfektion ausgerichteten Menschheit ginge alle Humanität abhanden; jeder befände sich in seinem sozialdarwinistischen Daseinskampf.

Man kann an einem fiktionalen, gleichwohl von den seinerzeit diskutierten Streitfragen saturierten Werk wie Abbotts *Flatland* die zeitgenössischen intellektuellen Auseinandersetzungen und den wissenschaftskulturellen Konflikt ablesen, wie er im Europa des 19. Jahrhunderts begann und im 20. Jahrhundert fortgesetzt wurde. Denn *Flatland* erweist sich vor dem bis hier dargelegten Hintergrund als deutliche Stellungnahme gegen einen allzu starken Materialismus und Utilitarismus, wie er im viktorianischen England seitens der oben erwähnten Intellektuellen-Kreise häufig propagiert wurde. Der Kontrast, der zwischen Teil I (als Realität) und Teil II (als Idealität und Norm) aufgebaut wird, ist getragen von der Kritik an einer rein szientifischen, glaubens-entleerten Weltsicht. In ihr wird den Individuen die Fähigkeit zum geistig/geistlichen Denken aberzogen (und damit auch die Fähigkeit zum Staunen). Es ist kein Zufall, wenn Abbott A. Square besonders in Teil I immer wieder auf verschiedene natürliche Gesetzmäßigkeiten ("natural law") eingehen läßt, die als apriorischer Regelbestand vorausgesetzt werden, aber jede Transzendenz ausschließen. Teil II hingegen führt vor, daß es diese Dimensionen gibt, auch wenn sie nicht in Begriffe zu fassen und also nicht kommunikabel sind. Sie sind dennoch nicht nur isolierte Parallelwelten, sondern werden als 'höhere' Wahrheit evident, für die ein Konvertit wie Square, der sich vom Flatland-typischen Denken in Äußerlichkeiten und Oberflächlichkeiten abwendet, ins staatliche Gefängnis geht. Wenn er dort schließlich seine Einsichten als "the offspring of a diseased imagination, or the baseless fabric of a dream" (*F* 197) bewertet und damit dem Wahrheitsgehalt, den er zuvor der spirituellen Erkenntnis zugemessen hatte, abschwört, so begibt er sich überdies ins mentale Diskursgefängnis.

Die Überhöhung natürlicher Gesetzmäßigkeiten, wie sie in Teil I vorgeführt und in Teil II Grundlage für Squares Verurteilung sind, können als Ausdruck des Bedürfnisses nach wissenschaftskonformem diskursiven "Gottesersatz" gedeutet werden, den Abbott anficht. Lance St. John Butler weist auf die Spannungen in den Äußerungen von Agnostikern hin, und er zeigt, wie sich auch bei Evolutionskritikern Entlehnungen aus dem nunmehr als "häretisch" begriffenen Glaubensdiskurs finden lassen:

> The avowedly religious discourse of the Victorians is shot through with the lexicon, the syntax and the imagery of doubt while the avowedly unreligious or antireligious discourse of the period is shot through with metaphysical assumptions, and with vocabulary and imagery that betray the cultural pervasion of religion.[1]

Die zunehmend verinnerlichte, sprachlose religiöse Praxis (die vom Zulauf für unterschiedliche Erweckungskonfessionen begleitet war) veranschaulicht Abbott in Teil II.[2] Er mahnt an, die materialistische Seite des Wissens und der Erkenntnis zu relativieren und statt dessen unter Wahrung der spirituellen Dimensionen die humanistische Qualität gesellschaftlichen Zusammenlebens zu restaurieren. Dies impliziert einen Aufruf zur Rückbesinnung auf Bacons empiristisches Wissenschaftsprogramm. Denn Abbott betrachtet es als eines, das von einem religiösen Impuls gesteuert ist, wie er 1885 unmißverständlich erklärt: "Physical Science, with Bacon, rises to the level of Religion."[3] Doch die Vereinigung beider Weltbilder ist eine Utopie, die in *Flatland* nicht einmal gedacht werden darf und die im viktorianischen England nicht praktikabel ist.

In der polaren Denkweise der alten Debatte um die so genannten "Two Cultures" (C.P. Snow) wäre Abbott wohl als vehementer Verfechter der Geisteswissenschaften zu stilisieren, der absichtlich alle negativen Folgen naturwissenschaftlichen Fortschritts hervorhebt, um die Überlegenheit von humanistischen Wahrheits- und Moral-Kategorien darzulegen. Aber Abbott beansprucht ausgerechnet die formale Grundlage der positivistisch-materi-

---

[1] Vgl. Lance St. John Butler, *Victorian Doubt: Literary and Cultural Discourses* (New York, 1990), S. 7, sowie Levine, "Scientific Discourse", S. 225 passim.

[2] Vgl. Frank Turner, "The Victorian Crisis of Faith and the Faith that was Lost", in: *Victorian Crisis in Faith*, ed. Helmstadter/Lightman, S. 9-38, S. 13 f.

[3] Abbott, *Francis Bacon*, S. 410.

alistischen Erfahrungswissenschaften, nämlich die Leitsprache "Mathematik", für die idealistischen Erkenntniswissenschaften. Er spricht ihr dort eine höhere Fähigkeit in erklärenden, sinnstiftenden Anwendungen des Kontinuitätsprinzips zu als der Biologie, die – als naturwissenschaftliche Leitdisziplin jener Zeit – sie allenfalls zur Hilfswissenschaft degradiert. Seiner Ansicht nach bietet die epistemologisch gewendete Mathematik mit ihrer bis in theologische Bereiche hineinragende Offenheit für die Deduktion, anders als die rein empiristisch-induktiven Methoden, die Möglichkeit, den Weg für eine transzendentale Erkenntnis und subjektive Wahrheitsfindung frei zu halten: Er projiziert seine eigene Wissenschaftsphilosophie auf Bacons Erkenntnisprogramm und reklamiert den ersten Empiristen als Apostel für imaginative Erkenntnis und die in seiner Nachfolge entwickelte formale Wissenschaftssprache als Medium. Abbott schließt: "The study of Physical Science [...] can hardly be described as vulgarly utilitarian or as ministering the merely material wants of men."[1]

Das Dilemma, vor das Abbott sowohl seinen verunsicherten Protagonisten aus *Flatland* als auch seinen Leser stellt, lautet, entweder die Ziele Bacons als unbedingten Perfektionsdrang mit einem als 'notwendig' propagierten *telos* zu mißverstehen, oder sich als neuplatonischer Idealist in ein gesellschaftliches Martyrium zu begeben. So betrachtet, birgt Abbotts (und das viktorianische) Dilemma die seither periodisch wiederkehrende wissenschaftskulturelle und -ethische Quadratur des Kreises, an der später die Figuren in Aldous Huxleys unvereinbaren Alternativwelten "Brave New World" und "Malpais" zerbrechen.[2]

---

[1] Ibid., S. 411.

[2] Sowohl Abbott (im Motto für Teil II von *Flatland*) als auch T.H. Huxleys Enkel (im Titel seines anti-utopischen Roman) stellen einen intertextuellen Bezug zu den Zeilen "O brave new worlds, / That have such people in 't" in Shakespeares *The Tempest* her. Das Dilemma, wie es sich in der scheinbar unausweichlichen Entscheidung zwischen wissenschaftsfeindlichem Humanismus und inhumanen Naturwissenschaften während des Viktorianismus abzeichnete, scheint seither noch gravierender geworden zu sein. C.P. Snows *Rede-Lecture* von 1959 und die sich daran entzündende Debatte um die "two cultures" in den 1960er und 1970er Jahren hob diese Fragen auf eine bildungspolitische Ebene. Mit den "science wars" – im Anschluß an Polemiken wie Paul R. Gross' und Norman Levitts *Higher Superstition* (Baltimore, MD, 1994) und Alan Sokals "Hoax", vgl. *Social Text*, 46/47 (1996), S. 217-252 – wurde in den 1990er Jahren ein vorläufiger Tiefpunkt in diesem nunmehr institutionalisierten Streit der Fakultäten erreicht.

The Pleasures of Men and the Subjection of Women

By *Michael Meyer* (Bamberg)

Debating the question as to whether women should be slaves to men's pleasure or equal companions[1], the Victorians took recourse to religious, moral, biological, economic, legal and political arguments. I will trace the major arguments for and against equality and will point out contradictions within the propositions against women's emancipation. The Victorian constructions of women had an enormous impact on the segregation of education and discrimination at work. However, working women in turn challenged the position of men in terms of performance, earnings, and masculinity. I will take a wider perspective of the Victorian age or rather of the 19th century from 1789-1918 because it is necessary to see the Victorian negotiation of gender as a transition between the containment of radical demands for women's emancipation in the late 18th century and the achievement of their national franchise in the 20th century. It is difficult to see women's history as a steady stream of progress because huge rocks of resistance to emancipation from both men and women of all classes rather suggest the image of a meandering river that has not yet reached its destination.

1. The "Failure" of Feminism

The restrictive construction of women's nature and position in the 19th century began with the end of feminism in the late 18th century. The figurehead of feminism, Mary Wollstonecraft, earned a negative reputation after the public learned that she had had an illegitimate child and had made an attempt to commit suicide. Her reputation impeded the influence of her work, and the conservative crackdown on radicals in the 1790s damped down women's fervour to clamour for emancipation. The times became less propitious for an advancement of women's rights.

In the context of the French Revolution and its conservative reaction in Great Britain, Mary Wollstonecraft claimed civil rights for women and

---

[1] Vera Nünning analyses the negotiation of gender that prefigures the Victorian discussions in: "'The slaves of our pleasures' oder 'our companions and equals'? Die Konstruktion von Weiblichkeit im England des 18. Jahrhunderts aus kulturwissenschaftlicher Sicht", *ZAA*, 44 (1996), 199-219.

criticized the fact that patriarchal rule reduced women to slaves because it denied them liberty, equality, and justice. Wollstonecraft seemed to confirm male prejudices about women as the weaker sex, but she denied the argument of innate inferiority because she attributed women's degradation to their repression by men. She regarded women's bondage to their bodies as a key impediment to emancipation. She conceded that men were naturally superior in physical strength, which justified the subordination of the female to the male in the animal world.[1] In spite of the subordination of bodily power to moral and mental power in civilized societies, men tended to ignore women's minds and to consider women primarily as bodily subjects. She added that a woman is made a slave to her body because male sensuality reduced her value to arbitrary and short-lived physical beauty.[2] Since marriage was the only way to rise in society, women turned themselves into "insignificant objects of desire"[3] in order to attract prospective husbands and so acquire their social status. A married woman, the feminist deplored, forfeited her status as a legal person under the law of coverture and "is reduced to a mere cipher".[4] Blackstone's *Commentaries on the Laws of England*, the lawyers' Bible in the 18th and 19th centuries, stipulated that man and wife were "one person in law", but that person was the man, because "the very being or legal existence of the woman is suspended during the marriage, or at least is incorporated or consolidated into that of her husband".[5] The law limited not only married women's management of their property, but almost turned wives into their husbands' private properties since it deprived them of their status as independent legal subjects. Wollstonecraft attacked marriage as an absolute male rule, which turned women into slaves, who were submissive or obtained power by cunning like children or favourites.[6] She demanded the liberation of women from male domination "in a physical, moral, and civil sense".[7] Instead of being kept in the state of "perpetual childhood"[8], women should become "rational creatures", "moral agents", and "free citizens".[9] Reason and judgement should be their guides to virtuous behaviour and replace coercion, which

---

[1] Mary Wollstonecraft, *A Vindication of the Rights of Woman*, ed. Janet Todd and Marilyn Butler, The Works of Mary Wollstonecraft, 5 (London, 1989), pp. 74, p. 108.

[2] Ibid., pp. 113, 115, 208.

[3] Ibid., p. 76.

[4] Ibid., p. 215.

[5] Robin Gilmour, *The Victorian Period. The Intellectual and Cultural Context of English Literature 1830-1890* (Harlow, 1993), p. 189.

[6] Mary Wollstonecraft, *Vindication*, pp. 77, 215, 226.

[7] Ibid., p. 266.

[8] Ibid., p. 75.

[9] Ibid., p. 250.

merely enforced the slavish fulfilment of duties. She considered moral and intellectual education as a prime instrument in order to improve women's characters and functions in the private and the public spheres. The feminist demanded a "revolution in female manners [...] to restore to them their lost dignity – and make them, as a part of the human species, labour by re-forming themselves to reform the world".[1] She considered the end of women's liberation as nothing less than the "progress of knowledge and virtue"[2] of mankind.

2. Backlash: Restrictive Constructions of Women

The early Victorian era between 1830 and 1848 has been called the period of reform or even a part of *The Age of Revolution* 1798-1848 by Eric Hobsbawm, who conceded that the institutional reforms lagged far behind the economic, technical and social changes.[3] If we take the position of women into consideration, Hobsbawm's suggestion of progress rather appears to be ironic because the first half of the 19th century saw the growing restriction of women's roles to domestic life and to the support of, and dependence on, men. Women took an active part in collective protests and strikes but could hardly advance their own position with regard to men within their class.[4] Central Victorian *discourses* continued and extended 18th-century arguments which narrowed down the range of women's capacities and activities: in spite of the egalitarian Protestant tradition that held

---

[1] Ibid., p. 114.

[2] Ibid., p. 66.

[3] Eric Hobsbawm, *The Age of Revolution, 1789-1848* (New York, 1996), p. 303.

[4] Karl Ittmann, *Work, Gender and Family in Victorian England* (Houndmills, 1995), p. 144. For example, women were active in the abolition of slavery and in the Chartist movement. Clare Midgley demonstrates that sentimentalism, economic and political action went hand in hand as abolitionist women boycotted West Indian sugar and handed in numerous petitions to Parliament (*Women against Slavery. The British Campaigns, 1780-1870* [London and New York, 1992], pp. 1-120). Moira Ferguson and Clare Midgley explain that the women's struggle against the slave trade and slavery negotiated gender positions at home and indirectly advanced their own emancipation (Moira Ferguson, *Subject to Others. British Women Writers and Colonial Slavery, 1670-1834* (New York, 1992), p. 299; Clare Midgley, *Women against Slavery*, pp. 202-203). Still, women who raised their voice in public had to face opposition. As late as 1872, a minister felt obliged to assure the public audience that the female speaker for suffrage was a respectable character (Lilias Ashworth, quoted in Patricia Hollis, *Women in Public, 1850-1900. Documents of the Victorian Women's Movement* [London, 1979], p. 7).

each individual responsible and accountable for his or her life in the eyes of God, *religious authorities* maintained that God designed woman to be man's helpmate.[1] If Christian meekness, charity, and compassion were thought to be predominantly female characteristics, Victorians increasingly foregrounded Christ's manliness and muscular Christianity, shifting moral esteem from women to men.[2] In 18th-century *biology and medicine*, the one-sex model, which assumed the basic similarity between men and women, was dismissed in favour of the two-sex model, which established the basic opposition and hierarchy between the sexes. Differences in physical gender were extended to psychological ones as women were held to be physically weaker than men, and more emotional, intuitive, and passive.[3] Phrenology and physiology suggested that women's smaller brains implied less intelligence and reason. Theories about the evolution of the human, or rather the English, race stipulated that survival and progress depended upon reproduction and education that required women's presence as wives and mothers at home. Domestic family life formed the core of society.[4] Conservative voices in *society and politics* maintained that the family was a microcosm of the commonwealth that must be headed by a patriarch, and any questioning of his authority or the hierarchy within the family had repercussions on the order and stability of the nation. (A woman as the head of state was not accepted as a counterargument because, after all, Queen Victoria had a husband to give advice to her.) The *law* codified the hierarchy between men and women. The First Reform Bill of 1832 extended the franchise to propertied male adults but excluded women who might be eligible due to their possession. The law of coverture, already criticized by Mary Wollstonecraft, still disempowered women. Frances Cobbe voiced her discontent with the legal degradation of women in an apt series of subjects excluded from equality: "'Criminals, Idiots, Women, and Minors' are the classes of people considered unfit for most legal and political rights at the time".[5] In addition, women did not necessarily have the moral right to paid work even if they saw the necessity to work for money. The sphere of *production* was supposed to be reserved for men, the sphere of reproduction for women. Women were thought to be guided by the morality of social

---

[1] J. Burgon, quoted in Patricia Hollis, *Women in Public, 1850-1900. Documents of the Victorian Women's Movement* (London, 1979), p. 8.

[2] Ina Schabert, *Englische Literaturgeschichte. Eine neue Darstellung aus der Sicht der Geschlechterforschung* (Stuttgart, 1997), p. 550.

[3] Ibid., pp. 40-42.

[4] Karl Ittmann, *Work, Gender and Family in Victorian England* (Houndmills, 1995), p. 142.

[5] Quoted in Robin Gilmour, *The Victorian Period*, p. 189.

relations in the household as a necessary counterbalance to the self-interest that drove men in the competitive economic market.[1] Female compassion and charity should compensate for the economic aggression and exploitation by middle-class men.[2] Due to a change from the middle-class family as an economic co-operative unit, in which everyone contributed to the family income, towards individual wage-earning, professional life became increasingly segregated from family life in the 18th century[3], and women were compelled "to consider marriage, not as a question of happiness, but of subsistence"[4] in spite of romantic ideals of marriage. An article in the *Saturday Review* of 12 November 1859 warned that women's economic independence would ultimately ruin the commonwealth:

> the greatest of social and political duties is to encourage marriage. The interest of the State is to get as many of its citizens married as possible. [...] Wherever women are self-supporters, marriage is, *ipso facto*, discouraged. The factory population is proof of this. In the manufacturing districts women make worse wives and worse helpmates than where they are altogether dependent on the man. And where there are fewer marriages there is more vice ...[5]

The writer continued that paid work tempted women to abandon the family and neglect the more tedious and unpaid domestic chores. So the needs of men to be served by women were as important as the social control of women according to this view of economics and society. Having identified key arguments in important Victorian discourses concerning gender, we proceed with the discussion of difficulties and contradictions in famous texts on gender by Sarah Ellis in the 1830s and 1840s, and by John Ruskin and Eliza Linton in the 1860s and 1880s.

Sarah Ellis was one of the most famous writers on women in spite of or because of her negative bias towards her sex. According to her, woman's nature was determined by the love of self-indulgence, vanity, indolence, a multiplicity of floating ideas, and the "constant overflow of her feelings"[6], which made women deviate from reason and propriety. Society did not

---

[1] Katrina Honeyman, *Women, Gender, and Industrialisation in England, 1700-1870* (Houndmills, 2000), p. 102.
[2] Ina Schabert, *Englische Literaturgeschichte*, p. 56.
[3] Ibid., p. 45.
[4] Maria Grey and Emily Shireff (1872), quoted in Patricia Hollis, *Women in Public*, p. 13.
[5] Quoted in Patricia Hollis, *Women in Public*, p. 11.
[6] Sarah S. Ellis, *The Women of England. Their Social Duties, and Domestic Habits* (London, 1839), p. 287, cf. p. 45.

need fashionable ladies but useful women at home.[1] Women had to subdue
their natural propensities in order to fulfil their central function in society
to promote others' happiness and morals, and to serve as "interesting and
instructive companions to men".[2] The essential qualities required from
women aimed at their secondary and domestic existence in their relationship to men. Her popular work *The Daughters of England* (1842) told
young women that

> the first thing of importance is to be content to be inferior to men – inferior in
> mental power, in the same proportion that you are inferior in bodily strength. [...]
> For a man it is absolutely necessary that he should sacrifice the poetry of his na-
> ture for the realities of material and animal existence; for women there is no ex-
> cuse – for women, whose whole life from the cradle to the grave is one of feeling
> rather than action; whose highest duty is so often to suffer and be still; whose
> deepest enjoyments are all relative; who has nothing, and is nothing, of herself;
> whose experience, if unparticipated, is a total blank. [...] Love is women's all –
> her wealth, her power, her very being.[3]

Her arguments of natural inequality fly in the face of Mary Wollstonecraft,
who rejected any inference from the physical inferiority of women to any
other characteristic or position of women. Sarah Ellis's statement that
women had "no excuse" to tamper with the material and animal existence
of reality seemed to qualify her embellishment of men's work as a "sacrifice" and ignored the vast majority of her sex, who had no excuse not to
feed their babies, wash their nappies, to scour the floors at home or as a
maid-of-all-work at other households. Victorian sources on social and
working conditions of the poor suggested that a middle-class man's sacrifice of "the poetry of his nature" could have led to the reckless exploitation
of workers due to starvation wages and the literal sacrifice of their lives for
his profit. But Ellis had the morals of middle-class husbands rather than the
lives of lower-class workers in mind when she complained that men are
exposed to "evils of competition"[4] and suffer from "degrading cares and
sordid views that occupy the working world"[5], as she told *The Women of
England*. Ellis saw no contradiction in her view that, for a gentleman, almost any degrading occupation was acceptable as long as it procured him
the means to support a "respectable establishment at home".[6] She even

---

[1] Ibid., p. 11.
[2] Ibid., p. 352.
[3] Quoted in Patricia Hollis, *Women in Public*, p. 16.
[4] Sarah S. Ellis, *The Women of England*, p. 255.
[5] Ibid., p. 340.
[6] Ibid., p. 345.

argued that women should help men to keep "a separate soul for his family, his social duty, and his God".[1] Women had to "assist in redeeming the character of English *men* from the mere animal, or rather, the mere mechanical state"[2], which the capitalist economy seemed to reduce them to. Implicitly, the hypocritical writer justified men's amoral behaviour towards others in business by the comfort and esteem provided for his own family. In turn, wives at home became the healing source for their corrupted and contaminated husbands. Women's corrective function was restricted to the moral supervision of the status quo rather than socio-economic reform because women were to support society and the commonwealth by serving as "the minor wheels and secret springs of the great machine of human life".[3] Sarah Ellis reversed the feminist evaluation of the gendered spheres as she attributed to women contradictory positions at the visible periphery of alienating public or professional life and at the invisible center of authentic life in the private homes of families, in which human beings came into their own.

In his popular lecture "Of Queen's Gardens", published as a part of "Sesame and Lilies" in 1865, John Ruskin did not share Sarah Ellis's annihilation of women's natures as ciphers apart from men but stressed that man and woman complement each other in an ideal way: "We are foolish, and without excuse foolish, in speaking of the 'superiority' of one sex to the other, as if they could be compared in similar things. Each has what the other has not; each completes the other, and is completed by the other."[4] However, the promise of equality was undermined by implicit value judgements in Ruskin's concept that harked back to the chivalrous medieval age:

> The man's power is active, progressive, defensive. He is eminently the doer, the creator, the discoverer, the defender. His intellect is for speculation and invention; his energy for adventure, for war and for conquest. [...] But the woman's power is for rule, not for battle and her intellect is not for invention or recreation, but sweet ordering, arrangement, and decision. She sees the quality of things, their claims, and their places. Her great function is praise; she enters into no contest, but infallibly adjudges the crown of contest. By her office and her place, she is protected from all danger and temptation. The man, in his rough work in the open world, must encounter all peril and trial – to him therefore must be the failure, the of-

---

[1] Ibid., p. 58.
[2] Ibid., p. 343.
[3] Ibid., p. 106.
[4] John Ruskin, "Sesame and Lilies", in: *The Works of John Ruskin*, ed. E.T. Cook and Alexander Wedderburn, Library Edition, 18 (London, 1905), p. 121.

fence, the inevitable error; often he must be wounded or subdued, often misled, and always hardened.[1]

Ruskin's pathos about wounded and hardened heroes bordered on the ridiculous as it suggested epic dimensions in male life, which according to Ellis had lost its poetic qualities in capitalist competition. We may assume that, returning from the daily fight with the dragon of capitalist forces, our Victorian hero found shelter from the hostile world in the sacred temple of the hearth. Ruskin may have had Queen Victoria in mind when he attributed rule and order to women, but at second glance, Ruskin's generous attribution of power to "ordinary" women looks far less attractive because they were to sympathize with and praise men but should not ask for any reward for themselves: women may award the crown to men but must not share their throne. For their domestic offices and their role as man's helpmate, women did not need extensive knowledge or elaborate education because, after all, they should not be turned into dictionaries and lose their charm of sweet, childish beauty.[2] Ruskin's idea of mutual dependency did not eliminate hierarchy: the husband should be obediently devoted to his wife, but the loving wife was truly subordinate to her husband.

Not only old-fashioned arguments looking back to some golden age, but also modern statements referring to the theory of social evolution served to restrict women's claim to emancipation. Eliza Linton managed to define ideal "Womanliness" (1883) in terms of the natural function of motherhood while denying its animal nature and "natural" or undisciplined qualities in women:

> She knows that part of her natural mission is to please and be charming. [...] She knows that she was designed by the needs of the race and the law of nature to be a mother. [...] She has no newfangled notions about the animal character of motherhood, nor about the degrading character of housekeeping. On the contrary, she thinks a populous and happy nursery one of the greatest blessings of her state; and she puts her pride in the perfect ordering, the exquisite arrangements, the comfort, thoughtfulness and beauty of her house. [...] She has taken it to heart that patience, self-sacrifice, tenderness, quietness, with some others, of which modesty is one, are the virtues more especially feminine; just as courage, justice, fortitude, and the like, belong to men. Passionate ambition, virile energy, the love of strong excitement, self-assertion, fierceness, an undisciplined temper, are all qualities which detract from her ideal of womanliness, and which make her less beautiful than she was meant to be.[3]

---

[1] Ibid., pp. 121-122.
[2] Ibid., pp. 122-128.
[3] Quoted in Patricia Hollis, *Women in Public*, p. 20.

Linton conceded that women may have strong passions but maintained that they should not indulge their feelings for the sake of beauty, expressed in the wife's meek subordination to, and devoted reverence of, her husband. June Purvis sums up the conservative construction of gender: "femininity became identified with domesticity, service to others, subordination and weakness while masculinity was associated with life in the competitive world of paid work, strength and domination".[1] In the eyes of most conservative Victorians, the domestic function of women as wives and homemakers required little education. "Married life is woman's profession; and to this life her training – that of dependence – is modelled. Of course by not getting a husband, of losing him, she may find that she is without resources. All that can be said of her is, she has failed in business; and no social reform can prevent such failures."[2]

In order to make women eligible for marriage, education had to be specified according to the categories of the "good woman", who worked for her own family and/or as a servant for other families, and the "perfect lady", the devoted wife and mother who created a decorative, loving and morally uplifting home.[3] Working-class education for most girls usually began and ended at home. Until 1851, only about 10 per cent of them had any formal schooling, and women who took care of children while their mothers were at work usually taught them the basics of reading, sewing and knitting, sometimes writing and arithmetic. The British and Foreign Society and the much more powerful Church of England National Society ran about two thirds of all schools which provided elementary education. The Sunday schools offered part-time education, which for almost half the children of the poor was the only education in reading, sometimes spelling and writing, and usually included religious teaching, that aimed at the moral formation and submission of the lower classes. In contrast to lower-class girls, who were taught very basic practical skills, middle-class girls whose parents could afford better schools learned about "ornamental knowledge that might attract and impress a suitor".[4] The emphasis was definitely not put on intellectual skills and knowledge but on "accomplishments", such as singing, dancing, playing the piano, drawing or painting, a smattering of languages, the art of pleasing conversation and deportment, and above all the

---

[1] June Purvis, *A History of Women's Education in England*, Gender and Education Series (Milton Keynes and Philadelphia, 1991), p. 4.

[2] *Saturday Review*, 12 November 1859, quoted in Patricia Hollis, *Women in Public*, p. 11.

[3] I am indebted to June Purvis, *Women's Education* (pp. 5-8, 12-21, 53, 64-71) for most of the subsequent information on education.

[4] June Purvis, *A History of Women's Education*, p. 64.

moulding of submissive characters to attract men in order to become a genteel *"ladylike wife and mother"*.[1] In the rather permissive 1860s, ladies went great lengths in order to provoke men's interest. At a time when it was considered to be indecent to wear loose pantaloons, it was acceptable to expose the shoulders and even the breasts to the male gaze at fashionable balls, which reminded the eye-witness Arthur Munby of "how thoroughly conventional, in such matters, is modesty".[2] Needless to say, education by parents, governesses or tutors, by small private day schools or boarding schools usually did not qualify women for highly skilled work. I will turn to reforms concerning women in the second half of the 19th century before I present how women at work shaped the negotiation of gender.

3. Reforms: The Struggle for Emancipation

In the second half of the 19th century, the conflict over gender roles sharpened. The "woman question" became the topic of the day in the 1860s, re-negotiating women's nature, proper sphere, education, and work. Resistance to emancipation was voiced by many, including Queen Victoria, who wrote in a letter of 29 May 1870 that she was

> anxious to enlist every one who can speak or write to join in checking this mad, wicked folly of 'Women's Rights', with all its attendant horrors, on which her poor feeble sex is bent, forgetting every sense of womanly feeling and propriety. [...] God created men and women different – then let them remain each in their own position.[3]

Of course, Queen Victoria's position as the head of state contradicted the ideology of the segregated spheres, which she endorsed in that letter. In reverse, Florence Nightingale, who appeared to Victorians as the ideal mythic "English Sister of Charity, the self-denying caretaker – a mother, a saint, or even a female Christ"[4], chafed about conservative restrictions of women and precepts of the homely housewife in a text that remained unpublished during her life-time, "Cassandra". Full of sarcasm, Nightingale

---

[1] Ibid., p. 65.

[2] Quoted in Michael Hiley, *Victorian Working Women: Portraits from Life* (London, 1979), p. 39.

[3] Quoted in Jan Marsh, "Votes for Women and Chastity for Men: Gender, Health, Medicine and Sexuality", in: *The Victorian Vision. Inventing New Britain*, V&A Publications, ed. John M. MacKenzie (London, 2001), p. 98.

[4] Mary Poovey, *Uneven Developments. The Ideological Work of Gender in Mid-Victorian England* (Chicago, 1988), p. 167.

condemned those of her own sex, alluding to Sarah Ellis, who told women that "trifles make the sum of human things"[1], and who praised domesticity as a tabernacle that was too sacred for sons and daughters, not to speak of sleeping husbands. She asked: "Why have women passion, intellect, moral activity – these three – and a place in society where no one of the three can be exercised?"[2] A job, she claimed, was a liberation from tedious domestic duties that encroached upon women's time, which was thus rendered value-less: "Women often long to enter some man's profession where they would find direction, competition (or rather opportunity of measuring the intellect with others), and, above all, time."[3] She complained that only "Widow-hood, ill-health, or want of bread, these three explanations or excuses are supposed to justify a woman in taking up an occupation."[4] Most of all, she resented that most women took marriage to be a sacrifice of all other things:

> That man and woman have an equality of duties and rights is accepted by woman even less than by man. Behind *his* destiny woman must annihilate herself, must be only his complement. A woman dedicates herself to the vocation of her husband; she fills up and performs the subordinate parts in it. But if she has any destiny, any vocation of her own, she must renounce it, in nine cases out of ten.[5]

Ironically, Florence Nightingale did not think that the time was right for the immediate publication of her trumpet call for women's role in public life at present: "The time is come when women must do something more than the 'domestic hearth'".[6]

Women found an important ally in John Stuart Mill, who wrote *The Sub-jection of Women* in collaboration with his stepdaughter Helen Taylor in 1861, but who also postponed its publication in order to wait for a more promising situation (1869). Mill summarized the issues of the woman question and demanded the full emancipation of women. He reiterated and expanded Mary Wollstonecraft's feminist arguments about 70 years after the publication of *A Vindication of the Rights of Woman* (1792), and met with similar scorn and defiance as his famous predecessor. John Stuart Mill was aware that his rational views of women would outrage his Victorian

---

[1] Florence Nightingale, "Cassandra", in: *Cassandra and other Selections from Suggestions for Thought*, ed. Mary Poovey (London, 1991), p. 229; cf. Sarah S. Ellis, *The Women of England*, p. 279.

[2] Ibid., p. 205.

[3] Ibid., p. 210.

[4] Ibid., p. 212.

[5] Ibid., p. 219.

[6] Ibid., p. 229.

contemporaries because he attacked "almost universal opinion".[1] The reviews of his essay were devastating, and he was even accused of immorality and madness.[2] What offended his contemporaries? Mill (1) fundamentally questioned that there were "natural" differences between the sexes, and (2) sharply criticized its consequences, such as women's *discrimination in education*, their *legal subordination* to men, especially in marriage, and their *political disenfranchisement*.

(1) Mill undermined the basis of the gendered power structure in Victorian society, the assumption that women were by nature different from, and inferior to, men. He argued that the concept of a God-given inferior nature was an ideological construction that had served masters of all historical periods to justify injustice and legitimize their own privileges. He said that the circumstances women suffered from distorted their characters to such an extent that their nature, if there was any, was nowhere visible and discernible: "What is now called the nature of woman is an eminently artificial thing – the result of forced repression in some directions, unnatural stimulation in others."[3]

(2) He criticized the fact that women's *education* lead to the enslavement of their minds and hearts:

> Men do not want solely the obedience of women, they want their sentiments. All men, except the most brutish, desire to have, in the women most nearly connected with them, not a forced slave but a willing one; not a slave merely, but a favourite. They have therefore put everything in practice to enslave their minds. [...] All the moralities tell them that it is the duty of women, and all the current sentimentalities that it is their nature, to live for others; to make complete abnegation of themselves, and to have no life but in their affections.[4]

Mill's attack on the Victorian sacred home and marriage as a site of domestic slavery, which reduced women to bondservants of despotic patriarchs[5], provoked those Victorians who maintained that benevolent husbands and fathers created a safe haven for their angels at home. He exposed the ideology of the self-less woman and her subordinate role as an old trick that led to male privilege and power. He revealed the contradiction between the ideal of the moral guidance of men by women and their expected sub-

---

[1] John Stuart Mill, *The Subjection of Women*, in: *On Liberty and Other Essays*, ed. with an introd. by John Gray (Oxford, 1991), p. 472.

[2] Kate Millet, "The Debate over Women: Ruskin vs. Mill", in: *Suffer and Be Still: Women in the Victorian Age*, ed. Martha Vicinus (Bloomington, 1972), p. 124.

[3] John Stuart Mill, *The Subjection of* Women, p. 493.

[4] Ibid., p. 486.

[5] Ibid., p. 503.

mission to men. Although Mill polemically remarked that women who read and write "are, in the existing constitution of things, a contradiction and a disturbing element"[1], formal education was advanced in the second half of the 19th century.

Educational reforms improved the basic skills of the masses but remained gendered, as it aimed at providing women's unpaid services within the family, raising healthy children and sustaining husbands for the sustenance of the skilled male labour force and the benefit of the nation.[2] In 1870, the Elementary Education Act stipulated schooling for all children but attendance between the ages of five and ten was made compulsory only in 1880. Gradually, evening schools added the instruction of domestic or vocational skills to elementary education. Scholarships for secondary and vocational schools were gender-biased: boys were to attend trade schools or junior technical schools, girls rather to go to domestic economy and domestic service schools. The Education Department gave grants to schools in 1878, demanding that girls be taught domestic economy, added grants in 1882 for the teaching of cooking and, in 1890, for laundry work; "the 'new' subjects should involve the learning of useful, practical skills *and* character training"[3], which meant discipline, cleanliness, carefulness, and order, to turn women not only into good housewives but "Home Managers" or even "Home Geniuses" according to *Longman's Domestic Economy Readers* in 1896.[4] Working men's and working women's colleges run in co-operation between the lower and middle classes added humanitarian education to that of basic skills offered by mechanics' institutes. Even if the Working Women's College founded in Queen's Street, London, in 1864, promoted the necessity of knowledge for women, it aimed rather at better domestic service than social mobility.

Middle-class girls had better opportunities to receive a good education, albeit with a gender bias. 1850 saw the foundation of the North London Collegiate School, which provided religious and liberal education to daughters of gentlemen in order to turn them into useful modern mothers, accomplished ladies, and philanthropic citizens. That institution formed the model for secondary schools for girls, which were established increasingly after the Endowed School Act of 1869, and which introduced mathematics and natural sciences but in general offered little or no vocational training, such as shorthand, typing, and book-keeping. Universities did not hurry to

---

[1] Ibid., p. 501.
[2] The subsequent information on education is based on June Purvis, *A History of Women's Education*, pp. 15-54, 77-83, and 109-120.
[3] Ibid., p. 26.
[4] Ibid., p. 27.

admit women. University extension classes began in 1867 upon the initiative of middle-class women, who invited a Cambridge professor for a series of lectures outside the institution. The fact that some universities accepted women for degree courses, such as London University in 1878, Victoria University in 1880, and the University of Durham in 1895, does not necessarily mean that they were on an equal footing with their male peers. Newnham College at Cambridge University provided a separate and different education for women, whereas Girton College at Cambridge offered the same education and examinations to female and male students with a decisive difference: in 1881, Cambridge University allowed women to take examinations but did not award them degrees. At Oxford University, women had to wait until 1919 to receive the same degrees as men, and at Cambridge until the middle of the 20th century. After all, a degree would officially recognize a woman's high quality of education, which, according to Sarah Sewell in 1868, was detrimental to her ordinary work:

> profoundly educated women rarely make good wives or mothers. The pride of knowledge does not amalgamate well with the every-day matter of fact rearing of children, and women who have stored their minds with Latin and Greek seldom have much knowledge of pies and puddings, nor do they enjoy the hard and uninteresting work of attending to the wants of little children.[1]

Unfortunately, the educational efforts of women did not lead to substantial progress in the job market. Lower-class women were better qualified for lower-class work, and middle-class women had better professional opportunities in teaching and in national bureaucracy at the beginning of the 20th century but had not been able to enter male professions in large numbers. However, the position of married women gradually improved due to legal reforms.

John Stuart Mill touched on a sensitive spot as he criticized the legal bondage of wives to husbands and their inability to escape sexual coercion since the law handed women over to men as "their thing, to be used at their pleasure"[2], and he demanded more legal reforms in the 1860s. If we consider that married women were not assumed to be legal subjects because the married couple was one person in law under the head of the husband, and that married women's property belonged to their husbands in common law, the legal reforms were large steps ahead but stopped short of women's equality. In 1857, the Matrimonial Causes Act established a civil divorce court in London and stipulated that wives could sue for divorce provided

---

[1] Quoted in June Purvis, *A History of Women's Education*, pp. 111-112.
[2] John Stuart Mill, *The Subjection of Women*, p. 508.

that they could prove two of three charges: cruelty, desertion, adultery – husbands, however, had only to prove one charge in order to obtain a divorce. The Matrimonial Causes Act of 1878 allowed for divorce for cruelty as a single offence and granted women the right to claim maintenance and the custody of children. In 1870, the Married Women's Property Act entitled women to 200 pounds of their own earnings but initiated more improvements concerning women's control of their possessions upon marriage. The act was extended in 1884 to ensure that married women had the same right to manage their own property as unmarried women. Wealthy fathers, however, had always been able to arrange marriage settlements for daughters, which established by contract the wife's control over her separate property. Still, wives had no reciprocal claim to the property of their husbands, which is significant since many a wife became the unpaid domestic servant to her husband if he was the only provider of an income. The denial of suffrage to women may have been a serious impediment to progress since it definitely curbed their influence on politics and therefore on the legislative body responsible for reform acts.

In the Victorian mid-sixties, the increasing demands for the female right to vote in national elections polarized the electorate. John Stuart Mill insisted on women's perfect equality and demanded their right to vote as a matter of justice beyond any allegations of inferior female faculties but his amendment to the Second Reform Bill in 1867 in order to extend the franchise to women was rejected in Parliament.[1] The opponents of female suffrage brought forth a series of mutually exclusive and contradictory arguments. Some maintained that women's fickle emotional and biological nature violated the necessity of a reliable electorate, others argued that suffrage would draw women into corruption and turmoil at elections, a fact that clearly speaks for an unreliable male electorate and, what is worse, corrupt political candidates. Women would not need franchise because they were represented by their husbands, but the implied unanimousness of husband and wife was destroyed by the argument that separate votes would spark quarrels between husband and wife. Radicals and liberals were afraid that women would vote for conservatives under the influence of clergymen, forgetting that women clamoured for progress by social and legal reforms. The arguments for female suffrage were based on the claim of women's equality to men, the need of a voice of their own because their husbands might not represent their wives' views and interests, and the necessity to have a say in politics since politics interfered with women's lives. Even if women gained opportunities to exert influence on local boards and elec-

---

[1] Ibid., pp. 526-527.

tions for county borough councils, resistance to their national franchise was too strong among Victorians. If suffragettes fought for legal reforms of the franchise, working women experienced legal bills relating to working conditions as a mixed blessing because laws that protected women from particular forms of work also reduced their competitiveness. Whereas restrictive constructions of women and the consequent lack of vocational training had a negative impact on women's opportunities and positions at work, their practical performance in particular jobs implicitly undermined gender constructions and challenged male authorities in the capitalist market.

4. Women's Work and Working Women's Challenge of Gender Constructions

Many women suffered from the obvious contradiction between the middle-class ideal of segregated spheres and the necessity for most women of the lower and the middle classes to make a living without having been qualified for it. The problem was particularly acute for the so-called redundant or surplus women, spinsters and widows.[1] The numbers of women exceeded that of men by half a million in the mid-19th century, and by one million at the end of the century, so that "ten to twenty percent of all adult women remained permanently unmarried".[2] In spite of the fact that the marriage bar meant the end to paid work for those women whose husbands earned a family wage, the majority of women had to work both at home and outside the home, which was particularly difficult for mothers: "for those with dependents, the choice was often restricted to part-time, poorly paid, home-based work that might be fitted around domestic duties".[3] Poor women's little monetary income was also "supplemented by non-wage earnings"[4], the preparation of food, the keeping of livestock, or the cultivation of kitchen crops.

Most of the women who had to work went into domestic service. In 1851, about 10% or 750,000 of the female population worked as domestic servants, doing the household chores for their superiors.[5] Education at home qualified most women for cleaning, sewing, and cooking, but working con-

---

[1] Sheila Ryan Johansson, "Demographic Contributions to the History of Victorian Women", in: *The Women of England. From Anglo-Saxon Times to the Present. Interpretive Bibliographical Essays*, ed. Barbara Kanner (London, 1980), p. 281.

[2] Ibid., pp. 277-278.

[3] June Purvis, *A History of Women's Education*, p. 53.

[4] Katrina Honeyman, *Women, Gender, and Industrialisation*, p. 45.

[5] Jan Marsh, "Votes for Women", p. 101.

ditions and wages varied: Johannsson optimistically maintains that "Domestic service paid relatively high wages, and it offered a young woman the opportunity to learn valuable social and household skills that might lead to better marriages and upward mobility".[1] Emma Paterson had a rather different point of view in 1879:

> domestic service is incessant hard work at all hours of the day and sometimes of the night also. It is at best but a kind of slavery, and when a girl has a home it is only a human feeling, and one that we should respect, if she prefers to undertake work in trades, because she can return at night and on Sundays to the home circle.[2]

The consideration that domestic service enabled a comfortable middle-class family life at the cost of their servants' own family lives probably escaped their employers. The difference between a poor domestic servant's rather bare room-and-kitchen home and the parlour she had to clean in a well-off household must have been considerable. The lady of the house decorated the parlour with an accumulation of objects in order to fulfil the demands of comfort and aesthetic experience as well as the construction and communication of identity via conspicuous consumption.[3] The parlour served as an interface between the private and the public, a site of intimacy for the family, from which servants were mostly excluded, *and* the display of identity and of social status to visitors, which included the number of servants in the household.[4]

The trades of sewing, weaving, and lace-making often allowed women to work at home but did not necessarily ensure their survival. In the ball season, ladies required seamstresses to toil without end in order to procure dresses for balls, which, at least in the case of Mary Ann Walkley, lead to death by overworking and starvation after she worked for more than 26 hours without a break.[5] Even if Walkley's case was extreme, most poor women certainly did not suffer from the want of work which Florence

---

[1] Sheila Ryan Johansson, "Demographic Contributions", p. 280.

[2] Quoted in Patricia Hollis, *Women in Public*, p. 64.

[3] Thad Logan, *The Victorian Parlour. A Cultural Study* (Cambridge, 2001), p. 76.

[4] Ibid., pp. 27-31. John Tosh points out that the Victorian home was as important to the gendering of (middle-class) men as of women since a man achieved his full social status as a bourgeois patriarch by the establishment, the protection, the control of and the provision for a household, which he could retreat to after work and which was supposed to fulfil his needs of affection, order, mastery, and social status (*A Man's Place. Masculinity and the Middle-Class Home in Victorian England* [New Haven and London, 1999], pp. 2-4, 47).

[5] Michael Hiley, *Victorian Working Women*, p. 24.

Nightingale in her upper-middle-class perspective described in an exaggerated way as the lot of women, who felt as if they were going mad at the end of day because "they suffer at once from disgust of the one and incapacity for the other – from loathing of conventional idleness and powerlessness to do work when they have it".[1] Poor women were rather hampered by weakness from want than from leisure if they became "incapable of consecutive or strenuous work".[2]

In order to survive, many women had to work hard for low wages outside their homes, for example in sweat shops or textile mills, in spite of concerns for the neglect and disintegration of their families, whose welfare they were held responsible for: "the factory tears her from all these duties: homes become no longer homes; children grow up uneducated and entirely neglected; the domestic affections are crushed or blunted, and woman is no longer the gentle sustainer of man, but his fellow-drudge and fellow-labourer".[3] Working women risked not only the integrity of their families but social esteem as well since some forms and conditions of work were considered to be unwomanly – but not necessarily inhumane. When the amateur inspector Arthur Munby saw young women dealing with offal in a slaughterhouse, he was afraid that this kind of work threatened to "coarsen and unsex a young woman and destroy all grace of form and character".[4] Munby was not at all concerned with poor women's health or wages but with the possible consequences of gross work in the shape of impudent or disrespectful behaviour towards middle-class gentlemen, for which he was glad not to find any evidence.[5] In general, middle-class gentlemen were less interested in the reform of working conditions than of working women, whose independence beyond the control of fathers or husbands gave rise to the fear of license and prostitution.[6] Women working outside their homes also provoked the renegotiation of gender in various ways. Mining, which seemed to violate womanliness, and nursing, which seemed to realize womanliness, raised disputes about gender roles that revealed various challenges to men's superiority and their responses in order to maintain "masculinity" and contain female competition.

---

[1] Florence Nightingale, "Cassandra", p. 221.

[2] Ibid.

[3] Samuel Smiles, quoted in June Purvis, *A History of Women's Education*, p. 8; see also Christopher Hibbert, *The English. A Social History, 1066-1945*, third edition (London, 1988), p. 592.

[4] Quoted in Michael Hiley, *Victorian Working Women*, p. 15.

[5] Ibid., p. 16.

[6] Karl Ittmann, *Work, Gender and Family*, pp. 150-152.

Patricia Hollis notes that 11,000 women laboured in mining in 1851.[1] Girls and women who worked in the mines and women who cross-dressed in order to earn male wages[2] contradicted prejudices about the weaker sex, implicitly questioned male superiority, and rivalled men for jobs. The explicit public debate on women workers in or at mines focused on morals rather than economic necessity, wages, or health. The *First Report of the Children's Employment Commission* in 1842 revealed that girls worked half-naked and in more or less tattered pants in mine shafts, which sent moral shockwaves through the middle-class public. The fact that girls pulling wagons in mines and women working at pit brows wore men's used trousers and coats, "queer clothes"[3] in the apt words of a pit brow girl, was considered to be almost as immoral as the exposure of breasts in mineshafts. The offense taken by the public can be measured by the fact that "the Great Breeches Question"[4] remained a topic of recurrent public debates in the 1860s, 70s, and 80s. Male miners joined middle-class inspectors in denouncing their fellow-labourers for three reasons: their presence and clothes gave rise to degrading contacts and acts of gross immorality with male workers; hard work unsexed women through their manliness in external appearance and behaviour, and their work interfered with women's domestic duties.[5] The outraged official report by middle-class men, which stressed those women's deterioration of character and loss of self-respect, stood in marked contrast to the women's own comments, which asserted the custom, convenience, and usefulness of male clothes, and expressed pride in the ability to perform well in their jobs.[6] In 1867, the Select Committee on Mines had to admit that no evidence of indecency was to be found and therefore did not see the need for legal interference.[7] In sum, the Factory Acts intended less to protect women from exploitation than to restrict their choice of work, their chance of earnings and their competitiveness, thus promoting women's domestic functions.[8] Miners and their unions opposed women workers in spite of or rather because of women's performance and competition at half the men's wages in order to enhance

---

[1] Patricia Hollis, *Women in Public*, p. 53.

[2] Michael Hiley, *Victorian Working Women*, pp. 41-43, 89; Camilla Townsend, "'I am the woman for spirit': a Working Woman's Gender Transgression in Victorian London", *Victorian Studies*, 36 (1992/93), 293-314.

[3] Quoted in Michael Hiley, *Victorian Working Women*, p. 87, cp. p. 92.

[4] Arthur Munby, quoted in Michael Hiley, *Victorian Working Women*, p. 85.

[5] Michael Hiley, *Victorian Working Women*, pp. 48, 50-52, 57.

[6] Ibid., p. 52.

[7] Ibid., p. 56.

[8] Ibid., 58-59; Katrina Honeyman, *Women, Gender, and Industrialisation*, pp. 69, 93.

their own definition of masculinity by being the sole providers of their families' incomes.

Whereas miners fought present competition by women, men in the medical profession rather tried to preempt future competition by women. Domestic nursing was considered to be a prime function of mothers but doctors claimed the authority to determine the nature of the disease and its cure. Sarah Ellis supported the strict professional segregation between nurses and doctors. She considered nursing to be one of the essential domestic duties in every woman's life because women had to attend to the sick-bed of children and parents, and she demanded women's education in health care but warned women not to interfere with the work of doctors.[1]

Florence Nightingale, the embodiment of the new middle-class nurse, extended the range of women's domestic work by leading a team of nurses at Scutari during the Crimean War, raising the public esteem for nurses.[2] In her writings, she defined nursing as hygienic and moral discipline, which aimed at reform by civilizing the poor, and "ultimately challenged the basis of medical men's power – the right to define who was a patient in need of health care".[3] Nightingale argued that nature rather than medicine cured human beings, and that nurses rather than doctors created conditions amenable to healing, but she did not advocate medical training for nurses in order to avoid conflicts with doctors.[4] Mary Seacole went even further than Florence Nightingale, who declined her offer to serve as a nurse in the Crimea. Mary Seacole, a creole of Scottish and Caribbean descent, pursued a double strategy, which asserted and challenged gender constructions at the same time. In her autobiography, she characterized herself (ironically?) as an "unprotected female"[5], and endorsed the dominant opinion that women could soothe the injured best as nurses in a motherly way.[6] She then debunked men when she described that the injuries unmanned the soldiers, who were in need of motherly care, and that she herself was "doing the work of half a dozen men"[7] in her incessant labour to relieve the

---

[1] Sarah S. Ellis, *The Women of England*, pp. 76-78.

[2] Jan Marsh, "Votes for Women and Chastity for Men: Gender, Health, Medicine and Sexuality", in: *The Victorian Vision. Inventing New Britain*, ed. John M. MacKenzie (London, 2001), p. 113.

[3] Mary Poovey, *Uneven Developments*, p. 166; see also pp. 191-192.

[4] Catherine Judd, *Bedside Seductions. Nursing and the Victorian Imagination, 1830-1880* (Houndmills, 1998), p. 25.

[5] Mary Seacole, *Wonderful Adventures of Mrs. Seacole in Many Lands*, introd. William L. Andrews, ed. Henry Louis Gates, Jr., The Schomburg Library of Nineteenth-Century Black Women Writers (Oxford, 1988), p. 8.

[6] Mary Seacole, *Wonderful Adventures*, p. 75.

[7] Ibid., p. 149.

pains of wounded troops. Finally, she asserted her own superiority not only as a nurse in implicit comparisons to the British ones, but also as a doctress due to her expertise in Afro-Caribbean medicine and some medical training by army surgeons: "I had gained a reputation as a skilful nurse and doctress".[1] As a nurse, she subordinated herself to the British doctors at their hospital, but she also set up her own practice as a rival doctor who helped patients with her own concoctions of medicine. Even if army doctors dismissed her authority, she cured many patients with great success if we may trust the testimonies she inserted in her autobiography.[2] Her lack of recognition by war officials in England before her departure to the Crimea and by the medical authorities in the theatre of war were easily countered by her demonstration of skills, which culminated in her cure of a surgeon who had given up the hope to survive.[3] Her success and her good reputation as a doctress, and her services to the British army were acknowledged in Great Britain after the war but did not allow her to work as a medical professional in the mother country. The British Medical Association was established in 1856 as a male preserve. In the same year, Jessie Meriton White was not admitted to examination for a diploma in midwifery and surgery at St. Bartholomew's Hospital simply for the reason that she was a woman.[4] Since its foundation in 1858, the General Medical Council, which was responsible for licensing doctors, refused to register women doctors.[5] But in the long run, they relented and admitted women to the profession, so that by 1901, Great Britain had 212 female physicians, 140 dentists, and 3 veterinarians.[6]

The examples of mining and healthcare show that in the field of unskilled labour, men opposed women because of their competitive performance, and in the field of skilled labour, men tried to preempt women's access to professional training, examination and practice in order to prevent future competition. Whereas well-educated women wormed their way into the professions towards the end of the Victorian age, unskilled women formed unions of their own in opposition to unions of skilled work force, who largely represented men and excluded women, who had a questionable advantage over men because they usually were paid half the wages. Wherever women had the opportunity, they proved to be equal to men, but it seemed to take the First World War for men to realize and accept that women did "men's"

---

[1] Ibid., p. 7; cf. p. 89.
[2] Ibid., pp. 101, 127-134, 171-172, 194.
[3] Ibid., pp. 69, 101, 78-79.
[4] Michael Hiley, *Victorian Working Women*, p. 41.
[5] Jan Marsh, "Votes for Women", p. 113.
[6] Ibid., p. 102.

work, at least as long as men were busy with warfare. It would be wrong to claim that by the end of the 19th century womanliness had become detached from domesticity, but it seems safe to say that working women dissolved the segregation of genders by mere practical performance as much as writers who clamoured for emancipation.

In 1972, Kate Millet stated that the Victorian woman question had not fundamentally changed, that apart from some new contemporary catchwords the Women's Liberation movement still battled against male prejudices and privileges.[1] Although it is true to say that even now, in 2002, women are still denied total equality, they have made some headway since the Victorian age. Disappointed by the failure of the moderate National Union of Women's Suffrage Societies (1897) to influence politics significantly, Emmeline and Christabel Pankhurst founded the militant Women's Social and Political Union in Manchester in 1903, which stepped up suffragist activities. They staged a protest in Hyde Park attended by about 250,000 people on 28 June 1908, and resorted to arson and bombing as the General Electoral Reform Bill was abandoned in 1913, and on 4 June 1913, Emily Davison died after having thrown herself under the king's horse in order to demonstrate how women were abused in Great Britain. The war of the sexes was temporarily displaced by World War I. The suffragettes suspended the militant campaign at home because they had decided that no longer British men but the Germans were the number one enemy. The war effort took pressure off politicians to battle against women at home. The front abroad triggered other changes on the home front: British women entered jobs that were better paid after these had been vacated by men drafted into the army. Historians have discussed whether militant suffragettes promoted or harmed the case for enfranchisement, and whether the changing position of women in World War I swayed politicians to favour women's franchise. I would argue for an accumulation of factors: the fact that women proved in World War I that they could adequately replace men as workers might have helped to promote their cause, but women did that before; the pressure of both moderate and radical suffragettes was possibly less decisive than the radical suffragettes' support of their country in the war effort, which seemed to have changed their image as lunatic anarchists into that of responsible citizens. In 1918, the Representation of the People Act granted all male citizens at 21 and women over 30 years of age the right to vote. Women had to wait for the fulfilment of their equal right to vote in national elections until 1928. Further reforms continued the gradual progress of the Victorian age. In 1969, the Divorce Reform Act acknow-

---

[1] Kate Millet, "The Debate", p. 139.

ledged the irretrievable breakdown of a marriage as a sufficient reason for divorce for both men and women. Women, however, still have to wait for equal pay, which the Equal Pay Act of 1970, which was put in force in 1975, should have ensured. The Sex Discrimination Act (1975), which was to safeguard equal opportunity in education, employment, housing, and the provision of public services, tells us as much about the legislative attempts to attain equality of the sexes as about the inadequate social reality which needs the law to enforce what does not go without saying. The ongoing series of further reform acts reveals that what was considered to be desirable by many women and some of their political representatives has not been put into current social practice. The woman question is, after all, also a question of man.

Prinz Albert und das universitäre Studium in Bonn und Cambridge[1]

Von *Franz Bosbach* (Bayreuth)

Als Prinz Albert im März 1847 zum Kanzler der Universität Cambridge gewählt worden war, gab er diese Nachricht in einem Brief der Herzogin von Sachsen-Gotha und Altenburg bekannt, in dem er in einer Federzeichnung sich selbst in der Kanzlerrobe porträtierte und dazu schrieb:

> Cambridge zwingt mich nicht die Perücke zu tragen sondern nur eine Mütze der Art mit langem Mantel. Ich gebe dir da das ganze Conterfey, daß etwas zwischen einem Pfaffen, einem Hoftrompeter, einem Ulahnen und einem Currentschüler steht. Es wird mir die Pflicht eine Lateinische Rede zu halten auferlegen, was aber nicht zu den größten Freuden gehört![2]

Es wäre verfehlt, wenn man aus der scherzenden Beschreibung schließen würde, dass Prinz Albert das ihm anvertraute Amt als nicht sonderlich wichtig einschätzte. Eher das Gegenteil war der Fall. Seit seiner Heirat mit Königin Victoria am 10. Februar 1840 hatte er seiner Stellung als Prince Consort[3] nicht zuletzt dadurch einen Sinn zu geben gesucht, dass er die Leitung einer ganzen Reihe von wissenschaftlichen Gesellschaften übernahm, die alle – mit Ausnahme von Cambridge – nicht-universitäre Institutionen waren. Die bedeutendste von allen war sicherlich die *Society of the Encouragement of the Arts and Sciences*, in der das Konzept der *Great Exhibition*, der ersten Weltausstellung, entwickelt wurde.[4] Seine weit ge-

---

[1] Dank gebührt Pamela Clark, Registrar, für hilfreiche Auskünfte über im folgenden zitierte Archivalien in den *Royal Archives* in Windsor Castle.

[2] Prinz Albert an Caroline Amalie, Herzogin von Sachsen-Gotha-Altenburg, 17. März 1847 (Royal Archives VIC/M35/116); Text und Zeichnung sind abgebildet bei Owen Chadwick, *Prince Albert and the University*, The Prince Albert Sesquicentennial Lecture (Cambridge, 1997), vor S. 1.

[3] So lautete ab 1857 sein offizieller Titel, unter dem er aber auch zuvor schon bekannt war, Robert Rhodes James, *Albert, Prince Consort* (London, 1983), S. 259; Theodore Martin, *The Life of HRH The Prince Consort*, fifth edition, vol. 4 (London, 1879), S. 63.

[4] Asa Briggs, "Politics and Reform: The British Universities", in: *Prinz Albert und die Entwicklung der Bildung in England und Deutschland im 19. Jahrhundert*, ed. Franz Bosbach, William Filmer-Sankey, Hermann Hiery und Thomas Brockmann, Prinz-Albert-Studien 18 (München, 2000), S. 119-127, S. 119; zur *Great Exhibition* und zur

streuten Interessen, sein Ehrgeiz und sein Arbeitsethos verhinderten, dass er solche Ämter als reine Auszeichnungen betrachtete; er traute sich vielmehr zu, jeweils auch seinen eigenen Beitrag zu leisten. Und es war das Kanzleramt in Cambridge, das ihm die erste Gelegenheit bot, etwas im eigenen Namen für seine neue Heimat zu tun, wie er seinem Bruder Ernst schrieb.[1]

Sein Engagement brachte ihm auch Spott ein. Zeit seines Lebens war er ein dankbares Objekt für Karikaturen im *Punch*, der im März 1847 die Wahl Alberts zum Kanzler der Universität Cambridge zum Thema machte.

PRINCE ALBERT "AT HOME."
WHEN HE WILL SUSTAIN (NO END OF) DIFFERENT CHARACTERS.

Abb. 1: "Prince Albert 'At Home.' When he will sustain (no end of) different characters", *Punch*, 12 (London, 1847), 225.

Society of Arts vgl. Schneider, *Die Weltausstellung von 1851 und ihre Folgen*, ed. Franz Bosbach und John R. Davis in Zusammenarbeit mit Susan Bennett, Thomas Brockmann und William Filmer-Sankey, Prinz-Albert-Studien 20 (München, 2002).

[1] Mit Brief vom 26. März 1847, vgl. Daphne Bennett, *King without a Crown* (London, 1983), S. 151.

In der Karikatur wird auf die Fülle der verschiedenen Ämter Alberts angespielt, in denen allen er eine gute Rolle spielen möchte, und zu denen nun als neueste Würde die des universitären Kanzlers kommt. Eine zweite Botschaft geht von dem mit einem Kreuz geschmückten Hut aus, der auf der Halterung auf dem Tisch zu sehen ist. Diese Kopfbedeckung war eine Erfindung Alberts aus dem Jahr 1843, der Entwurf eines neuen Helmes für die Infanterie.[1] Er war wegen seines unmilitärischen Aussehens in der englischen Öffentlichkeit sehr spöttisch aufgenommen worden und ging auch nicht in die Serienfertigung. *Punch* hat den Prinzen zehn Jahre lang fast nur noch zusammen mit diesem Hut karikiert.[2] Wenn er hier erwähnt wurde, so sollte der Betrachter wohl gewarnt werden, dass auch im Zusammenhang mit dem neuen Kanzleramt solche merkwürdigen Einfälle nicht auszuschließen seien.

Diese Erwartung ist allerdings nicht erfüllt worden. Die Forschung ist sich darin einig, dass Prinz Albert während einer für die Universität Cambridge außerordentlich wichtigen Reformphase eine konstruktive Rolle gespielt und damit der Universität genutzt hat. Die Meinungen gehen lediglich bei der Bewertung seiner Leistung auseinander. Biographische Darstellungen neigen dazu, diese hoch zu veranschlagen. 1932 rechnete Bolitho die Reformleistungen zuerst der Tatkraft des Prinzen zu: "Prince Albert had begun the reforms and he had given the greater energy and impetus which carried them through".[3] Dem folgte 1949 Fulford: "He proved an invaluable leader to Cambridge as it gingerly set its foot on the awkward paths of reform".[4] James sah 1983 die Reformtätigkeit des Prinzen weit über Cambridge hinausgehend:

> He was not only the greatest Chancellor Cambridge University has ever had, but he was the pioneer of the principles of enlightened scholarship and of the love of learning for its own sake.[5]

Und diese Beurteilung wurde 1997 von Weintraub noch einmal bekräftigt, der ausgehend von den für Prinz Albert teilweise unerquicklichen Vorgängen im Zusammenhang mit der Kanzlerwahl den Ausblick anschließt:

---

[1] Ein erhalten gebliebenes Muster ist abgebildet bei Hermione Hobhouse, *Prince Albert: His Life and Work* (London, 1983), S. 46.

[2] Hans-Joachim Netzer, *Ein deutscher Prinz in England* (München, 1992), S. 207.

[3] Hector Bolitho, *Albert the Good* (London, 1932), S. 161.

[4] Roger Fulford, *The Prince Consort* (London, 1949), S. 201.

[5] R.R. James, *Albert, Prince Consort*, S. 181.

For the Prince, it was the prelude to the real work of reforming the hidebound Ox-bridge system and dragging university education in England into the nineteenth century.[1]

Daneben gibt es aber auch zurückhaltendere Einschätzungen. Bereits 1983 hob Bennett auf den Umstand ab, dass die Studienreformen, soweit sie von der Universität ausgingen, erst durch die Kooperation ("conspiracy") des Prinzen mit Reformkräften in Cambridge verwirklicht wurden und aus der Sicht der Regierung immer noch unzulänglich blieben.[2] Solche Einschrän-kungen werden gestützt von Ergebnissen, die Searby 1997 in seiner Ge-schichte der Universität Cambridge vorgelegt hat, wo er über die Person Prinz Alberts hinausgreifend die allgemeinen Rahmenbedingungen und Entwicklungen in der Universität und in der Politik in den Blick nahm.[3] Zuletzt hat Beales dazu festgestellt, dass der Beitrag des Prinzen zu den Veränderungen im wesentlichen mit den neuen Examina verbunden sei, die 1849 von der Universität eingeführt wurden; danach habe er nicht mehr viel bewirkt.[4] Bei dem gegenwärtigen Forschungsstand scheint es nicht angebracht, einen erneuten Beitrag zu der Diskussion über das Ausmaß der Bedeutung Alberts als Kanzler beizusteuern. Dazu müßte zunächst die Quellengrundlage breiter sein, auf Grund derer solche Aussagen erarbeitet werden können. Das ist zur Zeit aber noch ein Desiderat, wie auch Beales feststellt: "The evidence of his activity lies in the royal archives, which no one has yet used systematically".[5]

Wie die folgenden Ausführungen zeigen sollen, läßt der jetzige Stand der Forschung aber zu, Antworten zu geben auf die Frage, welche Erfahrungen mit Studium und Universität Prinz Albert selbst besaß, was sich vor allem auf sein Studium an der Universität Bonn bezieht, und worin die Tätigkeit für die Universität Cambridge bestand. Diese doppelte Fragestellung ist nicht willkürlich gewählt, sondern rechtfertigt sich dadurch, dass die Arbeit des Prinzen für Cambridge deutliche inhaltliche Bezüge erkennen läßt zu dem universitären Lehr- und Forschungsbetrieb, den Prinz Albert in Bonn kennengelernt hatte. Um dies zu zeigen, wird zunächst nach den Erfahrun-gen gefragt, die Prinz Albert während seines eigenen Studiums mit der Universität gemacht hat (1.), dann werden die Verhältnisse in Cambridge

---

[1] Stanley Weintraub, *Albert. Uncrowned King* (London, 1997), S. 187.

[2] D. Bennett, *King without a Crown*, S. 152.

[3] Peter Searby, *A History of the University of Cambridge*, vol. III: *1750-1870* (Cam-bridge, 1997).

[4] Derek Beales, "The Prince Consort and the University of Cambridge", in: *Prinz Albert und die Entwicklung der Bildung*, S. 157-167, S. 164-166.

[5] Ibid., S. 163.

und die Kanzlerwahl betrachtet (2.), und schließlich die Entwicklung der Universität in der ersten Zeit seiner Kanzlerschaft (3.).

1. Studium in Bonn

Prinz Albert hat bis zu seinem 20. Lebensjahr, bis zu seiner Heirat mit Victoria, nahezu ununterbrochen eine auf den Erwerb von Wissen und Bildung gerichtete Erziehung genossen. 1823, im Alter von 4 Jahren, begann für ihn und für seinen älteren Bruder Ernst der Unterricht. Christoph Florschütz, Sohn eines Coburger Gymnasiallehrers, wurde für die nächsten fünfzehn Jahre, in denen die Brüder ihre Jugend gemeinsam verlebten, ihr Erzieher und Lehrer.[1] Er war allein für die Erziehung verantwortlich; der Unterricht wurde teils von ihm selbst erteilt, teils wurden andere Lehrer hinzugezogen. Unterricht und Lerninhalte entsprachen den damals für adelige Erziehung üblichen Maßstäben.[2] Abgesehen von den Kernfächern Deutsch, Mathematik und Geschichte wurde besonderer Wert gelegt auf den Unterricht in Fremdsprachen. Die Prinzen sprachen schließlich Englisch und Französisch und beherrschten Latein. Hinzu kamen naturwissenschaftliche Lerninhalte und die musische Erziehung. Wenn man das spätere Auftreten Alberts zum Maßstab nimmt, so hat die häusliche Bildung offenbar eine solide Grundlage an Kenntnissen und Fertigkeiten vermittelt und günstige Voraussetzungen für das Universitätsstudium geschaffen.

Eine zweite Ausbildungsphase schloß sich an, als Prinz Albert und sein Bruder Ernst sich 1836 auf Einladung ihres Onkels, des belgischen Königs Leopold I., für zehn Monate in Brüssel aufhielten. Betreut von Florschütz und dem Oberstleutnant Baron Wichmann sollten sie hier, wie es in einer Weisung ihres Vaters hieß, französischen und englischen Sprachunterricht erhalten, in die militärische Wissenschaft eingeführt und auf einen Universitätsbesuch vorbereitet werden.[3] Sie nahmen noch nicht am Lehrbetrieb der dortigen Universität teil, erhielten aber von ausgesuchten Professoren Unterricht, unter denen der Mathematiker Lambert A. Quetelet, der damals

---

[1] Er hatte in Jena Philosophie und Theologie studiert. 1815 hatte er die als sehr schwer geltende Prüfung als Predigtamtskandidat in Coburg bestanden und bereits als Hauslehrer Erfahrung gesammelt, H.-J. Netzer, *Ein deutscher Prinz in England*, S. 65.

[2] Dazu jetzt, auch aufgrund neuer Quellen, die in den Besitz der Kunstsammlungen der Veste Coburg gekommen sind: Kristin Wiedau, "Eine adlige Kindheit in Coburg. Fürstenerziehung und Kunstunterweisung der Prinzen Ernst und Albert von Sachsen-Coburg und Gotha", *Jahrbuch der Coburger Landesstiftung*, 45 (2000), 1-112.

[3] Ernst I., *Instruktion für Obristleutnant v. Wichmann als Gouverneur und den geheimen Hofrat Florschütz als Studiendirektor*, Gotha 1836, II 20, Kopie: Staatsarchiv Coburg, LA. A. nr. 6867 fol. 1-3', hier fol. 1.

schon Weltruf genoß, den nachhaltigsten Eindruck hinterließ. Von ihm wurde Prinz Albert in die vergleichende Statistik und die statistische Analyse eingeführt, zu der er Zeit seines Lebens eine besondere Vorliebe hegte.[1]

Nach dem Brüsseler Aufenthalt folgte das Studium an der Universität Bonn; zunächst war an zwei Semester gedacht, schließlich verbrachte Prinz Albert zusammen mit seinem Bruder dort insgesamt drei Semester vom Sommer 1837 bis zum Spätsommer 1838. Die Universität war eine preußische Gründung aus dem Jahr 1818, d.h. sie war vergleichsweise jung, aber sie hatte bereits einen hervorragenden Ruf, da sie als eine Gründung im Sinne der Humboldtschen Ideale galt und weil die dorthin berufenen Professoren hervorragend waren.[2]

Es dürften mehrere Gründe für die Wahl dieser Universität ausschlaggebend gewesen sein. Aus den vorangehenden Beratschlagungen ist ein anonymes Memorandum erhalten, das ein Schüler des in Berlin lehrenden Friedrich Carl von Savigny als Antwort auf eine Reihe von Fragen gefertigt hatte. Die Fragen sind nicht erhalten, doch läßt sich aus dem erhaltenen Schriftsatz erschließen, dass eine Art Evaluation und "Ranking" der Universitäten Berlin und Bonn erfolgen sollte, um zu entscheiden, wo die beiden Brüder als Prinzen aus einem regierenden Haus studieren sollten.[3] Es behandelt zunächst die Fragen

> ob auf den Universitäten Berlin und Bonn die Fächer des römischen und modernen Civilrechtes, des Staatsrechtes, der Staatswirthschafts-Lehre, der Politik, Geschichte und anderen verwandten philosophischen Wissenschaften gut und durch wen sie besetzt sind.

Generell wird dazu festgestellt, dass Berlin

> in den genannten Fächern ein größeres und ausgezeichneteres Lehrerpersonal und Bonn wenigstens ein ebenso gutes besitzt, wie jede andere unter den mir bekannten beßeren Universitäten in Deutschland.

---

[1] Theodore Martin, *The Prince Consort*, sixth edition, vol. 1 (London, 1879), S. 21-22.

[2] Zu Bonn vgl. Max Braubach, *Kleine Geschichte der Universität Bonn 1818-1968* (Bonn, 1968); zur Universitätsidee Humboldts und ihrer Geschichte vgl. Rainer A. Müller, "Vom Ideal der Humboldt-Universität zur Praxis des wissenschaftlichen Großbetriebes. Zur Entwicklung des deutschen Hochschulwesens im 19. Jahrhundert", in: *Prinz Albert und die Entwicklung der Bildung*, S.129-143.

[3] Auszug aus einem Briefe S. S. [salvis servandis] Berlin 9. Jan. 1837, in: Staatsarchiv Coburg, LA. A. nr. 6868, fol. 1-2'.

Unter den namentlich angeführten Professoren werden zwei Vertreter der Rechtswissenschaften besonders gewürdigt: unter den Bonnern Moritz A. v. Bethmann-Hollweg, der Großvater des späteren Reichskanzlers, als "an Gelehrsamkeit, Lehrtalent und moralischem Werthe ein wahrer Schatz für die dortige Universität", und unter den Berlinern dessen akademischer Lehrer Friedrich Carl von Savigny. Savigny erschien dem anonymen Gutachter wegen seiner Reputation und langjährigen Erfahrung darüber hinaus am besten geeignet, ein Urteil abzugeben über eine weitere Frage des Fragenkatalogs, "ob und in wie weit die Gefahren, deren sie ad no. 4 erwähnen, für junge Herren hohen fürstlichen Standes wirklich vorhanden oder doch zu vermeiden sind?". Bei dieser Frage ging es, wenn man von der Antwort her schließt, um Gefährdungen sowohl für die moralisch-sittliche Lebensführung als auch für den wissenschaftlich-intellektuellen Ertrag des Studiums. Savigny, dessen Stellungnahme das Memorandum sodann referiert, unterscheidet zwischen der Studiensituation bürgerlicher und kleinadeliger Studenten einerseits und der von "jungen Prinzen aus einem regierenden Hause". Für die zuerst genannten stelle sich die Frage so nicht, weil die Situation für sie in Berlin nicht anders sei als an kleineren Universitäten, vielleicht sogar günstiger[1], und der Studienerfolg letztlich von der Einstellung abhänge:

> Nicht einmal die Zerstreuung, welcher man in einer so großen Stadt wie Berlin ausgesetzt ist, pflegt den hiesigen Studierenden, wenn sie wirklich etwas lernen wollen und einige Characterfestigkeit mitbringen, besonders gefährlich zu werden.

Für die Fürstensöhne sei die Lage insofern anders, als sie unvermeidlich am Leben der Hofgesellschaft teilnehmen müßten und daher nicht zu ihren Studien kämen. Als Beispiel wird der bayerische Kronprinz Maximilian genannt, der 1830/31 in Berlin studiert hatte:

> der Kronprinz von Bayern, welcher aus eigener Erfahrung hierüber urtheilen kann, dürfte wohl schwerlich behaupten wollen, daß er von Berlin eine große wissenschaftliche Ausbeute mitgebracht habe.[2]

---

[1] Ibid., fol. 1'-2: "Für Studierende aus dem Mittelstande (wohin ich auch den gewöhnlichen Adel, den höhern Beamtenstand zähle), ist die Gefahr der Verführung in Berlin nicht größer und vielleicht weniger groß, als auf kleineren Universitäten, wo sie den jungen Leuten meistens viel näher auf den Leib rückt, und wo es für dieselben nicht so gute Gelegenheit giebt, ihre Musestunden im Kreise anständiger Familien zuzubringen, als es hier der Fall ist".

[2] Die Berliner Historiker von Raumer und Ranke haben darüber ganz anders geurteilt, was vielleicht damit zu erklären ist, dass Maximilian sich nicht für Rechtswissen-

Man erfährt sodann, dass wegen dieser Gegebenheiten der Großherzog von Mecklenburg-Strelitz seinen Sohn zum Studium nach Bonn schicken werde.[1] Abgesehen davon, dass deutlich wird, dass demnach die Coburger Prinzen nicht als erste den Weg Bonns zur "deutschen Prinzenuniversität"[2] bereitet haben, ist hier zugleich ein offenbar wichtiger Grund genannt, warum die Universität diese Entwicklung genommen hat: Aus der Sicht des am Studienerfolg interessierten Savigny war das fehlende Hofleben ein entscheidender Vorteil. Für die Gestaltung der Studien und der sozialen Kontakte wird schließlich der Rat Bethmann-Hollwegs empfohlen,

> der sich mit treuer Gewißenhaftigkeit angelegen seyn laßen würde, so weit es in seiner Macht stände, dafür zu sorgen, daß der Zweck ihres Aufenthaltes in Bonn ohne Beeinträchtigung ihrer moralischen Reinheit vollständig erreicht würde.

Es ist vielleicht auf Bethmann-Hollweg zurückzuführen, dass die sorgfältige und bis in kleine Details gehende Studienplanung mit vorzüglichen Informationen über die Situation in Bonn arbeitete. Dabei fällt auf, dass so lange noch keine Entscheidung über den Studienort getroffen war, der Coburger Herzog und sein Hof das Studium offenbar nach den damals für Angehörige des hohen Adels üblichen Grundsätzen geplant hatten, was deshalb eher mager ausfiel: Die herzoglichen Brüder sollten Kenntnisse in den Bereichen erwerben, denen für die Tätigkeit als Herrscher und Landesherren Bedeutung zugemessen wurde. Ein Examen als Studienabschluß war nicht vorgesehen. Dazu hatte der Vater in der oben erwähnten Instruktion im Februar 1836 angeordnet, dass Jura und Volkswirtschaft sowie Geschichte die Inhalte des künftigen Studium sein sollten:

> Das Studium unserer Prinzen auf der Universität, soll außer einem allgemeinen Cursus der Rechtswissenschaft, sich hauptsächlich auf die Vorlesungen über Staats-Wirthschaft, Statistik, Politik und Staats- und Völkerrecht erstrecken. Das Studium der Geschichte ist in allen Verhältnissen in Brüssel sowohl, als auf der Universität nicht zu versäumen und hauptsächlich dahin zu wirken, daß solches unsern Prinzen zur besonders angenehmen Selbstbeschäftigung werde.[3]

---

schaft, sondern für Geschichte interessierte. Vgl. Michael Dirrigl, *Maximilian II.*, vol. I (München, 1984), S. 470.

[1] Erbprinz Friedrich Wilhelm von Mecklenburg-Strelitz (1819-1905); eingeschrieben als stud. jur. zum Sommersemester 1837.

[2] Zu dieser Charakterisierung vgl. Th. Becker, "Prinz Albert als Student in Bonn", in: *Prinz Albert und die Entwicklung der Bildung*, S. 145-156, S. 156.

[3] Ernst I., *Instruktion*, fol. 1-1'; die Worte von "hauptsächlich" bis "erstrecken" sind in der Quelle unterstrichen.

Nachdem die Entscheidung für Bonn gefallen war, sah der Studienplan aber sehr viel bunter aus und schloß weitere Fächer der Geistes- und der Naturwissenschaften ein. Auch diesen Plan hatte der Vater erstellt, aber nun wies er nicht nur auf die Rechts- und Staatswissenschaften als passende Inhalte des Studiums hin, sondern auch auf die Sprachen und auf die "Philosophie und einige andere zur allgemeinen Bildung gehörige Gegenstände".[1] Im Unterschied zur ersten Anweisung wird hier mit der "allgemeinen Bildung" die damals gebräuchliche Terminologie der Universitäts- und Bildungsreformer aufgegriffen, deren Bildungskonzept offenbar in Bonn befolgt werden sollte. Auf diese Weise kam ein "allgemeinbildendes Studium mit juristischem Schwerpunkt"[2] zustande, was damals keineswegs selbstverständlich war. Für den Erbprinz von Mecklenburg-Strelitz waren bei weitem nicht so viele Vorlesungen aus der Philosophischen Fakultät vorgesehen, und aus dieser Tatsache wurde sogar ein Vorwurf gegen Florschütz abgeleitet, dass er die Prinzen Albert und Ernst einem zu großen Einfluß liberalen Gedankengutes aussetze.[3]

---

[1] Herzog Ernst I. von Sachsen-Coburg und Gotha: *Bestimmungen über den bei dem beabsichtigten Studium der Prinzen Ernst und Albert [...] auf der Universität zu Bonn zu beobachtenden Studien-Plan, Gotha 1837*, IV 19; Kopie in Staatsarchiv Coburg, LA. A. nr. 6867 fol. 7-8: "Die höchste Absicht ist bei dem Studium der Durchlauchtigsten Prinzen dahin gerichtet, daß Höchstdieselben eine übersichtliche Kenntnis der Rechtswissenschaft im Allgemeinen und einen ausführlichen Unterricht im Staatsrecht der neueren Zeit, in der Staatswirthschaftslehre, und in der Politik erhalten; zugleich müssen die neuen Sprachen fortbetrieben, und über Philosophie und einige andere zur allgemeinen Bildung gehörige Gegenstände der Unterricht verbreitet werden".
[2] Th. Becker, "Prinz Albert als Student in Bonn", S. 145.
[3] Georg von Wangenheim an Ernst I., Hannover 11. April 1838, Kopie, in: Staatsarchiv Coburg, LA. A. nr. 6867, fol. 17: "Wiewohl ich nicht zweifle, daß meiner verehrten Exzellenz längst genaue Nachrichten über alles, was unsere beiden hoffnungsvollen Prinzen Ernst und Albrecht anbetrifft, zur Kunde gekommen seyn wird, so halte ich als treuer Gothaner es doch für meine Pflicht, Ihnen auch das zu bestätigen, was wahrscheinlich auf officiellem Wege längst zu Ihrer Kenntniß gekommen ist, und die Bestätigung dessen enthält, was ich leider im vorigen Winter Ihnen in Gotha mitzutheilen die Ehre hatte. Ich fürchtete schon damals, daß mein Verdacht, daß die Prinzen liberale Grundsätze eingesogen, gegründet sey. – Wie ich aber kürzlich aus Bonn vernehme, so ist hierzu nicht so sehr der Grund in Brüssel gelegt, als die Bearbeitung des Herrn Florschütz hieran Theil haben soll. Graf Finck[enstein], Gouverneur des Erbgroß-Herzogs von Mecklenburg-Strelitz, sagte mir außerdem vor einigen Tagen, daß sein Prinz in diesem Sommer wohl nicht in so genauem Verhältnisse wie bisher zu unsern beiden Prinzen stehen würde – nicht mehr so viel Collegia mit ihnen hören – weil Florschütz zu viel auf philosophische Collegia Rücksicht nehme, welche er für seinen Prinzen nicht so nothwendig erachte"; der Schreiber des Briefes war nicht, wie in der biographischen Literatur zu Prinz Albert oft behauptet, der ehemalige Coburgische Minister gleichen Namens, vgl. zuletzt H.-J. Netzer, *Ein deutscher Prinz in England*, S. 97, sondern der

Diese haben ihr Studium, das nach den Planungen ihres Vaters zwischen 13 bis 17 Semesterwochenstunden umfassen sollte, wozu noch der Fremdsprachenunterricht kam, offenbar mit immensem Fleiß und Eifer betrieben. Ein Teil des schriftlichen Niederschlages ihrer Studien ist in Form von Kolleghaften erhalten geblieben. Die des Prinzen Albert werden im königlichen Archiv in Windsor verwahrt.[1] Es handelt sich überwiegend um Mitschriften von Vorlesungen, die teilweise noch einmal sorgfältig ausgearbeitet und in Leder gebunden wurden. Nach Mitteilung der *Royal Archives* sind hier als Studienthemen aus den Rechts- und Staatswissenschaften genannt: Juristische Enzyklopädie, Rechtsphilosophie, Deutsche Rechtsgeschichte, Rechtsaltertümer, Deutsches Staatsrecht, Deutsches Privatrecht, Volkswirtschaftslehre; aus den Geistes- und Naturwissenschaften ist die Philosophie am häufigsten vertreten mit Schriftsätzen zur Logik, Anthropologie und Psychologie sowie Neuerer Philosophie. Die übrigen geisteswissenschaftlichen Themen sind Geschichte des Mittelalters, Kunstgeschichte und Harmonielehre.

Es wäre eine lohnende Arbeit, die Inhalte der Mitschriften unter gleichzeitiger Berücksichtigung des in Windsor verwahrten Materials auszuwerten, um sie in den Kontext der zeitgenössischen universitären Lehre und Forschung zu stellen, wobei auch die akademischen Lehrer einzubeziehen wären. Aus den Aufschriften der Kolleghafte läßt sich ersehen, dass Clemens Perthes über Deutsche Rechtsgeschichte, Deutsches Staatsrecht und Deutsches Privatrecht las. Bei dem Professor für Römisches Recht und Römischen Zivilprozeß Moritz A. v. Bethmann-Hollweg hörten die Prinzen Juristische Enzyklopädie, bei dem Professor für Staatsrecht, Rechtsphilosophie, Enzyklopädie und Strafrecht, Gustav Friedrich Gärtner, Rechtsphilosophie, bei dem Kirchen-, Staats- und Privatrechtler Ferdinand Walter Rechtsaltertümer.[2] Die Staatswirtschaftslehre schließlich wurde von dem außerordentlichen Professor der Staatswissenschaft Peter K. Kaufmann gelehrt.[3] Die Philosophievorlesungen wurden von Immanuel Hermann

---

hannoverische Obersthofmarschall; wegen seiner Besitzungen in Thüringen gehörte er der Gothaischen Landschaft an, worauf er in dem Brief anspielt; *ADB*, vol. 41, S. 151.

[1] Vgl. die Liste bei K. Wiedau, "Eine adlige Kindheit in Coburg", S. 101; die von Alberts Bruder Ernst angelegten Hefte liegen im Staatsarchiv Coburg, LA. A. nr. 6871-6882.

[2] Zu den Professoren vgl. Cornelie Butz, *Die Juristenausbildung an den preußischen Universitäten Berlin und Bonn zwischen 1810 und 1850*, Diss. phil. (Berlin, 1992), S. 170-174.

[3] Zu ihm vgl. Paul Egon Hübinger, *Das Historische Seminar der Rheinischen Friedrich-Wilhelms-Universität zu Bonn* (Bonn, 1963), S. 264 n. 1.

Fichte gehalten, ein Sohn des Philosophen Johann Gottlieb Fichte.[1] Kunstgeschichte hörten sie bei Eduard d'Alton und Geschichte des Mittelalters bei Johann Wilhelm Loebell.[2] Der Schwerpunkt der Studien lag bei den Veranstaltungen der juristischen Fakultät. Prinz Albert nannte in einem Brief an seinen Vater das Römische Recht, das Staatsrecht und die Staatswirtschaftslehre mit Finanzwissenschaft als "Hauptgegenstand" für das Wintersemester 1837/38.[3] Die Lehrveranstaltungen umfaßten aber noch mehr Themen und Fächer, so dass das Studium tatsächlich als "Studium generale" angelegt war, wie es als Ideal an einer preußischen Reformuniversität verwirklicht werden konnte. In seiner Autobiographie, die fünfzig Jahre später erschienen ist und für die Bonner Zeit nicht frei von Irrtümern und Widersprüchen ist, hat Herzog Ernst das Studium der Brüder so beschrieben:

> Bei aller Geselligkeit waren wir aber doch alle sehr fleißig, und es war eine Art Lesewuth unter uns vorhanden, so daß wir eine Unmasse von Büchern verschlangen und hierin eine Art von wetteiferndem Ehrgeiz befriedigten. Die zahlreichen Collegien, welche wir meist als Privatissima hörten, wurden mit der größten Gewissenhaftigkeit in den beliebten Heften nachgeschrieben und nachstudirt. Bei einigen Professoren, wie insbesondere bei Fichte, waren Conversatorien gebräuchlich, in welchen viel und tapfer gestritten wurde. Wir hörten an der juristischen Fakultät fast den ganzen Cyclus von Vorlesungen, welche zum Staatsdienst vorzubereiten pflegten: Bethmann-Hollweg, Nissen, Gärtner, Perthes und Walter, außerdem wurde Finanzwissenschaft bei Kaufmann, Philosophie bei Fichte, Geschichte bei Löbell, Litteratur bei Schlegel, Kunstgeschichte bei Alten, französische Litteratur bei Lasson besucht. Wir dilettirten auch in der Anatomie bei Wurzer und in den Naturwissenschaften bei Nöggerath und Rehfuß. Bei Professor

---

[1] Vgl. *Lexikon für Theologie und Kirche*, third edition, vol. 3 (Freiburg, 1995), S. 1270.

[2] Zu diesen vgl. *Verzeichnis der Professoren und Dozenten der Rheinischen Friedrich-Wilhelms-Universität zu Bonn 1818-1869*, ed. Otto Wenig (Bonn, 1968).

[3] Albert an Herzog Ernst I., Bonn 12. November 1837, in: Charles Grey, *Die Jugendjahre des Prinzen Albert von Sachsen-Coburg-Gotha, Prinzgemahls der Königin von England* (Gotha, 1868), S. 123: "Das vorige Semester war uns verflossen, noch ehe wir recht daran denken konnten. In das neue haben wir uns schon ganz gestürzt. Dieser Winter wird für uns ein angestrengter werden (da wir mit Collegien und Ausarbeitungen ganz überhäuft sind). Hauptgegenstand unserer jetzigen Beschäftigungen ist das Römische Recht, das Staatsrecht und die Staatswirthschaftslehre mit Finanzwissenschaft. Daneben hören wir noch zwei historische Collegien bei Löbell und A.W. Schlegel, und ein philosophisches bei Fichte (Anthropologie und Philosophie), und werden zugleich an unserm Eifer von den neueren Sprachen nicht ablassen".

Breitenstein nahmen wir Unterricht in der Musik und beschäftigten uns nicht bloß mit ihrem geschichtlichen Teil, sondern auch mit der Generalbaßlehre.[1]

Einen bleibenden Eindruck vermittelten auch die Vorlesungen von August Wilhelm Schlegel über Shakespeare und über die moderne Literaturgeschichte seit Schiller.[2] Aus den Studienplänen geht hervor, dass die beiden herzoglichen Brüder auch ein Kolleg über experimentelle Physik hören sollten, und außerdem hatten sie weiterhin englischen sowie französischen Sprachunterricht;[3] schließlich betrieben sie auch noch das akademische Fechten[4] und Schwimmen.[5] Alles zusammen genommen, war das von ihnen wahrgenommene universitäre Bildungsangebot also denkbar weit gespannt.

Der Nutzen der drei Bonner Semester bestand für Prinz Albert demnach wohl zuerst darin, dass er sich in einer großen Bandbreite von akademischen Unterrichtsfächern ein fachliches Wissen aneignen konnte und zwar unter der Vermittlung von in der Regel führenden Wissenschaftlern des jeweiligen Faches. Sein Bruder Ernst hat in seinen Memoiren, also sehr viel später, auch die Vorlesungsinhalte einzelner Professoren kommentiert, wobei er zum Teil kritische Ausführungen machte.[6] Elisabeth Scheeben hat aber darauf hingewiesen, dass diese Einschätzungen mit Sicherheit nicht sein Urteil aus der Studentenzeit darstellen, sondern erst als ein Ergebnis

---

[1] Ernst II., Herzog von Sachsen-Coburg-Gotha, *Aus meinem Leben und aus meiner Zeit*, vol. I (Berlin, 1887), S. 67. Biographische Angaben zu den genannten Professoren in *Verzeichnis der Professoren*, ed. Otto Wenig; Nissen, der erst später in Bonn lehrte, ist in den Memoiren des Coburger Herzogs wohl irrtümlich genannt, ebenso Lasson, der bei Wenig nicht aufgeführt ist; wahrscheinlich ist der ao. Professor für Altindische Sprachen und Literatur Christian Lassen gemeint, der den beiden Prinzen Vorlesungen in Englisch hielt und dafür bezahlt wurde, vgl. Staatsarchiv Coburg, LA. A. nr. 6883 fol. 119. Bei Rehfuß könnte es sich um den Kurator der Universität, Philipp Joseph von Rehfues, handeln, vgl. zu ihm Gottfried Stein von Kamienski, "Bonner Kuratoren 1818 bis 1933", in: *Verfassungsgeschichte der Universität Bonn*, S. 527-563, 532-537.

[2] Ernst II., *Aus meinem Leben*, S. 69; freilich sind dazu – soweit bekannt – keine Vorlesungsmitschriften angefertigt worden, was seinen Grund darin haben kann, dass Schlegels Vorlesungen bereits veröffentlicht waren, vgl. Christian Renger, *Die Gründung und Einrichtung der Universität Bonn und die Berufungspolitik des Kultusministers Altenstein* (Bonn, 1982), S. 222.

[3] Vgl. Ernst I.: *Bestimmungen über den Studien-Plan* sowie [...] *gnädigst genehmigter Studienplan* [...] *für das Semester von Ostern bis Michaeli 1838 in Bonn, Gotha 1838*, IV 18; Kopie in Staatsarchiv Coburg, LA. A. nr. 6867 fol. 13; weitere Kopien ibid. fol. 14-15.

[4] Th. Becker, "Prinz Albert als Student in Bonn", S. 151.

[5] Staatsarchiv Coburg, LA. A. nr. 6883 fol. 92'.

[6] Th. Becker, "Prinz Albert als Student in Bonn", S. 150.

der späteren Auseinandersetzungen mit den politischen Zeitströmungen anzusehen sind.[1] In der Bonner Zeit dürfte die Anerkennung der fachlichen Autorität der akademischen Lehrer jede Kritik an ihnen überwogen haben.

Über die Studienfächer hinaus lernte Prinz Albert in Bonn die damals in Deutschland modernste und attraktivste Form des universitären Lehrbetriebes kennen, da sich die junge Universität ja im wesentlichen an Wilhelm von Humboldts Konzeption der Verbindung von Lehre und Forschung sowie der akademischen Selbstverwaltung anlehnte. Freilich war die Universität keineswegs von politischer Einflußnahme befreit, denn neben dem Prinzip der akademischen Selbstverwaltung und der Autonomie von Forschung und Bildung galt überall in Preußen der Grundsatz der staatlichen Universitätshoheit.[2] Diese war seit den Karlsbader Beschlüssen von 1819 noch verschärft worden, und es kann den Studenten kaum verborgen geblieben sein, dass die politischen Einflüsse "eine freie Entfaltung des Geistes behindern mußten" – wie es Max Braubach einmal formuliert hat.[3] Die studentischen Verbindungen waren verboten; vor der Immatrikulation hatte jeder Student ein Revers zu unterzeichnen, mit dem er auf die entsprechenden Beschlüsse des Bundestages verpflichtet wurde.[4] Darüber hinaus wurde die Freiheit der universitären Selbstverwaltung durch einen Regierungskommissar beschränkt, und der als akademischer Lehrer zu gefährlich erscheinende Ernst Moritz Arndt war von der Lehre suspendiert worden. Der bereits erwähnte denunziatorische Brief Wangenheims mit der Warnung vor liberalen Ideen ist vielleicht auch aus dem Umstand zu erklären, dass er in Hannover geschrieben wurde. Dort war die politische Lage im Jahr 1837 wegen des Verfassungskonfliktes besonders angespannt und eskalierte im Herbst desselben Jahres mit dem Protest der sieben Göttinger Professoren.

Davon wird in der Korrespondenz der beiden Coburger Prinzen allerdings nichts erwähnt; vielleicht weil im Rheinland gerade zu dieser Zeit die Aufmerksamkeit ganz den heftigen Auseinandersetzungen zwischen katholischer Kirche und preußischer Regierung galt. Hier dürfte Prinz Albert zum ersten Mal die konfessionelle Problematik in der preußischen Politik aus eigener Anschauung kennen gelernt haben. Das Coburger Herzogtum verstand sich stets als eine Keimzelle der lutherischen Reformation, und so fühlte sich auch Albert dem Protestantismus zutiefst verbunden. In Bonn

---

[1] Elisabeth Scheeben, *Ernst II., Herzog von Sachsen-Coburg und Gotha* (Frankfurt u.a., 1987), S. 41.

[2] Ernst Rudolf Huber, *Deutsche Verfassungsgeschichte seit 1789*, second edition, vol. I (Stuttgart, 1960), S. 289.

[3] M. Braubach, *Kleine Geschichte der Universität Bonn*, S. 13.

[4] Ein gedrucktes Exemplar ist erhalten in Staatsarchiv Coburg LA A nr. 6869.

erlebte er nun aus der Nähe, wie neben dem Protestantismus auch der Katholizismus Geltung beanspruchte. An der Universität wurde dem mit dem Prinzip der konfessionellen Toleranz begegnet. Es gab keine konfessionellen Beschränkungen bei der Zulassung zum Studium, es gab zwei theologische Fakultäten, eine evangelische und eine katholische, und es wurden auch Katholiken auf Professuren und Lehrstühle berufen.[1] Im allgemeinen war aus der Sicht des rheinischen Katholizismus die rechtliche, soziale und politische Lage freilich unbefriedigend, und Prinz Albert stand dem Verhalten der Bevölkerung bei dem Zusammenstoß von preußischem Staat und katholischer Kirche in den sog. Kölner Wirren mit Unverständnis gegenüber. Im Streit um die Kirchenzugehörigkeit von Kindern konfessionsverschiedener Eltern und um die geistliche Aufsicht über katholische theologische Fakultäten hatten die preußischen Behörden im Winter 1837 den Kölner Erzbischof in Haft nehmen lassen. Prinz Albert schrieb darüber an seinen Vater:

> Du wirst auch bestimmt Antheil an den Cölner Ereignissen genommen haben. Hier ist es die Lebensfrage geworden und zeigt sich sehr deutlich, dass die viel gepriesene Anhänglichkeit der Rheinlande erstaunlich locker ist. 'Preuss' und 'Lutherischer Ketzer' sind gewöhnliche Schimpfreden. Wie es scheint, ist die Priesterpartei ausserordentlich stark; sie findet ihre Hauptstütze in dem Adel und den Landleuten. Namentlich der Adel ist hier sehr bigott.[2]

In der Tradition einer protestantischen Landesherrschaft groß geworden, fehlte Prinz Albert für öffentliche Kritik am Landesherrn oder gar für Formen des Widerstandes, wie er sie nun erlebte, jedes Verständnis.[3]

Abgesehen von diesen Ereignissen, die sich eher im Umfeld der Universität als in ihr selbst abspielten, ist sicherlich die Annahme berechtigt, dass die intensiven und eindrucksreichen Studiensemester in Bonn die Vorstellungen beeinflußt haben, die Prinz Albert später selbst zur Universität und zu ihren Aufgaben entwickelt hat und die insbesondere auf seine Erwartungen und Ziele einwirkten, die er als Kanzler der Universität Cambridge hatte.

---

[1] M. Braubach, *Kleine Geschichte der Universität Bonn*, S. 12-13; vgl. Paragraph 8 der Universitätsstatuten von 1827, *Verfassungsgeschichte der Universität Bonn, 1818 bis 1968*, ed. Karl Th. Schäfer (Bonn, 1968), S. 424-425.

[2] Albert an Ernst I., Bonn 26. Dezember 1837, in: Ch. Grey, *Die Jugendjahre des Prinzen Albert*, S. 128.

[3] Dazu auch Frank Eyck, *Prinzgemahl Albert von England* (Erlenbach-Zürich und Stuttgart, 1961), S.19.

2. Kanzlerwahl in Cambridge

Die Wahl Prinz Alberts zum Kanzler der Universität Cambridge im Jahr 1847 war keineswegs selbstverständlich. Aus zeitgenössischer Sicht waren seine Wahlchancen zunächst äußerst gering, weil vieles gegen ihn sprach. Seine Stellung als Ehemann der Königin machte ihn in England zwar zu einer bekannten Erscheinung, aber vornehmlich aus zwei Gründen waren daraus keine Argumente für seine Qualifikation zu dem Amt abzuleiten. Der erste Grund bestand darin, dass die Monarchie selbst immer noch belastet war durch das schlechte Image der letzten Könige aus dem Haus Hannover. Die Regierungszeit Georg III. (1760-1820), seines Sohnes Georg IV. (1820-1830) und dessen Bruder William IV. (1830-1837) hatten das Ansehen der Krone verspielt. In der Biographie der Königin Victoria von Sidney Lee aus dem Jahr 1902 heißt es dazu sarkastisch: "Der englische Thron war nacheinander von einem Schwachsinnigen, einem Sittenlosen und einem Hanswurst besetzt"[1], und die Erinnerung daran wurde auch nach dem Übergang der Monarchie auf Victoria im Jahr 1837 nicht weniger wirkungsvoll wachgehalten durch die Eskapaden, die sich die noch lebenden Söhne Georgs IV. leisteten.[2] Als zweiter Grund ist die Tatsache zu nennen, dass es nicht üblich war, dass ein Mitglied der königlichen Familie das Kanzleramt bekleidete. Vielmehr wählte Cambridge wie auch Oxford stets Hochadelige, die nicht der königlichen Familie angehörten.[3] Dafür waren politische Gründe maßgebend. Der Kanzler sollte Interesse am Wohlergehen der Universität haben, sie ab und zu besuchen und im übrigen im Parlament für ihre Belange eintreten. Wichtig war daher, dass er Mitglied eines der beiden Häuser des Parlaments war. Das war bei Prinz Albert nicht der Fall. Und darüber hinaus bestand die Gefahr, dass er in Loyalitätskonflikte geriet, wenn er als Ehemann der Königin zugunsten der Universität gegen Maßnahmen der königlichen Regierung streiten mußte.[4] Abgesehen davon galt Prinz Albert im Land ohnehin als ein Fremder, denn er war ja weder im Lande geboren, noch hatte er an einer der alten Universitäten Englands studiert. Fremde hatten es auch in England von vornherein nicht einfach. Aus Sicht der Universität Cambridge mit ihrem traditionellen Studienprogramm und ihren engen Beziehungen zur Kirche von England

---

[1] Sidney Lee, *Queen Victoria* (London, 1902), S. 53.
[2] D. Beales, "The Prince Consort and the University of Cambridge", S. 158.
[3] O. Chadwick, *Prince Albert and the University*, S. 1.
[4] Denys Arthur Winstanley, *Early Victorian Cambridge* (Cambridge, 1940), S. 98, S. 107.

schienen zudem seine deutsche Bildung und seine Konfession suspekt.[1]
Wie empfindlich man hierin war, hatte sich schon unmittelbar vor seiner
Heirat gezeigt, als er sich gegen Verdächtigungen verteidigen mußte, ent-
weder Katholik oder Angehöriger einer protestantischen Sekte zu sein.[2]
Schließlich sprach auch nicht für ihn, dass er mit gerade 27 Jahren noch
jung war.

Dass er trotz dieser auf den ersten Blick nachteiligen Qualitäten dennoch
zum Kanzler gewählt wurde, lag daran, dass zu der Zeit, als das vakant ge-
wordene Kanzleramt zur Besetzung anstand, in England und in Cambridge
hochschulpolitische Entwicklungen in den Vordergrund traten, die sich als
überaus günstige Voraussetzungen für die Kandidatur Prinz Alberts erwie-
sen. Damit ist vor allem der zunehmend lauter werdende Ruf nach Reformen gemeint, die im Studiensystem Cambridges Platz greifen sollten. Die
Universität hatte im Gegensatz zu den Universitäten in den deutschen Ter-
ritorien keinerlei Brüche durch französische Revolution und napoleonische
Herrschaft erleben müssen. Im Unterschied zu den preußischen Universitäten bestand hier das College-System unverändert fort, was weit mehr als
einen Unterschied in der Organisationsstruktur bedeutete. Vielmehr kam
damit eine andere Auffassung von universitärer Bildung zum Ausdruck.
Während an den preußischen Universitäten die Studenten allein über ihre
Studientätigkeit in die Hochschule eingebunden wurden und weitgehend
eigenständige soziale Organisationsformen zur Gestaltung ihres studentischen Alltags entwickelten, erwartete die Studenten in Cambridge in den
Colleges ein ganzheitlich verstandenes Bildungsprogramm, das sich neben
der Wissensvermittlung auch auf die moralische und soziale Bildung er-
streckte.[3] Diese ganzheitliche Einbindung und Betreuung der Studenten
machte somit Überlegungen überflüssig, wie sie am Coburger Hof wegen
der "Gefahren für junge Herren fürstlichen Standes" angestellt wurden. Es
war auch nicht dieses traditionelle universitäre Erziehungsmodell, das sich
zunehmend der Kritik ausgesetzt sah, sondern es war vornehmlich die Universitätsverfassung, weil sie – so schien es – von den *Colleges* und deren
partikularen Interessen dominiert wurde, und es waren die Studieninhalte.
Die Verfassung bestand aus den unter Elisabeth I. im Jahr 1570 verab-
schiedeten Statuten und einigen Verfügungen aus der ersten Hälfte des 17.
Jahrhunderts.[4] Die Statuten waren eine Art Bestandsschutz für Verhält-

---

[1] Ibid., S. 22; D. Beales, "The Prince Consort and the University of Cambridge", S.
159.

[2] Th. Martin, *The Prince Consort*, vol. 1, S. 56-58.

[3] O. Chadwick, *Prince Albert and the University*, S. 29.

[4] George Peacock, *Observations on the Statutes of the University of Cambridge*
(London, 1841), S. 1-74; P. Searby, *A History of the University*, S. 46.

nisse, die – nach Auffassung von Derek Beales – selbst für Zeitgenossen
einen bizarren Eindruck vermittelten und drei charakteristische Merkmale
besaßen:[1] 1. die Universität bestand im wesentlichen aus 17 *Colleges*, die
die *Fellows* auswählten und bezahlten und für die akademische Lehre ihrer
jeweiligen Studenten sorgten. Eine untergeordnete Rolle sowohl in der
Lehre als auch in der Höhe der Besoldung spielten hingegen die lediglich
17 Universitätsprofessoren, obwohl sie zum Teil einen sehr guten Ruf hatten. 2. Die *Fellows* waren nahezu alle Kleriker der Kirche von England.
Die meisten von ihnen warteten darauf, Cambridge zu verlassen, besser be-
zahlte kirchliche Funktionen zu erhalten und dann auch heiraten zu können.
Nicht anders verhielt es sich bei den Studenten. In den 10 Jahren vor Beginn von Prinz Alberts Kanzlerschaft nahm Cambridge ca. 4000 Studenten
auf, von denen 3000, also drei Viertel, einen Abschluß erwarben. Dazu war
nur berechtigt, wer sich zur Anglikanischen Kirche bekannte; 70 Prozent
der Examinierten wiederum erhielten einen Weihegrad, d.h. dass von allen
Studenten Cambridges in den 10 Jahren ungefähr die Hälfte in den Klerus
der Kirche von England ging.[2] 3. Unter den Prüfungen und Lehrangeboten
spielten die theologischen Fächer aber keineswegs die besondere Rolle, die
man aufgrund der genannten Zahlen erwarten könnte. Vielmehr waren die
beiden wirklich bedeutenden und dementsprechend nachgefragten Prüfungen die in Mathematik und in *Classics*. Ein *Honours Degree* war nur in
Mathematik möglich, und nur wer dabei gut abschnitt, konnte sodann noch
die Prüfung in *Classics* ablegen. Da dies wenige taten, ergab sich in Cambridge eine ausgesprochen enge Verbindung von Klerus und Mathematik;
diese Wissenschaft besaß an der Universität seit Newton höchstes Renom-
mee, und ihr Studium sollte die Fähigkeit zu strikt logischem und rationa-
lem Denken vermitteln.[3]

Als die Wahl Alberts zum Kanzler erfolgte, war bereits seit langem eine
Diskussion im Gange zwischen Verteidigern dieser traditionellen Verhältnisse und denen, die darauf verwiesen, dass eine solch einseitige universitäre Bildung nicht mehr den Anforderungen der Lebenswelt entspreche und
daher zu verändern sei.[4] Peter Searby zeichnet in seiner Darstellung der
Geschichte der Universität den Weg der Reform nach, deren Beginn er
spätestens im Jahr 1835 ausmacht, als eine Regierungskommission sich mit

---

[1] D. Beales, "The Prince Consort and the University of Cambridge", S. 159-162.

[2] Das bedeutete aber nicht, dass stets ein Priesteramt übernommen wurde, sondern
Kleriker waren z. B. auch Schulmeister, vgl. ibid., S. 161; O. Chadwick, *Prince Albert
and the University*, S. 6.

[3] P. Searby, *A History of the University*, S. 166-167.

[4] Dazu ein sehr detaillierter Überblick bei D.A. Winstanley, *Early Victorian Cambridge*, S. 148-233.

der Reform der Verwaltung der Kirche von England befaßte. Angesichts der engen Verbindungen zur Kirche war zwangsläufig auch die Universität einbezogen. Den vorläufigen Endpunkt der Reform markierte die Königliche Reformkommission von 1850, deren Arbeitsergebnisse die Grundlage für den *Cambridge University Act* von 1856 bildete.[1]

Die Kommission ging im wesentlichen auf John Russell zurück, der 1846 *Prime Minister* eines liberalen Kabinetts wurde und seit langem einer der prominentesten politischen Befürworter von Universitätsreformen war. Wie Prinz Albert hatte auch er keine Ausbildung in Cambridge oder Oxford erfahren, sondern hatte seine Studien drei Jahre lang an der schottischen Universität in Edinburgh betrieben, weil sein Vater der Meinung war, dass man an englischen Universitäten nichts lernen könne.[2] Es wurde allgemein erwartet, dass unter Russell von politischer Seite aus die Reform energisch in Gang gesetzt würde.

Diese Erwartung war auch in Cambridge weit verbreitet, als im Februar 1847 die Wahl Prinz Alberts zum Kanzler erfolgte. Eine starke Gruppe hatte einen Gegenkandidaten präsentiert, den Earl of Powis, der das eher traditionelle Bild eines Kanzlers abgab: Er war Mitglied von St John's, seit 23 Jahren Tory-Abgeordneter, und kürzlich hervorgetreten als Verteidiger der Anglikanischen Kirche gegen Versuche des Kabinetts Peel, die Bistumsstruktur zu verändern. Das Wahlergebnis war mit 953 Stimmen für Prinz Albert gegen 837 Stimmen für Powis ausgesprochen knapp, war aber für die Stimmungslage in der Universität selbst nur bedingt repräsentativ, denn drei Viertel der in Cambridge residierenden *Masters of Arts* hatten für Prinz Albert gestimmt. Die Stimmen für Powis kamen überwiegend von den aus dem ganzen Land zur Abstimmung angereisten *MAs*; unter ihnen war die Zahl der Tory-Anhänger offensichtlich größer, was das genannte Ergebnis erklärt.[3] Weniger deutlich auszumachen sind die Erwartungen, die zu der Entscheidung der Mehrheit für Prinz Albert geführt hatten, aber sicherlich zählten dazu die Überlegungen, die den Master von *Trinity*, William Whewell, zu einem der Wortführer der Kandidatur des Prinzen werden ließen. Er sah in Prinz Albert den geeigneten Kanzler, der – gerade weil er keine engen Verbindungen zu den Tories besaß – besser mit der liberalen Regierung zurecht kommen werde. Zudem übte er, obwohl er den Parteien neutral gegenüberstand und obwohl er keinen Sitz im Oberhaus hatte, erheblichen politischen Einfluß aus. Das mochte den Ausschlag ge-

[1] P. Searby, *A History of the University*, S. 430, S. 530.
[2] Spencer Walpole, *The Life of Lord John Russell*, vol. I (London, 1889), S. 44; cf. P. Searby, *A History of the University*, S. 508.
[3] Ibid., S. 508; die Details der Wahl sind nachgezeichnet bei D.A. Winstanley, *Early Victorian Cambridge*, S. 106-121.

geben haben für viele, die sich der Einsicht nicht verschlossen hatten, dass Reformen unvermeidlich sein würden, und die von ihrem neuen Kanzler erwarteten, dass er seine Universität so gegen politische Pressionsversuche abschirme, dass sie in der Lage sei, diese Reformen selbst auf den Weg zu bringen.[1]

3. Studienreform in Cambridge

Diese Erwartungen der Wähler sind in den nächsten Jahren auch erfüllt worden, wie der *Punch* im Jahr 1848 treffend illustriert hat mit einem Cartoon, dessen Titel lautet: *H.R.H. Field Marshal Chancellor Prince Albert taking the Pons Asinorum. After the manner of Napoleon taking the bridge of Arcola.*

H.R.H. FIELD-MARSHAL CHANCELLOR PRINCE ALBERT TAKING THE PONS ASINORUM.
AFTER THE MANNER OF NAPOLEON TAKING THE BRIDGE OF ARCOLA.

Abb. 2: "H.R.H. Field-Marshall Chancellor Prince Albert Taking the Pons Asinorum. After the Manner of Napoleon Taking the Bridge of Arcola", *Punch*, 15 (London 1848), 225.

---

[1] D. Beales, "The Prince Consort and the University of Cambridge", S. 163.

Das Thema ist die Auseinandersetzung um neue Studiengänge, hier als *Moral Sciences* und *Physical Sciences* tituliert, deren Gegner auf der linken Bildseite das alte System von Mathematik und Classics offenbar vergeblich gegen den Ansturm der Truppen des Prinzen Albert zu verteidigen suchen, der persönlich mit der Fahne seinen Truppen so voranstürmt, wie es nach populären Darstellungen Napoleon auf seinem Italienfeldzug tat, als er am 15. November 1796 bei Arcoli in scheinbar aussichtsloser Lage auf diese Weise die Schlacht für sich entschied. Es wird vorausgesetzt, dass der Leser diese Anspielung versteht.[1]

In einer ersten Phase der Amtszeit Russells gelang es Prinz Albert tatsächlich, den auf Reformen drängenden Prime Minister dazu zu bewegen, staatliche Initiativen aufzuschieben, um der inneruniversitären Reform Gelegenheit zur Entfaltung zu gewähren. Er war daran meist selbst beteiligt und unterstützte, wie Owen Chadwick formuliert hat, im wesentlichen drei Ziele einer Reform: eine Ausweitung der Zahl der Studienfächer, eine Schmälerung des Einflusses der Colleges auf das universitäre Geschehen und eine Erhöhung der Hörerzahl in den Lehrveranstaltungen der Professoren.[2] Seinen Vorstellungen lagen sicherlich die befriedigenden Erfahrungen zu Grunde, die er in seinen Bonner Jahren mit einem weitgespannten und von Professoren verantworteten Studienangebot gemacht hatte. So waren seine Pläne nicht reine Theorie. Es war aber von ebenso großer Bedeutung, dass auch einflußreiche Universitätslehrer aus Cambridge das Reformbedürfnis verspürten und deshalb die Kooperation mit ihm suchten. Seine engsten Ratgeber in Cambridge waren dabei der Master von St Catherine's Henry Philpott und der Professor für Geologie Adam Sedgwick; ein wichtiger Berater wurde außerdem der von Russell im Jahr zuvor als Prime Minister abgelöste Robert Peel. Bereits im Oktober 1847 beschrieb Philpott, der zu diesem Zeitpunkt Vice-Chancellor war, dem Prinzen in einem ausführlichen Memorandum die Lehrsituation. Als Problem wurde dabei deutlich, dass die Professoren zwar Vorlesungen hielten, dass diese aber nur von wenigen Studenten besucht wurden, da ihr Besuch freiwillig war und selten Bedeutung für die Examina hatte.[3] Nach einem Vorschlag Philpotts, dem Prinz Albert zustimmte, sollte die allmähliche Einführung von Prüfungen in neuen Fächern neben den traditionellen in Mathematik und Classics Abhilfe schaffen, denn nur durch den Prüfungsdruck wurde erfahrungsgemäß das Interesse der Studenten am Besuch von Lehrveranstaltun-

---

[1] Auch der Ausdruck "Pons Asinorum" konnte bei einem in Mathematik geschulten Zeitgenossen Assoziationen wecken, da die fünfte Proposition in den *Elementen* des Euklid als eine Eselsbrücke galt, vgl. St. Weintraub, *Albert*, S. 208.

[2] Chadwick, *Prince Albert and the University*, S. 23f.

[3] P. Searby, *A History of the University*, S. 509.

gen in anderen Fächern geweckt. Tatsächlich kamen an der Universität Reformbemühungen dieser Art in Gang, deren Befürwortern sicherlich zustatten kam, dass Prime Minister Russell im Herbst 1847 mit seinem Vorschlag für eine königliche Reformkommission hervortrat. Prinz Albert hat sich in einem Brief an Russell persönlich dafür verwendet, dass die Regierung sich zunächst noch zurückhalte, damit die Reformbemühungen der Universität selbst sich entwickeln könnten.[1] Die Universität brauchte tatsächlich einige Zeit. Die sich darüber entzündenden, erregten Debatten zeigten, dass die Reformbereitschaft unter den Fellows keineswegs allgemein verbreitet war. Die Gegner argumentierten konservativ, indem sie auf die Bedeutung verwiesen, die Mathematik und klassische Sprachen für eine intellektuelle Schulung besaßen. Ihnen schien nicht gewiß, dass ein stärker auf der Vermittlung von Forschungserkenntnissen beruhendes Studium dieselben Zwecke erreichen und übertreffen würde. Der bedeutende Mineraloge William Whewell, der ohne Zweifel ein grundsätzlicher Befürworter der Reformbemühungen war, erhob hinsichtlich der Studieninhalte die Forderung, dass naturwissenschaftliche Entdeckungen erst nach einhundert Jahren im akademischen Unterricht gelehrt werden sollten. Er fürchtete, dass das Ansehen der Professoren bei den Studenten leiden könnten, wenn vermeintlich sicheres Wissen ständig revidiert werden müßte. Robert Peel trat dieser Forderung schroff entgegen und sah in ihr eine Absurdität, die der schlimmste Feind der Universität hätte ersinnen können.[2] Hier zeigten sich tiefgreifende Meinungsverschiedenheiten über die Frage, in welchem Ausmaß die Lehre forschungsorientiert gestaltet werden sollte.

Das Ergebnis der Reformbemühungen waren eine Reihe von Änderungsbestimmungen für die bestehenden Studiengänge und vor allem zwei neue *Triposes* in Naturwissenschaften und in Geisteswissenschaften, die erstmals 1851 geprüft wurden. Der naturwissenschaftliche *Tripos* (*Natural Sciences*) umfaßte als Teilfächer Anatomie, Vergleichende Anatomie, Physiologie, Chemie, Botanik und Geologie; der geisteswissenschaftliche *Tripos* (*Moral Sciences*) bestand aus den Fächern Ethik, Volkswirtschaft, Neuere Geschichte, Allgemeine Rechtswissenschaften und Englisches Recht.[3] Als ihre Einführung 1848 von der Universität beschlossen wurde,

---

[1] Prinz Albert an Lord John Russell, Windsor Castle 13. November 1847, in: Th. Martin, *The Prince Consort*, fourth edition, vol. 2 (London, 1877), S. 121-124; vgl. P. Searby, *A History of the University*, S. 511.

[2] "[...] exceeds in absurdity anything which the bitterest enemy of University Education would have imputed to its advocates", Robert Peel an Prinz Albert, 27. Oktober [1847], Th. Martin, *The Prince Consort*, vol. 2, S. 117-119; vgl. D.A. Winstanley, *Early Victorian Cambridge*, S. 202.

[3] Ibid., S. 208.

schrieb Prinz Albert sichtlich zufrieden in sein Tagebuch: "My plan for a reform of the studies at Cambridge is carried by a large majority".[1] Dies zeigt, wie engagiert er an dem Vorhaben Anteil genommen hatte. Und tatsächlich ist es vornehmlich die Einführung dieser Studiengänge, wofür er unmittelbare öffentliche Anerkennung fand und mit der der Name des Prinzen Albert verbunden geblieben ist. Kurze Zeit danach ging die Phase zuende, in der die Universität ohne staatlichen Druck Reformen auf den Weg bringen konnte, und eine vergleichbare Situation, die eine fruchtbare Kooperation von Kanzler und Universität begünstigt hätte, hat sich nicht noch einmal ergeben.

Die Initiative ging 1850 vielmehr auf Russell und sein Kabinett über, die eine königliche Kommission für Reformen in Oxford und Cambridge einsetzten. Prinz Albert hat die Arbeit dieser Kommission unterstützt, vor allem dadurch, dass er in engem Kontakt mit Russell stand und gleichzeitig auf die Universität einwirkte, mit der Kommission zu kooperieren und eigene Mitglieder für sie zu benennen. Die Kommission hat die Grundlage erarbeitet für das Gesetz von 1856, durch das die Universitätsverfassung reformiert wurde.[2] Gemessen an den Mitteln, die Prinz Albert zur Verfügung standen, um die Studienreform voranzubringen, war die Kommission Russells weit machtvoller und hat schließlich auf dem Wege der Gesetzgebung ihre Ziele regelrecht erzwingen können. Prinz Albert war hingegen auf Kooperation mit der Universität angewiesen, die immerhin soweit gebracht werden konnte, dass sie das Angebot an Studiengängen und Prüfungen erweiterte. Auch das war schon ein Fortschritt und entsprach der Idee einer breit gefächerten universitären Bildung, für die Prinz Albert weiterhin Werbung gemacht hat. Sie war für Cambridge wie für ganz England ungewohnt und hat sich erst ganz allmählich durchsetzen können. 1855 hat er sich dazu einmal öffentlich in einer Grundsatzrede geäußert, die geradezu eine Reflexion seiner in Bonn und in Cambridge gemachten Erfahrungen darstellte: Er betonte die Bedeutung der fortwährenden wissenschaftlichen Erkenntnisgewinnung, die für alle nachvollziehbar sein sollte, und führte dann aus, dass Mathematik und klassische Sprachen, die traditionellerweise als die klassischen Lernfelder einer nationalen Erziehung gelten, sicherlich wissens- und bildungsmäßig wichtige Bereiche seien. Aber hierzu müßten unbedingt andere treten, ohne die es einfach nicht mehr gehe, und er zählte davon einige auf: Logik und Metaphysik, Physiologie und Psychologie, Politische Wissenschaften, Rechtswissenschaft und Staatswissenschaften;

---

[1] Eintrag vom 1. November 1848, in: Th. Martin, *The Prince Consort*, vol. 2, S. 114.
[2] P. Searby, *A History of the University*, S. 522.

und er schloß die Ergänzung an: "und viele andere".[1] Wissen und Bildung waren aus seiner Sicht vielfältig, ohne dass diese Vielfalt abschließend zu definieren war.

4. Schlußbemerkung

Asa Briggs hat auf die Tatsache hingewiesen, dass Oxford und Cambridge im 19. Jahrhundert einen fundamentalen Wandel durchliefen. Während sie zu Beginn des Jahrhunderts im wesentlichen klerikale Institutionen der Kirche von England waren, präsentierten sie sich am Ende des 19. Jahrhunderts nicht mehr als religiöse, sondern als weitestgehend säkularisierte Institutionen. Dieser Wandel lasse sich nicht mit dem Geschehen in der universitären Erziehung selbst erklären, sondern sei zurückzuführen auf Veränderungen wirtschaftlicher, politischer und sozialer Art. Was sich in den Universitäten ereignete, war also Funktion und nicht Ursache der allgemeinen Entwicklung.

Dieser Beobachtung entsprechen die Ergebnisse der hier ausgebreiteten Betrachtung. Wenn man die drei von Chadwick festgehaltenen Ziele, die Prinz Albert bei seiner Kanzlerschaft in Cambridge verfolgte, als Maßstab nimmt, so hat er sie nicht in allem erreicht. Eine Schmälerung des Einflus-

---

[1] Rede zur Grundsteinlegung des *Birmingham and Midland Institute*, 22. November 1855, *The Principal Speeches and Adresses of HRH The Prince Consort* (Leipzig, 1866), S. 146-155, S. 152-154: "It is sometimes objected by the ignorant that science is uncertain and changeable, and they point with a malicious kind of pleasure to the many exploded theories which have been superseded by others, as a proof that the present knowledge may be also unsound, and, after all, not worth having. But they are not aware, while they think to cast blame upon science, they bestow, in fact, the highest praise upon her [...]. The study of the laws by which the Almighty governs the Universe is therefore our bounden duty. Of these laws our great academies and seats of education have, rather arbitrarily, selected only two spheres or groups (as I may call them) as essential parts of our national education: the laws which regulate quantities and proportions, which form the subject of mathematics, and the laws regulating the expression of our thoughts, through the medium of language, that is to say, grammar, which finds its purest expression in the classical languages. These laws are most important branches of knowledge, their study trains and elevates the mind, but they are not the only ones; there are others which we cannot disregard, which we cannot do without. There are, for instance, the laws governing the human mind, and its relation to the Divine Spirit (the subject of logic and metaphysics); there are those which govern our bodily nature and its connection with the soul (the subject of physiology and psychology); those which govern human society, and the relations between man and man (the subjects of politics, jurisprudence, and political economy); and many others"; vgl. dazu auch Chadwick, *Prince Albert and the University*, S. 30.

ses der Colleges auf das universitäre Geschehen ist nicht ihm, sondern erst mit Hilfe der 1850 eingesetzten Royal Commission gelungen. Hingegen war er aktiv beteiligt an der tatsächlich statthabenden Ausweitung der Zahl der Studienfächer, was wiederum auf längere Sicht das dritte Ziel erreichbar werden ließ, die Erhöhung der Hörerzahl in den Lehrveranstaltungen der Professoren. Die hiermit eingeleitete Erweiterung der Prüfungs- und Fächerstruktur war erst langfristig von größerer Bedeutung, weil sich erst allmählich Studierende fanden, die sich den neuen Prüfungen unterzogen. Gleichwohl bildeten sie – von heute aus gesehen – doch einen fundamentalen Wandel: An die Stelle der Pflege formaler Bildung an traditionellen Stoffen trat die Vermittlung aktueller, mit fortschreitendem Erkenntnisgewinn sich ständig erneuernder Inhalte. Es war zugleich der Anfang einer fortschreitenden Spezialisierung der Studiengänge, wodurch die universitäre Bildung in Cambridge in einer damals noch ungewohnten Vielfalt der Fächer und Prüfungen angeboten wurde. Nicht mehr die allgemeine Schulung in mathematischer Logik und klassischen Sprachen sollte allein den *Master of Arts* heranbilden, sondern daneben sollten gleichwertige Angebote der Geistes- und Naturwissenschaften treten, die als Gegenstand des Studiums und der Prüfung jeweils ein breites Fächerspektrum abdeckten.

Dass Cambridge damit ein zukunftsweisendes Studienangebot entwickelt hatte, mußte sich erst noch erweisen. Denn es war für die im *Oxbridge System* angebotene akademische Bildung etwas ungewohnt Neues. Dies läßt sich auch ablesen an der Bewertung des Herzogs von Wellington, Kanzler der Universität Oxford, der 1850 in einer Rede im Oberhaus beteuerte, dass auch seine Universität erforderliche Verbesserungen vornehmen werde, jedoch ohne die Absicht zu haben, "to introduce German projects, or any system of that kind, into the system of education now in force in the University of Oxford".[1] Mochten diese Ausführungen auch "discourteous" sein, wie im Jahr 1940 der *Vice-Master* von *Trinity College*, D.A. Winstanley, meinte[2], so sind sie doch ein Beleg, wie in der Zeit selbst öffentlich und an prominenter Stelle das Ausmaß und die Art des Einflusses wahrgenommen wurde, den Prinz Albert auf die jüngsten Reformen in Cambridge genommen hatte.

---

[1] *Hansard's Parliamentary Debates*, third series, vol. 110 (London, 1850), S. 1373-1374.

[2] D.A. Winstanley, *Early Victorian Cambridge*, S. 225 n. 3.

Victorian Christmas: or, "What have the Victorians ever done for us?"

By *Kenneth Wynne* (Bamberg)

For a number of years now, there has been a definite Victorian revival in connection with celebrations, cuisine, clothing and furniture, not only in Britain, but also in the United States[1], which makes it necessary to digress occasionally into the present-day celebration of Christmas as the two concepts of enjoying this festive period are not entirely unrelated. It seems strange perhaps, in these days of high technology, to observe whilst strolling through the British high street such shops as 'Past Times', a chain specialising in selling replicas of items from days gone by. But it is not only such phenomena which give rise to parallels between the Victorian celebration of Christmas and the present-day one. As an answer to the slightly adapted question from a well-known Monty Python film[2], "What have the Victorians ever done for us?", we can identify a number of the current features of the typical Christmas celebration as having their origins in the reign of Queen Victoria.

Some of the Victorian ways of celebrating Christmas are undoubtedly revivals of even older traditions, of course. The festive season, as we know from Germany too, is littered with remnants of rituals from Pagan, Roman, Germanic and Nordic times. It was during the Victorian era, however, that many of these rituals became firmly anchored in the British way of life. By taking a more or less chronological view of the preparations for the celebration of the birth of Christ, many of these features can best be illustrated.

It should first be mentioned that many of the more elaborate aspects of the Victorian celebration were clearly restricted to the urban, middle and upper classes. As a passage from *Godey's Lady's Book* of 1860 indicates, a clear distinction was made between the celebrations of city people and those from the country:

---

[1] One such example is the North Star Chapter of the Victoria Society, which is based in Minnesota. Reference is made to their Twelfth Night Gala on the website www.victoriana.com, a site which contains a wealth of related material on all things Victorian (here at www.victoriana.com/christmas/Twelfthnight.htm).

[2] The allusion is to the question "What have the Romans ever done for us?", which is repeatedly asked in Monty Python's film, *Life of Brian* (1979) and which leads to the realisation that so much of the infrastructure of Britain was influenced by Roman society.

City people [...] look on their "country cousins" as victims of routine and narrow-mindedness and general stupidity.

We present these [...] claims in what may be supposed to be the chief enjoyment of each separate life. Christmas, the general holiday, has its charms for each. In town there is much consultation as to toilet, for though the children absorb the morning, and it is proper to be seen at church, it is not less certain that the intimate male gentleman friends of the family will make their appearance by the time a demi-toilet can be dispatched [...]. There are symptoms of it in the well spread lunch table of the luxurious drawing-room, in the *impromptu* grouping of ladies of the house with the first tinkle of the door bell. [...]

Their county cousins, meantime, have already dined! – unfashionable creatures – and have enjoyed with keen appetites the ample bountiful Christmas dinner the barn yard and the garden's latest gifts of crisp celery, winter vegetables and fruit have contributed to. The air is keen and clear, the sky unclouded sapphire, the roads in the prime of sleighing from yesterday's travel over the last cheerful snow storm. They, too, have "gentleman friends" who are only too happy to pay their *devoirs* in the clear open air, and in much merriment the sleighing party is made up, to dash along with chiming bells and song and laughter. [...]

We leave our lady friends to choose for themselves in which scene lies the best opportunity for amusement and – a proposal![1]

Valerie Janitch comments further on this urban society and prefaces her book with the following assessment of the Christmas celebration:

In 1837 Queen Victoria came to the throne and soon afterwards she and her con-sort, Prince Albert, set about changing the moral attitude of the nation. Family values, the home and a more caring society were their aims and Christmas pro-vided a perfect opportunity to promote these ideals.[2]

Whilst some of these noble aims can be considered to be realistic and even to have been achieved, they did not apply to the whole of Victorian society, of course. The working class usually continued to work over the festive period and could only afford a rabbit to eat for Christmas dinner or maybe pigeon pie, if they were lucky to catch one or the other of these animals! They did not have the facilities to roast a whole turkey or goose anyway, and often took their meat to the local baker's to cook it in his larger ovens for their Christmas dinner. The Victorian Age and especially the Industrial Revolution had created a well-to-do middle class, but the effects of this development also resulted in a degree of poverty never experienced before in Britain. The British comedy series *Blackadder*[3], an irreverent re-

---

[1] Quoted under www.victoriana.com/christmas/godeys-99.htm.

[2] Valerie Janitch, *Victorian Christmas* (London, 1995), p. 7.

[3] *Blackadder's Christmas Carol*, written by Richard Curtis and Ben Elton. BBC Enterprises, 1981.

view of British history in the person of the eponymous hero, was able to tap into this misery in true British style in its version of the Dickens classic *A Christmas Carol*.[1] In the *Blackadder* version, Scrooge is initially a pleasant, charitable character who is corrupted by the visions of a happy, successful and completely uneventful future offered by the ghost!

As already established above, in largely middle and upper-class homes, great attention was paid to decoration. In the period before Christmas, a cart bearing holly branches would rumble through the streets and the open hearths would be decorated accordingly – all these decorations being brought inside before Christmas Eve, as it was considered unlucky to bring evergreens into the home afterwards. Carol singers would visit the houses in the manner of wandering players and be rewarded by the chance to warm themselves at the open fire and eat a traditional mince pie.

Not only holly featured prominently in the decorations, but ivy, laurel wreaths and other evergreens recall to mind the Pagan associations of the Winter Solstice, eternal life and the Roman festival of Saturnalia – in other words, an excuse was given for much drinking, eating and outrageous misconduct, which is largely reflected today in the notorious office party!

The ladies and children of the Victorian household would take great trouble and invest copious amounts of time in making their decorations by hand as the following instructions for making a chimney ornament reveals:

> Select a crooked twig of white or black thorn; wrap some loose wool or cotton round the branches, and tie it with worsted.
> Suspend this in a basin or deep jar.
> Dissolve two pounds of alum in a quart of boiling rain water and pour it over the twig.
> Allow it to stand twelve hours. Wire baskets may be covered in the same way.[2]

The centrepiece of the home, then as now, was the Christmas tree, which is frequently cited as being a Victorian 'invention' imported to Britain from Germany as a result of Victoria's marriage to Albert. This common opinion is not entirely accurate as Christmas trees in their 'naked state', that is, as trunks from the fir tree, were used for many years in the form of Yule logs and the then Princess Victoria described having a Christmas tree in her diary entry of 1832, well before she met Albert and five years before she actually became Queen.[3] The Yule log was traditionally cut down on Christmas Eve and dragged home in procession from the forest. It was liberally

---

[1] Charles Dickens, *A Christmas Carol*, in: Charles Dickens, *Christmas Books* (London, 1966).

[2] *Peterson's Magazine*, Dec. 1864, at www.victoriana.com/christmas/craft2-99.htm.

[3] Quoted in Valerie Janitch, *Victorian Christmas*, p. 44.

sprinkled with wine and oil, dressed with bristles from the wild boar for luck and set on fire. Victorian and modern-day echoes of this traditional celebration, which was still attested in Britain as late as 1880[1], can still be seen in people setting fire to the Christmas Pudding and in the burning of candles, notably Yule candles, which were often given as presents by grocers to their customers.

Another typical decoration used before the tree became established was a Kissing Bough, a garland of greenery with ivy, willow and mistletoe. This decoration, as its name betrays, provided an excuse for kissing people freely in the festive season and is still in existence today in the somewhat reduced form of a mere branch or twig of mistletoe which is held over the head of the chosen victim or placed over doorways to ensure maximum effectiveness!

As mentioned already, the Christmas tree increasingly started to form the centrepiece during the Victorian era. In 1841, Prince Albert decorated a large Christmas tree in Windsor Castle and thus launched a trend for the rest of Britain. Albert was very pleased that a picture showing him and Victoria with their tree was published and thus started a fashion throughout Britain for having such trees.[2]

The early trees, which Dickens referred to as the "new German toy"[3], were decorated with sweets, cakes and lighted candles. These tree candles were actually only lit for about an hour a day and there are several accounts of them having burnt down the tree, in some cases resulting in the whole house going up in flames, too! The trees were originally quite small, sitting on a table with presents lying underneath, the latter being a feature of Christmas which up to this time was largely unknown in Britain. Later, during Victoria's reign, the trees were larger and they stood on the floor. It is also not surprising that the concept of the Christmas tree was exported to the United States and that store-bought decorations started to replace the handmade ones as early as in 1870 in America. Albert and Victoria had separate trees erected in their rooms and it is recorded that they each placed presents there "with which each took pleasure in surprising the other."[4]

The decorations were left in the home, as they are now in many British households, until 6th January, Twelfth Night, and by many it is still con-

---

[1] Quoted in Margaret Baker, *Discovering Christmas Customs and Folklore*, p. 18.

[2] The coloured lithograph from 1848 is reproduced in: Dorothy Fraser, *The Life and Times of Victoria* (London, 1972), p. 79.

[3] Quoted in Margaret Baker, *Discovering Christmas Customs and Folklore* (Princes Risborough, Buckinghamshire, 1999), p. 50.

[4] Quoted in Valerie Janitsch, *Victorian Christmas*, p. 45.

sidered unlucky to take them down before this date. Similarly, it was also considered bad luck not to eat a mince pie on each of the Twelve Days of Christmas! Quite a feat, considering the modern, rather sweet and sickly mixture which, incidentally, has little to do with the sweet and savoury minced meat and other ingredients contained within the pastry cases of the original Christmas pies.

Along with establishing the tradition of the mince pie, the Victorians also have a great deal to answer for, in my opinion, with a further development that, in part, resulted from technological progress made in the printing industry during this period: the Christmas Card. Although there had been religious woodprints in the Middle Ages, the first commercial Christmas card is believed to have been designed and printed in London in 1843 at the suggestion of Sir Henry Cole, the first director of the Victoria and Albert Museum. This first card was produced in an edition of 1,000 cards and depicted a family party scene with the greeting "A Merry Christmas and Happy New Year to You" below the picture. The card was not without its critics, however, firstly because of its price of one shilling and secondly because the children were portrayed with wine glasses in their hands.[1]

The spread of the Christmas card is also attributed to the development of the Penny Post and later the Halfpenny Post, which made the sending of these cards much cheaper. This development today has resulted in the veritable flood of some 50 million cards sent around Britain and from the United Kingdom to the rest of the world. The Yule Log of the past has been made into wood pulp from which to produce the copious amounts of card and paper needed to wish those people that are seen every day of your life a "Merry Christmas", a fact that helps to explain why only 5% of the United Kingdom is now forested!

The designs and images on the cards during the Victorian era can often be deemed inappropriate for the occasion from today's perspective: naked children sitting with Santa, Santa creeping out of the sleeping child's bedroom and an array of cards with bare-breasted nymphs! The Victorian love of the 'language of flowers' then took over and eventually we find the usual snow scenes and the highly sentimental messages inside the cards. Religious themes only appeared later, but the British obsession with the robin on the Christmas card stems from Victorian times, too, as this bird was variously accredited with having a red breast due to being scorched by flames from either attempting to rescue sinners from Hell or, rather less plausibly for such a small bird, fanning the dying embers of the fire Mary was using to keep the baby Jesus warm!

---

[1] The first Christmas card is reproduced and commented upon in Valerie Janitsch, *Victorian Christmas*, p. 60.

Without going into too much theological detail about the decision of when Christmas should be celebrated, the adoption of the Gregorian calendar in 1752 decreed that the Twelve Days of Christmas began on Christmas Eve and ran through until 6th January. In Britain, in Victorian times and also today, Christmas Eve was still a time of planning and preparing rather than the time of family celebration it is in Germany. Initially, of course, due to the lack of a Father Christmas figure, who only reappeared on the Christmas scene around the mid-1800s, children would not go to bed with the same degree of excitement and anticipation as they did, and still do when they knew that Santa was on his way. The tradition of the German *Nikolaus* on 6th December was, and is not celebrated, either, so for many years the idea of children enjoying Christmas as the time for receiving that Gameboy or Barbie they always wanted was entirely unknown and Christmas was more a time for adults to enjoy the bawdy mummer plays and revel in pseudo-pagan celebrations.

The 'invention' of Father Christmas resulted from a combination of St. Nicholas, whose logic of rewarding good behaviour and punishing the bad appealed to the Victorians, and the more Americanised figure of Santa Claus, inspired by the drawings by Thomas Nast in 1863. *The Legend of St Nicholas*[1], written by the New York Professor of Divinity, Clement Clarke Moore in 1822, also played its role in establishing the present-day image. The English Old Father Christmas, under Prince Albert's tutelage, we are told by Margaret Baker, "took on a Teutonic character, acquiring new skills as night rider, sleigh driver, chimney descender, stocking filler, gift-bringer *par excellence*, resident of department stores and darling of the advertising industry."[2]

Thus, it was Christmas Day which would start the celebrations off – not perhaps as is now the case with children waking their parents just after five o'clock to see if Father Christmas has been, but with the Christmas Day service in church. It was only after that duty had been done that presents and the midday meal could be enjoyed in full.

The Victorian invention of the Christmas cracker added to the wealth of decoration placed on and around the tables. By the mid-1800s the tables were cleared after every course in the Continental manner and there was more space for table decoration. In wealthier homes and certainly in the Royal Court, the tables were piled with fruit bowls, flowers and, in the case of Queen Victoria's table, three Christmas trees hung with gingerbread. The Christmas cracker, which today is a cardboard tube filled with

---

[1] Quoted in Margaret Baker, *Discovering Christmas Customs and Folklore*, pp. 63-64.

[2] Ibid., p. 62.

an embarrassing paper hat, a motto and a cheap plastic gift, started off life as a 'bon bon', a wrapped sugared almond, which the London confectioner Tom Smith had seen on a trip to France in 1840. Almonds and other sweets were not wrapped in England at this time and he thought it would be a novel way to offer these products. He is said to have been further inspired by the cracking sound of an open fire and, after experimenting with various chemicals, managed to create a strip of paper that, when pulled and rubbed together with a friction strip, would create a snapping sound. Until the 1920s, these decorations were still known as bonbons; afterwards they became known as the Christmas crackers which are still in use today.

The undoubted highlight of the Victorian Christmas was the cuisine – richly supplemented with the help of the famous cookbook by Mrs Beeton, *The Book of Household Management*[1], originally published in 1861, which became the Bible for the Victorian cook and which is enjoying popularity again today in the light of Britain's current interest in cookbooks and TV chefs. Maybe, in the years that followed, the cookery Bible was read about as much as the real Bible, thus resulting in the well-known clichés about British food, but there was no excuse for not putting on a real spread if one followed the advice of this and many other cookbooks of the time! The food offered in the Victorian home was not hastily prepared beans-on-toast or microwaved steak and kidney pie, either. Preparation weeks, if not months in advance was the secret to success. As one account of 1898 tells us:

> Our greatest observance of custom is, as it should be, in connection with Christmas-tide. Indeed, preparation for the same really commences some weeks in advance. There is the pudding to make and partly boil; all the ingredients for the plum cake to order; the mincemeat to prepare for the mince-pies; the goose to choose from some neighbouring farmer's stock; the cheese to buy; ...[2]

The procedure for making the Christmas cake is still observed carefully by some families today with a typical Victorian recipe (requiring flour, sugar, butter, eggs, peel, almonds, cherries, raisins, sultanas, brandy or rum) still being used in a largely unchanged form. The mixture results in a very rich cake which was dowsed regularly in the weeks before Christmas with rum to stop it from drying out.

---

[1] *Mrs Beeton's Book of Household Management – Abridged Edition*, ed. Nicola Humble (Oxford, 2000).

[2] Richard Blakeborough's account of Christmas on his Yorkshire farm in 1898, quoted in Margaret Baker, *Discovering Christmas Customs and Folklore*, p. 31.

The family would then all gather, rather in the manner described by Dickens in *A Christmas Carol*:

> By this time it was getting dark, and snowing pretty heavily; and as Scrooge and the Spirit went along the streets, the brightness of the roaring fires in kitchens, parlours, and all sorts of rooms was wonderful. Here, the flickering of the blaze showed preparations for a cosy dinner, with hot plates baking through and through before the fire, and deep red curtains, ready to be drawn to shut out cold and darkness. There, all the children of the house were running out into the snow to meet their married sisters, brothers, cousins, uncles, aunts, and be the first to greet them. Here, again, were shadows on the window-blinds of guests assembling; and there a group of handsome girls, all hooded and fur booted, and all chattering at once, tripped lightly off to some near neighbour's house; where, woe upon the single man who saw them enter – artful witches: well they knew it – in a glow they would appear.[1]

Then the typical menu would be served such as this one taken from *Godey's Lady's Book* of 1890:

Raw Oysters
Bouillon
Fried Smelts   Sauce Tartare
Potatoes à la Maitre d'Hotel
Sweetbread Pate   Peas
Roast Turkey   Cranberry Sauce
Roman Punch
Quail with Truffles   Rice Croquettes
Parisian Salad
Crackers and Cheese
Christmas Pudding   Fancy Cakes
Fruit   Coffee[2]

Turkey, as the main dish of the dinner, only became affordable in Britain towards the end of the 19th century and gradually replaced the goose or side of beef. Other, nowadays more exotic birds had been eaten previously such as the swan or even the peacock (taken out of its skin and sewn back in again complete with tail feathers!), but, whilst the turkey was imported from America in the mid-sixteenth century, it still remained a luxury dish for much of the Victorian era.

The meal was rounded off by the Christmas pudding, which is also sometimes referred to as plum pudding, thus hinting at its origins as a kind

---

[1] Charles Dickens, *Christmas Books*, p. 49.
[2] Quoted at www.victoriana.com/christmas/menu-99.htm.

of plum porridge served in the manner of a soup earlier on in the meal. The plum pudding was later adapted to its present-day recipe of suet, sugar, raisins, lemon and orange peel, spices, eggs, flour and milk. The pudding was also prepared in advance and stirred by each member of the family for luck, often following the distinct hierarchy of the Victorian household. The other lucky feature of the pudding was the silver coins hidden in it with the person who managed not to choke to death on the coin they found in their portion being the lucky one! A further typical problem of the Victorian days was that the pudding was often so large it had to be cooked in a wash boiler – after carefully removing the washing from the water first, of course.

The meal was rounded off by the giving of presents and then the Victorians indulged in their much-loved party games. A great number of these games still exist today such as Blindman's Buff, Forfeits or Charades.[1] Thankfully, however, some have gone out of fashion such as the highly amusing game of 'snapdragon' where raisins were set alight in brandy, the lights were turned off and the point of the game was to grab the raisins out of the flames! A variation on this theme was 'flapdragon', where a lighted candle was placed in a mug of cider and the participants had to drink the contents – quite a feat in the days of the Victorian side-whiskers! The Royal Family is also known to have engaged in the singing of duets and to have watched pantomimes and magic lantern shows. Card games and petty gambling are also said to have amused Victoria and Albert in the festive period. The Christmas scene was then completed by the women retiring and the men indulging in port and cigars.

It should also be said in this context of the rather smug and self-satisfied family home that many of the less well-off members of society also benefited from the Victorian spirit of giving, which largely centred on the donations given to the workhouses and prisons, but also took the form of 'Christmas boxes', that is, presents given to those who had served the household during the year. This custom gave rise to the name used for 26th December in Britain even today: namely, Boxing Day. This day was in Victorian times as well as today also associated with sporting events; the Victorians were great fans of horse racing, for example, and it gave others the chance to indulge in such pastimes as the English have become famous for: eccentric ones such as the Boxing Day swim in the Serpentine in Hyde Park! In 1870, the *Daily Telegraph* reported of such a swim: "In no country but happy England could such a scene be witnessed as the breaking of 3 inches of ice to give enough water for the race to take place."[2]

---

[1] See *Victorian Parlour Games*. Compiled by Patrick Beaver (Wigston, 1995).

[2] Quoted in Margaret Baker, *Discovering Christmas Customs and Folklore*, p. 94.

In conclusion, it must be said that the Victorians seemed to have no trouble in selecting the best-loved and most attractive of the Christmas traditions and I have largely followed their lead in choosing the elements I liked most, too, or which reminded me most of things I am familiar with from my own childhood. All that remains is to repeat the wishes for the festive period contained in the poem mentioned earlier, the *Legend of St Nicholas*:

> T'was the night before Christmas,
> When all through the house
> Not a creature was stirring, – not even a mouse;
> The stockings were hung by the chimney with care,
> In hopes that St. Nicholas soon would be there.
> The children were nestled all snug in their beds,
> While visions of sugar-plums danced through their heads;
> And mamma in her 'kerchief, and I in my cap,
> Had just settled our brains for a long winter's nap,
> When out on the lawn there arose such a clatter,
> I sprang from my bed to see what was the matter.
> Away to the window I flew like a flash,
> Tore open the shutters and threw up the sash.
> The moon on the breast of the new-fallen snow
> Gave a lustre of mid-day to objects below,
> When, what to my wondering eyes should appear,
> But a miniature sleigh, and eight tiny reindeer,
>
> With a little old driver, so lively and quick,
> I knew in a moment it must be St. Nick.
> More rapid than eagles his coursers they came,
> And he whistled, and shouted, and called them by name;
> "Now, Dasher! now, Dancer! now, Prancer and Vixen!
> On, Comet! on Cupid! on, Donner and Blitzen!
> To the top of the porch! to the top of the wall!
> Now dash away! dash away! dash away all!"
> As dry leaves that before the wild hurricane fly,
> When they meet with an obstacle, mount to the sky,
> So up to the house-top the coursers they flew,
> With the sleigh full of toys – and St. Nicholas too.
> And then, in a twinkling, I heard on the roof
> The prancing and pawing of each little hoof.
> As I drew in my hand, and was turning around,
> Down the chimney St. Nicholas came with a bound.
> He was dressed all in fur, from his head to his foot,
> And his clothes were all tarnished with ashes and soot;
> A bundle of toys he had flung on his back,
> And he looked like a peddler just opening his pack.

His eyes – how they twinkled! his dimples how merry!
His cheeks were like roses, his nose like a cherry!
His droll little mouth was drawn up like a bow,
And the beard on his chin was as white as the snow;
The stump of a pipe he held tight in his teeth,
And the smoke it encircled his head like a wreath;
He had a broad face and a little round belly,
That shook, when he laughed, like a bowlful of jelly.

He was chubby and plump – a right jolly old elf –
And I laughed when I saw him, in spite of myself;
A wink of his eye and a twist of his head,
Soon gave me to know I had nothing to dread;
He spoke not a word, but went straight to his work,
And filled all the stockings; then turned with a jerk,
And laying his finger aside of his nose,
And giving a nod, up the chimney he rose;
He sprang to his sleigh, to his team gave a whistle,
And away they all flew like the down of a thistle.
But I heard him exclaim, ere he drove out of sight,
"HAPPY CHRISTMAS TO ALL, AND TO ALL A GOOD-NIGHT"

READING AND WRITING IN VICTORIAN ENGLAND

The Bourgeois Pleasures of a Queen: Late-Victorian Fiction

By *Julia Kuehn* (London)

Victoria was apparently not an avid reader. It seems that she was hardly a reader at all and that she preferred dancing, her favourite pastime until old age, needlework, riding, painting and music to the perusal of a book. As Lytton Strachey, her first biographer, says in his *Queen Victoria* (1921), reading "was not an occupation that she cared for".[1] Indeed, if we extract the list of books mentioned in the most influential biographies of the Queen, it appears rather sparse with about forty titles. And even though the inference that Victoria barely read a book a year would be premature (and depend entirely upon the rather questionable premise that the biographers list *every* book Her Majesty ever read), it seems fair to sustain Strachey's statement.

Consequently, critics have ignored Victoria as a reader. Margaret Homans' excellent study *Royal Representations* (1998) looks at Victoria as a writer and author of the highly successful publications *Leaves from the Journal of Our Life in the Highlands* (1868) and *More Leaves from the Journal of a Life in the Highlands* (1884), the two autobiographical accounts in diary form of the life of the royal family in Scotland.[2] It is surprising that Homans fails to comment upon the connection between Victoria as author and as reader. Or scholars have looked at other pastimes the Queen enjoyed, such as the theatre. George Rowell's *Queen Victoria Goes to the Theatre* (1978) and Michael Booth's "Queen Victoria and the Theatre" (1967) present interesting and thorough information, but, again, her interest in books (or painting and music, for that matter) is ignored in these studies.[3]

For various reasons, however, I believe that a systematic account of Victoria as a reader should be written. Fully aware that this enterprise would require a more extensive study, my intention in this essay is to simply open up discussion in an interesting field of research. My focus is on the

---

[1] Lytton Strachey, *Queen Victoria* [1921] (London, 1948), p. 26.

[2] Margaret Homans, *Royal Representations. Queen Victoria and British Culture, 1837-1876* (Chicago, 1998).

[3] George Rowell, *Queen Victoria Goes to the Theatre* (London, 1978); Michael R. Booth, "Queen Victoria and the Theatre", *University of Toronto Quarterly: A Canadian Journal of the Humanities*, 36 (1967), 249-258.

Queen's reading habits during the last two decades of the nineteenth century – a period which saw fascinating changes in the publishing industry
and which therefore cannot go unnoticed in an account of Victoria's taste
in literature. But before we turn to the latter part of the century, we have to
briefly outline Victoria's reading habits between 1819 and the last quarter
of the nineteenth century. Given the sketchy information available from the
biographies, and because it is impossible to fully understand another person's motivation for reading a particular book, my short overview is necessarily painted with a rather broad brush. But even as such, it gives some
interesting insights.

1. The Books She Read

As part of the young princess's education, reading amounted to whatever
her governess, teachers and the very headstrong Victoria could agree upon.
Elizabeth Longford's seminal biography *Victoria R.I.* (1964) provides the
most inclusive overview of the literature Victoria read – although she does
not make it her business to draw any conclusions from this list, either.[1]
Apart from the scripture and conduct books, Longford lists the poetry of
Pope, Gray, Cowper, Goldsmith and Scott (Victoria's favourite author in
her younger years) as part of her reading. The princess also read Scott's
romances, such as *Kenilworth* and *The Bride of Lammermoor*, Edgeworth's
Tales (i.e. *Tales of Fashionable Life* and *Moral and Popular Tales*), Cooper's *Last of the Mohicans*, and Washington Irving's *Conquest of Granada*,
which introduced her to the wide range of literatures in English.[2]
   Victoria's years with Albert, whom she married in 1840, familiarised her
with a broader scope of reading, including continental literature. Albert, a
genuine booklover and academic, influenced his wife's reading habits to a
large extent so that for the marriage years, Longford lists Dumas' *Trois
Mousquetaires*, Shakespeare's *King John* and Goethe's *Faust*.[3] Victoria,
however, seemed to have preferred simplicity and English romance to
complexity and foreignness – although she grew up speaking German and
French with more proficiency than English. The novels of Charles Dickens,
Austen's *Northanger Abbey*, Charlotte Brontë's *Jane Eyre* and Trollope's
Barchester Towers were apparently more to her taste.[4] Of the novelists of

---

[1] Elizabeth Longford, *Victoria R.I.* (London, 1964).

[2] See Elizabeth Longford, *Victoria R.I.*, p. 43.

[3] Ibid., pp. 164 and 221.

[4] Ibid., p. 186. For Queen Victoria's reading of Dickens see also Dieter Mehl's essay
in this volume.

her reign only George Eliot, in particular her *Adam Bede*, did – for obvious reasons – not at all find favour with the married Queen. She could probably ignore the moral ambiguity in Isabella Thorpe's flirtations with Captain Tilney while engaged to another man, Rochester's bigamy, and even a clergyman's – Slope's – dubious marital ambitions, but it does not seem surprising that Eliot's accumulation of (moral) disasters – seduction with pregnancy, infanticide, escape from the gallows, transportation – proved too much for Victoria's rather conservative taste.

After Albert's death in 1861 the Queen's reading taste returned to what seemed to be hers naturally. Although Longford lists Disraeli's *Coningsby* and *Endymion* and Gaskell's *Life of Charlotte Brontë* among the reading for 1878-1880 – another two novelists of her reign the Queen approved of although it requires explanation why Victoria would only read their books up to thirty years after their first publication – Victoria seems to have preferred literature that we would have to evaluate as rather second-rate. Books that she read, and apparently with much pleasure, include *Aunt Margaret's Trouble* and *The Unkind Word*. [1]

Aunt Margaret's Trouble (1866) by Frances Eleanor Trollope (Ternan)[2] and *The Unkind Word* (1870) by Dinah Mulock (better known as Dinah Craik)[3] are stories about sentimental love and loss. The first book tells in a retrospective account the events of sixty years ago, when (now Aunt) Margaret and the young Horace Lee fall in love, who, however, betrays her with her own sister Anna. Anna and Horace's life is one of misery and guilt, but Margaret forgives Anna and takes her and her two children into her own house after Horace has died. *The Unkind Word* is a moralistic

---

[1] Ibid., p. 418. See Frances Eleanor Trollope, *Aunt Margaret's Trouble* [1866] (London, 1884) and [Dinah Craik], *The Unkind Word and Other Stories*, 2 vols. (London, 1870).

[2] Yet another Fanny Trollope (Ternan), who was the daughter-in-law of the famous writer Fanny Trollope (Milton) (1780-1863), the popular writer of the first half of the nineteenth century and author of such novels as *The Vicar of Wrexhill* (1837) or *The Widow Barnaby* (1839). Beside *Aunt Margaret's Trouble*, her first novel, the younger Fanny Trollope wrote three more novels: *Mabel's Progress* (1867), *The Sacristan's Household. A Story of Lippe Detmold* (1869) and *Veronica* (1870), which was first published in *All the Year Round*. She is, however, remembered for the biography of her mother-in-law, *Frances Trollope, her Life and Literary Work* (1895). Frances Eleanor Trollope died in 1913.

[3] Dinah Mulock, afterwards Craik, lived from 1826 to 1887. Coming to London in 1846, she had the luck to meet two men who became good friends and who would help her achieve her popular success: the publisher Alexander Macmillan and the king of the circulating libraries, Charles Edward Mudie. Craik is best known for her novels *The Ogilvies* (1849), *Olive* (1850) and *John Halifax, Gentleman* (1857).

story about the consequences an inconsiderate word might have. Young Dick tells his brother Maurice that he considers him a selfish, domineering and ill-natured brute, just before Maurice takes off on a journey from which he will never return. Dick has to bear feelings of guilt for the rest of his life. The same night before Maurice's leave, he declares his love to his cousin Jessie. After years of waiting for the brother and lover, another brother, Richard, proposes to Jessie, but she rejects him: she remains faithful to the man who has now officially been declared dead but whose memory Jessie will cherish forever.

It is well-known that Victoria truly *loved* the poetry of Scott – mentioned earlier – and Tennyson whom she chose as laureate after the death of Wordsworth. The Queen's correspondence with Tennyson communicates not only true friendship but also admiration for the perfect poet of "love and loss". His *In Memoriam*, written in memory of his dead friend, it is said, helped Victoria through the loss of her beloved husband and thus remained a favourite with her until her death.[1] As for the rest of her library cited above, we must assume that most of the books were imposed upon her by either her teachers, Albert or political circumstances – Disraeli, for instance, being her Prime Minister between 1874 and 1880 and her favourite Prime Minister of all – rather than chosen and genuinely enjoyed by the Queen. It is the last two novels mentioned, however, that is, *Aunt Margaret's Trouble* and *The Unkind Word*, books of an ephemeral nature and popular character, that lead me to enquire further into the profile of Queen Victoria as a reader in the late nineteenth century.

2. The Nineteenth-Century Reading Public

In their introduction to the essay collection *Remaking Queen Victoria* (1997), Margaret Homans and Adrienne Munich reclaim Victoria as part of the cultural history of the era. Rather than seeing the figure of the Queen at the margin of an age that bears her own name, which many scholars have done, they argue that "Victoria was central to the ideological and cultural signifying systems of her age".[2] Following their claim that Victoria was central to the cultural production, it is my contention that Victoria is also an important factor in the nineteenth-century history of reading and the reading public. I believe that her reading taste, in particular the taste of the elderly Queen, is as much a *result* of the contemporary literary scene as an

---

[1] Margaret Homans, *Royal Representations*, p. 180.

[2] *Remaking Queen Victoria*, ed. Margaret Homans and Adrienne Munich (Cambridge, 1997), p. 2.

influence on it. More precisely, I want to argue that Victoria can be considered an exemplary late nineteenth-century reader.

But again we have to move back a few years in the nineteenth century before we can look at the late-Victorian era: reading is probably one of the most important cultural and social phenomena in the nineteenth century, as Richard Altick shows in his *English Common Reader* (1957).[1] The development of a potential reading public (through a growing population in general, improvements in the education system and an increase of leisure time through industrialisation), the technological progress in the printing industry, the solidification and expansion of the circulating library system, and the introduction of the one-volume novel which replaces the more expensive three-decker, provide the basis for an expanding book market and a growing readership. The breakdown of the lending library system in 1894/95 is caused by the introduction of the six-shilling one-volume novel which puts it for the first time into the financial reach of the broader public who start to buy rather than borrow novels. At the same time, the publishers can sign up more authors and thus provide a wider range of literature. Consequently, the 1880s and 1890s are swamped with new authors and their books. John Sutherland, in his *Victorian Fiction* (1995), provides the figure of roughly 50,000 novels for the entire nineteenth century and about 3,500 novelists, of whom more than two thirds still rest in obscurity.[2] A vast majority of these authors emerges in the late nineteenth century; and as such, the less renowned authors of *Aunt Margaret's Trouble* and *The Unkind Word* have been sadly neglected in scholarship and been largely forgotten. They were, however, for some reason important or representative enough in Queen Victoria's (sparse) reading history to be mentioned by her biographer Longford.

Given the list of books extracted from the biographies, we can characterise Victoria as a reader who read whatever she enjoyed but who was unaware of the difference between what we now label as high literature and popular literature. This, Queenie Leavis argues in *Fiction and the Reading Public* (1932), is characteristic of the nineteenth century.[3] The nineteenth-century reading public, according to Leavis, was still homogeneous, which basically means that anybody read anything. As such, the Queen would have read the same books that her kitchen maids read – and that was anything from Austen to *Aunt Margaret*. But it was at the very end of the

---

[1] Richard Altick, *The English Common Reader. A Social History of the Mass Reading Public 1800-1900* (Chicago, 1957).

[2] John Sutherland, *Victorian Fiction. Writers, Publishers, Readers* (Houndmills, 1995), p.153.

[3] Q.D. Leavis, *Fiction and the Reading Public* [1932] (London, 1990).

nineteenth century – after George Eliot, Leavis argues, who was the last writer with a homogeneous readership – that the reading public split into high-brow and low-brow, and literature into elite and popular.

It is the low-brow, popular books, which emerged in the late nineteenth century that I now want to focus on. They show a change in the literary scene and tell a whole story about the emergence of the modern bestselling novel – a story in which Victoria plays an important role.

Titles like *Aunt Margaret's Trouble* and *The Unkind Word* lead us directly into this scene of popular writing. The late nineteenth century had provided all the necessary conditions to let the modern one-volume bestseller arise: a cheap book production, a mass reading public, and the abolishment of the three-decker and the subscription libraries. People now bought books and could thus turn a novel into a bestseller. And it is the very first English bestselling author of the one-volume novel that I want to draw attention to: her history is an essential part in an analysis of Queen Victoria's reading habits.

With regard to Victoria's reading taste after 1880, Strachey writes enigmatically that "[t]here is reason to believe [...] that the *romances* of another female writer, whose *popularity* among the humble classes of Her Majesty's subjects was at one time enormous, secured, no less, the approval of Her Majesty".[1] Strachey's concealment of this author's name is, at best, mysterious and, at worst, a sign of embarrassment.

With regard to his possible uneasiness with the concept of *popularity*, we have to remember that he wrote Victoria's biography in 1921 after the aesthetic of high modernism had long been developed. The modernists claimed that good literature aimed at and was read by the select few. If popularity was a positive quality in early and high Victorianism as it allowed the author to represent the whole of society and interact with it, popularity towards the end of the nineteenth century was more and more considered a negative quality incompatible with the emerging stance of the artist as an isolated but superior character in a society that failed to understand him. Literature was no longer popular entertainment, but a philosophical, subtle, complicated and demanding concept.

Secondly, regarding Strachey's possible embarrassment with the *romance* genre, we must remember that ever since the intellectual debate in the 1880s and 1890s about the superiority of realist fiction over romance, the imaginary romance genre had lost its supporters. Authors like Henry James in his article on Zola's *Nana* (1880) and George Moore in *Literature at Nurse, or Circulating Morals: A Polemic on Victorian Censorship* (1885)

---

[1] Strachey, *Queen Victoria*, p. 238, emphasis added.

propagated a turning away from the pure but unsophisticated nature of the English novel and an attempt at an aesthetically demanding form, which they claimed to find in the French realist tradition of authors such as Zola, Flaubert and Balzac.[1] And although the use of the term "realism" is rather confused and open in the late nineteenth century, as Jane Eldridge Miller argues in her 1994 study *Rebel Women*, the adaptation of French naturalism through English authors – such as George Gissing in *New Grub Street* (1891) and George Moore in *A Modern Lover* (1883) or *A Mummer's Wife* (1885) – basically meant to present an authentic record of the details of a blemished social reality, including a scrutiny of codes of morality and social institutions and a graphic depiction of poverty, crime and sex.[2] To the advocates of realism, only the characteristics of (scientific) objectivity, lack of emotion, sexual openness, and breadth of experience would provide the novel with the intellectual respectability and high aesthetic purpose which they felt it had hitherto lacked.[3] And although romancers like Stevenson, for instance in "A Gossip on Romance" (1882), celebrated the imaginary, unreal, and dream-like atmosphere of romance and its overall wholesome nature, romance literature was mostly considered a second-rate escapist and extravagant form of narration.[4]

So there were, after all, good reasons why Strachey would avoid mentioning the name of Marie Corelli, the popular romance author of the late Victorian age and the first English bestselling author of the modern volume novel, in his account of Victoria's favourite reading.

---

[1] Henry James, "*Nana*", in: *The House of Fiction. Essays on the Novel by Henry James*, ed. and intr. Leon Edel (London, 1957), pp. 274-280. Originally published in *The Parisian* (26 February 1880); George Moore, *Literature at Nurse, or Circulating Morals: A Polemic on Victorian Censorship*, ed. and intr. Pierre Coustillas (Hassocks, 1976). "Literature at Nurse" originally published by Vizetelly in London, 1885.

[2] Jane Eldridge Miller, *Rebel Women. Feminism, Modernism and the Edwardian Novel* (London, 1994), pp. 204-205, n.1.

[3] Ibid., p. 12.

[4] R.L. Stevenson, "A Gossip on Romance", in: *A Victorian Art of Fiction. Essays on the Novel in British Periodicals 1870-1900*, ed. John Charles Olmsted (New York, 1979), pp. 189-199. Originally published in *Longman's Magazine* 1 (November 1882), 69-79.

3. Marie Corelli

Born in 1855 as Mary ("Minnie") Mackay[1], the illegitimate daughter of
Charles Mackay, a minor poet but friend of Charles Dickens's, Corelli assumed her pseudonym before the publication of her first successful novel,
A Romance of Two Worlds (1886), and lived her own imaginary romance
until her death in 1924. She created a myth around her own person which
included a noble Italian mother (in lieu of her English mother who was a
servant in the Mackay household), connections to the Italian royalty, an
education in France and the adoption through Charles Mackay after the
death of her relatives. Between the early 1880s and 1924, Corelli produced
26 novels, 2 major non-fictional publications in which she explored her
aesthetics (*The Silver Domino*, 1892 on the fin-de-siècle literary scene and
Free Opinions Freely Expressed, 1905 on various subjects of art and literature), over 100 speeches and articles, about 50 short stories and various
poems and reviews. Her novel *The Sorrows of Satan* (1895), a romantic
story about the unsuccessful novelist Geoffrey Tempest who sells his soul
to the Devil to gain a reputation as an artist and marry a society beauty,
published shortly after the breakdown of the three-decker in 1895 in a one-
volume format, can be considered the first modern English bestseller. It
sold, according to an advertisement for Corelli's works in 1920, 202,000
copies until then. Corelli's *The Master Christian* (1900) sold 186,000
copies until 1923, *God's Good Man* (1904) 164,000;[2] numbers which were
phenomenal and unprecedented.

With increasing popularity and financial freedom, Corelli's life style became more and more glamorous and included social encounters with eminent authors, actors and politicians such as Oscar Wilde, Robert Browning,
George Meredith, Mark Twain, Ellen Terry, Henry Irving, Ella Wheeler
Wilcox and William Gladstone. Her readership comprised – in addition to

---

[1] For accounts of her life and work see, among others, Kent Carr, *Marie Corelli*, Bi-
jou Biographies 8 (London, 1901); Thomas F.G. Coates and R.S. Warren Bell, *Marie
Corelli. The Writer and the Woman* (London, 1903); Bertha Vyver, *Memoirs of Marie
Corelli* (London, 1930); Eileen Bigland, *Marie Corelli. The Woman and the Legend*
(London, 1953); Brian Masters, *Now Barabbas was a Rotter. The Extraordinary Life of
Marie Corelli* (London, 1978), and, most recently, Teresa Ransom, *The Mysterious
Marie Corelli. Queen of Victorian Bestsellers* (London, 1999). Carr, Coates and Bell's
are sheer hagiographies. Similarly, Vyver, Corelli's life-long companion, presents a
rather idealised picture of her friend; Masters' biography is well researched and very
detailed, yet it begs for a feminist revision. His condescending, misogynist tone and his
constant deprecation of Corelli as a writer mar the otherwise most reliable biography.

[2] All sales numbers from Marie Corelli, *The Life Everlasting. A Reality of Romance*
[1911] (London, 1923), Appendix.

the names mentioned above – Alfred Lord Tennyson, James Joyce, William Butler Yeats, Theodore Watts, Canon Wilberforce of St. Paul's Cathedral, the Empress of Austria, the Tsarina of Russia, the Queen of Italy, and the Queen of Romania. One of her biographers, Brian Masters, says that "[w]hile Queen Victoria was alive, Miss Corelli was the second most famous Englishwoman in the world".[1] The myth built around her, however, was much bigger than her actual life would justify. It was an ingenious creation by an average woman who decided to become a somebody, and who employed all means of publicity to achieve her goal.

Corelli's connection to Victoria is a case in point. As Masters explains, the names of Marie Corelli and Queen Victoria became inextricably linked when the Dowager Duchess of Roxenburghe "had [in 1890] brought to the Queen's attention a copy of *The Romance of Two Worlds* [sic] which Her Majesty had read with real enjoyment".[2] [*A Romance* is one of Corelli's many supernatural stories about a woman's enquiry into the mysteries of the universe and the nature of God.] After an expensive presentation copy had been sent to the Queen, bound in royal red morocco with the English coat-of-arms and V.R. underneath, Corelli received "a telegram with a royal command that all Marie Corelli's books should be sent to [the Queen]".[3] And it was then – through the dissemination of the news that Corelli had received royal favour – that Corelli's progression from a very popular novelist to a bestselling author was assured. And even though George Bentley, her publisher, refused to advertise Corelli's novel of 1892, *The Soul of Lilith*, with the added subtitle "Accepted by her Majesty the Queen"[4], Corelli's fame and financial success was sealed.

A visit to the Queen at Windsor was planned in May 1892, but it is hard to determine from the Corelli-Bentley correspondence whether this visit was Corelli's wishful thinking or whether it actually was intended but unfortunately never took place. In a letter to Bentley Corelli expressed how overwhelmed she was with the honour, and she addressed matters of etiquette, for instance "I am told that I am to be perfectly frank and unaffected in my conversation as that is what the Queen likes".[5] There is no further mention in the correspondence about the planned visit; had it actually taken place in the expected form, it is likely that Corelli – being the woman that she was – would have made it public. As things are we can only speculate that the visit was either called off, that it turned out to include a mere visit

---

[1] Brian Masters, *Now Barabbas was a Rotter*, p. 6.

[2] Ibid., pp. 103-104.

[3] Ibid., p. 104. See also Eileen Bigland, *Marie Corelli*, p. 125.

[4] See Brian Masters, *Now Barabbas was a Rotter*, p. 105.

[5] Ibid., p. 106.

to the Queen's library without actually seeing the Queen (reminiscent of Jane Austen's disappointing experience when invited by George IV), or that it was in the end the mere brainchild of a very imaginative writer.

A visit to Vicky, the Empress Frederick of Germany, however, took place in 1893 in Buckingham Palace, as Bertha Vyver, Corelli's life-long friend and companion, writes in her Corelli biography from 1930. The Emperor Frederick had read Corelli's sentimental love romance *Thelma* (1887) on his death-bed in 1888, and he "had admired it".[1] The Empress arranged for a private interview with Corelli and was enchanted with the authoress. As another biographer, Kent Carr, in his 1900 Corelli hagiography points out, the Empress received Corelli "with especial courtesy and kindness" and the "private interview last[ed] nearly an hour".[2] Vyver stresses that Vicky and Corelli met afterwards "on several occasions"[3], and that in 1921, Vicky expressed her admiration for Corelli's eulogy on her mother in *The Passing of the Great Queen*, published shortly after Victoria's death in 1901.

But there are more than just historical meeting-points between the Queen and the English bestselling author. In the second half of this article, I want to point out the ideological connections, and enquire into the reasons why Victoria read so many of Corelli's novels with such pleasure and – apparently – fervour, given that she was not a great reader after all. It is three themes in Corelli's novels – love, religion and the Woman Question – that, I believe, appealed to Victoria in particular.

3.1. Love

The courtship of the young Queen Victoria and Albert, Prince of Saxe-Coburg and Gotha, is probably one of the best-known romances of the nineteenth century. And nobody needs to be reminded of the happiness of their marriage years with an exemplary domestic life with their nine children. Similarly, we need not call to mind the intensity of Victoria's mourning after Albert's death in 1861 and the long period of her widowhood which characterises her image in the latter part of the century until her death.

It is not surprising, then, that Victoria would be susceptible to the love plots in Corelli's romances. *Thelma* (1887)[4] was a well-known novel in Buckingham Palace, and not only because Vicky and the German Emperor

---

[1] Bertha Vyver, *Memoirs of Marie Corelli*, p. 116.
[2] Kent Carr, *Marie Corelli*, p. 59.
[3] See Bertha Vyver, *Memoirs of Marie Corelli*, p. 116.
[4] Marie Corelli, *Thelma. A Norwegian Princess* [1887] (London, 1896).

read it. As Masters notes, Princess Beatrice, Victoria's youngest daughter, read *Thelma* aloud to the Queen in November 1891.[1] [Again, we come across the curious fact that Victoria read books several years after they were first published.]

Thelma is a love story about an English aristocrat, Sir Philip Bruce Errington, who travels to Norway and there falls in love with the country girl Thelma Güldmar, the incarnation of the perfect, innocent and pure woman. He takes her back to London, but Thelma's spotless character clashes with the corrupted and sexually perverted London high society. When Thelma receives the false information that Philip is having an affair with a famous dancer, she flees in panic back to Norway. After a series of tragic events, which include the death of her beloved father and a miscarriage resulting from the psychological strains, Philip finds her, is forgiven, and they return to England: a couple grown closer, which can now face the evils of society together – and which will hopefully bring some of their love and moral values into a fin-de-siècle society that desperately needs ethical guidance.

One could argue rather simply along psychological lines why Queen Victoria would have enjoyed happy love romances in general; any romance would then recreate for her the love story between herself and Albert. Romantic fiction is an instance of wish-fulfilment for the reader as recent critics such as Laurie Langbauer, Tania Modleski and Janice Radway have convincingly argued in their critical studies *Women and Romance* (1990), *Loving with a Vengeance* (1982), and *Reading the Romance* (1984).[2] Or, as Queenie Leavis puts it much earlier and much more simply in *Fiction and the Reading Public*, bestselling love romances appeal to "the great heart of the public" as they respond to unconscious desires.[3] They eliminate a rational response, but trigger an emotional reaction through certain signals and techniques. In her article "My First Book" (1893), Corelli admits to this emotional manipulation and acknowledges that her aim was always to "*write straight from my own heart to the hearts of others*".[4] This, she rightly sees as the key to her success. Leavis pins down the emotional re-

---

[1] Brian Masters, *Now Barabbas was a Rotter*, p. 104.

[2] Laurie Langbauer, *Women and Romance. The Consolations of Gender in the English Novel* (Ithaca, 1990); Tania Modleski, *Loving with a Vengeance. Mass-Produced Fantasies for Women* (New York, 1982); Janice Radway, *Reading the Romance. Women, Patriarchy, and Popular Literature* (Chapel Hill, 1984).

[3] Q.D. Leavis, *Fiction and the Reading Public*, p. 156.

[4] Marie Corelli, "My First Book. *A Romance of Two Worlds*", in: *My First Book: The Experience of Walter Besant* (London, 1894), pp. 206-220, p. 206. First published in *The Idler*, 4 (1893), 239-252.

sponse through an author's use of certain signal words ("life, death, love, good, evil, sin, home, mother, noble, gallant, purity, honour"), and clichés and stereotypes[1], which evoke feelings. I do agree with Leavis, but rather than laying it down to the use of individual words, I would argue that it is a generally non-rational and hyperbolic style which creates an emotional response in the reader, the use of certain words being only one factor. This non-rational language is signifier of the non-rational, unconscious, hidden, or forbidden wish which lies underneath. An author succeeds with his or her fiction if (s)he responds to people's wishes and makes public what others only dare to dream of. In Victoria's case, I want to argue that Corelli made public what Victoria could only write about secretly in her diaries – the desire for a passionate, transcendental love relationship which went far beyond the nineteenth-century feeling for decorum.

Victoria's diary entry on her wedding day on 10 February 1840 provides valuable clues as to Victoria's dreams and desires. This entry, indeed, reads itself like part of a love novel with its use of hyperbole which grasps the non-rational character of romantic writing that appeals directly to the emotions.

> I NEVER NEVER spent such an evening!!! My DEAREST DEAREST DEAR Albert sat on a footstool by my side, and his excessive love and affection gave me feelings of heavenly love and happiness, I never could have *hoped* to have felt before! He clasped me in his arms, and we kissed each other again and again! His beauty, his sweetness and gentleness – really how can I ever be thankful enough to have such a *Husband*! [...] To be called by names of tenderness, I have never yet heard used to me before – was bliss beyond belief! Oh! This was the happiest day of my life![2]

Compare this to an excerpt from Corelli's *Thelma* which bears striking similarities (although it is Philip proposing to Thelma and not Victoria to Albert), in particular in its surprisingly erotic content and its use of a non-rational, hyperbolical, almost hysterical, style:

> In one second she was caught in his arms, and clasped passionately to his heart. "Thelma! Thelma!" he whispered, "I love you, my darling – I love you!" She trembled in his strong embrace, and strove to release herself, but he pressed her more closely to him, scarcely knowing that he did so, but feeling that he held the world, life, time, happiness, and salvation in this one fair creature. His brain was in a wild whirl [...]; there was nothing any more – no universe, no existence – nothing but love, love, love, beating strong hammer-strokes through every fibre of his frame. [...] "Quick, Thelma!" and his warm breath touched her cheek. "My

---

[1] See Q.D. Leavis, *Fiction and the Reading Public*, pp. 64 and 255.

[2] Quoted in Giles St. Aubyn, *Queen Victoria. A Portrait* (New York, 1992), p. 146.

darling! My love! if you are not angry, – kiss me! I shall understand!" She hesitated. [...] Then came a touch – soft and sweet as a rose-leaf against his lips.[1]

Hyperbole is the stylistic device that best expresses the ideal of a non-rational, excessive (desire for) love and both Victoria, in her private diary, and Corelli, in her public novel, employ this style. Victoria's use of hyperbole in the wedding day entry, visible in expressions such as "never never", "dearest dearest" and "the happiest day", her acknowledgement of the excessive and non-rational aspect of her love ("excessive" and "beyond belief") and her shifting it into a transcendental sphere ("heavenly love") find a similar manifestation in Corelli: transcendence (love being the "world, life, time, happiness, and salvation") and excess ("hammer-strokes") are expressed accordingly. In contrast, Victoria's writing that was made public, that is, the extracts from her diaries published as *Leaves from the Journal of a Life in the Highlands* (1868) and as *More Leaves* (1884) is much more subdued and less immediate. In public, she simply could not give way to her unconscious desires and fantasies about a passionate love relationship, but had to pay attention to decorum, both in the use of topics and of style. Thus, she would rather proclaim family values in her writing on the life in Scotland than indulge in excessive love fantasies written in an irrational language of excess.

In a way, we could then argue that Corelli was the public spokesperson for all the unspoken feelings of love that both the Queen and many nineteenth-century women had, but that decorum forbad them to utter. *Thelma* made passion public and hysterical language acceptable.

3.2. Religion

Many of Marie Corelli's romances were labelled and marketed as religious novels. In a period at the end of the nineteenth century that saw a crisis in orthodox religion, Corelli's mission to bring Christ back into people's lives through fiction was laudable yet not unusual as the immense output of religious novels suggests. Most interestingly, Corelli's novels, such as *A Romance of Two Worlds* (1886), *Ardath* (1889), *The Soul of Lilith* (1892), *The Sorrows of Satan* (1895), *Ziska* (1897) and *The Life Everlasting* (1911) combine a rather orthodox faith in Christ the Saviour, the life everlasting, and the truth of the Scripture with many of the pseudo-religious branches people were interested in throughout the nineteenth century, such as spiritualism, mesmerism, and theosophy. Janet Oppenheim and Alex Owen

---

[1] Marie Corelli, *Thelma*, p. 203.

have argued in their studies *The Other World: Spiritualism and Psychic Research in England, 1850-1914* (1985) and *The Darkened Room. Women, Power and Spiritualism in Late Nineteenth-Century England* (1989) that the late nineteenth century showed a cultural turn towards the supernatural and fantastic.[1] Yet, I would argue, it is the combination of these pseudo-religions with orthodox religion, rather than an absolutist embracing of them, which seemed to be most appealing to the majority of Victorians, including Queen Victoria.

Corelli's *Ardath*[2] is the story of a disheartened English poet, Theos Alwyn, who travels to the Caucasus where the Chaldean sage Heliobas lives. The monk is a devout Christian, but also uses his magnetic powers to heal Theos' fin-de-siècle malady – although he proclaims popular quasi-religions to be nonsense. Theos falls asleep and dreams of the angel Edris – his soul's other half – who leads him symbolically to God and inspiration which will create lasting poetry. Theos' story shows the logic of a modern Pilgrim's Progress: he travels to the field of Ardath, a place by the former Babylon (Corelli took the idea and title for her novel from the apocryphal book of Esdras) and has a vision of the pre-Christian city Al-Kyris which is governed by the femme fatale Lysia, the priestess of the deity Nagâya, and her lover, the king Zephorânim. In his vision (which is set in 5,000 BC), Theos realises the truth of Christianity (suggested to him in the visions of Jewish prophets), the value of true love (he understands Edris to be his soul's mate) and transcendence as the way to good, lasting poetry. Theos befriends the poet laureate of the city, Sah-lûma, a selfish and self-indulgent person who values momentary fame higher than the possibility of creating eternal poetry. He, too, considers himself in love with the pagan priestess Lysia whose corrupt nature he does not seem to care for. Waking up from his dream-vision, Theos realises that Sah-lûma was his former incarnation: God-denying and incapable of feeling transcendental love and producing eternal poetry. Back in the London of the 1880s, Theos sets out on his mission to proclaim the truth of Christ through religious poetry, with Edris – who has become woman through Theos' selfless love – by his side.

On 9 November 1891 Corelli writes in a letter to her publisher George Bentley: "The Queen is intensely absorbed in 'Ardath' – it is her favourite one of all."[3] So why did the Queen like *Ardath* when her other religious

---

[1] Janet Oppenheim, *The Other World: Spiritualism and Psychic Research in England, 1850-1914* (Cambridge, 1985); Alex Owen, *The Darkened Room. Women, Power and Spiritualism in Late Nineteenth-Century England* (London, 1989).

[2] Marie Corelli, *Ardath. The Story of a Dead Self* [1889] (London, 1925).

[3] Marie Corelli, "To George Bentley" (9 November 1891). MS Marie Corelli Collection, Beinecke Rare Book and Manuscript Library, Yale University.

reading experiences had so far included the *Barchester* novels and Edge-worth's Catholic tales?

Victoria, too, had a rather interesting religious life. Not that she was not considered an exemplary and convinced orthodox Anglican by her people, but her biographer St. Aubyn stresses her growing tolerance and then de-fence of religious minorities over the years.[1] More interesting than her de-fence of non-Anglican Christian denominations, however, is how Victoria incorporated non-orthodox beliefs and customs into her religious system which apparently did not pose any contradiction for her. Longford speaks of Victoria's interest in magnetism, table-rapping and the intermediate life – as imagined by the spiritualists – especially after Albert's death.[2]

I want to argue that it is the orthodoxy of both Corelli's and Victoria's beliefs and, paradoxically, the simultaneous embracing of unorthodox pseudo-religions which drew Victoria (and the rest of the reading public) to Corelli. All of Corelli's religious works are written in the spirit that intends to lead the crisis-ridden England back to Christianity. Popular pseudo-re-ligions are used as a foil for the discussion of Christianity, but paradox-ically, they are often an essential part of the plot. The plot of Corelli's *A Romance of Two Worlds*, for instance, is based on hypnosis, that of *Lilith* on soul migration and that of *Ziska*, like that of *Ardath*, on reincarnation.

Ardath illustrates what I consider the late nineteenth-century crisis in orthodox religion. Theos visits Heliobas in his order of the Cross and Star in the Caucasus. Here, Heliobas tells him that he is neither a "mesmerist or magnetizer [...] [or] 'spiritualist' whose enlightened intelligence and heaven-aspiring aims are demonstrated in the turning of tables and general furniture-gyration".[3] In contrast, his powers trust solely in the strength of his soul that the Creator has given him. Heliobas and also the angel Edris lead Theos to the Bible and thus define his mission as a Christian pilgrim-age. Nevertheless, Corelli forgets the orthodox religious principles, which seem to be at the heart of her novel, on several occasions: first and fore-most, Theos is the nineteenth-century embodiment of Sah-lûma, the poet of Al-Kyris; familiar vocabulary and symbolism of orthodox Christianity is fused with Eastern doctrines of reincarnation. Later, magic drugs, Diony-sian dances, sacrifices of virgins and the worship of the snake deity Nagâya create the pagan vision against which Theos has to evaluate the truth of Christianity.[4] But even after he has accepted the Christian faith and after Corelli has given weighty sermons on Christianity, supernatural elements

---

[1] Giles St. Aubyn, *Queen Victoria*, pp. 526ff.
[2] Elizabeth Longford, *Victoria R.I.*, pp. 339 and 343.
[3] Marie Corelli, *Ardath*, p. 15.
[4] See Marie Corelli, *Ardath*, pp. 135, 233ff., 385ff.

recur. Edris, the angel, for instance, becomes human. So even though Corelli denounces the pseudo-religious tendency of her age, she still incorporates it into her novels.

In summary, we can conclude that in a period that experiences a crisis in orthodox religion, Corelli presents "the best of two worlds" and thus captures the spirit of the time. And Victoria, again, is also representative of this inclination to experience the metaphysical through approaches other than orthodox religion.

3.3. The Woman Question

Paradoxical notions of women's emancipation and women's rights characterise the latter part of the nineteenth century. An anecdote from Victoria's life exemplifies how her idea of woman is also one of paradoxes. As Strachey recounts, the legend goes that one night Victoria was refused entry into Albert's room who, in wrath, had locked himself in. He refused to act upon her royal command to open the door to "the Queen of England" and only let her in when she answered his question as to who was at the door and desired to be let in with the humble answer "Your wife, Albert".[1] Victoria was Queen and wife, the mother of a nation and mother to her nine children, a political person and a private woman.

Paradoxical notions of womanhood were not unusual at a time that saw the beginning of the fight for women's rights. The first militant suffragette Millicent Fawcett published a life of Her Majesty in 1895 – the first in a new series on *Eminent Women* – and although Victoria did not object to either the book or the writer personally, it was well known that she considered the women's suffrage movement in the shape it had taken rather regrettable since women had apparently forgotten all sense of propriety.[2] Victoria openly defended a feminine version of woman and objected to the way some militant suffragettes tried to achieve woman's emancipation.[3] And yet, in their essay on Victoria in *The Woman Question: Society and Literature in Britain and America 1837-1883* (1983), Elizabeth K. Helsinger, Robin Lauterbach Sheets and William Veeder open a feminist discourse of Victoria by examining how in her writing and her actions she undermined yet endorsed the so-called Victorian ideal of feminine asexual

---

[1] Lytton Strachey, *Queen Victoria*, p. 96.
[2] See Millicent Garrett Fawcett, *Life of Her Majesty Queen Victoria*, Eminent Women Series (London, 1895) and Giles St. Aubyn, *Queen Victoria*, p. 605.
[3] See Lytton Strachey, *Queen Victoria*, p. 246.

domesticity. Victoria's image of woman and womanliness was one of para-dox.[1]

Paradox is also central to Corelli's presentation of women in her fiction, as Janet Galligani Casey has argued in her "Marie Corelli and Fin de Siècle Feminism" (1992) and another reason for the wide appeal of the novels. Corelli's fictional women are strong, (financially) independent women who, however, also celebrate their feminine qualities rather than aspire to be like men. In a time of change it is Corelli who "reflects the confusion of an entire generation of women"[2], that is, a generation that faces at the same time the suffragette movement and the decline of the Angel in the House ideal.

But rather than reiterate Casey's argument and look at Corelli's fictional representations of women, I want to look at Corelli's non-fictional eulogy of Queen Victoria in *The Passing of the Great Queen* (1901)[3], which is ex-emplary of Corelli's view on the Woman Question. It not only supports my theory that it is Corelli's paradoxical representation of women that must have appealed to Victoria, but it also creates the closest connection be-tween the two women, being Corelli's only piece of writing on the Queen.

In Corelli's pamphlet, Victoria is taken as the representative of all women, in that she is presented as a woman who lived a life full of para-doxes as a powerful ruler and a submissive wife and devoted mother. In her argument, Corelli presents femininity as a superior form of womanhood and as complimentary to sovereignty, rather than as contradictory to it.[4]

As a (political) remedy to the ills of the early twentieth century, Corelli suggests a return to "'old-fashioned' virtues", such as those proclaimed by Queen Victoria. For women, this means that "simple goodness is best".[5] The Queen, Corelli argues, lived an exemplary life of simplicity:

> Occupying the proudest position on earth, her days were passed in the quietest pleasures, – and she stood before us, a daily unmatched example of the inesti-mable value of Home and home-life, with all its peaceful surroundings and sacred influences. There was nothing her Majesty so greatly disliked as vulgar show and

---

[1] Elizabeth K. Helsinger, Robin Lauterbach Sheets and William Veeder, "Queen Vic-toria and The Shadow Side", in: *The Woman Question: Society and Literature in Britain and America 1837-1883*, 3 vols. (Chicago, 1983).

[2] Janet Galligani Casey, "Marie Corelli and Fin de Siècle Feminism", *English Litera-ture in Transition 1880-1920*, 35 (1992), 163-178, p. 164.

[3] Marie Corelli, *The Passing of the Great Queen. A Tribute to the Noble Life of Vic-toria Regina* (London, 1901).

[4] See also Gail Turley Houston, *Royalties. The Queen and Victorian Writers* (Charlottesville, 1999), pp. 33-35.

[5] Both quotes Marie Corelli, *The Passing of the Great Queen*, p. 10.

ostentation – nothing she appreciated so thoroughly as quiet and decorous conduct, simplicity in dress, gentleness of manner. The extravagance, loose morals, and offensive assertion of flaunting wealth, so common to London society nowadays, met with her extreme disapproval ...[1]

Subsequently, Corelli retraces the different stages of life in order to eulogize the supreme woman of the age. "[A]n incarnation of womanhood at its best", the young princess was "simple and modest, unaffected and graceful". As wife and mother, she was "devoted to her duties, and adored her husband and children". And finally, as a widow, she fulfilled her feminine task by being the "faithful worshipper of a beloved memory".[2]

Not only her simplicity and womanliness were factors which made Victoria into a supreme monarch, but there was also her reverence for God. The "purity of her faith" and the "steadfast simplicity and candour of the Queen's religious faith" not only set a shining example in an age where religion faltered, but it was also an important aspect in her ruling, Corelli argues.[3] Her open-mindedness and willingness for compromise had consequences for Victoria's political reign: her faith in Christian virtues, such as tolerance, "enabled her to hold the delicate balance of things aright, and to maintain the equilibrium of national policy by the mere fact of her existence."[4]

In summary, Corelli argues that it was the Queen's personality, that is, her simple, religious and feminine character, which made her into the successful political ruler and powerful monarch that she was. In a singular step, Corelli deconstructs the notion of a holding on to "old-fashioned" female virtues, such as femininity, and faith in God as a "woman's weakness".[5] Instead, Corelli argues that it is exactly this supposed weakness that "made [Victoria] stronger than many armed hosts, and more potent than all other rulers of the kingdoms of this world".[6] The virtues of a woman's true heart and her trust in God create sovereignty. And, consequently, Corelli argues that women should return to the femininity exemplified by Queen Victoria rather than forget it in their useless fight for parity. The suffragettes' cause, she argues, will fail if difference between the sexes is not acknowledged.

To Corelli, the suffragette movement is "un-womanly", as she explores in later pieces, as women forget decorum and give up their natural feminine

---

[1] Ibid., p. 8.
[2] Ibid.
[3] Ibid., pp. 8 and 18.
[4] Ibid., p. 18.
[5] Ibid.
[6] Ibid.

powers, including moral superiority, for the cause of claiming equal political rights, which, however, will never be achieved as men and women can simply never be equal. For Corelli, departing from femininity is a sacrilege. Nature, she explains in her essay "The Women's Vote" of 1918, "insists on contrasts".[1] Thus, as representatives of the common opinion on the suffragettes, Corelli and also Victoria, would detest the – however falsified – masculine image of the suffragettes that *Punch*, for instance, would make popular. Women, Corelli argues, cannot be like men and should not wish to be: "'Equality of the sexes' is one of the advanced feminine war-cries, when every one with a grain of common sense knows there is and can be no such equality. Nature's law forbids."[2]

I cannot agree with Casey's conclusion that Corelli did not understand the feminist spirit of her time and its cry for parity. Instead, I would argue that she was a more complex thinker who proclaimed – in a rather skilful way – *difference* and not *equality* as a tool of empowerment. Thus, she went in certain ways far beyond the feminist spirit of her time. And I think it is exactly this defence of womanliness and its translation into political power which must have made Corelli's feminism attractive to Victoria.

4. Conclusion

In the Conclusion, we are confronted with two separate questions. Firstly, how can we evaluate the most popular author of the late nineteenth century? And, secondly, how can we evaluate the fact that Queen Victoria indulged in her books when she didn't like reading that much?

It poses a challenge to the literary scholar to recuperate Corelli; she can surely not be considered a great writer in the canonical sense. But she must be judged one of the greatest among the writers who were directly in touch with their readership and who had a feeling for what the readers wanted. As for literary quality, the fact that she was admired and read by Victoria does, unfortunately, not mean anything. On the contrary, an anecdote tells us that the fact *that* Victoria read Corelli sadly proves her literary deficiencies. Sir Frederick Ponsonby, for many years Victoria's Private Secretary, captures in his memoirs a scene at Balmoral when Corelli was the subject of royal dinner-table conversation. He writes in his *Recollections of Three Reigns* (1951):

---

[1] Marie Corelli, "The Women's Vote. Nature versus Politics", in: *My "Little Bit"* (London, 1919), pp. 292-296, p. 294.

[2] Ibid., p. 294.

> In literature the Queen's taste was said to be deplorable, and although she had lit-
> tle time for reading she never liked the works of the great authors.[1] I remember a
> discussion taking place once at Balmoral between Queen Victoria and the Em-
> press Frederick on the subject of Marie Corelli. The Queen said she would rank as
> one of the greatest writers of the time, while the Empress thought that her writings
> were trash. I was seated at the other end of the large dining-room table and there-
> fore had not, unfortunately, heard the commencement of the discussion. The Em-
> press suddenly called across the table to me and asked me what I thought of Marie
> Corelli. Quite unconscious of the fact that the Queen was an admirer of this
> authoress, I replied that her books undoubtedly had a large sale, but I thought the
> secret of her popularity was that her writings appealed to the semi-educated.
> Whereupon the Empress clapped her hands, and the subject dropped with startling
> suddenness. It was not till afterwards that I learnt how I had put my foot in it.[2]

Victoria's fondness of Corelli's books does not prove the writer's literary
worth. We have seen that Victoria was a rather indiscriminate reader. But,
what is more important, the popularity of Marie Corelli among the royals
proves Leavis' theory about the "homogeneous" readership at the end of
the nineteenth century.[3] Corelli's romances were indeed read from the scul-
lery maid to the Queen. And it was only later with the beginning of the
twentieth century that the reading public, and with it, literature, split into
what Leavis terms high-brow and low-brow. High-brow literature then
opened the way to high modernism, whereas low-brow literature was first
condemned, then devalued by what high modernists established as the
literary canon, and subsequently written out of literary history altogether.
And it has only been an interest in cultural history which has made Marie
Corelli into a subject worthy of academic interest.

With regard to Queen Victoria, she must be considered of cultural significance insofar as she was also an exemplary nineteenth-century reader. She
is representative of the age that encountered the rise of the bestseller in the
1890s (such as Corelli's); a phenomenon which was so obsessive and all-
encompassing in nature that it necessarily had to capture the Queen.

I hope to have shown in this essay that a study of the books that Victoria
read gives more insight into the politics and practices of reading in the
nineteenth century than one would assume. Queen Victoria was not at all
detached from her subjects when it came to reading. On the contrary, she
was also representative in the choice of themes that caught her attention
and that were very much of current interest, as Corelli's novels show: the

---

[1] Ponsonby seems too rash here in his conclusion. Cf. Victoria's reading of Scott,
Tennyson, Austen, Brontë, Edgeworth, Anthony Trollope, Cooper …

[2] Sir Frederick Ponsonby, *Recollections of Three Reigns* (London, 1951), pp. 51-52.

[3] Q.D. Leavis, *Fiction and the Reading Public*, p. 132.

reconsideration of sexuality and desire, ways of experiencing and understanding the metaphysical, and the Woman Question. Really, deep inside, the Queen was quite *bourgeois*.

Charles Dickens und Queen Victorias England

Von *Dieter Mehl* (Bonn)

Am 9. April 1870, fast genau zwei Monate vor seinem Tod, wurde Charles Dickens von Königin Victoria empfangen. Der enge Freund und Biograph des Dichters, John Forster, nennt ihn bei dieser Gelegenheit

> the author whose popularity dated from her accession, whose books had enter-tained larger numbers of her subjects than those of any other contemporary writer, and whose genius will be counted among the glories of her reign.[1]

Ein Biograph unserer Tage spricht von einer Begegnung der "two greatest representatives of the Victorian era"[2], und der Schriftsteller Angus Wilson bezeichnet den Besucher der Königin als "surely her most world-famous citizen".[3] Die Begegnung dauerte eineinhalb Stunden; vom Inhalt ist jedoch nur der Austausch von freundlichen Gemeinplätzen überliefert. Her Majesty überreichte dem Dichter ein signiertes Exemplar ihres *Journal of Our Life in the Highlands* und wünschte sich noch am selben Nachmittag eine Ausgabe seiner Werke. Dickens erbat sich etwas Zeit, um seiner Herr-scherin ein angemessen gebundenes Exemplar überreichen zu können und schickte ihr kurz darauf eine in rotes Marokkoleder gebundene Gesamt-ausgabe.

Soweit wir wissen, war dies die einzige persönliche Begegnung des Dichters mit der Königin, die sich schon dreißig Jahre früher als eifrige Leserin seiner Romane bekannt hatte. So notierte sie 1839 in ihrem Tage-buch ein lebhaftes Interesse für *Oliver Twist,* den gerade erschienenen zweiten Roman von Dickens: "liked it so much and wished [Melbourne] [Lord Melbourne, ihr Premierminister] would read it ...". Drei Monate spä-ter, nachdem er offensichtlich ihrem Wunsch nachgekommen war, schrieb sie: "'It's all among Workhouses, and Coffin Makers and Pickpockets,' he said; 'I don't like that low debasing style'. [...] We defended Oliver very much, but in vain."[4]

---

[1] John Forster, *The Life of Charles Dickens*, The Fireside Dickens (London, o.J.), S. 918.

[2] Peter Ackroyd, *Dickens* (London, 1991), S. 1126.

[3] Angus Wilson, *The World of Charles Dickens* (Harmondsworth, 1972), S. 290.

[4] *The Letters of Charles Dickens*, The Pilgrim Edition, ed. Madeline House and Gra-ham Storey, Volume Two 1840-1841 (Oxford, 1969), S. 26-27, n. 6.

Dickens seinerseits gab anlässlich von Victorias Hochzeit im Februar 1840 in mehreren burlesken Briefen an Freunde gemeinsam mit dem Maler Maclise eine komisch-theatralische Leidenschaft für die junge Königin vor: "Maclise and I are raving with love for the Queen – with a hopeless passion whose extent no tongue can tell, nor mind of man conceive."[1] An Forster schrieb er am Tag nach der königlichen Hochzeit einen Brief, dessen groteske Ausgelassenheit sicher mehr über die ungehemmte Freude an der eigenen Sprachvirtuosität aussagt als über die persönlichen Gefühle gegenüber der jungen Königin:

> The presence of my wife aggravates me. I loathe my parents. I detest my house. I begin to have thoughts of the Serpentine, of the regent's-canal, of the razors upstairs, of the chemist's down the street, of poisoning myself at Mrs. –'s table, of hanging myself upon the pear-tree in the garden, of abstaining from food and starving myself to death, of being bled for my cold and tearing off the bandage, of falling under the feet of cab-horses in the New-road, of murdering Chapman and Hall and becoming great in story (SHE must hear something of me then – perhaps sign the warrant [...]), of turning Chartist, of heading some bloody assault upon the palace and saving Her by my single hand – of being anything but what I have been, and doing anything but what I have done. Your distracted friend, C. D.[2]

Zum Glück für die englische Literatur blieb es bei diesem literarischen Ausbruch, mit der Aufzählung blutrünstiger Szenarien für eine ganze Bibliothek von Sensationsromanen.

In späteren Jahren war es wiederum die Königin, deren Wunsch, den berühmten Autor persönlich kennen zu lernen, zweimal von ihm respektvoll und zugleich entschieden abgebogen wurde. So besuchte Victoria 1857 eine der mit großem Aufwand vorbereiteten Amateuraufführungen, in denen Dickens maßgeblich mitwirkte: Wilkie Collins' Melodrama *The Frozen Deep*. Nach der offensichtlich sehr erfolgreichen Vorstellung bat sie den Dichter zu sich. Die Szene, in des Dichters Worten, ist für beide charakteristisch:

> My gracious sovereign was so pleased that she sent round begging me to go and see her and accept her thanks. I replied that I was in my Farce dress, and must beg to be excused. Whereupon she sent again, saying that the dress 'could not be so ridiculous as that', and repeating the request. I sent my duty in reply, but again hoped her Majesty would have the kindness to excuse my presenting myself in a costume and appearance that were not my own. I was mighty glad to think, when I woke this morning, that I had carried the point.[3]

---

[1] Ibid., S. 25.
[2] Ibid., S. 24.
[3] *The Life of Charles Dickens*, S. 917-18.

Später, als die Königin den Wunsch äußerte, Dickens möge eine seiner gefeierten Lesungen des *Christmas Carol* für sie persönlich wiederholen, erklärte der Dichter, er könne nur vor Publikum lesen, und lud sie zu einer seiner öffentlichen Auftritte ein, wozu es jedoch nicht kam. Immerhin erwarb die Königin eine Kopie des *Christmas Carol* mit Dickens' eigenhändiger Widmung aus dem Nachlass Thackerays für ihre Privatsammlung.

Von einem sonderlich nahen oder persönlichen Verhältnis zwischen der Monarchin und dem bekanntesten Chronisten ihrer Epoche kann also kaum die Rede sein. Für Generationen von Lesern aber, nicht nur im eigenen Land, sondern weltweit, ist das Zeitalter Königin Victorias eng mit den Romanen von Charles Dickens verbunden, ja diese Romane haben recht eigentlich ein Bild der viktorianischen Gesellschaft geschaffen und der Nachwelt weitergereicht, jedenfalls weit mehr als wissenschaftliche Darstellungen oder andere "authentische" Zeugnisse. In seiner klassischen, noch heute sehr lesenswerten Darstellung *The Dickens World* hat Humphry House es treffend formuliert, freilich mit dem notwendigen *caveat*: "He made out of Victorian England a complete world, with a life and vigour and idiom of its own, quite unlike any other world there has ever been."[1] Der Nachsatz beschreibt mein eigentliches Thema.

Die Feststellung, dass Dickens die Welt Victorias beschreibt, gilt streng genommen freilich nur für die erste Hälfte ihrer langen Regierungszeit. Ihre Krönung, 1837, fand im selben Jahr statt wie das Erscheinen der ersten Buchausgabe der *Pickwick Papers*, die seit März des vorausgehenden Jahres in monatlichen Fortsetzungen erschienen und zu einem beispiellosen Leser- und Verkaufserfolg geworden waren. Schon frühe Kritiker, wie viele spätere Leser, sahen das Werk als ein getreues Panorama des vorviktorianischen England. Der große Erfolg verführte den Dichter jedoch keineswegs zu einer Wiederholung desselben literarischen Rezepts: Noch während die monatlichen Fortsetzungen der *Pickwick Papers* erschienen, entstand der nächste Roman, *Oliver Twist*, der einen völlig anderen Ton anschlägt und in ganz andere soziale Bereiche einführt. Von da an schrieb Dickens mit wachsendem Erfolg Romane, Erzählungen und Betrachtungen über die verschiedensten Probleme der Gesellschaft seiner Zeit, an der er als aktiver Bürger höchst intensiven und auch praktisch tätigen Anteil nahm. Seine immense Korrespondenz zeigt dies besonders eindrucksvoll, aber auch seine engagierte journalistische Aktivität über fast vierzig Jahre bestätigt es in vielfältiger Weise.

Vom Beginn der Rezeption der Dickens'schen Romane war die Frage nach der spezifischen Qualität seines literarischen "Realismus" heftig um-

---

[1] Humphry House, *The Dickens World*, Second Edition (Oxford, 1942), S. 224.

stritten. Während viele Leser in den Romanen und ihrem Personal ein getreues Abbild der Welt sahen, wie sie ihnen auf den Straßen Londons, Ro-
chesters oder unterwegs begegnete, gab es schon früh Stimmen, die energisch das Gegenteil feststellten. So verglich der scharfsinnige George
Henry Lewis zwei Jahre nach dem Tod des Dichters seine Charaktere mit
Holzfiguren auf Rädern und stellte darüber hinaus lapidar fest: "The world
of thought and passion lay beyond his horizon"; noch härter fährt er fort: "I
do not suppose a single thoughtful remark on life or character could be
found throughout the twenty volumes. [...] He never was and never would
have been a student."[1] In ganz ähnlichem Sinne äußert sich 1882 der in den
letzten Jahrzehnten gerade als Gesellschaftsschilderer wieder neu ge-
schätzte Zeitgenosse von Dickens, Anthony Trollope. Er spricht von "the
peculiarity and the marvel of this man's power, that he has invested his
puppets with a charm that has enabled him to dispense with human nature"[2], und er begründet damit seine Präferenz für Thackeray und George
Eliot, mit der er sich in der Minderheit befinde. In einem seiner frühen
Romane, *The Warden* (1855), karikiert er den Autor als "Mr. Popular Sentiment", der öffentliche Affären oder Mißstände aufgreife und simplifizie-
rend als Sensation verkaufe. Wesentlich subtiler hatte George Eliot selbst
bereits zu Lebzeiten des Autors auf die für sie entscheidenden Grenzen
seiner Menschenschilderung hingewiesen:

> We have one great novelist who is gifted with the utmost power of rendering the
> external traits of our town population; and if he could give us their psychological
> character – their conceptions of life, and their emotions – with the same truth as
> their idiom and manners, his books would be the greatest contribution Art has ever
> made to the awakening of social sympathies [...] he scarcely ever passes from the
> humorous and external to the emotional and tragic, without becoming as transcen-
> dent in his unreality as he was a moment before in his artistic truthfulness.[3]

Es ist nicht schwer zu erkennen, dass George Eliot die Romane nach Maßstäben beurteilt, die für ihre eigene, sehr viel intellektuellere Erzählpraxis
zutreffen, aber kaum mit Dickens' extrovertiertem Fabuliertemperament in
Einklang zu bringen wären. Ob Dickens weniger erfolgreich war in dem,
was George Eliot so treffend als das oberste Ziel der Kunst bezeichnet,
"the extension of our sympathies", ist kaum zu entscheiden. Zweifellos war

---

[1] Zitiert nach *The Dickens Critics*, ed. George H. Ford and Lauriat Lane, Jr. (Ithaca,
NY, 1961), S. 62-63, S. 69.

[2] Nach *The Dickens Critics*, S. 75.

[3] "The Natural History of German Life" (1856), zitiert nach George Eliot, *Selected
Essays, Poems and Other Writings,* ed. A.S. Byatt und Nicholas Warren (Harmondsworth, 1990), S. 111.

dies aber auch für ihn ein vordringliches Anliegen. Besonders heftig reagierte er immer wieder, wenn die Wahrheit seiner Gesellschaftsschilderungen angezweifelt wurde, im besonderen wenn dies gerade von Vertretern dieser Gesellschaft ausging, die sich betroffen fühlen sollten. Das Vorwort zur dritten Auflage von *Oliver Twist*, drei Jahre nach Erscheinen des Romans, ist ein charakteristisches Beispiel. Der Autor verteidigt sich darin gegen Einwände, wie sie ja auch von Victorias Premierminister, Lord Melbourne, erhoben worden waren:

> It is, it seems, a very coarse and shocking circumstance, that some of the characters in these pages are chosen from the most criminal and degraded of London's population; that Sikes is a thief, and Fagin a receiver of stolen goods; that the boys are pickpockets, and the girl is a prostitute.[1]

Im folgenden beschreibt er ironisch die attraktiven Verbrechergestalten der ihm bekannten Literatur; nie, außer bei Hogarth, habe er "the miserable reality" angetroffen. Und er fährt fort:

> It appeared to me that to draw a knot of such associates in crime as really do exist; to paint them in all their deformity, in all their wretchedness, in all the squalid poverty of their lives; to show them as they really are, [...] it appeared to me that to do this, would be to attempt a something which was greatly needed, and which would be a service to society.[2]

Dies zu Dickens' eigener Definition von "Realismus". Zwei Seiten weiter freilich folgt eine Einschränkung, die spätere Leser, oft in etwas unhistorischer Voreingenommenheit, als kritischen Einwand benutzt haben. Sie betrifft vor allem die Sprache:

> No less consulting my own taste, than the manners of the age, I endeavoured, while I painted it in all its fallen and degraded aspect, to banish from the lips of the lowest character I introduced, any expression that could by possibility offend.[3]

Der ganze Abschnitt fehlt in der Neuauflage des Romans im Rahmen der Charles Dickens Edition von 1867, drei Jahre vor dem Tod des Dichters. Dieser mag den Eindruck gewonnen haben, dass "the manners of the age" sich inzwischen geändert hätten oder dass ein entsprechender Hinweis überflüssig wäre. Wichtiger ist, dass jedenfalls nach der Intention des Autors die abwertende Kritik Trollopes, George Eliots und vieler anderer

---

[1] *Oliver Twist*, ed. Kathleen Tillotson, The Clarendon Dickens (Oxford, 1966), S. lxi.
[2] Ibid., S. lxii.
[3] Ibid., S. lxiv.

nicht unreflektiert übernommen werden darf. Die für heutige Leser leicht irritierende Prüderie ist für Dickens in erster Linie ein sprachliches Problem, offensichtlich begründet in der nötigen Rücksicht auf die Leserschaft. Seiner Überzeugung nach beeinträchtigt dies in keiner Weise die Wahrheit seiner Schilderungen, jedenfalls nur für den oberflächlichen Leser. Er spricht in diesem Zusammenhang von "the unavoidable inference"[1], d.h. die für den Kundigen selbstverständliche Vorstellung des Schlimmsten, die der Ausbuchstabierung vorzuziehen sei. Es ist dies, so scheint mir, die unausgesprochene Voraussetzung jeder intelligenten bzw. historisch informierten Dickens-Lektüre. Sie gilt *mutatis mutandis* für den frühen wie für den späten Dickens, auch wenn er sich in *Our Mutual Friend* selbst über diese Form der viktorianischen Sprachregelung in einer Weise lustig macht, die seither sprichwörtlich geworden ist. So heißt es dort von Mr. Podsnaps neunzehnjähriger Tochter:

> A certain institution in Mr. Podsnap's mind which he called 'the young person' [...] It was an inconvenient and exacting institution, as requiring everything in the universe to be filed down and fitted to it. The question about everything was, would it bring a blush to the cheek of the young person.[2]

Bei allem selbstkritischen Spott war der Autor sich freilich bewusst, dass "the young person" letztlich auch ein Maßstab war, nach dem seine eigenen Texte beurteilt und gekauft wurden, nicht zuletzt von den mächtigen Leihbibliotheken. Im Vorwort zu den *Pickwick Papers* klingt er selbst ja nicht sehr viel anders als Mr. Podsnap: "He [der Autor] trusts that, throughout this book, no incident or expression occurs which could call a blush into the most delicate cheek, or wound the feelings of the most delicate person."[3] Wie dies in der literarischen Praxis aussieht, könnte etwa ein Vergleich zwischen zwei Szenen aus Fieldings fast genau ein Jahrhundert älterem Roman *Joseph Andrews* und den *Pickwick Papers* anschaulich machen. Sie folgen fast dem gleichen komödienhaften Muster: Parson Adams und Mr. Pickwick verirren sich in das falsche Schlafzimmer: Parson Adams "without [...] a rag of clothes on" gerät zunächst in eine handfeste Auseinandersetzung mit einer Bediensteten, bis er den Irrtum erkennt, "discovered, by the two mountains which Slipslop carried before her, that he was concerned with a female", anschließend verläuft er sich

---

[1] Ibid., S. lxiv.

[2] Charles Dickens, *Our Mutual Friend*, ed. Michael Cotsell, Oxford World's Classics (Oxford, 1989), S. 129. Alle Zitate nach dieser Ausgabe.

[3] Charles Dickens, *The Pickwick Papers*, ed. James Kinsley, Oxford World's Classics (Oxford, 1988), S. xxxv. Alle Zitate nach dieser Ausgabe.

nochmals und verbringt die Nacht an der Seite der unschuldigen Fanny, "ignorant of the paradise to which he was so near", so dass er am Morgen glaubhaft versichern kann, "As I am a Christian, I know not whether she is a man or a woman."[1] Das Kapitel, wie der ganze Roman, wären kaum eine geeignete Lektüre für Miss Podsnap. Mr. Pickwick dagegen, "one of the most modest and delicate-minded of mortals", überrascht im Schlafzimmer einer fremden Dame, reagiert, man ist versucht zu sagen "viktorianisch": "almost ready to sink, Ma'am, beneath the confusion of addressing a lady in my night-cap", und verlässt den Raum, Schuhe, Weste und Gamaschen auf dem Arm, unter höflichen Entschuldigungen und Verbeugungen. (S. 277-79) Ob man den Kontrast als Verlust an unverklemmter Vitalität oder Beweis für zivilisierte Verfeinerung der Sitten versteht, hängt vom subjektiven Standpunkt ab. Jedenfalls lässt er sich als literarisches ebenso wie als kulturhistorisches Phänomen erklären.

So kontrovers der Rang und die spezifische literarische Qualität von Dickens' Realismus auch von Anfang an diskutiert werden, so unbestreitbar ist die Tatsache, dass seine Romane in einer Welt spielen, die der größte Teil seiner Leser als die ihre erkannten und die spätere Generationen häufig mit dem historisch belegbaren England Queen Victorias gleichsetzen. In recht offensichtlicher Weise gilt dies zunächst für die Schauplätze seiner Romane, für ihre Topographie und speziell für die Metropole London. Nur wenige Werke der klassischen englischen Literatur sind in dieser Hinsicht so konkret nacherlebbar. Im Jahr des *Dickens Centenary 1970* erschien eine Publikation, die dies besonders anschaulich belegt, *The London of Charles Dickens*, herausgegeben von "London Transport" in Zusammenarbeit mit der Dickens Fellowship; es ist eine Art Führer zu all den noch identifizierbaren Örtlichkeiten in London, die in Dickens' Erzählungen eine Rolle spielen, mit kurzen Zitaten aus den Romanen und Angabe der nächstgelegenen Tube-Station. Dickens ist zwar nicht der einzige Dichter, dem diese Art der nostalgischen Pilgerreisen gewidmet sind, in seinem Fall ist es aber doch ein deutliches Indiz dafür, welch wichtige Rolle gewisse Örtlichkeiten in den Romanen spielen und wie die Romanwelt ihrerseits wieder auf die Lokalitäten zurückwirkt. Ein Beispiel von vielen ist das "George and Vulture Inn" in Lombard Street. Im Vorwort schreibt die Urenkelin des Meisters, Monica Dickens, dazu:

> We lunch at the George and Vulture Inn, off Cornhill, not only because it is very old, not only because Dickens lunched there, but because Mr Pickwick, when

---

[1] Henry Fielding, *Joseph Andrews* and *Shamela*, ed. Martin Battestin, Riverside Editions (Boston, 1961), S. 286-289.

asked by Bob Sawyer where he *hung out*, replied that he was at present *suspended at the George and Vulture.*[1]

Es gibt unzählige solcher topographischer "landmarks", viele freilich heute nicht mehr erhalten, die sich in der Phantasie vieler Leser festgesetzt haben und die der Dickens'schen Romanwelt einen qualitativ anderen Realitätsbezug geben als etwa Trollopes Barchester oder Hardys Egdon Heath. Durch die Fiktion einer als bekannt vorausgesetzten Szenerie wird der Leser deutlicher dazu animiert, auch die *dramatis personae* als Repräsentanten seiner eigenen, erfahrenen Welt zu akzeptieren, zumal wenn sie in Situationen gezeigt werden, die ihm aus der öffentlichen Publizistik bekannt sind, und die Rhetorik des Erzählers um Empathie wirbt und ein persönliches Vertrauensverhältnis zum Rezipienten zu schaffen sucht. Es ist dies ein wesentliches Element von Dickens' epischer Strategie.

Die ersten Jahrzehnte von Victorias Regierung waren eine Zeit dramatischer gesellschaftlicher Veränderungen, die viele Zeitgenossen beunruhigten. Sie fanden einen deutlichen Niederschlag in den zwischen 1836 und 1870 entstandenen Werken: das England von Dickens' späten Romanen stellt sich in vielerlei Hinsicht anders dar, als die Anfänge erwarten ließen.[2] Das ist natürlich auch das Resultat literarischer Entwicklungen, an denen er als Autor wie als Herausgeber und Leser lebhaften Anteil nahm; doch lassen sich solche vielfältigen Einflüsse ja kaum von dem historischen Kontext trennen.

Schon an Dickens' erstem Roman, den von März 1836 bis Oktober 1837 in monatlichen Fortsetzungen erschienenen *Pickwick Papers*, läßt sich das wachsende Bedürfnis des Autors ablesen, von unverbindlich humoristischen Genreskizzen zu präziser und durchaus auch aggressiver Gesellschaftskritik weiterzugehen. Selten noch dürfte ein so spontan erfolgreiches Buch mit weniger vorausschauender Planung entstanden sein. Es begann bekanntlich als nicht sonderlich vielversprechendes Auftragswerk, ein humoristischer Begleittext zu Stichen des wesentlich bekannteren Künstlers Robert Seymour. Als die erste Nummer erschien, hatte Dickens selbst kaum die folgende Fortsetzung geschrieben, geschweige denn eine Konzeption für das ganze Werk entwickelt. Nur etwa vierhundert Exemplare waren jeweils von den ersten vier Nummern abgesetzt, als fast

---

[1] *The London of Charles Dickens*, Foreword by Monica Dickens, Published by London Transport in Association with the Dickens Fellowship (London, 1970), S. xi.

[2] In dem Vorwort, das Dickens für die Charles Dickens Edition, 1867, schrieb, geht er auf Veränderungen ein, die seit dem ersten Erscheinen des Buches festzustellen seien. "Legal reforms" hätten eine Reihe von Mißständen beseitigt, aber noch genug bleibe für Zukunftshoffnungen übrig. Vgl. Kinsleys Ausgabe, S. 725.

schlagartig der Erfolg einsetzte: Von den letzten Fortsetzungen wurden je 40.000 Exemplare verkauft, und von da an war fast jedes seiner Bücher ein "best-seller", ein Begriff, der vielleicht erst seit den *Pickwick Papers* seine Berechtigung im heutigen Sinne hat.

In diesem Zusammenhang ist festzustellen, dass erst nach dem Tod des Illustrators, für den noch vor Erscheinen der dritten Nummer in aller Hast ein Ersatz gefunden werden mußte, Dickens wirklich freie Hand hatte und das Buch seinen eigentlichen Charakter annahm. Er weicht erheblich von dem ab, was in den ersten Kapiteln angelegt war. Angus Wilson nennt die *Pickwick Papers* schlicht "an exceptional, a truly wonderful book".[1] Das wurde es erst, als das ursprüngliche Konzept, "comic plates, 'illustrative of life in the Country'" zugunsten eines sehr viel breiteren Panoramas aufgegeben wurde. Aus den lebendig erzählten, komischen, aber nicht sonderlich originellen Abenteuern von Mr. Pickwick und seinen Begleitern wächst unerwartet eine Serie von Begegnungen und Episoden, die dem Roman erst eine über zahllose ähnliche humoristische Publikationen hinausgehende Aktualität verleihen und den oft gebrauchten Vergleich mit *Don Quichote* rechtfertigen, ein Vergleich übrigens, den Dickens selbst im Vorwort zu *Oliver Twist* aufgriff, wie Henry Fielding hundert Jahre vor ihm.

In erster Linie geschieht diese Ausweitung durch die Einführung des "Plot" um die Witwe Bardell, durch den Mr. Pickwick und der Leser unerwartet Einblick in die zeitgenössische Rechtspraxis und ihre Vertreter, sowie in das Innere des Gefängniswesens erhält, was anfangs allenfalls in einigen melodramatischen, in die Handlung eingestreuten Geschichten geschieht. Von da an werden nicht mehr nur vertraute Klischees aufgewärmt, sondern auch wesentlich bedrohlichere Aspekte der viktorianischen Realität sehr konkret vorgeführt, ohne dass, so wenig wie bei Cervantes, der komödiantische Grundtenor des Buches verleugnet wird. Schon die Lustspielszenen um Mr. Pickwicks erste Begegnungen mit den Ordnungshütern in Ipswich enthalten gezielteren Spott als der ausgelassene Erzählton zunächst suggeriert, auch wenn Dogberry aus dem Hintergrund grüßen läßt. Wichtiger scheint mir, dass durch den ganzen Roman altbewährte Komödienmotive durch die Adaptation an ein zeitgenössisches Milieu gewissermaßen aktualisiert werden, selbst wenn dies gelegentlich zu anachronistischen Diskrepanzen führt, worauf schon frühe Kritiker hingewiesen haben.

So sind die *Pickwick Papers* auf den ersten Seiten explizit auf das Jahr 1827, also fast zehn Jahre vor ihrer Entstehung, datiert, aber wie Humphry

---

[1] *The World of Charles Dickens*, S. 116.

House im einzelnen ausgeführt hat, beschreiben sie teilweise Verhältnisse, die schon damals überholt waren.[1] Gleichzeitig aber setzen sie die Kenntnis von Erscheinungen der Gegenwart voraus, d.h. der Autor gibt seiner fiktiven Welt etwas von der nostalgischen Patina einer vergangenen Zeit, aber zugleich schließt er sich mit den Lesern ein in die Gemeinschaft der Zeitgenossen. Ein unscheinbares, aber charakteristisches Beispiel ist die Überschrift zum achten Kapitel: "Strongly illustrative of the position, that the course of true love is not a railway" (S. 87). Die Eisenbahn war um 1836 noch im Stadium der ersten Erprobung, und ihre rasante Entwicklung im Laufe der folgenden Jahrzehnte war kaum vorauszusehen. Im späteren Werk und im Leben des Autors spielte sie jedoch eine höchst bedeutende Rolle. An dieser Stelle des Buches hat der Vergleich noch etwas zugleich Komisches und Prophetisches, in einem Werk, das oft als besonders lebendiges Zeugnis der "old coaching days" zitiert wird. Wie in den klassischen englischen pikaresken Romanen von Fielding und Smollett ist in den *Pickwick Papers* ja noch die Kutsche das wichtigste Beförderungsmittel. Ihre Tage waren zwar bald gezählt, aber sie hatte bereits in den zwanziger Jahren einen technischen Stand erreicht, der die altväterlichen Schilderungen von Weller Senior als etwas "out of date" erscheinen ließ. Die Diskrepanz läßt sich künstlerisch begründen; sie trägt jedenfalls zu dem Effekt bei, den Humphry House für *Great Expectations* feststellt, der auch für die Mehrzahl der Dickens'schen Romane gilt: "The mood of the book belongs not to the imaginary date of its plot, but to the time in which it was written."[2] Dies erklärt zu einem guten Teil, warum schon die *Pickwick Papers* trotz mancher historischen Ungenauigkeit den Eindruck eines authentischen Gesellschaftspanoramas vermitteln. Mr. Pickwick selbst könnte nach Alter, Temperament und sozialer Position kaum verschiedener von seinem agilen jungen Schöpfer sein. Was beide jedoch gemeinsam haben, ist die unbekümmerte Neugier, der Drang, möglichst viel über die Lebensverhältnisse und Biographien seiner Mitmenschen zu erfahren. Selbst in dem alles andere als gemütlichen Milieu des Fleet Prison scheint dieser Zug anfangs zu überwiegen, bis der Held sich mit dem Seufzer "I have seen enough" (p. 578) für drei Monate in sein einsames Gefängniszimmer zurückzieht. Doch am Ende blickt er zurück und beschreibt dabei das Grundthema des ganzen Buches:

> I shall never regret having devoted the greater part of two years to mixing with different varieties and shades of human character, frivolous as my pursuit of novelty may have appeared to many [...] numerous scenes of which I had no previous

---

[1] Vgl. *The Dickens World*, S. 24-27.
[2] Ibid., S. 159.

conception have dawned upon me – I hope to the enlargement of my mind, and the improvement of my understanding. (S. 714)

Das pikareske Schema wird so einem Bildungsroman für Senioren untergeordnet, wobei die Welt, anders als bei Cervantes oder Fielding, wesentlich präziser als Abbild der politischen und sozialen Gegenwart konzipiert ist, auch wenn sich Karikatur und Kritik nicht immer an den aktuellen Zuständen orientieren, so dass es jedenfalls unvorsichtig wäre, das Buch im Detail als historische Quelle heranzuziehen.

Ähnliche Diskrepanzen sind bei fast allen Romanen festgestellt worden, die spezifische Bereiche der viktorianischen Kultur kritisch-satirisch in den Mittelpunkt der Handlung stellen, sei es die Armengesetzgebung, das Gerichtswesen, das Erziehungssystem, der Zustand der Gefängnisse, das Gebaren der neuen Geschäftsplutokratie, des Industriekapitalismus oder gesellschaftlicher Moden. Dies, zusammen mit Dickens' theatralisch-hyperbolischer Rhetorik, hat dazu geführt, dass man ihn einmal als erfolgreichen Reformer öffentlicher Mißstände idealisiert, ein andermal als reißerischen Vertreter längst erledigter populärer Gravamina abgetan hat. Die überaus kontroverse Dickenskritik ist diesen Fragen zeitweise mehr oder weniger aus dem Weg gegangen, indem sie sich vielfach mit den eklatant unrealistischen Elementen der Dickens'schen Erzählkunst, namentlich seines Gebrauchs suggestiver Symbole und der Rolle des Unterbewussten in seinem Werk beschäftigt haben. Parallel dazu vollzog sich eine dezidierte Abwendung vom frühen Dickens und eine ganz neue Einschätzung der späten Romane. Charakteristisch für die ältere Einschätzung ist der gerne zitierte Satz von Chesterton: "Do not, if you are in the company of any ardent adorers of Dickens [...] insist too urgently [...] on the splendour of Dickens's last works, or they will discover that you do not like him."[1] Das hat sich seit 1913 gründlich geändert und zuweilen fast ins Gegenteil verkehrt. Doch hat der Methodenpluralismus der Dickenskritik, so scheint mir, inzwischen einen Punkt erreicht, von dem aus man die unvergleichlich straffere Struktur und poetische Geschlossenheit der späten Romane ebenso hervorheben kann wie ihren ganz unsymbolischen Realismus und die wenig optimistische Analyse der viktorianischen Gesellschaft.

Our Mutual Friend (1865), Dickens' letzter vollendeter Roman, macht deutlich, welchen Weg er als Erzähler wie auch als Beobachter der viktorianischen Gesellschaft seit den *Pickwick Papers* zurückgelegt hatte. Peter Ackroyd nennt das Buch "a full-frontal assault on English life" und stellt

---

[1] G.K. Chesterton, *Charles Dickens: A Critical Study* (New York, 1913), S. 185, zitiert nach George H. Ford, *Dickens and His Readers: Aspects of Novel-Criticism since 1836* (New York, ⁵1965), S. 242.

fest, "Dickens moved away from the demands and standards of conventional mid-Victorian society".[1] Die persönlichen, privaten Krisen des Autors, die Ackroyd wie viele andere Kritiker in diesem Zusammenhang erwähnt, sind allenfalls eine oberflächliche Erklärung. "[M]id-Victorian society", nicht nur ihre Konventionen, sondern ihre wirtschaftlichen, sozialen und menschlichen Grundlagen, sind in *Our Mutual Friend* einer radikalen Diagnose unterzogen, die durch die Gesten märchenhafter Utopie oder individuellen Optimismus nicht entscheidend abgemildert wird. Der letzte Satz des Romans zeigt einen bisher eher als zynisch-distanziert charakterisierten Zeitgenossen plötzlich froh gestimmt durch die mutig unkonventionelle Äußerung eines ganz und gar unscheinbaren Mitglieds der Gesellschaft. Es ist Mr. Twemlow, anfangs beschrieben als "a piece of innocent dinner-furniture" (S. 6), dann als "little feeble grey personage" (S. 409) und "Knight of the Simple Heart" (S. 569). Er hatte den verachtungsvollen Zorn von Mr. Podsnap und der ganzen Dinnergesellschaft der Veneerings erregt durch die entschiedene Verteidigung der ganz unstandesgemäßen Liebesheirat, die einen der beiden zentralen Handlungsstränge beschließt. Der Roman endet mit dem Satz: "Mortimer sees Twemlow home, shakes hands with him cordially at parting, and fares to the Temple, gaily." (S. 820)

Dies mag als Ausdruck der Stimmung aller guten, in das "happy end" eingeschlossenen Charaktere des Buches zutreffen, aber es scheint mir mehr Teil der utopischen Märchenrealität, die ein wichtiger Aspekt der Rhetorik des Buches ist, als des sehr viel weniger zuversichtlichen Befundes. In Mr. Podsnaps England sind es nicht die Twemlows oder die "Golden Dustmen", die den Ton angeben, und Dickens selbst weist in seinem Nachwort darauf hin, dass all die Mißstände, die in *Our Mutual Friend* für so viel menschliches Elend und Verzweiflung verantwortlich sind, von ihm keineswegs übertrieben wiedergegeben seien. "There is sometimes an odd disposition in this country", so führt er aus, "to dispute as improbable fiction what are the commonest experiences in fact." (S. 821) Als Beispiel führt er seine Darstellung der juristischen Auseinandersetzungen um das Harmon-Testament und der bedrückenden Anwendung der Armengesetzgebung an. So verläßt er bei der pathetischen Schilderung von Betty Higdens "long journey" auf der Flucht vor dem Armenhaus die Rolle des objektiven Erzählers und schlägt einen anklagend-warnenden Ton an, der die Intensität des sozialen Engagements bezeugt und sich kaum als Effekt des Mr. Popular Sentiment abtun läßt:

---

[1] *Dickens*, S. 997.

My lords and gentlemen and honourable boards, when you in the course of your dust-shovelling and cinder-raking have piled up a mountain of pretentious failure, you must off with your honourable coats for the removal of it, and fall to the work with the power of all the queen's horses and all the queen's men, or it will come rushing down and bury us alive. (S. 503)

Das Bild von "dust-shovelling" und "cinder-raking" nimmt eine der zentralen Metaphern des Romans auf, die "Dust-heaps": Sie sind oft genug in ihrer vieldeutigen (oder auch eindeutigen) Symbolik interpretiert worden, als gewinnträchtiger Großstadtmüll, in der viktorianischen Praxis der Entsorgung durchaus auch reich an unappetitlichen Bestandteilen euphemistisch tituliert, aber gleichzeitig auch Metapher für alles, was der neue Kapitalismus der aufstrebenden britischen Wirtschaft an Besitz zusammenrafft. Finanzielle Machenschaften spielen in diesem Zusammenhang durch den ganzen Roman eine schicksalhafte Rolle. Sie entscheiden über Aufstieg und Fall der Neureichen, aber auch vieler anderer Betroffener. Der ebenso beschränkte wie gewissenlose Fascination Fledgeby hat als einzige Befriedigung den Umgang mit "L. S. D. – not Luxury, Sensuality, Dissoluteness, which they often stand for, but the three dry letters [...] he was known secretly to be a kind of outlaw in the bill-broking line", und von seinem Umgang heißt es: "all had a touch of the outlaw, as to their rovings in the merry greenwood of Jobbery Forest, lying on the outskirts of the Share Market and the Stock Exchange" (S. 272). Sein Kapital kommt, wie fast alles Geld in diesem Roman, aus äußerst zweifelhaften Quellen, in diesem Fall aus Kreditgeschäften (e.g. "buying up queer bills", S. 278); anderswo wird das Geld aus den Müllbergen gegraben, aus dem Schlamm der Themse gefischt und in bildlichem Sinne aus schmutzigen Spekulationen oder den "money-mills" gewonnen, die die City beherrschen.[1] Als Bella Wilfer ihren Vater, den kleinen Angestellten in der Firma Chicksey, Veneering and Stobbles, aufsucht, führt ihr Weg ins Zentrum der Geldwirtschaft:

The City looked unpromising enough, as Bella made her way along its gritty streets. Most of its money-mills were slackening sail, or had left off grinding for the day. The master-millers had already departed, and the journeymen were de-

---

[1] Michael Cotsell spricht in diesem Zusammenhang von "the novel's theme of waste recycled" (vgl. seine Ausgabe des Romans in den "World's Classics", S. xx). Er verweist auch auf die komisch-satirischen Figuren von Mr. Venus, der mit Skeletten, präparierten anatomischen Objekten und anderen Kuriositäten handelt, sowie auf Jenny Wren, die aus Materialabfällen Puppen bekleidet.

parting. There was a jaded aspect on the business lanes and courts, and the very pavements had a weary appearance, confused by the tread of a million of feet. (S. 603)

Dem düsteren Bild der vom Geld beherrschten Realität wird im selben Kapitel das idyllische Märchenszenario vom Festschmaus der drei Kobolde entgegengesetzt, einem Familienidyll mitten in dem Büroraum Chicksey, Veneering and Stobbles, das in einer anderen Welt zu spielen scheint, einer Welt der verklärenden Phantasie, ohne Habgier, Standesneid und betrügerischem Egoismus. Die wiederholten Verweise auf diesen Bereich, auf Märchenfiguren und Kinderreime, dazu auf Zitate aus Shakespeare, der Bibel und volkstümlichem Versgut, schaffen einen intertextuellen Bezugsrahmen, an dem die Verirrungen der Gegenwart gemessen und mögliche Auswege oder Alternativen angedeutet werden. Der Dickens'sche Spätstil betont diese oft groteske Konfrontation von kritisch-satirischer Beobachtung, der Anprangerung von sozialen Schandflecken und daneben dem Rückzug in einen Raum der Phantasie, der Erinnerung an das Kinderzimmer, an frühe Lektüre und selbstvergessenes Rollenspiel. Die originellste Figur in diesem Zusammenhang ist die verkrüppelte Jenny Wren, "the doll's dressmaker", die sich über den Straßen der Stadt einen kleinen Dachgarten eingerichtet hat. Ihr Refrain "Come up and be dead!" (S. 282) ist ein originelles *memento mori* in einem Buch, in dem der Tod in so vielen ungewöhnlichen Formen auftritt. Sie wird Cinderella genannt, apostrophiert ihren betrunkenen Vater als bösen Buben und den Juden Riah, der sie mit Materialresten versorgt, als "godmother". Als sie ihn mit einer bedrohlichen Entwicklung der Handlung in Verbindung bringt, hält sie ihm vor: "You are not the godmother at all! [...] You are the Wolf in the Forest, the wicked Wolf!" (S. 574) Es braucht hier kaum an die besondere Vorliebe der Viktorianer für Märchen erinnert zu werden, in denen das Phantastische eine besonders prominente, nicht selten beängstigende Rolle spielt. Daneben ist freilich das in *Our Mutual Friend* am meisten zitierte Werk Edward Gibbons' achtbändige Geschichte *The Decline and Fall of the Roman Empire,* die sich Boffin, "the golden dustman" regelmäßig vorlesen läßt (S. 52-60). Offensichtlich ist dabei der Bezug zu dem in diesen Jahrzehnten entstandenen Begriff vom "British Empire". In seinen Arbeitsnotizen zum Roman vermerkt Dickens bei der ersten Einführung von Webbs Lektüre: "This to go through the Work", doppelt unterstrichen.[1] Und so heißt es bei einer späteren Erwähnung der Lektüre: "the Roman Empire usually declined in the morning" und "Boffin [...] would there,

---

[1] Vgl. Michael Cotsell, *The Companion to* Our Mutual Friend (London, 1986), S. 53.

on the old settle, pursue the downward fortunes of those enervated and corrupted masters of the world who were by this time on their last legs."[1]

Neben solchen indirekten Kommentaren zur viktorianischen Gegenwart dient Dickens' metaphorisch-allegorische Erzählweise oft auch der direkten Satire, etwa wenn es um Mr. Veneerings Einzug in das Parlament geht. Die Episode greift damit einen beliebten Gegenstand der politischen Karikatur in den Jahrzehnten der Wahlreformdebatten auf. Die Wahl in Eatanswill ist eine der besonders ausgelassenen Episoden in den *Pickwick Papers*; aggressiver ist der Artikel "Our Honourable Friend" aus Dickens' Zeitschrift *Household Words* vom 31. Juli 1852. Er beginnt:

> We are delighted to find that he has got in! Our honourable friend is triumphantly returned to serve in the next Parliament. He is the honourable member for Verbosity – the best represented place in England.

Seinen Wählern versichert er "England has been true to herself."[2] Auch Mr. Veneering, der Verkörperung viktorianischen Neureichentums in *Our Mutual Friend*, gelingt es, für seinen neuen Hausstand das M.P. hinter seinem Namen zu erwerben. Das Bild, mit dem dies vom Erzähler angekündigt wird, ist wiederum ein Beispiel für die satirisch-allegorische Rhetorik des Romans:

> Britannia, sitting meditating one fine day (perhaps in the attitude in which she is represented on the copper coinage), discovers all of a sudden that she wants Veneering in Parliament. It occurs to her that Veneering is a 'representative man' – which cannot in these days be doubted – and that Her Majesty's faithful Commons are incomplete without him." (S. 244)

Mit Geld und seinen "oldest friends" wird dieses Ziel bald erreicht. Im letzten Kapitel freilich verrät der Erzähler, welch charakteristisches Ende Veneerings Karriere nehmen wird: "it is written in the Book of the Insolvent Fates that Veneering shall make a resounding smash next week" (S. 887). Die Veneerings werden sich nach Calais zurückziehen und dort von den Diamanten Mrs. Veneerings leben, in die Veneering als guter Ehemann reichlich investiert hat.

Die neue Rolle des Geldes, vor allem der bargeldlosen Transaktion, Existenzgründung und Existenzvernichtung, ist ein Aspekt, in dem sich

---

[1] Vgl. dazu und zu anderen hier behandelten Aspekten des Romans, J. Hillis Miller, *Charles Dickens: The World of His Novels* (Cambridge, MA., 1958), S. 278-327, hier S. 296.

[2] *Reprinted Pieces*. Charles Dickens, *Complete Works*, Centennial Edition (London, o.J.), S. 229.

das Gesellschaftsbild der späten Romane von dem der frühen spürbar unterscheidet. Die gerade für diese Jahre der viktorianischen Konjunktur charakteristische Atmosphäre der hitzigen finanziellen Spekulation, in der schneller gesellschaftlicher Aufstieg und jäher Absturz sehr nahe beieinander lagen, ist selten so drastisch – und im ganzen zutreffend – beschrieben worden wie hier, jedenfalls kaum in so eingängiger Form.[1]

Dasselbe gilt für die Schauplätze: *Our Mutual Friend* kann als einer der frühesten und eindrucksvollsten Großstadtromane der englischen Literatur bezeichnet werden. Man hat das Buch mit Joyces *Ulysses* und mit T.S. Eliots *Waste Land* verglichen, dessen frühe von Ezra Pound gestutzte Fassung einen Untertitel aus *Our Mutual Friend* entnahm.[2] Wir verfolgen fast ständig die Figuren des Romans auf ihrem Weg durch London oder auch aus der Stadt heraus, wobei die Sprache immer wieder die Stadt als eigenständiges Wesen behandelt, das den Menschen unpersönlich gegenübersteht. So wird ein Nebeltag beschrieben:

> Animate London, with smarting eyes and irritated lungs, was blinking, wheezing and choking; inanimate London was a sooty spectre, divided in purpose between being visible and invisible and so being wholly neither. (S. 420)

Es folgt eine Schilderung des Nebels, der sich auf dem Weg vom offenen Land in das Zentrum der City von grau über gelb zu schwarz färbt. An anderer Stelle wird die "suburban Sahara" beschrieben, die die Stadt von den nördlichen Vororten trennt, "where tiles and bricks were burnt, bones were boiled, carpets were beat, rubbish was shot, dogs were fought, and dust was heaped by contractors." (S. 33)[3]

---

[1] Im letzten Kapitel, charakteristischerweise überschrieben "The Voice of Society", heißt es nach der Prophezeihung von Veneerings Fall: "It shall likewise come to pass, at as nearly as possible the same period, that society will discover that it always did despise Veneering, and distrust Veneering, and that when it went to Veneering's to dinner it always had misgivings – though very secretly at the time, it would seem, and in a perfectly private and confidential manner." (S. 887)

[2] Vgl. S. 198: "He do the police in different voices"; siehe T.S. Eliot, *The Waste Land. A Facsimile and Transcript of the Original Drafts*, ed. Valerie Eliot (London, 1971), S. 4-5 und S. 125, Anm. Siehe Cotsells Ausgabe, S. xxi, und Paul Goetsch, "The Thames River Valley and London. An Ecological Theme from *Our Mutual Friend* to *The Waste Land*", in: *Modernisierung und Literatur. Festschrift für Hans Ulrich Seeber zum 60. Geburtstag*, ed. Walter Göbel, Stephan Kohl und Hubert Zapf (Tübingen, 2000), S. 127-138.

[3] Siehe die Anmerkung zu dieser Stelle in der Ausgabe des Romans, ed. Stephen Gill, Penguin English Library (Harmondsworth, 1971 u.ö.), S. 904. Gill hebt die faktische Basis der meisten Schilderungen hervor: "Dickens' scholarship continues to show

Auch wenn sich Dickens äußerlich weithin im Rahmen einer vormodernen realistischen Erzähltechnik bewegt, gewinnt das viktorianische London durch seine eigenwillige intertextuelle Rhetorik und andere narrative Strategien deutlich Züge, die eine Assoziation mit *Waste Land* keineswegs weit hergeholt erscheinen lassen:

> Unreal City
> Under the brown fog of a winter dawn,
> A crowd flowed over London Bridge, so many,
> I had not thought death had undone so many.[1]

Es ist hoffentlich deutlich geworden, dass dies nur eine Seite von Dickens' düsterem Gesellschaftspanorama ist; die reißerischen, komischen und, jedenfalls nach heutigem Geschmack, nicht weit von Kitsch entfernten Aspekte des Romans haben zweifellos auch zu seinem Erfolg beigetragen: 30.000 Exemplare wurden in den ersten drei Tagen nach Erscheinen der ersten Nummer verkauft. Ob Königin Victoria den Roman auch gelesen hat, ist nicht überliefert.

Dabei enthält er doch eine ausdrückliche Würdigung der Königin: Als die geläuterte Bella Wilfer den entlassenen Sekretär des "Golden Dustman" heiratet, der unter dem Namen John Rokesmith fast das ganze Buch hindurch ihre moralische Prüfung und Bewährung beobachtet hat, teilt sie ihr neues Glück der Mutter in einem Brief mit, den der Gatte frankiert: "John Rokesmith put the queen's countenance on the letter – When had Her Gracious Majesty looked so benign as on that blessed morning! –" (S. 666). So düster, raffgierig und reformbedürftig die viktorianische Gesellschaft in Dickens' Roman auch erscheint, die Königin selbst sanktioniert gütig das märchenhafte *happy end*, wenigstens auf der Briefmarke.

---

that, although his marvellous imagination heightened and bewitched, it usually worked from an observed detail or topical detail."

[1] *The Waste Land*, ll. 60-63.

Alice's Adventures in Wonderland:
Eine Kuriosität der viktorianischen Kinderliteratur

Von *Ingeborg Boltz* (München)

Es gibt einige geflügelte Worte, die sich in vielen Lebenslagen anwenden lassen. Alices Ausruf zu Beginn des 2. Kapitels ihrer Abenteuer, "Curiouser and curiouser!" gehört dazu. Mehr noch als dieser einprägsame Komparativ, Ausdruck der Verwirrung des Kindes, deretwegen sie einen Moment lang vergißt, "how to speak good English", verbinden sich mit *Alice's Adventures in Wonderland* eine Reihe von Superlativen. Es gilt als originellstes Kinderbuch aller Zeiten, als einziges Kinderbuch, das auch Erwachsenen unvermindertes Vergnügen bereitet, als erstes Kinderbuch, das keine aufdringliche Moral, dafür aber die Freiheit des Denkens verkündet. Kurios, um bei dem Wort zu bleiben, mag auch erscheinen, daß der Autor dieses Werkes, in mancher Hinsicht Quintessenz eines Viktorianers, sich zu Beginn des 21. Jahrhunderts als veritabler 'global player' präsentiert. In weit mehr als 50 Sprachen übersetzt, hat er mühelos kulturelle und historische Grenzen überschritten, die vielen seinerzeit berühmteren Autorenkollegen verschlossen blieben. Sein Erfolg wurde von mehreren Voraussetzungen begünstigt, die nur kurz skizziert werden können.

Zum einen leistete die regierende Monarchin in ihrer mustergültigen Ehe mit Prinz Albert, der neun Kinder entstammten, einen wichtigen Beitrag zur Verklärung des Familienlebens in der Schicht des aufstrebenden Bürgertums, deren Wertekodex sich am königlichen Vorbild orientierte. Dank medizinischer Fortschritte konnte die Kindersterblichkeit gesenkt werden. Die Familien wurden kleiner und Mütter, die nicht kontinuierlich schwanger waren, konnten sich ihren Kindern widmen. Statistisch gesehen war die viktorianische Gesellschaft eine junge Gesellschaft. Von 1851 bis 1881 machten Jugendliche unter 15 Jahren mehr als 35% der Bevölkerung von England und Wales aus; dieser Prozentsatz übertraf die Gruppe der erwachsenen Männer und Frauen.[1]

Die Anfänge des Kapitalismus und die Ausweitung des Empire brachten größeren Wohlstand für breitere Gesellschaftsschichten, die in ihren Kindern Hoffnungsträger für eine noch erfolgreichere Zukunft sahen und mehr

---

[1] Claudia Nelson, "Growing up: Childhood", in: *A Companion to Victorian Literature and Culture, ed.* H.F. Tucker (Oxford, 1999), S. 69-81, S. 69.

in Bildung und Erziehung investierten. Die zunehmende Lesefähigkeit der Bevölkerung und Verbesserungen in Drucktechnik und Vertriebsmöglichkeit brachten eine Expansion des Marktes für Kinderliteratur mit sich, auf den sich nun auch kommerzielle Interessen richteten. Das Angebot, das bis zur Jahrhundertmitte von fiktionsfeindlichen, utilitaristischen Lehrmitteln dominiert war, begann sich aufzufächern und mit Abenteuer-, Reise- und Schulgeschichten auch kindlichen Unterhaltungsbedürfnissen zu entsprechen.

Daß die Phantasie, das Irrationale, das zweckfreie Spiel mit der Imagination für die seelische Entwicklung des Kindes unverzichtbar seien, war Gedankengut, das bereits die Dichter der Romantik proklamiert hatten, doch das sich erst allmählich durchzusetzen begann. Die 60er Jahre des 19. Jahrhunderts markierten den Beginn des 'goldenen Zeitalters' der Kinderliteratur, das sich bis um die Jahrhundertwende erstreckt.[1] Innerhalb dieses Zeitraums entstehen Kinderbücher, die zu den Klassikern der Weltliteratur gehören. Ohne den Durchbruch, den *Alice's Adventures* innerhalb des Genres bewirkte, wären sie nicht vorstellbar. Werfen wir zunächst einen Blick auf den Verfasser dieses Textes.

Charles Lutwidge Dodgson wurde am 27. Januar 1832 in Daresbury (Cheshire) als drittes von elf Kindern eines Landpfarrers geboren, der es, tatkräftig und gebildet, bis zur Position des Erzdiakon von Richmond brachte. Die Lebensleistung des Vaters als Patriarch und Prediger war für seinen ältesten Sohn so respekteinflößend, daß er darauf verzichtete, ihm auf diesen beiden Gebieten nachzueifern. Schon als Heranwachsender tat er sich jedoch als Unterhaltungskünstler hervor, der sich zum Amüsement seiner Geschwister Spiele und Scharaden ausdachte und familieninterne Magazine verfaßte. Deren Rezeptur orientierte sich am Mischcharakter viktorianischer Zeitschriften und bot Erbauliches neben Populärwissenschaftlichem, Rätsel und logische Knobeleien neben lyrischen Versuchen. Wenn bei diesen, für viktorianische Pfarrhäuser durchaus typischen Aktivitäten, etwas ins Auge fällt, so ist es die ausgeprägte Tendenz zur Parodie. In *The Rectory Magazine* (1848-50) persiflieren zahlreiche kleine Aufsätze den humorlosen Stil didaktischer Abhandlungen ('Reasonings on Rubbish', 'Musings on Milk', 'Twaddle on Telescopes') oder führen moralische Nutzanwendungen ad absurdum ("Never stew your sister"). Die pädagogischen Ermahnungen, mit denen ein Mittelstandskind dauerberieselt wurde, inspirierten den Dreizehnjährigen zu dem Gedicht *Rules and Re-*

---

[1] Eine chronologische Auflistung der Texte in: *Children's Literature. An Illustrated History*, ed. Peter Hunt (Oxford, 1995), S. 352-359.

gulations, in dessen Litanei von Imperativen sich manch beliebiger Nonsense eingeschmuggelt findet, wie etwa "starve your canaries" und "be rude to strangers". Die wiederholte Aufforderung "And never stammer", "Once more, don't stutter" verweist dagegen auf persönliche Erfahrungen. Dieses Familienleiden (sieben der Geschwister stotterten), brachte ihn später nicht nur auf dem gesellschaftlichen Parkett in Verlegenheit, sondern behinderte ihn auch in seiner beruflichen Laufbahn als Dozent für Mathematik und Logik am Christ Church College, Oxford, sowie in seinem Predigeramt als Diakon, dem er nach ersten Debakeln entsagte. Dodgson legte seine Sprechhemmung nur im vertrauten Umgang mit kleinen Mädchen ab. In ihrer Gesellschaft fühlte er sich glücklich und gelöst, und bei ihnen versprühte er jenen originellen Charme und Einfallsreichtum, der seinen Lehrveranstaltungen eher abging. "Boys are not in my line. I think they are a mistake" erwähnte er einem Studienfreund gegenüber;[1] umso mehr langweilten ihn seine männlichen Studenten.

Die atemberaubende Zahl sechs- bis zwölfjähriger Mädchen, die er im Laufe seines Lebens ansprach, die er auf Bahnfahrten, Strandpromenaden, im Kollegenkreis kennenlernte, und mit skurrilen Briefen bezauberte, die er photographierte (gelegentlich auch unbekleidet), wobei er zu einem der außergewöhnlichsten Porträtphotographen des 19. Jahrhunderts wurde, hätte dem schüchternen, lebenslangen Junggesellen im Zeitalter postfreudianischer Aufgeklärtheit zumindest wohlmeinende Therapieangebote eingetragen, womöglich aber auch Abmahnungen und Berufsverbot, wenn nicht sogar Hetzkampagnen in den Medien. Seine viktorianischen Zeitgenossen, mit ihrer neugeschärften Sensibilität für die Anziehungskraft der Kindheit, empfanden sein Verhalten offensichtlich als weniger befremdlich. Vielmehr schuf der viktorianische Kult des Kindes, besonders des jungen Mädchens, dessen Unschuld eine reinigende Wirkung zugeschrieben wurde, die Rahmenbedingungen für Dodgsons 'child-friendships'. Sie wurden zu einer Notwendigkeit für ihn – "three quarters of my life", wie er einmal bemerkte[2], da sie ihm die Regression in *die* Phase seines Lebens ermöglichten, die er eigentlich nie verlassen wollte. Das Gedicht des Ein-

---

[1] Brief an George Charles Bell vom 19. Februar 1882, in: *The Letters of Lewis Carroll*, ed. Morton N. Cohen (London, 1979), Vol. I, S. 455.
[2] Bemerkung zu Arthur Girdlestone, zitiert in: Isa Bowman, *The Story of Lewis Carroll* (o.O., 1899), S. 60. Repr. in: *Lewis Carroll. Interviews and Recollections*, ed. Morton N. Cohen (London, 1989), S. 96.

undzwanzigjährigen (!), *Solitude*[1], verdeutlich dies mit unverhohlener Sentimentalität:

> I'd give all wealth that toil hath piled
> The bitter fruit of life's decay
> To be once more a little child
> For one short sunny day.

So fungierten all die präpubertären Musen, die er mit Geschichten und Geschenken umwarb, und an denen er, sobald sie älter wurden, meist das Interesse verlor, gleichsam als Medien, mittels derer er sich in jene Kindertage im Kreise seiner sieben ihn vergötternden Schwestern zurückversetzen konnte. Seine Libido entfaltete sich als sublimierte Ersatzerotik im Ausreizen der Konventionen, die er selbst, dank seines Stützkorsetts aus Erziehung und religiöser Prägung, ganz und gar verinnerlicht hatte.

In der Enklave seines Oxforder College, in der er fast ein halbes Jahrhundert verbrachte, pedantisch bestrebt, die Reglements zu erfüllen, erzkonservativ in seiner Grundeinstellung zu Fragen des politischen, sozialen und kulturellen Lebens[2], verfaßte er eine respektable Zahl von mathematischen Fachpublikationen, die heute vergessen sind. Seine Nebentätigkeit als Kinderbuchautor, deretwegen er Weltberühmtheit erlangte, betrieb er unter dem Pseudonym Lewis Carroll ('Lewis' als englische Form des eher ungewöhnlichen 'Lutwidge', 'Carroll' als Abwandlung von 'Charles' mit einem Anklang an die als 'carols' bekannten englischen Weihnachtslieder). Die Schärfe, mit der er den Dichter und Kinderfreund von seinem akademischen Alltag zu trennen bemüht war, läßt an Bewußtseinsspaltung denken. "This curious child was very fond of pretending to be two people" (S. 33)[3] heißt es von Alice, der Reflektorfigur der Lewis-Carrollschen Hälfte eines 'homo duplex par excellence', wie ihn Klaus Reichert bezeichnete.[4] In späteren Jahren äußerte er sich irritiert über Fanpost, die seine Privat-

---

[1] Lewis Carroll, *The Complete Illustrated Works*, ed. Edward Guiliano (New York, 1982), S. 840.

[2] Bekannt ist sein Plan "of bowdlerising Bowdler" mit der Absicht, eine von sämtlichen Anstößigkeiten gereinigte Shakespeare-Ausgabe herzustellen, "absolutely fit for *girls*", den er in einem Brief an die Mutter eines Mädchens, Mrs. Richards, vom 13. März 1882 entwickelte (siehe *Looking-Glass Letters*, sel. and introd. by Thomas Hinde [London, 1991], S. 130).

[3] Zitiert wird nach Lewis Carroll, *The Annotated Alice*, ed. Martin Gardner, rev. ed. (London, 1970).

[4] Klaus Reichert, *Lewis Carroll. Studien zum literarischen Unsinn* (München, 1974), S. 47.

sphäre störte und sandte an 'Lewis Carroll, Christ Church, Oxford' adressierte Briefe als unzustellbar an den Absender zurück.[1] In diesem Kontext konnte auch eine Anekdote entstehen, die hartnäckig in populärwissenschaftlichen Darstellungen tradiert wird, vielleicht weil Dodgson sie erst spät und an wenig bekannter Stelle dementiert hat.[2] In ihr wird berichtet, daß Königin Victoria mit so großem Vergnügen *Alice's Adventures in Wonderland* gelesen habe, daß sie Mr Carroll um sein nächstes Buch bitten ließ. Sie erhielt postwendend *Condensation of Determinants*, eine gelehrte mathematische Abhandlung, die unter Carrolls richtigem Namen Charles Dodgson erschienen war.

Im Gegensatz zu anderen Autoren seines Bekanntenkreises, wie Tennyson oder Kingsley, wurde Dodgson nie die Ehre einer persönlichen Audienz bei seiner Monarchin zuteil. Da er Kontakte zu höheren Kreisen durchaus zu schätzen wußte, und in mancher Hinsicht sogar als Snob bezeichnet werden kann, mag ihn dies etwas gekränkt haben. Um verschiedene seiner 'child-friends' zu amüsieren (oder um ihnen zu imponieren?), behauptete er jedenfalls mehrmals, mit der Königin in Briefverkehr zu stehen. So fingierte er eine handschriftliche, mit "Yours truly, Victoria R." unterzeichnete Einladung zu einer Gartenparty[3], und scherzte in einem anderen Brief, daß ihn die Königin schriftlich um eine Photographie von sich gebeten habe.

Für die Literatur war es ein besonderer Glücksfall, daß sich Dodgsons dichterisches Talent an den Erlebnissen mit einem wirklichen, geliebten Kind entzündete, dem der Verfasser Vergnügen bereiten und dessen Zuneigung er sich sichern wollte. Aus ähnlichen Beweggründen entstanden auch andere Kinderbuchklassiker, wie *The Wind in the Willows* oder *Winnie the Pooh*, die sich aus Kenneth Grahams und A.A. Milnes 'Gutenachtgeschichten' für ihre Söhne entwickelten. John Ruskin verfaßte *The King of the Golden River* für die zwölfjährige Effie Gray, Charles Kingsley *The Water Babies* für sein jüngstes Kind Grenville und Thackeray *The Rose and the Ring* als Weihnachtsgeschenk für seine Töchter.

Unendlich viel ist schon über jenen denkwürdigen Ausflug in einem Ruderboot vom 2. Juli 1862 geschrieben worden, den der dreißigjährige Dodgson mit den kleinen Liddells, den drei Töchtern des Dekans seines

---

[1] Morton N. Cohen, *Lewis Carroll. A Biography* (London, 1995), S. 297.
[2] Als Postskript zu seinem 'Advertisement', das seinem 1896 erschienenen Buch *Symbolic Logic* vorangeht. Vgl. Derek Hudson, *Lewis Carroll. An Illustrated Biography* (London, 1976), S. 133.
[3] Faksimilewiedergabe bei Cohen, *Lewis Carroll*, S. 297.

College, unternahm.[1] Befreit von der Gouvernante Miss Prickett, und nur begleitet von seinem Kollegen, dem Reverend Robinson Duckworth, bestürmte ihn das Trio, die dreizehnjährige Lorina, die zehnjährige Alice und die achtjährige Edith, mit Aufforderungen, eine Geschichte zu erzählen, über deren improvisierten Charakter er später in dem Aufsatz "Alice on the Stage" (1887) berichtete:[2]

> I remember, how in a desperate attempt to strike out some new line of fairy-lore, I had sent my heroine straight down a rabbit-hole, to begin with, without the least idea what was to happen afterwards.

Und es war die mittlere der Schwestern, Alice Pleasance Liddell, sein Idealbild eines Kindes, auf deren Verlangen er die Stegreifgeschichte niederschrieb, sie ausarbeitete und ihr schließlich 1864 in einer in Reinschrift ausgeführten und mit eigenen Zeichnungen versehenen Geschenkfassung auf den weihnachtlichen Gabentisch legte.[3] Mit dieser 'labour of love' hätte es wohl sein Bewenden gehabt, wenn nicht inzwischen verschiedene Freunde Kenntnis von der Erzählung erlangt und ihre ganze Überredungskunst aufgewendet hätten, den Verfasser zu einer Veröffentlichung des Büchleins zu bewegen. Eine maßgebliche Rolle spielte dabei der mit Dodgson befreundete George MacDonald, selbst Autor berühmter viktorianischer Kinderliteratur, dessen sechsjähriger Sohn Greville zu den ersten begeisterten kindlichen Rezipienten des Werkes gehörte.

Für die geplante Druckfassung kamen weitere, in sich geschlossene Episoden hinzu, wodurch der Umfang fast verdoppelt wurde (von 18.000 auf 35.000 Wörter). Der ursprüngliche Titel *Alice's Adventures Under Ground* wurde verworfen, da er den Autor zu sehr an ein Sachbuch über Bergbau erinnerte, und nach verschiedenen Anläufen, die 'elves' und 'goblins' im Titel führten, hieß das 1865 erschienene Buch schließlich *Alice's Adventures in Wonderland* (was sicher auch Anteil am Erfolg hatte).

Mit Bedauern mußte sich Carroll (wir bleiben im folgenden bei dem Pseudonym) die Unzulänglichkeit seiner zeichnerischen Bemühungen eingestehen, deren verstörende Originalität trotz mancher Unbeholfenheit je-

---

[1] Forschungsüberblick und gute Einführung in das Werk bei Eberhard Kreutzer, *Lewis Carroll: 'Alice in Wonderland' und 'Through the Looking Glass'* (München, 1984).

[2] Nachgedruckt in: *'Alice in Wonderland'*, ed. Donald Gray, Norton Critical Edition, Second Edition (London, 1992), S. 280-283, S. 280.

[3] *Alice's Adventures Under Ground*, Facsimile edition, 1886. Repr. with Introd. by Martin Gardner (New York, 1965).

doch sofort ins Auge sticht. Da er sich der wesentlichen Bedeutung von Illustrationen auf dem expandierenden Kinderbuchmarkt nur allzu bewußt war – schließlich fragt ja auch Alice gleich zum Auftakt "What is the use of a book without pictures or conversations" –, schätzte er sich glücklich, John Tenniel für eine strapaziöse, im Endergebnis jedoch kongeniale Zusammenarbeit gewonnen zu haben. Tenniel, der 1864 die Position des wichtigsten politischen Karikaturisten des Magazins *Punch* innehatte, verdanken wir die unvergeßliche Visualisierung von Figuren, deren äußeres Erscheinungsbild Carroll nur angedeutet hatte (etwa der 'ugly duchess', für die ein Gemälde des flämischen Malers Quinten Massys in der National Gallery als Modell diente). Gelegentlich ersparte sich der Autor die Mühsal der Beschreibung und verwies gleich auf die Illustration ("If you don't know what a Gryphon is, look at the picture", S. 124). Anläßlich der Gerichtsszene (Kap. 14) wird auf das Frontispiz hingewiesen, wo zu sehen sei, wie der König seine Krone über der Perücke getragen habe. Tenniel, dessen besondere Stärke seine Tierkarikaturen waren, gelang es auch bei dieser Illustration, zusätzliche satirische Momente einzubauen – so ist einer der Rechtsanwälte ein Raubvogel, der andere ein Papagei. Die hybride Natur der 'mock turtle' wird erst durch Tenniels Beitrag vermittelt. Sogar für das Äußere der Heldin gab Carroll nur spärliche Instruktionen. Erwähnt werden 'shiny shoes', 'a skirt', 'small hands', 'bright eyes' und 'long straight hair', wenig aussagekräftige Attribute eines 'every girl', aus denen Tenniel die vertraute Ikone eines selbstsicheren viktorianischen Mittelstandkindes schuf, das die Wunderlandwesen und auch den Betrachter gelassen, fast kühl observiert. Die von Carroll gezeichnete Alice wirkt weicher, traumverlorener als die Tenniels, die einem gefühlloseren Stereotyp weiblicher Anziehungskraft entspricht. Und obwohl *Alice in Wonderland* allein in England inzwischen von weit über 100 zum Teil hochberühmten Illustratoren neu bearbeitet wurde, die dem jeweiligen Zeitgeschmack huldigten, bleibt Tenniel in vieler Hinsicht unerreicht.[1] Selbst die faszinierenden, mit tagespolitischen Anspielungen gespickten Karikaturen Ralph Steadmans Ende der 60er, Anfang der 70er Jahre des letzten Jahrhunderts, können sich nicht völlig von dem großen Vorbild lösen, dessen Bilderfindungen, einmal gesehen, die Vorstellungskraft der Leser nachhaltig besetzen.

---

[1] Siehe *The Illustrators of 'Alice in Wonderland'*, ed. Graham Ovenden (London, 1972) sowie Michael Hancher, *The Tenniel Illustrations to the 'Alice' Books* (Ohio, 1985).

Heutige Kinder kommen mit Carrolls Erzählung fast nur noch im Medium des Films oder Bilderbuchs in Berührung. Der an der Vermarktung seines Spitzenerfolgs durchaus interessierte Autor hatte bereits 1889 eine Version für Kleinkinder unter fünf Jahren herausgebracht. *The Nursery Alice* enthält mit seinen 6.500 Worten hauptsächlich einen Kommentar zu Tenniels Abbildungen, die stark vergrößert und in Farbe die Buchseiten dominieren. Der Tenor des Begleittextes ist kindertümelnd und verharmlosend – Eigenschaften, die man mit dem Text von 1865 gerade nicht verbindet. Kinder des ausgehenden 20. Jahrhunderts kennen am ehesten die immer noch beliebte Trickfilmversion von Walt Disney (1951), in der die Komik der Sprache durch bildhafte Situationskomik ersetzt wird. Auch hier ist der Modellcharakter Tenniels unübersehbar, bis in die Konzeption der Titelfigur, die allerdings zu einer barbiehaften Retortenschönheit transformiert ist.

Carrolls beträchtliches intellektuelles Potential, seine Vertrautheit mit Paradoxien der Logik, die ihn zu Verwirrspielen mit den Regelsystemen der Sprache animierten, begeistern mittlerweile eher ein erwachsenes Publikum, das jedoch hinsichtlich der spezifisch viktorianischen Referenzen, der Gedichtparodien und Zitate auf Kommentierung angewiesen ist.[1] Unter der Fangemeinde befinden sich auffällig viele Mathematiker, Philosophen, Naturwissenschaftler, Psychoanalytiker und Linguisten. Der Einfluß des Buches auf Literaten des 20. Jahrhunderts wird von diesen selbst immer wieder hervorgehoben. Juliet Dusinberre sieht Carroll z.B. als Katalysator für die skeptische Generation Virginia Woolfs – nicht, weil er sich über Gott lustig gemacht, sondern weil er sich im Gegensatz zu anderen Kinderbuchautoren seiner Zeit geweigert habe, eine religiöse Botschaft zu propagieren.[2] Wie revolutionär dies auf manche Zeitgenossen gewirkt haben muß, läßt sich heute, wo das Buch längst im angelsächsischen Kulturgut etabliert ist, kaum mehr nachvollziehen. Der passionierte Sprachexperimentator Arno Schmidt erhob Carroll gar zum "Kirchenvater aller modernen Literatur".[3] In *Finnegans Wake* assoziierte Joyce mit dem wortspielerischen Anklang an die Heilige Dreifaltigkeit "Dodgfather, Dodgson & Coo" die vom viktorianischen Autor vollzogene Wendung von rigiden

---

[1] Besonders hilfreich *The Annotated Alice. The Definitive Edition*, ed. Martin Gardner, Update der rev. ed. 1970 (London, 2001). Siehe auch Jo Elwyn Jones and J. Francis Gladstone, *The 'Alice' Companion. A Guide to Lewis Carroll's 'Alice' Books* (London, 1988).

[2] Juliet Dusinberre, *Alice to the Lighthouse. Children's Books and Radical Experiments in Art* (London, 1999), S. 73.

[3] *Trommler beim Zaren* (Karlsruhe, 1966), S. 257.

patriarchalen Denkweisen zu 'art for art's sake' im zweckfreien kindlichen Spiel.[1]

Daß Carroll damit wirklich eine Pionierleistung vollbrachte, mag der kurze Blick auf einen anderen Klassiker verdeutlichen, mit dem gerne das goldene Zeitalter der Kinderliteratur eingeläutet wird – Charles Kingsleys *The Water Babies. A Fairy Tale For a Land Baby* (1863), ein Buch, das Carroll zur Zeit seiner Abfassung von Alices Abenteuern zweifellos bekannt war.[2] Die ersten zwei Kapitel befassen sich durchaus realistisch mit dem zehnjährigen Waisen Tom, der seinen Unterhalt als 'lebender Besen' mit dem Fegen von Schornsteinen fristet. Obwohl William Blake bereits 1789 ein anrührendes Gedicht über das harte Los der 'chimney sweeps' verfaßt hatte, waren deren Arbeitsbedingungen weitgehend unverändert geblieben. Erst 1864, nicht zuletzt auf Grund von Kingsleys populärem Erfolg, wurde diese Tätigkeit für Kinder gesetzlich verboten. Toms Vorstellungskraft reicht nicht weiter als bis zur Antizipation derselben Existenzform, die ihm sein brutaler Dienstherr, ein Trunkenbold namens Grimes, vorlebt. Er hofft, auch einmal ein eigenes Geschäft zu haben, in dem er dann ebenfalls seine Lehrlinge ausbeuten kann. Bei der Arbeit in einem großen Herrschaftshaus verirrt er sich in das blütenweiße Schlafzimmer eines engelgleichen Mädchens, der Tochter des Hauses, und macht eine verstörende Erfahrung. Denn zum ersten Mal in seinem Leben sieht er in einem Spiegel sein rußiges Äußeres und kommt sich neben dem vollkommenen Geschöpf wie ein häßlicher schwarzer Affe vor. Er flüchtet, verfolgt vom Hauspersonal, in die Yorkshire Moors, wo ein kristallklarer Fluß in ihm das Verlangen weckt, hineinzuspringen, und ihn ausrufen läßt: "I will be a fish; I will swim in the water; I must be clean" (Kap. 2). Dies klingt nach mehr als einem banalen Säuberungsakt, und in der Tat nimmt die Handlung alsbald symbolischen Fahrtwind auf. In Toms Kopf läuten imaginäre Glocken, die Wasseroberfläche scheint sich wie eine Kirchentür zu öffnen. Er wirft seine schmutzigen Lumpen ab und taucht ein in eine magische Unterwasserwelt. Während seine Verfolger glauben, daß er ertrunken sei, verwandelt sich Tom in ein winziges Wasserbaby, gerade einmal 4 Zoll groß, mit Kiemen an den Schultern. In der Folge erlebt er in dieser, von sprechenden Fischen und fabulösen Kreaturen bevölkerten Welt, eine Serie phantastischer Abenteuer, die darauf abzielen, ihn vom

---

[1] Robert Polhemus, "Lewis Carroll and the Child in Victorian Fiction", in: *The Columbia History of the British Novel*, ed. John Richetti (New York, 1994), S. 579-607, S. 581.

[2] John Goldthwaite, *The Natural History of Make-Believe* (Oxford, 1996), S. 74-169, interpretiert *Alice's Adventures* sogar als eine Art Gegendarstellung zu Kingsleys Buch.

Stadium roher Wildheit in einen Zustand geistiger Regeneration zu befördern. Er, der um seine Kindheit betrogen wurde, ja noch nicht einmal gelernt hat, ein Gebet zu sprechen, bekommt die Chance eines Neubeginns. Er begegnet auch dem schönen Mädchen Miss Ellie wieder, die ihm Privatunterricht in den Regeln gesitteten Verhaltens erteilt. Ihm wird in Aussicht gestellt, Ellie auf ihren sonntäglichen Ausflügen in ihr Zuhause begleiten zu dürfen, einen als paradiesisch beschriebenen Ort. Vorher muß er sich jedoch auf einer großen Reise in verschiedenen Prüfungssituationen bewähren, in denen Selbstüberwindung und Versöhnungsbereitschaft, z.B. gegenüber seinem früheren Meister, gefordert sind. Toms Wasserbabyexistenz wird so zu einer Parabel für das Fegefeuer, in dem sündige Christen die seelische und moralische Reife erlangen können, die Voraussetzung für das Eingehen in Gott ist. Was diese dürre Zusammenfassung ausspart, sind die skurrilen Beschreibungen der Unterwasserwesen, die Kingsleys Faszination von meeresbiologischen Phänomenen widerspiegeln, oder Toms Erfahrungen mit zwei Feen, einer Mrs. 'Bedonebyasyoudid', und einer wesentlich liebreicheren Mrs. 'Doasyouwouldbedoneby', deren sprechende Namen ahnen lassen, daß sie den Geist des Alten und des Neuen Testaments repräsentieren. Wie bereits erwähnt, nahm Kingsley zum Schreibanlaß, daß er seinem jüngsten Sohn eine Gutenachtgeschichte schenken wollte, die neben einem sozialkritischen Ansatz auch eine evangelikale Mission erfüllen sollte. Immer wieder wendet sich der Erzähler an einen kindlichen Adressaten, der mit 'my dear little man' tituliert, ermahnt und examiniert, verspottet, freundlich oder herablassend herumkommandiert wird. Noch häufiger allerdings kokettiert der Erzähler mit erwachsenen Lesern, die er mit einer Flut von Fremdwörtern, Rabelaisschen Katalogen und kaum aussprechbaren Namen traktiert und auch an intertextuellen Anspielungen auf Dante, die Bibel, Shakespeare, romantische Dichter etc. partizipieren läßt. Entsprechend sind heutige Kritiker über das Buch geteilter Ansicht – John Rowe Townsend findet nur noch eine gekürzte Fassung zumutbar, wie sie seit 1961 im Handel ist;[1] andere meinen, daß dann aber der "quaint charm", den dieses Werk trotz aller Irritationen vermittle, verloren gehe.

Auch Carroll hat ein doppelsinniges Kinderbuch verfaßt[2], das Kinder wie Erwachsene anspricht, doch gegenüber der unverhüllt patriarchalen Er-

---

[1] J.R. Townsend, *Written for Children*, 5th rev. ed. (London, 1990), S. 75.

[2] Hans-Heino Ewers, "Das doppelsinnige Kinderbuch", in: *Kinderliteratur – Literatur für Erwachsene?*, ed. Dagmar Grenz (München, 1990). Siehe auch Paul Goetsch, *Monsters in English Literature: From the Romantic Age to the First World War* (Frankfurt, 2002), S. 222-237, S. 222.

zählinstanz in *Water Babies* fällt die erzählerische Vermittlung in *Alice's Adventures* aus dem üblichen Rahmen viktorianischer Kinderliteratur. Mit "Hand in Hand: A Partnership" hat Barbara Wall das Carroll-Kapitel in ihrem Buch *The Narrator's Voice* überschrieben.[1] Diese, in der Mitte des 19. Jahrhunderts noch ungewöhnliche Partnerschaft beruhte auf der Empathie, mit der sich der Autor in die Psyche kleiner Mädchen hineinversetzen konnte. "No novelist has identified more intimately with the point of view of his heroine" konstatierte Harry Levin.[2] Die in den ersten Kapiteln noch häufigeren auktorialen Kommentare werden im Verlauf der Handlung deutlich zurückgenommen und durch die Perspektive der Reflektorfigur ersetzt, die ihre Gedanken enthüllt, indem sie laut vor sich hindenkt oder mit sich selbst Zwiesprache hält. Im übrigen sind die meist in Parenthese eingefügten Erzählerreflektionen über Schwächen, Widersprüchlichkeiten oder seltsame Assoziationen der Heldin von milder Ironie und Mitgefühl bestimmt ('poor' ist das am häufigsten auf sie angewandte Epitheton); sie üben keine explizite Kritik oder ziehen didaktische Schlußfolgerungen, wie es bei *Water Babies* häufig vorkam. Bei der Abfassung der Erzählung mag der Altersunterschied zwischen der im Buch erst siebenjährigen Heldin und der zehnjährigen Alice Liddell ebenfalls zu dem vertraulichen Einverständnis beigetragen haben, das dem Erzähler erlaubt, sich über den Kopf seiner Heldin hinweg über manche ihrer altklugen Fehlleistungen zu belustigen. Auch Carroll verwendete komplizierte Wörter und intellektuelle Konzepte, die den kindlichen Horizont überschreiten. Er bettete diese Wörter jedoch in eine verständliche Abenteuerfolge ein und vertraute wohl auch auf die Hilfestellung der Eltern, die häufig als Vorlesende involviert waren. Ihnen gibt der Kursivdruck Hinweise auf Emphasen, mit denen sich die mündliche Aura des Erzählens vermitteln läßt. Zweifellos werden erwachsene und kindliche Leser unterschiedlich auf die gleichen Textimpulse reagieren – mit Bangen oder Amüsement beispielsweise – doch niemand vorher hatte die Kluft zwischen Kind und Erwachsenem so erfolgreich überbrückt wie Carroll in *Alice's Adventures*.

Das *quest*-Motiv, das die komplexe Handlung von *The Water Babies* zusammenhält, gehört zum Grundbestand der europäischen Literaturtradition. Tom, der in diversen Prüfungsritualen seine Läuterung unter Beweis stellen mußte und dabei auch Unterstützung von Helferfiguren erfuhr, wird

---

[1] Barbara Wall, *The Narrator's Voice: The Dilemma of Children's Fiction* (London, 1991), S. 40.

[2] Harry Levin, "Wonderland revisited" (1965), repr. in: *Aspects of Alice. Lewis Carroll's Dream Child as seen through the Critics' Looking-Glasses, 1865-1971* (New York, 1971), S. 175-197, S. 179.

zur Belohnung mit Miss Ellie vereint und darf sich auf himmlische Sonntagsausflüge freuen. Auch Carroll greift auf dieses traditionelle Strukturmuster von Bewährung in abenteuerlichen Situationen zurück, doch verwandelt es sich unter seiner Feder zur Parodie. Schon daß es sich um eine Heldin, ein wohlerzogenes kleines Mädchen aus gutbürgerlichem Hause handelt, widersetzt sich den Erwartungen an heroische Konfliktbewältigung. Zwar werden auch Alice Prüfungen auferlegt, doch sind diese eher bizarrer Natur und verwickeln die Heldin in peinliche Situationen von unfreiwilliger Komik.

Mit ihren sieben Jahren befindet sich Alice in einer Entwicklungsphase, in der sich die kindliche Phantasie besonders intensiv mit körperlichen Veränderungen befaßt, und Befürchtungen über zu langsames oder zu schnelles Wachstum die kindliche Erlebnissphäre bestimmen. Insofern dürften Alices spektakuläre Metamorphosen, die sie schrumpfen oder in die Höhe schießen lassen, für ein jugendliches Publikum besonders faszinierend sein. Irritation bereitet jedoch, daß sich das eigentlich gewünschte Format nicht einrichten läßt. Der herbeigesehnte Zustand eindrucksvoller Größe führt zur Klaustrophobie im Kaninchenhaus, das ihre wachsenden Glieder zu sprengen drohen, oder zur Konfrontation mit der Taube, die ihr unterstellt, eine eierfressende Schlange zu sein. Im Tränenteich, den sie als Riesin geweint hat, befürchtet sie als Zwergin zu ertrinken, und die Episode mit dem kleinen Hund, der normalerweise ein harmloser Spielgefährte wäre, nähert sich in ihrem liliputanerhaftem Zustand einem Alptraum an, der an vergleichbare Ereignisse in *Gulliver's Travels* erinnert. In Alices Sorge, so reduziert zu werden, daß sie wie eine Kerze erlöschen müßte, klingt das in viktorianischen Kinderbüchern selten ausgesparte Thema des Todes an, freilich wesentlich subtiler als in evangelikalen Schriften, die den Aspekt der Todesangst didaktisch aufbereiten. Alices Fährnisse sind nicht wie in *The Water Babies* Sühne für Fehlverhalten, sondern auf den Konsum von Eß- und Trinkwaren und den Kontakt mit magischen Objekten zurückzuführen (Fächer des Kaninchens, Kiesel, mit denen sie bombardiert wird). Allerdings veranlassen sie die Heldin zu ernsthaften Zweifeln an ihrer Identität, was durch den Kontrollverlust über antrainierte Fertigkeiten noch verstärkt wird. Der 'obstacle and survival course', den Alice ohne wohlwollende Helfer- und Führerfiguren hinter sich bringt, vermittelt ihr keine tieferen Einsichten und läßt sich nicht einmal als notwendiger Lernprozeß einer Heranwachsenden begreifen. Selbst das Ziel ihrer 'Quest', der wunderschöne Garten, den sie bereits im 1. Kapitel durch das Schlüsselloch der Miniaturtür erspäht hat und nach zahlreichen Ablenkungen im 8. Kapitel erreicht, erweist sich keineswegs als 'locus amoenus'. Die Rosenbüsche bestehen aus angemalter Pappe, das

Kroquetspiel endet im Chaos, und die Herzkönigin terrorisiert ihre Gäste mit Exekutionsbefehlen. Selbst wenn es sich nur um leere Drohgebärden handelt, wird eine Atmosphäre der Angst und Verunsicherung (vor allem auch für kindliche Leser) beschworen. Blicken wir noch einmal auf Kingsley zurück, der seinem Freund F.D. Maurice die Intentionen, die ihn bei *The Water Babies* leiteten, folgendermaßen darlegte:

> I have tried, in all sorts of queer ways, to make children and grown folks understand that there is a quite miraculous and divine element underlying all physical nature; and that nobody knows anything about anything.

Die "Tom-fooleries", mit denen er seine Parabel verpackt habe, fügte er apologetisch hinzu, seien nichts anderes als der Zuckerguß, mit dem man eine bittere Pille präpariere, damit sie williger eingenommen werde, "by a generation who are not believing with anything like their whole heart, in the Living God."[1]

Auch den bereits erwähnten George MacDonald bewegten religiöse Themen, die er in seinen für Kinder und Erwachsene konzipierten Kunstmärchen, wie z.B. *The Princess and the Goblin* (1872) allegorisch verschlüsselt präsentierte. Auch ihm war der Gedanke der Besserung wichtig. So waren die im Berginnern hausenden bösartigen Kobolde ursprünglich Menschen, die unter dem Druck von Repressalien im Laufe der Zeit degenerierten. Wie Kingsley war MacDonald von Darwins Evolutionstheorie überzeugt, die auch die Möglichkeit der Regression einschloß, während gefestigte moralische Grundsätze als ein Movens der Evolution galten. Bemerkenswerterweise verzichtete der Verfasser von *Alice's Adventures*, der wie Kingsley und MacDonald eine gediegene theologische Ausbildung erhalten hatte, im Kontext des Wunderlandes gänzlich auf die Diskussion religiöser Themen. Wenn Carroll das Thema der Evolution aufgriff, dann auf komische Weise, etwa wenn sich das Baby in Alices Armen in ein grunzendes Schwein verwandelt (S. 87) und sie zur nüchternen Feststellung veranlaßt, daß die Rückentwicklung im Falle dieses Exemplars als Fortschritt anzusehen sei: "If it had grown up [...] it would have made a dreadfully ugly child: but it makes rather a handsome pig, I think." Fragen der Moral werden nur unter satirischem Vorzeichen angeschnitten, etwa wenn die häßliche Herzogin verkündet "Everything's got a moral if you only can find it" und diese Maxime sogleich auf den abstrusen Begriff einer 'mustard mine' appliziert: "And the moral of that is – 'The more there

---

[1] Barbara Wall, *The Narrator's Voice*, S. 56.

is of mine, the less there is of yours'" (S. 121/2). Carrolls Abstinenz, was
die Vermittlung einer moralischen Botschaft anging, wurde bereits von
einer der frühen Rezensionen als Novum erkannt:

> This pretty and funny book ought to become a great favourite with children. It has
> this advantage, that it has no moral and that it does not teach anything. It is, in
> fact, pure sugar throughout, and without any of that bitter foundation which some
> people imagine ought to be at the bottom of all children's books.[1]

Was hier wie eine (unbewußte) Erwiderung auf Kingsley klingt, deutet die
veränderte Einsicht an die Bedürfnisse der kindlichen Psyche an, die sich
allmählich durchzusetzen begann.

Dodgsons Obsession, Details seines Alltags zu katalogisieren, ist bekannt – so wissen wir von etwa 100.000 Briefen, die er mit Angabe des
Empfängers und Betreffs registrierte, von Menüfolgen, die er seinen
'child-friends' vorsetzen ließ, sowie Rätseln und Witzen, deren Rezipienten er sich notierte, um nicht dieselbe Person mit Wiederholungen zu
langweilen. Es mag kurios erscheinen, daß ausgerechnet ein so überstei-
gerter Ordnungsfanatiker den Atlas der Weltliteratur um zwei[2] Regionen
bereichert hat, in denen die Ordnungsprinzipien des vertrauten Alltags auf
den Kopf gestellt, bzw. die Defizite der realen Welt durch Inversion und
Übertreibung erst eigentlich zur Anschauung gebracht werden. Doch darf
vermutet werden, daß temporäre Exkursionen in die Sphäre des Nonsense
für den Autor eine Art Überlebensstrategie darstellten. Die Lizenz für sein
subversives Treiben bezog er aus der Rahmenhandlung, durch die Alices
Aufenthalt im Wunderland als Traumgeschehen markiert wird. Dabei griff
er nicht die alte Tradition der visionären Traumallegorie auf, für deren didaktische Komponente in der Nachfolge von Bunyans *Pilgrim's Progress*
(1864) sich etwa MacDonald in seinem Buch *At the Back of the North
Wind* (1871) so empfänglich zeigte. Dort wird der arme Kutscherjunge
Diamond von der Verkörperung des Nordwinds, einer mütterlichen Ge-
stalt, nächtens in Sphären entführt, in denen sich ihm Visionen des Jenseits
erschließen, in das er schließlich eingeht. Vielmehr ließ sich Carroll von
der Neubelebung der Traumdichtung durch die Romantiker inspirieren, die
damit die Entfesselung der Imagination verbanden und in Träumen bereits

---

[1] *The Sunderland Herald*, 25 May 1866. Repr. in: *Looking-Glass Letters*, ed. T.
Hinde, S. 70.

[2] Zu den Absonderlichkeiten des Lands jenseits des Spiegels vgl. Donald Rackin,
'Alice's Adventures in Wonderland' and 'Through the Looking Glass' (New York,
1991).

unterschwellig sich manifestierende psychische Motivationen vermuteten. Über den Grenzbereich zwischen Träumen und Wachen und die Verwandtschaft von Traum und Wahnsinn hat sich Carroll schon früh Gedanken gemacht, wie der Tagebucheintrag vom 9. Februar 1856 zeigt:

> Query: when we are dreaming, and as often happens, have a dim consciousness of the fact and try to wake, do we not say and do things which in waking life would be insane? May we not then sometimes define insanity as an inability to distinguish which is the waking and which the sleeping life?[1]

Wie aus den Erinnerungen von Ethel M. Arnold, einer Nichte Matthew Arnolds, hervorgeht, hielt der Autor stets Bleistift und Papier neben seinem Bett bereit, "for he found that his most absurd ideas generally came to him on the borderland of dreams."[2] Carrolls Wunderland schöpft aus dem anarchischen Potential des 'sleeping life'. Wenn die Cheshire Cat mit sardonischem Grinsen verkündet "we're all mad here. I'm mad. You're mad" (S. 89), faßt sie damit die Grundkonstellation aller Wunderlandvorgänge zusammen, die Alice zu diesem Zeitpunkt noch nicht akzeptieren kann. Erst unter dem Druck der an Kafkaesker Absurdität nicht mehr zu überbietenden Gerichtsverhandlung (Kap. 12), als die Herzkönigin verkündet "sentence first – verdict after", reißt dem stets um Contenance bemühten Kind der Geduldsfaden und sie wird ungewöhnlich deutlich. "'Stuff and nonsense' said Alice loudly" (S. 161) und befreit sich mit diesem Fazit in einem Willensakt aus ihrem Traum.

Genau genommen wird erst mit Alices Erwachen im Schoß ihrer Schwester expliziert, daß es sich bei den vorausgegangenen Abenteuern um einen Traum gehandelt hat. Mit ihrem Ausruf "You are nothing but a pack of cards" hatte Alice die Macht der auf sie niederflatternden Spielkarten gebrochen. Bei ihrer Rückkehr in die Realität wird dieser Vorgang mit den vom Baum auf sie herabfallenden Blättern in Verbindung gebracht, die ihr die Schwester sanft vom Gesicht streicht. Wenn die Schwester dann über den von Alice rekapitulierten Traum selbst in Träumereien verfällt, und die wichtigsten Episoden noch einmal an ihr vorbeiziehen, wird impliziert, daß die fernen Geräusche des Bauernhofs als akkustische Reizauslöser für die Traumbilder gewirkt haben. Diese nachträgliche Reduktion der phantastischen Impressionen auf erkliche Kausalzusammenhänge mögen wir bedauern. Doch zur Entstehungszeit

---

[1] *The Diaries of Lewis Carroll,* ed. R.L. Green (London, 1953), Vol. I, S. 76.

[2] Repr. in: *Lewis Carroll. Interviews and Recollections,* ed. Morton N. Cohen, S. 165.

des Werkes war dies wohl eine unvermeidliche Rücksichtnahme auf realistisch-pragmatische Erwartungen, die mit Kinderliteratur verknüpft wurden.

Umso bemerkenswerter ist der Auftakt des Buches, in dem Carroll seine Heldin in einem gleitenden Übergang von der empirischen Wirklichkeit in ein Zwischenstadium des Tagträumens versetzt und nur durch ihre veränderte Wahrnehmung den Wechsel zur irrealen Ebene andeutet. Alice – schon das erste Wort etabliert sie im Zentrum des Geschehens –, die gelangweilt und schläfrig in der Sommerhitze neben ihrer Schwester döst, sieht plötzlich ein weißes sprechendes Kaninchen. Dieses als Faktum hingestellte Ereignis erregt noch nicht ihre Aufmerksamkeit. Schließlich reden Tiere in Kinderbüchern fast immer; erst als das offensichtlich menschlich gekleidete Tier eine Taschenuhr aus seiner Westentasche zieht, erscheint dies Alice verwunderlich, und von unbändiger Neugier (ihrer hervorstechendsten Eigenschaft) getrieben, folgt sie dem Wesen ohne zu zögern in das Kaninchenloch. Der Eintritt in die phantastische Dimension bewirkt offensichtlich bereits eine erste Größenveränderung (ähnlich wie Tom beim Eintauchen in das Wasser zu einem Miniaturbaby wurde). Daß die Ordnungskategorien Raum und Zeit hier eigenen Regeln unterworfen sind, wird indirekt vermittelt. Das Kaninchenloch verwandelt sich in einen Brunnenschacht, der sich wiederum zu einem als Bibliothek möblierten Wohnraum verändert, in dem die Gesetze der Schwerkraft aufgehoben sind. Denn Alice schwebt so gemächlich in die Tiefe, daß sie ein Marmeladenglas aus einem Regal entnehmen und in ein anderes zurückstellen kann. Bei ihrem langsamen Fall bleibt ihr Zeit für verschiedene Spekulationen, z.B. ob man sich die in Australien lebenden Menschen mit dem Kopf nach unten hängend vorzustellen habe. Hier klingt bereits der Topos der verkehrten Welt an, der als Motto über dem Wunderland stehen könnte.[1] Sie findet Zeit für das Memorieren angelernten Faktenwissens (was den Erzähler veranlaßt, sich über die viktorianische Praxis der Wissensvermittlung zu mokieren, die kleinen Kindern lateinische Fachtermini wie *Latitude* und *Longitude* einbläute, ohne daß sie deren Bedeutung begriffen hätten). Und sie findet Zeit, während ihres Gleitflugs einen Knicks zu üben, ein Verweis auf ihre Sozialisation im bürgerlichen Verhaltenscodex. Als erste Fehlleistung, der zahlreiche weitere folgen werden, unterläuft ihr die Verwechslung des Wortes *antipodes* mit *antipathies*. Noch weiß sie nicht, daß mit *antipathies* sehr zutreffend die Haltung der Wunderlandwe-

---

[1] Ronald Reichertz, *The Making of the Alice-Books. Lewis Carroll's Uses of Earlier Children's Literature* (Montreal, 1997).

sen bezeichnet werden könnte, die diese dem Eindringling entgegenbringen. Schließlich sinniert sie über die Frage nach "Do cats eat bats? [...] Do bats eat cats?", bei der Sprache vom Informationsträger zum reinen Lautspiel wird. Damit ist die Grenze zwischen Wachen und Träumen überschritten. "She felt that she was dozing off" (S. 28). Offensichtlich versinnbildlicht ihr Fall das Eintauchen ins Unbewußte.

In ihrer Zwitterstellung zwischen kindlichem Erwachsenen und erwachsenem Kind bietet Alice Identifikationsangebote für jugendliche und ältere Leser. Mit ihrem arglos staunenden Blick auf eine "brave new world" erinnerte sie Harry Levin an eine Mischung aus Miranda und Daisy Miller, "resolved not to miss the tourist attractions".[1] Ihre Wißbegierde und Belastbarkeit in gefährlichen Situationen entspricht dem Forscherdrang, mit dem viktorianische Anthropologen ferne Länder erkundeten. Doch die Logik der fremden Welt bleibt Alice verschlossen. Als Vertreterin des gesunden Menschenverstandes wird sie mit einem Raritätenkabinett von Sonderlingen konfrontiert, die vernünftigen Argumenten nicht zugänglich sind. Vergeblich bemüht sie sich, die 'rules and regulations' zu ergründen, die das paradoxe Verhalten ihrer Gesprächspartner bestimmen. Durch die aggressive Grundstimmung, die ihr seitens der Wunderlandbewohner entgegenschlägt, werden ihre wohlerzogenen Kommunikationsversuche auf eine harte Probe gestellt. Vom weißen Kaninchen wird sie für das Hausmädchen gehalten und mit Botengängen beauftragt – für ein standesbewußtes Kind besonders irritierend, ganz zu schweigen von der außer Kraft gesetzten Hierarchie zwischen Mensch und Tier. Die schulmeisterlich herablassende Raupe stößt sie vor den Kopf, die verrückte Teerunde legt keinen Wert auf ihre Gesellschaft, die Herzogin schockiert sie durch rüde Babypflege, die Herzkönigin durch noch rüderen Umgang mit ihren Untertanen. Es mangelt gänzlich an erwachsenen Vorbildfiguren, und Alices eigentlicher Triumph besteht darin, sich von der angemaßten Autorität dieser egozentrischen Wesen nicht unterkriegen zu lassen.

Allerdings wird in neueren kritischen Beiträgen auch die Ansicht vertreten, daß die hier vorgeführten 'interkulturellen Kontakte' scheitern müßten, weil Alice die Kriterien und Denkformen ihrer Alltagswelt unbedenklich auf das Wunderland übertrage und gar nicht die nötige Offenheit für dessen Andersartigkeit aufbringe. Alice wird als "ethnocentric intruder" bezichtigt oder als "the most impressive comic critique of British

---

[1] Harry Levin, "Wonderland Revisited", S. 179.

ethnocentrism in the age of imperialism" gesehen.[1] In der Tat läßt sich nicht leugnen, daß Alices wiederholte Hinweise auf die Jagdgewohnheiten ihrer Katze Dinah nicht eben Empathie mit den Existenznöten ihrer vorwiegend aus Mäusen und Vögeln bestehenden Hörerschaft beweisen (3. Kap.). Ähnliche unabsichtliche Taktlosigkeiten unterlaufen ihr in der Unterhaltung mit der Suppenschildkröte, deren Unterwassergefährten 'lobster' und 'whiting' ihr nur vom elterlichen Mittagstisch vertraut sind. Alices Einstellung zu Nutztieren ist unsentimental; der animalische Selbsterhaltungstrieb des Fressens und Gefressenwerdens ist diesem viktorianischen Mittelstandskind geläufig. Gleich zwei ihrer Rezitationsfehlleistungen verwandeln die erbaulichen Erziehungsverse von Isaac Watts (1674-1748) in Gedichte mit darwinistischer Freßmoral. Das arbeitsame Bienchen wird durch das faule räuberische Krokodil ersetzt (S. 38) und das warnende Beispiel vom Faulpelz schlägt unversehens in eine Fabel von roher Gewalt um, in der die Eule vom Panther verspeist wird (S. 140). Derartige, von Alice als peinlich empfundene Gedächtnisstörungen reflektieren das in der viktorianischen Tagespolitik viel diskutierte Thema des Kampfes ums Dasein, in dem nur die Stärkeren überleben, das vom immer aggressiver werdenden Kolonialismus durchaus instrumentalisiert wurde.[2]

Andererseits läßt sich ein Großteil der gewalttätigen Handlungen, die im Wunderland so beiläufig begangen werden, auf das Konto des 'schwarzen Humors' verbuchen, der nach Petzold[3] ein Charakteristikum der Epoche ist. Wenn die Haselmaus ohne besonderen Anlaß kopfunter in die Teekanne gestopft wird (S. 103), wenn beim Kroquetspiel Flamingos als Schläger und Igel als Bälle mißbraucht werden (S. 111), wenn man Meerschweinchen 'unterdrückt', indem man sich auf sie draufsetzt (S. 149), oder die Eidechse Bill in hohem Bogen zum Kamin hinaus katapultiert wird (S. 62), dann entspricht dies Gepflogenheiten der Farce oder des Comic. Die Gelassenheit der 'Opfer' und die Folgenlosigkeit der Mißhandlung tragen wesentlich zur komischen Distanzierung bei.

---

[1] Daniel Binova, *Desire and Contradiction. Imperial Visions and Domestic Debates in Victorian Literature* (Manchester, 1990), S. 72. Vorher bereits James R. Kincaid, "Alice's Invasion of Wonderland", *PMLA,* 88 (1973), 92-99.

[2] Einer der ersten, der auf darwinistisches Gedankengut in *Alice's Adventures* hingewiesen hat, war William Empson in *Some Versions of Pastoral* [1935] (New York, repr. 1960), Kap. 7.

[3] Dieter Petzold, *Formen und Funktionen der englischen Nonsense-Dichtung im 19. Jahrhundert* (Nürnberg, 1972), S. 241, empfindet dies als Abwehrreaktion der Viktorianer gegen die wirklichen Schrecken der Welt.

Eine Ingredienz der Erzählung war für Carrolls berühmteste Muse, Alice Liddell, besonders wichtig. Die dritte Strophe des persönlichen Widmungsgedichts verrät uns ihre Hoffnung, "there will be nonsense in it". Daß Nonsense häufig mit pädagogischen Konventionen in Verbindung gebracht wird, zeigt, wie gut sich der Autor in die kindliche Psyche einfühlen konnte, zu deren zentralen Erfahrungsbereichen Schule und Unterricht gehören. Dementsprechend dürfte das Kapitel IX, in dem die 'mock turtle' die Schulfächer wortspielerisch verunglimpft und die Unterrichtsstunden 'lessons' heißen, "because they lessen from day to day" (S. 129-130), den direktesten Weg zum Herzen eines Kinderpublikums nehmen. Da Alices Vater, Henry George Liddell, der berühmte Herausgeber des *Greek-English Lexicon* war, könnte die Verballhornung des Schulfachs 'Greek' als 'Grief' als besonderer 'inside joke' belacht worden sein. Das trifft auch auf den staubtrockenen Extrakt aus Havilland Chapmells *Short Course of History* (1862) zu, mit dem die Maus ihre durchnäßten Gefährten zu 'trocknen' versucht, ein Lehrbuch, das zum Pensum der Liddell-Kinder gehörte (S. 30-31 und Anm. 1). Bereits die kurze Passage gibt einen Eindruck von der Beschaffenheit viktorianischer Lehrmaterialien. Obwohl Carroll inzwischen selbst der lehrenden Profession angehörte, hatte er wenig Sympathie für die zu dieser Zeit immer noch vorherrschende phantasiefeindliche Tendenz in der Kinderliteratur. Das erste Buch, das er den Liddell-Geschwistern als Geschenk überreichte, war Catherine Sinclairs Geschichtensammlung *Holiday House* (1839), die in ihrem Vorwort Einspruch erhebt gegen Drill und Didaxe, mit denen Kindern jede Individualität ausgetrieben wurde. Die potentiell tragischen Konsequenzen einer derartigen Erziehung prangerte Charles Dickens in seinem Roman *Hard Times* (1854) an. "Now, what I want is, Facts. Teach these boys and girls nothing but facts. [...] Plant nothing else and root out everything else" (Kap. 1) ist das utilitaristische Credo des Schulleiters Thomas Gradgrind, der jegliche Unterweisung, die über die Vermittlung von Faktenwisssen hinausgeht, als Zeitverschwendung ansieht. Nicht wenige viktorianische Verleger machten sich diese Devise zu eigen und offerierten ein umfangreiches Sortiment von Sachtexten. Neben den ab 1839 monatlich erscheinenden *Peter Parley Magazines*, in denen Nützliches und Wissenswertes immerhin in eine schlichte Erzählung eingekleidet wurde (z.B. 'Uncle John's Visit to the Polytechnic Institute, Regent Street'), gab es, wie Catherine Sinclair aufzählte, "Conversations on Natural Philosophy, – on Chemistry, – on Botany, – on Arts and Sciences, – Chronological Records of History, – and travels as dry as a road-book". Zu jedem Wissensgebiet erschienen Katechismen, die den Lehrstoff in bewährter Frage- und Antwortmanier einpaukten und die Kinder zum Memorieren langer Listen anleiteten. Auch die von Privatlehrern und einer Gouvernante unterwiesenen Liddell-Kinder waren mit derartigen mnemotechnischen Übungen vertraut, die zur Erhöhung der Konzentration in vorgeschriebener Körperhaltung absolviert wurden – im Sitzen mit verschränkten Armen, im Stehen mit gefalteten Händen.[1] In ihrer Verwirrung über die abrupten Veränderungen ihres Körpers sucht Alice Halt bei ihrem angelernten Faktenwissen, muß sich jedoch eingestehen, daß sie weder die Multiplikationstabelle, noch die Geographielisten, noch das Sprüchlein von der fleißigen Biene korrekt repetieren kann. Statt dessen kommt es ihr vor, als flüstere ihr ein Kobold schieren Unsinn ein, ein Alptraum, mit dem sich jedes Schulkind identifizieren kann.

Im Hinblick auf die Charakterbildung durften auch in keiner besseren Kinderstube 'cautionary tales' fehlen, warnende Beispiele von kindlichem Fehlverhalten, das drastisch bestraft wird. Die größte Verbreitung auf diesem Sektor erzielte Mrs. Mary Martha Sherwood mit *The Fairchild Family* (1818), die in revidierten Ausgaben noch bis zur Jahrhundertwende gerne als Schulpreis für gute Leistungen vergeben wurde. Mrs. Sherwood war Spezialistin für die instruktive Aufbereitung von tödlichen Unfällen, etwa jenem Exemplum von der unfolgsamen Augusta Noble, die sich bei Kerzenlicht in ihrem neuen Kleid im Spiegel bewundert und dabei in Flammen aufgeht. Alice beweist ihre Kenntnis derartiger Ratschlagliteratur, wenn sie in einer ersten Reaktion die auf dem Fläschchen stehende Aufforderung 'drink me' ablehnt:

> "No, I'll look first", she said, "and see whether it's marked *'poison'* or not": for she had read several nice little stories about children who had got burnt, or eaten up by wild beasts, and other unpleasant things, all because they *would* not remember the simple rules their friends had taught them (S. 31).

Der Erzähler zeigt mit zurückhaltender Ironie, wohin die Ratschlaggläubigkeit der "wise little Alice" führen kann, wenn sie das Fläschchen, da es ja nicht als 'poison' gekennzeichnet ist, leert und zur Größe von 25 Zentimetern zusammenschnurrt (S. 31).

Die Ratschlagsatire, die vielleicht den engsten Bezug zu Carrolls doppelbödiger Persönlichkeit hat, ist die Parodie des Gedichts von Robert Southey, 'The Old Man's Comforts and How He Gained them'. Ihr besonderer Reiz erschließt sich in Martin Gardners Ausgabe, der die uns mittlerweile unbekannten Vorlagen abdruckt (S. 69-71). Bei Southey berichtet

---

[1] Vgl. *The Annotated Alice*, S. 38, sowie *The Annotated Alice. The Definitive Edition*, S. 51, Anm. 3.

ein salbungsvoller, selbstzufriedener Greis, daß er sich dank Askese, Triebverzicht und Fleiß in der Jugend nun eines rüstigen, abgesicherten Alters erfreue. Carrolls 'Father William' dagegen ist geradezu die Verkörperung der auf den Kopf gestellten Altersweisheit. Während sein Sohn als altkluger Moralist auftritt, der beim Vater die Gebote der Schicklichkeit anmahnt, präsentiert sich letzterer voll anarchischer Vitalität. Er steht auf dem Kopf, macht Purzelbäume rückwärts und wirkt wesentlich jugendfrischer als sein Sprößling. Die utilitaristische Botschaft Southeys, die einem Kind geradezu das Recht auf Lebensfreude abspricht, wird hier zu einer 'slapstick performance' im Stile von 'Monty Pythons Flying Circus' umgemünzt. Im schützenden Raum seiner Nonsense-Erzählung entwirft Carroll, der sich, wie Alice Liddell berichtete, stets so steif und gerade hielt, als habe er einen Schürhaken verschluckt[1], eine Utopie des Alters als heimlich ersehnten Prozeß der Selbstbefreiung von allen Rücksichten und Normen. Damit verkörpert er, wie ein Kritiker bemerkt hat,

> geradezu symbolhaft die widersprüchlichen Spannungen der Zeit, die Psychodynamik der Anpassungszwänge, Entfremdungsgefühle und Entlastungsbedürfnisse. Ist Dodgson der Teil seiner Persönlichkeit, der sich mit den hochgesteckten Ansprüchen des viktorianischen Kodex identifiziert, so [ist] Carroll der Teil, der sich – unter anderem – erholsame Befreiung aus solcher Rigidität verschaffen kann.[2]

Leser in aller Welt haben die therapeutische Wirkung dieses Kinderbuches erfahren; sie ist bis heute ungebrochen.

---

[1] Caryl Hargreaves, "Alice's Recollections of Carrollian Days", *The Cornhill Magazine*, July 1932. Repr. *Alice in Wonderland*, ed. Donald Gray, S. 272-278, S. 277.

[2] Eberhard Kreutzer, *Lewis Carroll: 'Alice in Wonderland'*, S. 101.

Oscar Wilde and Shakespeare's Secrets

By *Russell Jackson* (Birmingham)

This essay (which has a beginning, a middle and at least two endings) addresses an aspect of Oscar Wilde's self-fashioning, and the way it operates in his writing on Shakespeare. Wilde's career as a writer includes several 'respectable' personae, openly adopted – he presented himself as a poet, a journalist, a pseudo-Jacobean dramatist (*The Duchess of Padua*), a French symbolist dramatist (*Salome*), a crafter of exquisite short fictions and poems in prose and a West-End playwright. Oddly enough, although there are good reasons for thinking of him as such, he did not put himself forward as a specifically Irish writer, and – most important for my present purposes – unlike many fellow-Victorians he never imitated Shakespeare directly. (*The Duchess of Padua* is would-be Webster). But the topic of Shakespeare allowed Wilde to co-opt the Elizabethan in one of his own favourite games: playing off public and private writing against each other. In this Wilde was nourished by the project of Victorian Shakespeare criticism, particularly as defined by Edward Dowden's *Shakspere: A Study of his Mind and Art* (1875): the elucidation of an 'inner life' through the evidence of the playwright's works.

Two quotations to begin with. The first is from the first act of *The Importance of Being Earnest*:

> JACK: [...] It is a very ungentlemanly thing to read a private cigarette case.
> ALGERNON: Oh! It is absurd to have a hard and fast rule about what one should read and what one shouldn't. [...] More than half of modern culture depends on what one shouldn't read.[1]

Despite this admonition, Algernon not only reads the inscription on the private cigarette case – 'From little Cecily, with her fondest love to her dear Uncle Jack'[2] – but produces from it one of Jack's cards, which reveal him as Mr Ernest Worthing, the name Algernon has always known him by. Who is this Jack? What is this double life that Ernest is leading?

---

[1] Oscar Wilde, *The Importance of Being Earnest*, in: *Collins Complete Works of Oscar Wilde. Centenary Edition*, ed. Merlin Holland (Glasgow, 1999), pp. 357-419, p. 360.

[2] Ibid.

The second quotation is from W.H. Auden's introduction to the 1964
Signet edition of Shakespeare's *Sonnets*:

> A great deal of what today passes for scholarly research is an activity no different
> from that of reading somebody's private correspondence when he is out of the
> room, and it doesn't really make it morally any better if he is out of the room be-
> cause he is in the grave.[1]

On 24 April 1895, 'at one o'clock precisely', took place one of the saddest
literary auctions ever held. Its lots included a rabbit hutch, 'a very large
quantity of toys,' and a framed autograph poem by Keats.[2] The contents of
16, Tite Street, Chelsea, home of the disgraced Oscar Wilde, were being
sold. The owner was now in prison, beginning a sentence for offences
against the Criminal Law Amendment Act of 1885, which forbade private
or public sexual relations between men, and he had been declared bankrupt
by his wife's solicitors. The catalogue of the auction provides a remarkable
but partial testimony to the breadth and quantity of Wilde's reading. The
clerk who drew up the lists was thorough in his work, but after a few items
he tired, and one senses that he might have known the price of everything
and the value of nothing. Very soon the lots become less and less specific,
and the seeker of sources for lines or ideas in Wilde has to be content with
such unhelpful references as those to bundles of 40 and 100 French novels.
However, one notable feature of the list is the considerable number of
works on Shakespeare. Wilde's personal library included (in their order of
appearance in the catalogue) Massey's book on Shakespeare's sonnets, the
translation of Gervinus's commentaries, Mary and Charles Cowden-
Clarke's *Shakespeare-Key*, Dowden's *Shakspere his Mind and Art*, Moul-
ton's *Shakespeare as a Dramatic Artist*, the Transactions of the New
Shakspere Society, Stopes on Bacon's authorship of Shakespeare's works
(appropriately bundled together with another work on the cultivation of
exotics, *The Orchid Grower's Manual*) and Abbott's *Shakespearean
Grammar*. In addition to an unspecified edition of the Sonnets, there were
Cassell's *Illustrated Shakespeare* and 'The Handy Volume of Shakespeare'
(12 volumes in one). There were also John Payne Collier's volumes on
English Dramatic Poetry and his *Annals of the Stage*, A.J.A. Symonds's
Shakespeare's Predecessors, A.W. Ward's *English Dramatic Literature*
and F.G. Fleay's *History of the London Stage*.

---

[1] William Shakespeare, *The Sonnets*, ed. Sylvan Barnet, introd. W.H. Auden (New
York, 1964), p. xviii.

[2] "Oscar Wilde, 24 April 1895", in: *Sale Catalogues of Libraries of Eminent Persons*, gen. ed. A.N.L. Munby, vol. 1: *Poets and Men of Letters*, ed. A.N.L. Munby (London, 1971), vol. 1, pp. 371-388, p. 388.

Wilde was not above passing off other people's expertise as his own – learned references to the history of jewellery in *The Picture of Dorian Gray* have been shown to derive from the intermediate source of a Victoria and Albert Museum Handbook – but the list of the sale reflects his extensive and first-hand acquaintance with current and recent scholarship on Shakespeare's works, life and times. When Wilde borrows, he does so with informed judgement: if he is occasionally silent about the borrowing, that is another matter. But then when Wilde writes as a critic he is nearly always using some fictional persona, who can be influenced without experiencing or arousing too much anxiety.

To consider Wilde's relationship with – and use of – Shakespeare we should take into account his debt to many authors not on the auction list, for a distinction must be made between authors Wilde (for all his scepticism about the institution of sage) venerated as teachers, and those in whom he merely found ideas, turns of phrase or whole paragraphs corresponding to his own. Plato, Huysmans, Whitman, Pater and Keats can certainly be included among those directly quoted but also imitated. Even authors whose opinions Wilde might have been supposed to have left behind by the 1890s turn up in the strangest places: a passage on the relative positions and mentalities of men and women in *An Ideal Husband* (written in 1894-5) seems to derive from one of Ruskin's more reactionary statements. Wilde's knowledge of the ancient authors, and of French literature seem genuinely wide and first-hand, whereas he seems to have known comparatively little of German literature. He quotes tags airily (Goethe, for example: 'In der Beschränkung zeigt sich erst der Meister') in a way that suggests access to a good dictionary of quotations. But he also cites more knowingly, from what may be presumed to be more than a nodding acquaintance with a fashionable thinker:

> Schopenhauer has analysed the pessimism that characterises modern thought, but Hamlet invented it. The world has become sad because a puppet was once melancholy.[1]

From Shakespeare himself, interestingly, Wilde took very little – perhaps the loan would have been too obvious – but one can trace the influence of Wilde's attitudes to Shakespeare, and (perhaps more significant) to the idea of Shakespeare. More important, one can trace Wilde's co-option of Shakespeare's secrets – the information not available about his personal life and thought – to his own strategies as an author.

---

[1] Oscar Wilde, "The Decay of Lying", in: *Collins Complete Works of Oscar Wilde*, ed. Merlin Holland, pp. 1071-1092, p. 1083.

In addition to passages scattered throughout his letters and published critical works, Wilde wrote one essay, three performance reviews and two substantial pieces on Shakespeare. The essay 'Shakespeare on Scenery' and the reviews of productions appeared in the *Dramatic Review* in 1885. The essay claims Shakespeare as a potential supporter of the refinements of the modern scenic stage, frustrated by the limitations of his own theatre. It is characteristic of Wilde that his claims for the effectiveness of the scenic stage should be framed in terms of an enhanced aesthetic effect, rather than mere expediency.

> Yet lovely as all Shakespeare's descriptive passages are, a description is in its essence undramatic. Theatrical audiences are far more impressed by what they look at than by what they listen to; and the modern dramatist, in having the surroundings of his play visibly presented to the audience when the curtain rises, enjoys an advantage for which Shakespeare often expresses his desire. It is true that Shakespeare's descriptions are not what descriptions are in modern plays – accounts of what the audience can observe for themselves; they are the imaginative method by which he creates in the mind of the spectators the image of that which he desires them to see. Still, the quality of the drama is action. It is always dangerous to pause for picturesqueness. And the introduction of self-explanatory scenery enables the modern method to be far more direct, while the loveliness of form and colour which it gives us, seems to me often to create an artistic temperament in the audience, and to produce that joy in beauty for beauty's sake, without which the great masterpieces of art can never be understood, to which, and to which only, are they ever revealed.[1]

The three reviews praise university productions of *Twelfth Night* and *Henry IV, Part One*, and a 'pastoral' production of *As You Like It* staged by fashionable amateurs under the direction of E.W. Godwin. In this Lady Archibald Campbell played Orlando to the Rosalind of the American actress Eleanor Calhoun.[2] Wilde's review invokes the transvestite performance of the play described in chapter eleven of Theophile Gautier's novel of perverse desires, *Mademoiselle de Maupin* (1835) – a classic of 'decadent' transgressive literature – in which Théodore, the male object of the narrator's obsession, plays Rosalind. The longer pieces are a magazine article and a short story. The article is 'Shakespeare and Stage Costume', published in the journal *The Nineteenth Century* in May 1885, and subsequently revised for the volume *Intentions*, 1891, where it appeared as 'The Truth of Masks'. The short story was 'The Portrait of Mr W. H.' which appeared in *Blackwood's Magazine* for July 1889. A longer version of this

---

[1] Oscar Wilde, "Shakespeare on Scenery", *Dramatic Review*, March 14, 1885.

[2] See John Stokes, *Resistible Theatres: Enterprise and Experiment in the Late Nineteenth Century* (London, 1971), pp. 47-50.

was prepared but did not appear in print until 1923: the two authoritative editions of Wilde's *Shorter Fiction*, by Isobel Murray (Oxford) and Ian Small (Penguin), print the short version, but reference is made here to the longer text as it appears in the *Collins Complete Works*.

At first sight, there does not seem to be much to connect the two longer pieces with one another. The first is a response to adverse criticism of an elaborately 'archaeological' (that is, historically researched) production of *Romeo and Juliet* staged in London in 1884 for the American actress Mary Anderson. (In the revised version, this is replaced by Mrs Langtry's 1890 *Antony and Cleopatra*.) Drawing on his own reading in various authorities on the costuming of Shakespeare's plays, on the Elizabethan theatre and – most important – on his friend E.W. Godwin's writings on the modern staging of the plays, Wilde offers a detailed survey of references to dress in Shakespeare to support the contention that Shakespeare's own ideas and practice corresponded to the modern pursuit of historical detail in costume and mise-en-scène. Not only does Shakespeare refer to the significance of dress in terms of status, but he also uses it metaphorically and his interest in disguise depends on elaboration of costuming.

Although this is nominally a defence of Shakespearean production in the lavishly pictorial mode of the 1880s, Wilde is in fact offering a defence of his own views of the role and aims of the artist, in which Shakespeare is being enlisted as a supporting witness. Wilde attributes to Shakespeare his own interest in costume and connoisseurship in the archaeology of dress, and Shakespeare is described as defending himself (like Wilde) from the attacks of Philistines. The puritans who objected to stage finery, writes Wilde, appealed to 'those moral grounds which are always the last refuge of people who have no sense of beauty.'[1] One clothing reference gives Wilde the opportunity to remind readers that the alleged modern obsession with violence has a distinguished ancestry:

> When Cloten [in *Cymbeline*], stung by the taunt of that simile which his sister [*sic*: in fact Imogen is his step-sister] draws from her husband's raiment, arrays himself in that husband's very garb to work upon her the deed of shame, we feel that there is nothing in the whole of modern French realism, nothing even in *Thérèse Raquin*, that masterpiece of horror, which for terrible and tragic significance can compare with this strange scene ...[2]

Elsewhere, Wilde figures the Renaissance in terms similarly appropriate to the preoccupations of his own time. The sixteenth century's study of the

---

[1] Oscar Wilde, "The Truth of Masks", in: *Collins Complete Works of Oscar Wilde*, pp. 1156-1173, p. 1156.

[2] Ibid., p. 1158.

artefacts of the past had an agenda in which they were 'used as motives for the production of a new art, which was to be not beautiful merely, but also strange.'[1] At one point in the essay Shakespeare is recommended as an educational tool:

> ... if it be really necessary that the School Board children should know about the Wars of the Roses, they could learn their lessons just as well out of Shakespeare as out of shilling primers, and learn them, I need not say, far more pleasurably.[2]

This is one of the justifications commonly used for the introduction of Shakespeare into the examination system in the wake of the 1870 Education Act, but Wilde also attaches to the dramatist a doctrine of his own that would not be as likely to appeal to examiners: 'Truth is independent of facts always, inventing or selecting them at pleasure.'[3]

Many of the arguments and most of the evidence in Wilde's essay come more or less directly from his secondary sources, Godwin in particular, and the familiar teleological model of theatrical (indeed, cultural) history appears again: Shakespeare was impatient with his own theatre, fretted under its restrictions, would have welcomed modern staging techniques to realise the settings he imagined. The anachronisms in his plays are blemishes he would have corrected if told of them by a 'brother artist'.[4] The departures from routine defences of Victorian illusionistic stagings are mostly adapted from Godwin, adopting his position that (as Wilde phrases it) 'Archaeological accuracy is merely a condition of illusionist stage effect; it is not its quality' and arguing that 'as far as dramatic values goes, to confuse the costumes is to confuse the play.'[5] Wilde also quotes Victor Hugo's preface to his play *Cromwell* (1827), where the French dramatist insists that human life must always be in the foreground: 'L'homme sur le premier plan, le reste au fond.'[6]

In the conclusion of his essay, Wilde goes over the main points again, then remarks that in future dramatic critics will be required to cultivate 'a sense of beauty'.

---

[1] Ibid., p. 1162.

[2] Ibid., p. 1166.

[3] Ibid.

[4] Ibid., p. 1165 – Wilde pointedly avoids 'critic'.

[5] Ibid., p. 1169.

[6] Ibid., p. 1168.

And if they will not encourage, at least they must not oppose, a movement of which Shakespeare of all dramatists would have most approved, for it has the illusion of truth for its method, and the illusion of beauty for its result.[1]

This seems like a more or less graceful stroke by which a bread-and-butter piece of literary journalism on a current topic is turned into an essay identifiably by 'Oscar Wilde' the card-carrying aesthete and dealer in the paradoxical mysteries of beauty and truth (on loan from John Keats and others). However, it is followed in the revised version by a startling disclaimer:

Not that I agree with everything that I have said in this essay. There is much with which I entirely disagree. The essay simply represents an artistic standpoint, and in aesthetic criticism attitude is everything. For in art there is no such thing as an universal truth. A Truth in art is that whose contradictory is also true.[2]

Shakespeare has already faded into the background, while the author repeats one of his favourite tricks to *épater les bourgeois*: of course he is posing, but that is a necessary means for conducting an argument. 'Attitude', suggestive at once of both affectation and opinion, is a word either devalued or enhanced by this ambiguity. Commitment, earnestness – is by implication an over-valued commodity. In the final sentence Wilde seems to turn away from the essay altogether:

And just as it is only in art-criticism, and through it, that we can apprehend the Platonic theory of ideas, so it is only in art-criticism, and through it, that we can realise Hegel's system of contraries. The truths of metaphysics are the truths of masks.[3]

This is Wilde in 1891, bolder and more disorienting than the journalist of 1885: the arrival (by way of truth and beauty) of Keats, the sudden bursting into the room of Plato and the revelation that Hegel has been there all the time, have a disorienting almost Joycean here-comes-everybody effect. The Wildean *sprezzatura*, scattering great names knowingly, is a means of appropriation – taking Shakespeare's enlistment in the defence of the modern theatre a stage or two further. If we retrace our steps in the essay, we find Shakespeare's alleged preoccupation with costume described as his understanding of 'one of the essential factors of the means which a true il-

---

[1] Ibid., p. 1173.
[2] Ibid.
[3] Ibid.

lusionist has at his disposal';[1] then Wilde makes a leap into almost direct quotation from Keats's letters:

> Indeed to [Shakespeare] the deformed figure of Richard was of as much value as Juliet's loveliness; he sets the serge of the radical beside the silks of the lord, and sees the stage effects to be got from each: he has as much delight in Caliban as he has in Ariel, in rags as he has in cloth of gold, and recognises the artistic beauty of ugliness.[2]

If we compare this with its source in a letter by Keats, we find that Wilde's Shakespeare is taking pleasure in 'recognising' the beauty of ugliness, whereas Keats speaks of his having "as much delight in *conceiving* an Iago as an Imogen".[3] A characteristic critical or authorial process in Wilde's construction of the two interconnected roles, is the experience of unmasking, discovering or simply recognising a secret: time and again, it is the epiphany, the moment of insight, that is dramatised. Keats' definition of the 'poetical character' differs in the respect that its lack of 'self' ('it is everything and nothing – it has no character [...]') is a precondition of acts of creation rather than of acknowledgement.

At the same time, Wilde's use of this famous letter also suggests a source for that puzzling final paragraph in the 1891 version of his essay. Keats writes:

> It is a wretched thing to confess; but it is a very fact that not one word I ever utter can be taken for granted as an opinion growing out of my identical nature – how can it be, when I have no nature?[4]

Wilde's is a public utterance rather than a private one, an essay not a letter, and where Keats is tentative and self-questioning, Wilde is defiantly nonchalant: 'Not that I agree with everything that I have said [...]' The effect is not unlike Wilde's skilfully provocative (and nonchalant) interviews and curtain-speeches, offering a playful parody of frankness that denies access to what he is really thinking. In the light of the new title and the final paragraph 'Shakespeare on Stage Scenery' becomes not so much a personal manifesto, as an invitation to enquire into what might be the private significance of what has gone before. Just what is Shakespeare being co-opted into?

---

[1] Ibid., p. 1165.

[2] Ibid., p. 1161.

[3] John Keats, Letter to Richard Woodhouse, 27 October 1818, in: *The Letters of John Keats*, ed. H. Buxton Foerman, 2nd ed. (Oxford, 1935), pp. 227-228.

[4] Ibid., p. 228.

In the short story 'The Portrait of Mr W. H.' an elaborate frame surrounds a theory of the identity of the dedicatee of the Sonnets of Shakespeare. The common literary device for framing outlandish stories with seemingly scientific (or at least forensic) accounts by different contributors is hinted at by Wilde's narrator, who is prompted by a friend (Erskine) into the investigation of the theories of a third (Cyril Graham) about the mysterious Mr. W. H. (Willie Hughes, a boy actor). There is a picture in the case, which is both the clue to the theory and (we discover) a clever forgery: the distinctions between fiction and fact, historical investigation and lying, are blurred.

Wilde's homework for this story, both in the version published in his lifetime and the longer version prepared in the mid-1890s, was very thorough. As Horst Schroeder has shown, he drew on current commentary on the sonnets and (in the longer version) on Symonds and others.[1] The revised story expands the discussion of the text of the sonnets, and adds disquisitions on the honourable history of love between men and on Elizabethan culture – which is depicted as headily sensual, and with a deliberate anticipation of the characteristics of 'decadent' artistic life. Wilde claims, in the latter extended passage, that 'It is Art, and Art only, that reveals us to ourselves', and his account of the Elizabethan artistic world is introduced with a description of the experience of reading the sonnets of Shakespeare:

> As from opal dawns to sunsets of withered rose I read and re-read them in garden or chamber, it seemed to me that I was deciphering the story of a life that had once been mine, unrolling the record of a romance that, without my knowing it, had coloured the very texture of my nature, had dyed it with strange and subtle dyes. Art, as so often happens, had taken the place of personal experience. I felt as if I had been initiated into the secret of that passionate friendship, that love of beauty and beauty of love, of which Marsilio Ficino tells us, and of which the Sonnets in their noblest and purest significance, may be held to be the perfect expression.[2]

The sudden revelation is a life-changing experience: 'How curiously it had all been revealed to me! A book of Sonnets, published nearly three hundred years ago, written by a dead hand and in honour of a dead youth, had suddenly explained to me the whole story of my soul's romance.'[3] The no-

---

[1] See Horst Schroeder, *Oscar Wilde, 'The Portrait of Mr. W. H.': Its Composition, Publication and Reception* (Braunschweig, 1984), and *Annotations to Oscar Wilde, 'The Portrait of Mr W. H.'* (Braunschweig, 1986).

[2] Oscar Wilde, "The Portrait of Mr. W. H.", in: *Collins Complete Works of Oscar Wilde*, pp. 302-350, p. 343.

[3] Ibid., p. 344.

tion that a critic might experience and convey to his readers a perception of the artistic world of a past period, summed up in a vividly apprehended vision, was one of the lessons that Wilde had learned from Walter Pater – not least from the *Imaginary Portraits* collected in 1887. The technique can be traced back in the historiography of culture in Britain at least to Thomas Carlyle, and it has much in common with the historical novel, historical painting and illustration and the theatrical staging of plays on historical subjects – not least those of Shakespeare. In Wilde's case, it is not merely a turning point in the life of the subject of the story that is presented (the Paterian effect) but we are given to believe that the very apprehension of the past on the part of the narrator himself has effected a momentous change in his attitudes to life and (in this case) sexuality. In the longer version of 'The Portrait of Mr. W. H.' this is made more explicit by a passage[1] asserting the honourable tradition of love between men – similar to but not as concise and eloquent as a speech on the subject delivered by Wilde in court in 1895.

It is worth pausing here to recall the review of *As You Like It* in 1885. On a less obviously controversial level, Wilde's praise in 1885 of Lady Archibald Campbell celebrates the potential for sexual confusion of the role of Rosalind:

> Rosalind suffered a good deal through the omission of the first act; we saw, I mean, more of the saucy boy than we did of the noble girl; and though the persiflage always told, the poetry was often lost; still Miss Calhoun gave much pleasure; and Lady Archibald Campbell's Orlando was a really remarkable performance. Too melancholy some seemed to think it. Yet is not Orlando lovesick? Too dreamy, I heard it said. Yet Orlando is a poet. And even admitting that the vigour of the lad who tripped up the Duke's wrestler was hardly sufficiently emphasised, still in the low music of Lady Archibald Campbell's voice, and in the strange beauty of her movements and gestures, there was a wonderful fascination, and the visible presence of romance quite consoled me for the possible absence of robustness.[2]

In 'Mr. W. H.' it is central to Wilde's (or his narrator's) account of the mystery of the sonnets that the boy in question is an actor, and that the proponent of the theory, Cyril Graham, has also excelled as an amateur actor of women's roles while a student at Oxford. The problematics of theatricality and sincerity seem to appeal to Wilde, here and elsewhere, because they add a dimension of the questionable to the interpretation of art. Wilde is able to propose a sonnet-writer who begins with the pretence of

---

[1] Ibid., pp. 324-327.

[2] Oscar Wilde, "Review of *As You Like It*", *Dramatic Review*, June 6, 1885.

love, but finds himself unable to avoid the consequences of having assumed the lover's role: 'It is never with impunity that one's lips say Love's Litany. Words have their mystical power over the soul, and form can create the feeling from which it should have sprung.'[1] This deals neatly with the claim that Shakespeare's sonnets were informed more by literary convention than by personal experience.

Wilde's account of Shakespeare's theatre foregrounds the effect of the boy-player – 'Of all the motives of dramatic curiosity used by our great playwrights, there is none more subtle or more fascinating than the ambiguity of the sexes'[2] – and he appeals to the example of a franker, more sophisticated and sensual version of the Renaissance than more inhibited Victorian critics allowed themselves to contemplate. But it is the intensifying of the problematics of sincerity that seems particularly significant in Wilde's construction of Shakespeare's personality and circumstances. He claims Shakespeare as a supreme artist not in the conventional Victorian mode, a clear-sighted speaker of truths, or (in Edward Dowden's version) as a man struggling for self-mastery, but as a skilled deceiver. A passage on the sonnets in 'The Critic as Artist' concludes with a variation on a theme common in Wilde's work: 'Yes, the objective form is the most subjective in matter. Man is least himself when he talks in his own person. Give him a mask, and he will tell you the truth.'[3]

In 'The Portrait of Mr. W. H.' the frame of the story is complex. The narrator is shown a portrait by his friend Erskine, who says that he does not believe in the theory it seems to support – to be precise, he tells the narrator: 'I used to believe – well I suppose I used to believe in Cyril Graham and his theory'.[4] It was Erskine who was fascinated by Graham himself at Eton, where the boy had been sent by his guardian, who thought him effeminate and hoped he would be cured there: despite the disapproval of his enemies, who said he was merely pretty, Graham captivated Erskine. At Oxford Cyril's acting as Shakespeare's heroines confirmed the effect: 'Cyril Graham was the only perfect Rosalind I have ever seen.'[5] Even in the shorter version the eroticism of Erskine's relationship with Cyril is thinly veiled – if it is veiled at all: it seems surprising that the editors of Blackwood's accepted the story. However, the relationship between the two men is made to turn on the providing of evidence for his theories about

---

[1] Wilde, "The Portrait of Mr. W. H.", pp. 335-336.

[2] Ibid., p. 330.

[3] Oscar Wilde, "The Critic as Artist", in: *Collins Complete Works of Oscar Wilde*, pp. 1108-1155, p. 1142.

[4] Wilde, "The Portrait of Mr. W. H.", p. 303.

[5] Ibid., p. 305.

the sonnets, with which he has become obsessed: it is made the nexus between the two of them, as though it represents their sexual and emotional bond. Cyril has a forged painting made as material evidence of Mr W. H.'s identity, and when Erskine traces the fraud and confronts him with it, the young man shoots himself. The story fascinates the narrator in turn, and he sets about trying to prove the theory, in defiance of Erskine's scepticism. When he has done this to his own satisfaction he has arrived at a perception of Hughes as a muse:

> I could almost fancy that I saw him standing in the shadow of my room, so well had Shakespeare drawn him, with his golden hair, his tender flower-like grace, his dreamy deep-sunken eyes, his delicate mobile limbs, and his white lily hands. His very name fascinated me. Willie Hughes! Willie Hughes! How musically it sounded![1]

Hughes is added to a pantheon of muses – '... others whose beauty had given a new creative impulse to the age'[2] – and the solution of the mystery has its effect on the narrator. But the story's final section distances this: the narrator writes a long exposition of the theory's proof to Erskine, but the act of writing seems to deprive him of his own capacity for belief. 'Perhaps, by finding perfect expression for a passion, I had exhausted the passion itself.'[3] He subsequently receives a letter from Erskine which seems like a suicide note, of the kind Erskine claimed he had received from Cyril Graham. Arriving too late, he discovers that Erskine has in fact died of consumption, and had known himself to be dying for some time. In retrospect, the circumstances of Erskine's death suggest (though Wilde's narrator does not make this suggestion himself) that he may also have been lying about Cyril Graham's alleged suicide – the only evidence for which was Erskine's claim to have received a suicide note (destroyed by him). The rest of the world – except for the narrator, whom Erskine has told – thought Graham had died by accident, but it was this story, establishing him as 'the youngest and most splendid of all the martyrs of literature' (the narrator's words[4]) that launched the narrator on his quest. Shakespeare's secret – the identity of Mr W. H. – is enfolded in the secrets of Graham's death (still not clearly solved), Erskine's relationship with Graham (clearly homoerotic), the narrator's with Erskine (deceived by a forgery that in fact connects two alleged secrets) and the narrator's with the reader (how 'true' is any of this?). If, as the ending seems to require, the reader turns back to

---

[1] Ibid., p. 319.
[2] Ibid., p. 320.
[3] Ibid., p. 345.
[4] Ibid., p. 312.

the first page and re-reads the tale, the opening passage's references to Macpherson, Chatterton and the honourable status of literary forgery take on an additional significance, as does its assertion that 'all Art [is] to a certain degree a mode of acting'.[1]

The use of the 'clue' of the forged Elizabethan portrait in this short story differs from the more famous picture of Dorian Gray, a painting that holds the 'true' physical image of Dorian's degradation while he is alive, and reverts to his 'original' perfect state when he is dead. The portrait not only claims to be evidence corroborating a theory about the sonnets of the kind that at least one commentator had wistfully hoped for, but it is also, by being allegedly splashed with his blood, evidence of the self-sacrifice of Cyril Graham. He has died not for a forged work of art (as Chatterton could be imagined doing) but for a reading of it – a reading that was the penetration of a secret. And that forensic quest yielded, for those engaged in it, an imaginative vision of the Elizabethan past that was life-changing – implicitly by providing an honourable example of male love hidden in a series of publicly available private poems. That the martyr should be a beautiful boy, a gifted stage interpreter of Shakespeare's women, adds another level of meaning.

In conclusion, we should take account of two later occasions when public and private communications, life and works, sincerity and artifice were dramatised.

On 30 April 1895, during Wilde's trial on charges of gross indecency, the reading in court of a poem 'Two Loves', by Lord Alfred Douglas, prompted the defendant to an eloquent interpretation of it as a plea on behalf of 'the love that dare not speak its name' in terms corresponding to those in which the narrator of 'The Portrait of Mr W. H.' in the longer version describes his understanding of Shakespeare's love for his muse. 'It is that deep, spiritual affection that is as pure as it is perfect.'[2] In this non-fictional forensic quest, Wilde's letters, his own poems and those of his friends, his published writings and even the cigarette cases (private cigarette cases) he had given as gifts were mercilessly scrutinised to establish his guilt. The process had been precipitated by an act that might well have been kept private: Lord Alfred Douglas's father, the Marquis of Queensberry, left a card at Wilde's club 'To Oscar Wilde, posing as [a] Somdomite [*sic*].' A club servant discreetly noted the time and put the card in an envelope. By agreeing to sue for libel, Wilde opened the envelope, and converted the card into exhibit A in his own trial.

---

[1] Ibid., p. 302.

[2] H. Montgomery Hyde, "The Second Trial", in: *The Trials of Oscar Wilde* (New York: 1962), pp. 150-221, pp. 200-201.

On the afternoon of Thursday, 16 June 1905 (as reported by James Joyce in *Ulysses*) Stephen Dedalus was propounding his own theory of Shakespeare's life and works in the National Library in Dublin. One of his interlocutors, Mr Best, hazarded the opinion that

> – The most brilliant of all is that story of Wilde's [...] That *Portrait of Mr W. H.* where he proves that the sonnets were writtten by a Willie Hughes, a man all hues.
> – For Willie Hughes, is it not? the quaker librarian asked.
> Or Hughie Wills. Mr William Himself. W. H: who am I?
> – I mean, for Willie Hughes, Mr Best said, amending his gloss easily. Of course it's all paradox, don't you know, Hughes and hews and hues the colour, but it's so typical the way he works it out. It's the very essence of Wilde, don't you know. The light touch.
> His glance touched their faces lightly as he smiled, a blond ephebe. Tame essence of Wilde.[1]

Some time later, when Stephen had finished his disquisition on Shakespeare as the Ghost of Hamlet's father, John Eglinton asked him 'Do you believe your own theory?'

> – No, Stephen said promptly.
> – Are you going to write it? Mr Best asked. You ought to make it a dialogue, don't you know, like the Platonic dialogues Wilde wrote.
> John Eclection doubly smiled.
> – Well, in that case, he said, I don't see why you should expect payment for it since you don't believe it yourself.[2]

Stephen and the narrating Joyce clearly knew their Wilde, and could see the difference between 'tame essence of Wilde' and the duplicitous, doubly platonic, real thing.

---

[1] James Joyce, *Ulysses. The 1922 Text*, ed. Jeri Johnson (Oxford, 1993), p. 190.
[2] Ibid., p. 205.

Off the Beaten Track: Victorian Culture and the Refashioning of Late Romantic Travel Writing

By *Ralph Pordzik* (Munich)

In a stimulating paper delivered at the University of Munich, Christoph Bode once remarked that British travel writers of the eighteenth century were driven by the quest for unity and unified experience. Romantic explorers, he argued, went to Egypt in order to find the sources of the Nile and thus, in metaphorical terms, the mythic origins of western culture.[1] In this essay, I shall argue that the Victorians did the same on a more prosaic, matter-of-fact level of social experience. They wanted to have proof that their inclusive concept of society was the most accomplished of all, a useful model for other societies likewise driven by the wish to overcome the discontinuity of the modern age, its differentiation into ever more self-consciously distinct and separate moments. Writers as different as William Cobbett, Charles Lever, George Henry Borrow, Alexander Kinglake, Amelia Edwards and R.B. Cunninghame Graham sought to incorporate the fragments of their touristic experience into a meaningful whole or 'relevant' cultural situation in the sense of Raymond Williams' notion of a common "mode of interpreting all our existence"[2], of testing one's understanding of the other's ways of life according to the prevailing values and systems of belief.

In the following, I shall bring into focus some of the major moves in Victorian discourses about travel and travel writing between 1830 and 1900. My essay will be divided into five sections. In the first and second section I shall outline some of the differences between travel as a social practice in the late Romantic and the early Victorian age; in the third and fourth I shall try to confirm my argument by discussing a series of texts written and published at that time; and in the fifth section I will give a synopsis with a view to late Victorian travellers' most common responses to the social and epistemological crises of the modern age.

---

[1] "Ad fontes! Bemerkungen zur Verzeitlichung des Raumes, anhand einiger englischer Texte des Zeitraumes 1770-1830". Unpublished lecture, 29th February, 2000.

[2] Raymond Williams, *Culture and Society* (London, 1958), p. xviii.

1. Victorian 'Culture' and the Revision of Late Romantic Travel Discourse

In an illuminating passage of her travel classic *Untrodden Peaks and Unfrequented Valleys* (1873), Amelia Edwards (1831-92) chooses as her setting a North Italian landscape largely unspoilt by postcard Romanticism and the early success stories of travel consumerism. Inspired by the untouched wildness of the Dolomite district – "scarcely known even by name to any but scientific travellers"[1] – she takes South-eastern Tyrol as a springboard for redrawing the map of mid-Victorian travel discourse. What motivates her above all is the possibility of escape from "hackneyed sights, from overcrowded hotels, from the dreary routine of table d'hôtes [and] from the flood of Cook's tourists" and the pleasure of exploring freely a region in which it is still "natural to the natives [...] to be kind, and helpful, and disinterested."[2] In its purity and simplicity, her version of Tyrol offers a scenic route to familiarise writer and reader with genuine representations of landscape and society, promising a more direct and unmediated access to its history and native culture.

After the first chapters, however, it begins to transpire that the female explorer has failed to pursue her designated path. The wild Tyrolean landscape proves a no-man's-land in which there is nothing to describe but "wooded hills, vineyards, terraced gardens [and] gleaming villas bowered in orange-groves."[3] In order to make it more palatable to the educated and high-minded reader at home, the scenery needs cultural enrichment, needs, in fact, the pleasures of the "well-known" ancient routes, "so full of beauty, so rich in old romance, that the mere names [...] read like a page of poetry."[4] It needs the "old Palazzos decorated with fast-fading frescoes by Pordenone"; the "fine Annunciation of Titian to be seen in the Duomo", and the "ruined castles" of a more adventurous and sentimental age in order to justify such lengthy description at all.[5] Behind this impenetrable screen of cultural artefacts and learned excursions into history, south-eastern Tyrol as advertised on the first pages of the book threatens to fade out of sight completely, reduced to a geographical matrix for the writer's projections and reminiscences, a conglomerate of local mythographies, extended quotations and clichés ("school children of all ages, [...] as numer-

---

[1] Amelia Edwards, *Untrodden Peaks and Unfrequented Valleys* [1873] (London, 1986), p. xxx.

[2] Ibid., p. xxxi.

[3] Ibid., p. 8.

[4] Ibid., p. 9.

[5] Ibid., p. 16, 15 and 18. See also p. 21.

ous as the flies of Santa Croce") devised to please and instruct the western consumer.

In recent criticism of travel writing it has been argued that it was the Romantic age that gave rise to such obvious marks of self-contradiction, duplicity and ambiguity, to new representations aimed at distinguishing authentic from spurious or merely repetitive experience.[1] The end of the Napoleonic wars and the re-emergence of European travel as a cultural commodity made the new middle classes adopt the sentiments and ideals of Romanticism, turning tourism into an effective opportunity for self-staging and reviving the childlike sense of wonder at the world inherited from the early Romantics.[2] Licensing the notion of a superior emotional-aesthetic sensitivity which separates the inspired visitor from the vulgar tourist on the one hand and the enlightened Continental traveller on the other, travel literature began to redefine its position in the symbolic economy of nineteenth-century discourse about the purposes of culture and personal acculturation, claiming to readmit "into human life the imaginative, emotional, and moral energies [...] sacrificed in a Benthamite workaday world."[3] According to this more or less derivative model[4], the actual experience of travelling as depicted in a large body of writing is relevant only in terms of its being reflected in the moods and projections of the subjective 'I'.[5] Outer reality, the simple 'truth' of places visited and responded to, is reduced to a mere occasion for a highly original exploration of the individual's inner state of mind.

It will be the major task of this essay to evade such allegations and to relocate travel writing in the context of nineteenth century literature and culture. It is my thesis that the poetical impressionism exhibited in much travel writing, the constant vacillation between opposing and often contra-

---

[1] Cf. James Buzard, *The Beaten Track: European Tourism, Literature and the Ways to 'Culture' 1800-1918* (Oxford, 1993).

[2] C.P. Brand, *Italy and the English Romantics: The Italianate Fashion in Early Nineteenth-Century England* (Cambridge, 1957), p. 16.

[3] J. Buzard, *The Beaten Track*, p. 176.

[4] Derivative, because it reinforces Victorian complaints about the subjectivism of travel writing: "the majority of travellers [...] merely skim the surface, and bring back what are popularly called impressions, which mean, not an account of the things they saw and observed, but of the manner in which they were themselves affected by them." Anonymous reviewer, in: *Fraser's Magazine*, 42.247 (1850), p. 44.

[5] Cf. Christoph Bode, "Beyond/Around/Into One's Own: Reiseliteratur als Paradigma von Welt-Erfahrung", *Poetica*, 26 (1994), 70-87, p. 80; James Duncan, "Introduction", *Writes of Passage: Reading Travel Writing*, ed. James Duncan and Derek Gregory (London and New York, 1999), p. 6; Manfred Pfister, "Robert Byron and the Modernisation of Travel Writing", *Poetica*, 31 (1999), 464-475, p. 470.

dictory terms and attitudes, is not so much bound up with Romantic writing strategies as with the specific modes of constructing, sustaining and delimiting images of self and other in Victorian travel accounts. It derives from an *experiential attitude* to reality rather than from one celebrating the traveller as a fount of originality, a creative perambulating spirit obeying its unique inner dictates and moulding them into a distinctly Romantic experience. Quite clearly, travel writers of the Victorian period tried to refashion the genre in so far as they adopted literary techniques marking themselves off from prior representations, entering into a 'direct' and 'immediate' relationship with the places and objects they sought to describe. John Murray's famous *guide books* for travel played an important role in this process, stressing the "value of practical information gathered on the spot"[1] and the personal experience of the writer given to straightforward exposition of his material. It was this publisher who successfully made the "Weberian transition" from Romantic travel writing's charismatic authority to the "rational bureaucracy of editors and agents"[2], who initiated commodifying practices materialising in the investigative vocabulary and utilitarian practicality of so many nineteenth-century travel writers. Frances and Anthony Trollope, Charles Lever and Charles Dickens claimed to base much of their work on the rich uniqueness of personal impressions recorded directly from experience[3], working to create a mode of travel writing purportedly truer to lived experience. As I shall argue here, travelling for these writers represented a suitable way of acquiring a sense of 'culture' in a society almost entirely devoted to economic growth and materialism, a means of increasing 'social coherence' in an otherwise fragmented modernity.[4] Their view of culture was linked to a particular form of social activity intervening in a Victorian mental and institutional framework and directed against the forces of constriction and alienation and the attitudes

---

[1] John Murray, *Handbook for Travellers on the Continent* (London, [10]1854), p. v.

[2] Edward Mendelson, "Baedeker's Universe", in: *Yale Review*, 87 (1985), 386-403, p. 393.

[3] "The greater part of the descriptions were written on the spot, and sent home, from time to time, in private letters ..."; Charles Dickens, *Pictures From Italy* [1846] (New York, 1988), p. 2.

[4] Cf. Dean MacCannell, *The Tourist: A New Theory of the Leisure Class* (New York, 1976). For a full account of this remedial concept of culture in Victorian times see Raymond Williams, *Culture and Society*. A good example illustrating the notion of culture as a fully integrated way of life and the powerful positive charges it has taken on can be found in Edward Sapir's article "Culture, Genuine and Spurious", in: *Culture, Language and Personality: Selected Essays*, ed. David G. Mandelbaum (Berkeley, 1960), pp. 90-93. Sapir argues that "genuine" culture is "inherently harmonious, balanced, self-satisfactory", a unity "in which nothing is spiritually meaningless."

of the 'uncultured' middle classes. What they sought to establish was a representational contract enabling them to incorporate new and unfamiliar objects so as to control and integrate them according to the prevailing model of social coherence.[1] They saw the encounter with the other as a potentially disturbing and intervening force which needed to be made consistent with their preordained idea of culture as unified experience, as a 'common faith' and 'common way of life' in the sense of Raymond Williams' theory of culture. To achieve this, they turned travel writing into a cognitive instrument capable of testing prevailing concepts of self and other, the relationship between people and places and the social realities surrounding them, between the present and the accretions of history.

This is not to argue that there ever existed a single strategy of describing 'real' experiences of travel. The various writers had so many different ways of seeing the world that any attempt to posit a unified field must prove a gross distortion. But the variety of modes is not infinite, and in the face of often radically unfamiliar experiences – especially in the context of travels to Spain, to the Orient or the Far East – the different responses reveal shared assumptions and tropes of representations. And the most important of these assumptions is the faith in a common reality that can be experienced and interpreted by all and agreed upon in a kind of continued dialogue. The overarching cultural strategy attached to this framework is thus not so much one of 'foreignizing', as Romantic theories of travel put it, but rather one of familiarizing, of turning the other into a "useful and necessary agent in both developing and controlling our own personal and social self."[2]

In the end, however, this ambitious project failed, resulting in complication and paradox. As Samuel Rogers (1763-1855) wrote in his verse tale *Italy*: "in travelling we multiply events, and innocently. We set out, as it were, on our adventures."[3] Seeking consistent patterns underlying their travel experience, writers permanently uncovered new and unfamiliar objects which needed to be textualised yet resisted being accommodated to their imaginative geography. As a result, the ideal of social coherence became more elusive with each attempt purporting to reassert it. The specific

---

[1] This section is much indebted to Winfried Fluck's thoughts on the development of American realist fiction, "Fiction and Fictionality in American Realism", *Amerikastudien / American Studies*, 31.1 (1986), 101-112. See also the chapter on travel writing in my introduction to the nineteenth-century English novel, *Der englische Roman im neunzehnten Jahrhundert* (Berlin, 2001), pp. 74-81.

[2] Gerhard Stilz, "Dimensions of Identity Formation in the New English Literatures", in: *Anglistentag 1999 Mainz: Proceedings*, ed. Bernhard Reitz and Sigrid Rieuwerts (Trier, 2000), pp. 289-299, p. 289.

[3] Samuel Rogers, *Italy: A Poem* (London, 1830), p. 172.

mode adopted by travel writers to control their material unfolded its own dynamic, revealing an insoluble inner complication of the notion of coherence itself. Reshaping the received itineraries to include cultural material that threatened the prevailing value system bore the danger of unwelcome results and further complicated the process of symbolic exchange and mediation maintained in the texts – a contradiction that finally culminated in the search for altogether new forms of representation.

2. Victorian Travels and the 'Culture of Experience'

It has long been a commonplace to see the arrival of modernism on the literary stage as the major event inaugurating this renewal and repositioning travel writing within a discursive formation that involves formal innovation as well as the free play of desire and the possibility of transgression.[1] According to Manfred Pfister, "modern travel writing [...] reflects both the crisis of travelling and of travel writing as media of understanding oneself and the other."[2] True as this may be, it must not let us forget that the first inklings of this disaffection surfaced in travel records written as early as 1830. The theme of indescribability, for instance, the fear of no longer being able to truthfully render in words the culture of the other, runs through several writings of this period. Anna Jameson (1794-1860), in her *Diary of an Ennuyée* (1826), confessed to strong doubts about conveying a proper image of the world around her.[3] Struggling with the inherited code, she submits to the word-defying sublimity attached to scenes and landscapes: "The whole scene was – but how can I say what it was? I have exhausted my stock of fine words; and must be content with silent recollections, and the sense of admiration and wonder unexpressed."[4] Similarly, William Cobbett in his unforgettable *Rural Rides* anticipated the sense of the necessity to disrupt received conventions. What aroused his indignation was the breaking up of traditional society by mechanised labour and a ruthless taxing and funding system drawing national property into the hands of a few. Against the patronising attitude of Romantic agricultural tourism, he presented himself in the role of the traveller as ethnographer, competent to write authoritatively about the rural poor on the basis of his intimate

---

[1] Cf. Paul Fussell, *Abroad: British Literary Travelling Between the Wars* (Oxford, 1980), p. 95; Manfred Pfister, "Robert Byron", p. 466.

[2] Manfred Pfister, "Robert Byron", p. 467.

[3] Anna Brownell Jameson, *The Diary of an Ennuyée* (Boston, 1857).

[4] Ibid., p. 124.

knowledge of the country and its forms of communal life.[1] "The authority of the ethnographer over the 'mere traveller'", Mary Louise Pratt writes, "rests chiefly on the idea that the traveller just passes through, whereas the ethnographer lives with the group under study [...] producing accounts that are indeed full, rich, and accurate by ethnography's own standards."[2] Ironically, her neo-historicist point of view works to validate, albeit unknowingly, contemporary complaints about travellers rushing into print without the qualification of a long residence in the country and an acquaintance with the language:[3]

> To observe the habits of a people, and thoroughly investigate their social life and institutions, it is necessary to live long enough amongst them, not merely to become familiar with their modes of thinking, but to emancipate ourselves from our own.[4]

It is here, therefore, at the crucial point of transition from *familiarity* to *alterity*, from the weighty precedence of writings filled with regiments of fact or the outpourings of a self-professedly sensitive soul to the attempt at reconstructing and re-negotiating cultural difference, that we can begin to pursue the transformational process engendered by a predominantly experience-derived attitude to foreign places and cultures. With amazing frankness, mid-Victorian travel accounts register the distance enforced by established travel discourse and seek to diminish it by restaging the encounter with the other, with what has been removed from their own cultural grasp. Yet it is precisely at this point that the crucial paradox reveals itself: seizing a foreign culture by actual or imaginary acts of 'taking part' as an ethnographer strives to do, the writers and their accounts can never acquire the true 'standard' of accuracy they wish for. The other always speaks in the discourse, in the images and clichés, the whole mental framework, that seeks to construct, celebrate and catalogue it. It is therefore shot through with imaginary projections and associations displacing

---

[1] William Cobbett, *Rural Rides* [1830] (London, 1967).

[2] Mary Louise Pratt, "Fieldwork in Common Places", in: *Writing Cultures: The Poetics and Politics of Ethnography*, ed. James Clifford and George E. Marcus (Berkeley, 1986), pp. 27-50, p. 38.

[3] Complaints flourishing particularly in Victorian times, as James Buzard has shown. He quotes the example of the anonymously published *Italy as It Is: Or, a Narrative of an English Family's Residence for Three Years in that Country* (1828) whose author "distinguished his book from the many Italian-tour accounts by asserting that prolonged experience of the country had given him a true perception of its character." (J. Buzard, *The Beaten Track*, p. 61)

[4] "Recent Travellers", *Fraser's Magazine*, 42.247 (1850), p. 44.

any well-meant attempt to get hold of its 'authentic' or immediate reality. The result of this constantly renewed yet also constantly frustrated effort to construe alterity, to prevent oneself from 'translating' the foreign other into mere similarity or negativity, is a rupture in the narrative and, in effect, the emergence of an 'ambiguous subject of representation'[1] producing a tense 'space in-between' or interstitial zone sustained by relations of power and desire. As Wolfgang Iser puts it: "Whenever realities are transposed into the text, they turn into signs for something else, which indicates that their original determinacy has been outstripped."[2]

3. The Traveller as Adventurer: George Henry Borrow's *Bible in Spain*

This permanent criss-crossing of boundaries can be pursued in one of the most widely read examples of the genre, George Henry Borrow's *Bible in Spain*.[3] As a widely travelled and experienced writer of touristic accounts, Borrow has a peculiar way of inducing unique and memorable responses whenever he purports to meet the other on its own terms. Quite often, the unexpected clash of two patterns of experience evokes a response subject to the contingencies of the process of cultural mediation or a value judgment governed by the very assumptions Borrow seeks to evade. In a telling scene, the narrator is prevented from entering a picturesque Spanish fortress by the commanding officer. He erupts into a rancorous speech addressed to the Portuguese locals and their "miserable vanity", while at the same time praising the English for their courageous military engagement in a country much too "corrupt and unregenerate"[4] to appreciate this kind of

---

[1] Cf. Ulla Haselstein, *Die Gabe der Zivilisation: Kultureller Austausch und literarische Textpraxis in Amerika 1682-1861* (München, 2000), p. 19.

[2] Wolfgang Iser, "Fictionalizing Acts", *American Studies / Amerikastudien*, 31.1 (1986), 5-15, p. 7.

[3] The definitive 18th edition of the book contains a map showing Borrow's various travel routes across the Spanish peninsula. He made four journeys to Spain as major representative of the British Bible Society, partly in the unsuccessful attempt at obtaining permission to print the New Testament in the Castilian language. It is tempting to see this map as an icon of the book's zigzagging plot. According to Jurij Lotman, maps are examples of plotless texts, and once we draw a line from A to B, they acquire a plot: action is introduced. The rambling red lines of the travel routes on this map signify, so to say, the only textual event: namely that of the endless introduction of new events, landscapes, objects and characters.

[4] George Henry Borrow, *Bible in Spain*, p. 100.

support. This scene is balanced by a passage engaging the issue of "missionary labour"[1] in Spain:

> I will say nothing with respect to the doctrine of the Jesuits, for as you have observed, I am a protestant; but I am ready to assert that there are no people in the world better qualified, upon the whole, to be entrusted with the education of youth.[2]

Obviously, Borrow here gets into difficulties with his underlying ideal of faithfully reconstructing past experiences.[3] On the one hand, he has to make sure that his eyewitness report is not spoiled by a patronising gesture containing the alternative views necessary to produce it; on the other, he has to introduce ways of inspecting the alien domain from the comfort and security of the familiar. Always maintaining some minimum distance between himself and the local space he traverses thus enables him to modify previous judgements without putting at risk the coherence of the larger experience. This, in turn, produces new complications, as it requires him always to remain in some sort of protective isolation from the 'authentic' elements of the culture he investigates: he can no longer give himself 'bodily', as it were, with abandon, to the spirit of the place he is "mixed up" with.[4] In the quoted section, he not only modifies his observations on England's interventionist policy, but also reworks them in the light of subsequent encounters. Borrow's zigzagging path across the Peninsula thus produces a space in which each reference is mediated and modified by its shifting relationship with other judgements and assumptions. Nothing he describes to his readers is ever authentic or fully adequate, mysteriously connected with the spot or object it seems to designate. Where Robert Ford, author of Murray's *Hand-book for Travellers in Spain* (1845), arrogantly notes that there "is no via media, no Protestantism, no Bible in Spain [...] only two classes: infidels and bigots"[5], Borrow acknowledges the fact that the experienced 'truth' is not a neutral surface but a composite, fractured and spatialised construction. Viewed from this angle, the differences between Jesuits and Protestants in the aforementioned scene, previously marked as an instance of the perennial conflict between tolerance and fanaticism, enlightenment and superstition, are implicitly reduced to a minimum, their opposing creeds reduced to a mere stultifying sameness.

---

[1] Ibid., p. vi.

[2] Ibid., p. 66.

[3] Ibid., p. vi.

[4] Ibid., p. vi.

[5] Quoted in: David Williams, *A World of His Own: The Double Life of George Borrow* (Oxford, 1982), p. 97.

If it is thus the constructivity and narrativity of cultural identities which make it so difficult to return to the immediate object of one's experience, then a solution might lie in a mode of representation taking into account the materiality of the others' language and culture as presented by themselves. *The Bible in Spain* features long passages in which Borrow conjures up a host of terms taken from Romany, the Indic language of the Spanish Gypsies. The achieved effect is that of a series of bizarre and absorbing conversations which to understand without consulting the appended glossary is next to impossible. Quite obviously, Borrow here seeks to alienate the reader from a traditional understanding of the travel record as a site of self-promotion; removing the wall of prior language blocking the imaginative grasp of the 'real thing', he wheedles the reader into direct confrontation with the other, appealing to his sense of wonder while at the same time exerting some kind of physical authority over the object under study, yoking together the incongruous parts of the text's inner world. Here is an excerpt from a conversation taking place between the narrator and his 'brother' Antonio, in English, interspersed with Romany terms:

> It is an affair of Egypt, brother, and I shall not acquaint you with it; peradventure it relates to a horse or an ass, or peradventure it relates to a mule or a *macho*; it does not relate to yourself, therefore I advise you not to inquire about it – *Dosta*. With respect to my offer, you are free to decline it; there is a *drungruje* between here and *Madrilati*, and you can travel it in the *birdoche*; or with the *dromális*; but I tell you, as a brother, that there are *chories* upon the *drun*; and some of them are of the *Errate*.[1]

It is in passages like these that we can see the sense of wonder pass over to the narrator's own self, desiring as it does to merge and become one with the other culture, to be "one of the *Errate*" or Gypsies[2] – according to the glossary a "respectful appellation [...] used by them of their own race"[3] – who roam the countryside of a disintegrating nation in quest of a way to "become once more what they were in former times."[4] However, it is not only the fact that many translations of Romany terms as given in the record are inaccurate, conjectural or simply false, but also the failure of the narrative to provide a meaningful context for them which intensifies the

---

[1] George Henry Borrow, *Bible in Spain*, p. 109. *Dosta* = enough!; *drungruje* = the king's highway; *Madrilati* = Madrid; *birdoche* = stage-coach; *dromális* = muleteers, men of the road; *chories* = thieves; *drun* = road; *Errate* = gypsy. For further translations of Romany terms see the "Glossary", pp. 797–833.

[2] Ibid., p. 109.

[3] Ibid., p. 810.

[4] Ibid., p. 108.

reader's textual frustrations (e.g., what is he supposed to make of the re-peated announcement that the Gypsies have some important "business of Egypt to transact"?)[1]. A gap begins to open between the inner world of the record and that of the reader, threatening to block communication and to terminate the quest for the bedrock of truth, for the local 'other'.

On the other hand, this relative failure to contain the original sense of wonder and witness[2] may be reconsidered in the light of the narrative possibilities it offers. In this sense, Borrow's choice of Spain at a time when young men of property and other practitioners of tourism preferred Italy as a destination is in itself programmatic. It not only suggests the imaginative occupation of uncharted territory, thus clearing the path for a new sense of cultural difference; in fact, it also restores the disturbances and social wrongs to the discourse from which they have been removed. At one level, *The Bible in Spain* is a picturesque adventure story about rough encounters with zanies and bandits, about stop-overs in dubious inns, and about the misery of social rejects rubbing along in a country torn by vio-lence and war. Discrete though these cultural spaces appear to be, Borrow nevertheless travels through and between them, transgressing apparently immutable boundaries and betraying the instability of the ideological and cultural constructions underlying them.

One's interpretation thus depends on the way one defines the text's at-tempt to explore foreign space: as a failure to integrate and to render in meaningful terms the encounter with the other or as an inscription of radi-cally new and undreamed-of possibilities. On the whole, it seems to me that Borrow's entry into uncharted space devoid of fixed coordinates and definable boundaries spins a web of meanings and attributions in which his narrator runs the risk of becoming hopelessly entangled. As a result, he finds himself creating another screen of sovereign texts or archives through which the faint outlines of the world 'as it really is' can still just barely be discerned. The ensuing dilemma is double-edged: Throughout this rich account of events and encounters with life in nineteenth-century Spain, we can see our fearless polyglot resuming his attempts at 'writing the other culture' *from within*. Yet the opposing narratives of fantasy[3] and

---

[1] Ibid., p. 114.

[2] For a detailed account of the "primal act of witnessing around which virtually the entire discourse of travel is constructed", see Stephen Greenblatt, *Marvelous Posses-sions: The Wonder of the New World* (Oxford, 1992), p. 122-126.

[3] Fantastic renderings of the other emerge as a kind of *ersatz* or strategy, taking the place of the legitimising "articulating code" displaced in the process of revisioning the framework that produces it; Karl Ludwig Pfeiffer, "Gilbert and Sullivan, or the Cultural Poverty of Systems Theory", in: *Anglistentag 1997 Giessen: Proceedings*, ed. Raimund Borgmeier et al. (Trier, 1998), pp. 337-346, p. 340. As I conceive of it, the end of this

materiality emerging from this routine continue to prove a debilitating factor, threatening to subvert the integrity and assumed 'authenticity' or truth of the experience itself. The result is a composite and internally ambiguous site of negotiation and transculturation, a kind of multi-faceted 'inter-text' that folds itself into a series of different spatialities continuously interrogating their construction, thus preventing it from ever achieving the goal of a fully integrated record, or 'social coherence'.

4. Victorian Travellers at the Threshold of Modernity

In this densely packed record of Spain, Borrow's subliminal references to the perspective of the investigative traveller as somehow indispensable to the place raise the possibility that the place cannot exist without that traveller. To view this dilemma as prerequisite to a new representational contract in travel writing is a lesson modern and postmodern travellers in particular seem to have learned well.[1] However, it would appear prejudiced to deny George Borrow's influential role in this process of 'raising' travel writing to the standard of modern literature. What he has in common with a new generation of writers emerging at the end of the nineteenth century (Cunninghame Graham, *Mogreb-el-Acksa*, 1898; W.H. Hudson, *Idle Days in Patagonia*, 1893) is what Manfred Pfister has described as the "shared awareness that the old epistemological and psychological certainties of subject and object no longer hold."[2] Borrow expressed anxiety about the place of European culture during the period of colonialist expansion when 'exotic' cultures were becoming progressively familiar and vice versa, realising that his sympathies with the 'real' Spain as he conceived of it did not exempt him from implication in Britain's power and growing influence in the country. His diagnosis of an imperial compound of power and misunderstanding – constantly revised and readjusted in the ambiguous moves and vacillations of his account – led him to be uneasy with the medium in

---

process is embodied in postmodern travel writing which gives full license to the imaginary as a positive force unrestrained by formalistic considerations. Reactivating the signifiers' full potential for semantic difference, its practitioners seek to regain the sense of wonder co-opted by a rationalist framework of perception. Wonder, as Stephen Greenblatt puts it, "precedes, even escapes, moral categories. [It] depends upon a suspension or failure of categories." (Stephen Greenblatt, *Marvelous Possessions*, p. 20) In this sense it resembles nothing so much as the rapt attention we give to multiply affiliated signs and meanings in literary texts.

[1] Cf. Manfred Pfister, "Bruce Chatwin and the Postmodernization of the Travelogue", *LIT*, 7 (1996), 253-267.

[2] Manfred Pfister, "Robert Byron", p. 467.

which he had built a career. His later works which failed to be a success with the high-minded Victorian reading public reflect as well as rework the issues addressed in *The Bible in Spain* with a power unique in Victorian travel writing. In both *Lavengro* (1851) and *The Romany Rye* (1857) lies a strong and undeniable genius, both featuring enchanting and stylised dialogues and cultivating the "programmatic dilettantism"[1] later to become a characteristic trait of the travel writings of D.H. Lawrence. Both works are peculiar for their anticipating some of the formally innovative techniques employed by the early modernists in the decades shortly before the outbreak of the Great War;[2] their dreamlike quality and feverish excursions into foreign cultural and linguistic space, their fake-philosophising and unappeasable tendency to quote at great length from unknown texts and authors have earned Borrow the dubious reputation of being one of the most inaccessible and unreadable of nineteenth-century writers, unable to create plausible characters in credible surroundings and lacking the organisational ability to write a cogent and convincing narrative. The preceding attempt at putting into a cultural frame certain of the opposing moves and implicit ambiguities of Borrow's work has tried to correct this impression in order to arrive at a more sympathetic understanding of his work. It locates Borrow's travel records within the larger dynamic of Victorian travel discourse, a dynamic in which the discrete texts are strategically enabled but also inherently delimited by their underlying assumptions and demarcations, by their trying to get into a putatively direct and meaningful relationship with the other – an effort constantly thwarted by the "physicality" of the literary signs, the "multiple sites"[3] or spaces they create when introduced into the text. Distinguishing himself from the ideological web in which traditional travel writing seemed trapped, Borrow could only add new strands to that web, further isolating himself from the material realities and prospects of coherence he purported to grasp. Without necessarily intending to, he thus stimulated redefinitions of travel writing's *raison d'être* and ushered in a series of surprisingly fresh modes of voicing the

---

[1] Ibid., p. 470.

[2] Not unlike their Victorian precursors, modern writers looked for some kind of 'unified experience' in travelling. But they conceived of it more in the sense of a mythological experience or archetypal passage through life. Robert Byron, e.g., wanted to restore the primitive, phallic roots of civilization to his own time; Lawrence sought to restore the intense fullness, spontaneity and somatic dimension to life which he saw endangered by the modernising process. Postmodern travel writers seem to have fully incorporated into their writing what resulted from modernism's unrelenting critical examination of culture: the pervading sense of the constructivity and historicity of all human experience.

[3] James Duncan, "Introduction", *Writes of Passage*, p. 3.

encounter with the other, helping prepare the ground for later generations of travel writers who situated their work on the ambiguous borders of fiction, dream, reportage, and autobiography.

This is of course not to say that good travel writing ceased to exist after the death of George Henry Borrow. Due to the impending crisis of late Victorianism, the more self-assuredly provocative, more intense and 'imperial' travel accounts were still to come. If the 'capacity for wonder' must be seen as one of the most striking aspects of Borrow's writing, this capacity appears to have transformed itself into a different category, a separate goal, in many travel books published during the second half of the nineteenth century. Wonder, as Raymond William puts it, "overrides the determinism of the system [...] it is the kind of miracle that happens."[1] In later writings, wonder re-emerges as a miracle deliberately manufactured in order to gloss over the writers' difficulties in coming to terms with the foreign cultures they seek to portray. There is nothing of that kind of genuine faith, e.g., in Alexander Kinglake's *Eothen, or Traces of Travel brought home from the East* (1844), an extended narrative recording the English historian's experiences in the Middle East.[2] Again, the immediate shock of the individual encountering a foreign and 'marvellous' culture is reflected in the book's highly erratic style and vacillation between different forms of reportage, history and portrayal. Several times it sets out to explore a particular scene or observation in greater detail which attracts the traveller's attention for a time but then doesn't get meaningfully incorporated at all. For Kinglake, it seems, it has proved impossible to integrate the various 'traces of travel brought home' into a coherent narrative of cause and effect. Whereas Borrow offers some kind of release, which even at its most grotesque is irrepressible and above all spontaneous, Kinglake's account of the East provides the most fantastic and idiosyncratic kinds of growth in an almost purely supplementary fashion; what runs through it is a paradoxical energy, a loss of customary settlement, which in its constant repetition appears ludicrous because misplaced. The bloated face of the "extremely fat"[3] and white female slave who symbolises a distorted mirror for the writer's European (imperial) self, the 'fetishizing' of Early Chris-

---

[1] Raymond Williams, *The English Novel: From Dickens to Lawrence* (London, 1971), p. 52.

[2] Alexander Kinglake, *Eothen, or Traces of Travel Brought Home from the East* [1844]. With an Introduction by J.M. Scott (Geneva, 1969). Cf. also Christoph Bode, "Alexander Kinglake, *Eothen or Traces of Travel Brought Home from the East* (1844) oder Wie man sich nicht ansteckt", in: *West Meets East: Klassiker der britischen Orient-Reiseliteratur*, ed. Christoph Bode (Heidelberg, 1997), pp. 49-67.

[3] Alexander Kinglake, *Eothen*, p. 226.

tian beliefs in Palestine and the emptied symbols of the Church, the perennial conflict and struggle for power between East and West – these are vital areas of social and cultural experience that can no longer be implemented successfully in the traveller's isolated narrative. It is thus not without irony that Kinglake, failing to acknowledge the shortcomings of his own discursive system, provides us instead with the "Orientals'" explanation for European vagrancy, shifting its meaning from a plainly rational to an 'exoticized' level of explanation:

> The theory is that the English traveller has committed some sin against God and his conscience, and that for this, the Evil Spirit has hold of him, and drives him from his home like a victim of the old Grecian Furies, and forces him to travel over countries far and strange, and most chiefly over Deserts and desolate places, and to stand upon the sites of cities that once were, and are now no more, and to grope among the tombs of dead men.[1]

The representation of foreign cultures has been pursued in an even more supplementary fashion in R.B. Cunninghame Graham's notorious *Mogreb-el-Acksa*.[2] Graham's account of his trek into the Moroccan interior beyond Marrakech has become the classic example of late imperial British adventure travel. It is, however, much more than that; it is also a first tentative attempt at deconstructing British colonial travel discourse. Graham's purpose was to pay a visit to the forbidden city of Tarudant, where it was claimed no Christian has ever set foot, and which he attempted while disguised as a Turkish doctor and a sheikh from the city of Fez. In the end, his mission proved a failure: halfway to his goal, Graham was captured and held prisoner for four months in the medieval castle of Kintafi in the Atlas Mountains; a loss for the writer turning into the reader's gain, one feels tempted to add, as it is this book which throws a wholly new and critical light on western culture's preoccupation with itself and its own values and attitudes. Returning the encounter with deprivation and primitive conditions of life from the imperial explorer's 'Dark Africa' to the writer's English doorstep, it unmasks the heroic glamour of travelling and de-mythologizes the assumedly visionary spirit of discovery and exploration:

> [B]ut when so many savages still exist in Africa and in East London – not to speak of Glasgow and the like – it seems a pity to expend upon a people [i.e. the Orientals], civilized according to their needs, so much good faith, which might be used with good effect upon less stony ground. [...] How many an honest, hard-working

---

[1] Ibid., p. 199.

[2] R.B. Cunninghame Graham, *Mogreb-el-Acksa: A Journey in Morocco* [1898]. Introduction by Edward Garnett (Evanston, Illinois, 1997).

young man [...] thinks when he reads of Livingstone, Francisco Xavier, the Jesuits of Paraguay, and Father Damien, that he, too, would like to take his cross upon his back and follow them. It seems so fine [...] a self-denying life, lived far away from the comforts, without books; Bible and gun in hand, to show the heathen all the glories of our faith. [...]

[A]s I see the matter Europeans are a curse throughout the East. What do they bring worth bringing, as a general rule?[1]

There is not enough time, nor is this the place, to analyse Graham's deliberate yet also somehow ambiguous and self-undermining anti-imperialist stance. For we may ask ourselves as well, 'what does *he* bring worth bringing, as a general rule of travelling and appropriating the other's natural domain of life'? As Graham himself cheekily remarks, "truth [...] suffers by too much comprehension"[2], and a genuine attempt at understanding the other's ways along with a valid self-assessment of the British traveller's politics of 'negative identity' is precisely what the book lacks. There are, therefore, intriguing parallels between Graham's time and our own referring to which I would like to conclude: in *Mogreb-el-Acksa*, the traveller in his traditional role as male adventurer, as "magisterial polymath of the Other"[3], is preserved from undergoing a crisis of identity by spontaneously switching from one dramatic event to the next without further elaboration or discussion. There is not the slightest hint of self-doubt or self-critique in the narrator's account of his travels in Morocco. Drawing a parallel here between the Victorians' passion for sensation and our contemporary, self-justifying media culture, I cannot but question the western attitude of 'showing the heathen' the glories of 'enduring freedom'. I ask myself if we have really succeeded in putting a satisfyingly critical distance between Graham's colonial views and our own, his self-assuring statement and our modified liberal terms, if we still subscribe to the dualistic ideology voiced in his account of the East:

Christ and Mohammed never will be friends; their teaching, lives, and the conditions of the different peoples amongst whom they preached make it impossible; even their respective followers misunderstand each other quite as thoroughly as when a thousand years ago they came across each other's path for the first time.[4]

---

[1] Ibid., pp. 29-30.

[2] Ibid., "Preface", pp. xvii.

[3] Manfred Pfister, "Robert Byron", p. 469.

[4] R. B. Cunninghame Graham, "Preface", *Mogreb-el-Acksa*, p. 30.

Fish and Fetish: Mary Kingsley in West Africa

By *Silvia Mergenthal* (Constance)

When Mary Kingsley travelled to West Africa in the 1890s, her two journeys were, according to Sandra M. Gilbert and Susan Gubar[1], no longer "privileged" but "paradigmatic", and "representative" rather than "idiosyncratic". In other words, Kingsley was not, as she would have been before the nineteenth century, a rare specimen, but one of numerous Victorian women travellers, quite a few of whom "roam[ed] with the freedom of man in lands so very different and distant from their own."[2] Others accompanied their fathers, brothers, or husbands to distant outposts of the British Empire, thus participating, vicariously as well as often quite directly, in the British imperial enterprise.[3]

Mary Henrietta Kingsley was born in London on October 13, 1862.[4] Her father George was a physician, but like his better-known brothers Charles and Henry and his sister Charlotte he also nursed literary ambitions. Relations between the Kingsley siblings were strained, partly perhaps because of George's marriage to Mary Bailey, who may or may not have been his cook or housekeeper, but who certainly gave birth to Mary Henrietta only four days after the wedding ceremony. For the first sixteen years of Mary's life, the family lived in London; in 1883 they moved to Cambridge so that Mary's younger brother Charles, born in 1864, could take up his studies at the university. In a letter to her publisher, written in 1899, Mary will remark that "being allowed to learn German was all the paid-for education I ever had – 2,000 pounds were spent on my brother, I still hope not in vain."[5] Apart from these German lessons, which she was given in order to assist her father in his research, Mary was largely self-taught. In later

---

[1] Sandra M. Gilbert and Susan Gubar, *No Man's Land: The Place of the Woman Writer in the Twentieth Century. Volume 1. The War of the Worlds* (Yale, 1985), p. 17.

[2] Dea Birkett, *Spinsters Abroad. Victorian Lady Explorers* (London, 1989), "Preface".

[3] See for example *Western Women and Imperialism. Complicity and Resistance*, eds. Nupur Chaudhuri and Margaret Strobel (Bloomington, 1992).

[4] For biographical information on Kingsley see Dea Birkett, *Mary Kingsley. Imperial Adventuress* (Basingstoke, 1992); see also Alison Blunt, *Travel, Gender, and Imperialism. Mary Kingsley and West Africa* (New York, 1994); Katherine Frank, *A Voyager Out. The Life of Mary Kingsley* (Boston, 1986); Catherine Barnes Stevenson, *Victorian Women Travel Writers in Africa* (Boston, 1982).

[5] Quoted in Stevenson, *Victorian Women Travel Writers in Africa*, pp. 92-93.

years, she will repeatedly lament her lack of formal education and scientific training, and her inability to express herself properly in writing as well as in speech; she will attribute her social awkwardness to these educational deficiencies, and she will, throughout her life, defer to her brother. Charles, incidentally, will eventually abandon his project to write a biography of his sister, and will burn all the documents which he had collected for that purpose.

George Kingsley spent the greater part of Mary's childhood and youth abroad, as private physician to a series of wealthy aristocrats whom he accompanied to the Middle and Far East, the United States, and the Pacific. His letters home, brimful of adventures, narrow escapes and the like, proved, naturally enough, deeply distressing to his wife, while in his daughter they fostered a desire to travel herself, and an interest in ethnography. His projected comparative study of primitive sacrificial rites was, like his son's biography of Mary, destined never to be completed; a volume of his travel writings, *Notes on Sport and Travel*, did, however, appear in 1900 – edited by Mary, ever the obedient Victorian daughter. During the last years of their lives, both her parents were ailing, and had to be cared for by Mary, who was by now in her late twenties; they died in 1892. In her preface to *Travels in West Africa*, Mary describes her situation after her parents' deaths as follows:

> It was in 1893 that, for the first time in my life, I found myself in possession of five or six months which were not heavily forestalled, and feeling like a boy with a half-crown, I lay about in my mind, as Mr Bunyan would say, as to what to do with them. 'Go and learn your tropics,' said Science. Where on earth am I to go, I wondered, for tropics are tropics whenever found, so I got down an atlas and saw that either South America or West Africa must be my destination, for the Malayan region was too far off and too expensive. Then I got Wallace's *Geographical Distribution* and after reading that master's article on the Ethiopian region I hardened my heart and closed with West Africa.[1]

While it is tempting to explore Kingsley's psychological motivation in greater detail, it may suffice here to suggest that she must have experienced her parents' deaths as both liberating and threatening; this sense of an existential crisis, even panic, is barely concealed under the light-hearted jocularity of her opening paragraph. Years later, she will write to a friend:

---

[1] Unless otherwise indicated, quotations are from one of the more easily accessible abridged versions of *Travels in West Africa*: *Mary Kingsley. Travels in West Africa*, abridged and introduced by Elspeth Huxley (London, 1987), here p. 11.

Dead tired and feeling no one had need of me any more, when my Mother and Father died within six weeks of each other in '92, [...] I went down to West Africa to die. West Africa amused me and was kind to me and was scientifically interesting – and did not want to kill me just yet.[1]

At any rate, to West Africa Kingsley went, in order to collect, as she put it herself, *fish* and *fetish*, that is, to conduct zoological as well as anthropological studies: *fetish*, in her diction, refers to West African religious practices associated with animism. The first of her two journeys, from August 1893 to January 1894, took her from the Canary Islands to Senegal, Sierra Leone, and the Gold Coast (now Ghana), from thence to the delta of the Niger and to Luanda (now Angola), and back through French Congo to British Old Calabar (now Nigeria). In December 1894, Kingsley returned to West Africa, where she ascended the Ogowé River (in Gaboon), crossed the region between it and the Rembwé River, and descended the Rembwé; she also climbed the Mungo Lah Lobeh (12,000 feet) in Cameroon, then a German colony, and visited some islands off the coast of Africa. When she arrived back home in November 1895 her fame as intrepid woman explorer had already preceded her. In the four years following her second journey, she gave innumerable public lectures all over Britain, but she was also received by high-ranking colonial administrators, who sought her advice on West African affairs: her two books, *Travels in West Africa* (1897) and *West African Studies* (1899), not only record her West African experiences, but attempt to influence British imperial policy towards and in West Africa. By the time *West African Studies* was published, however, British attention had already begun to shift from West to South Africa. When the Boer War started in the same year, Kingsley volunteered as a nurse; on June 3, 1900, only two months after her arrival in South Africa, she contracted enteric fever and died. She was buried at sea.

As may have become evident from the trajectories of Kingsley's journeys, West Africa in the second half of the nineteenth century was a territory in which all the colonial powers of the period – Britain, France, Germany, Portugal, and Belgium – were trying to gain footholds. Even after

---

[1] Quoted in Stevenson, *Victorian Women Travel Writers in Africa*, p. 100. Stevenson comments on this letter as follows: "Although Stephen Gwynn takes this as a proof of a latent suicidal urge, later biographers have pointed out that this letter, written seven years after the fact, expresses Kingsley's exhaustion and depression in 1899, not her mood in 1892. Moreover, this statement must be juxtaposed both to Kingsley's precautions against contracting fever in West Africa and her remark in a lecture during the last years of her life that 'It was no desire to get killed and eaten that made me go and associate with the tribes with the worst reputation for cannibalism and human sacrifice; but just because such tribes were the best for me to study ...'." (ibid.)

the Berlin Conference of 1884-5, which had been organised to terminate the "Scramble for Africa" by dividing the continent into spheres of influence, tensions in West Africa continued to mount: between Britain and France on the upper reaches of the Niger, and between France, Portugal, and Belgium in the Congo. Furthermore, within each sphere of influence, explorers, missionaries, traders, the military, and colonial administrators pursued different and frequently contradictory goals, not least in their dealings with "the natives". In her journeys, Kingsley met representatives of each colonial power, and of each interest group; she compared their respective strategies, and eventually, and unsurprisingly, ended up supporting the British side – but also, for reasons which will be explored later, that of the traders, whose lobbyist and spokesperson she became after her return to Britain. She never questioned the European presence in Africa as such.

During the "Scramble for Africa", European attitudes towards "the African" began to change: while up to the middle of the nineteenth century the idea of the Noble Savage still played a prominent part in Africanist discourses of alterity, these positive constructions of "the African" began to be replaced by pseudo-evolutionary arguments which consigned the African Other to a lower rung in the evolutionary ladder and, in the process, served to justify European intervention on the African continent – another issue to which further reference will be made below.[1]

Thus, when Kingsley travelled in West Africa, she carried not only her famous "long waterproof sack"[2], but also the cultural baggage of her period. As Tim Youngs observes, perhaps stating the obvious:

> Travellers do not simply record what they see. They travel with a purpose. They journey with preconceptions. They observe and write according to established models, having those in mind even when they wish to query or depart from them. No one who travels and writes of their experience can be said to be writing purely as an individual. Descriptions and judgements reveal the values of class, gender, and nationality.[3]

It is, in particular, Youngs's "values of gender" on which this analysis of Mary Kingsley's travel writings will focus; it will take its departure from

---

[1] On Africanist discourse see Christopher L. Miller, *Blank Darkness. Africanist Discourse in French* (Chicago, 1985); see also David Ward, *Chronicles of Darkness* (London, 1989), and *Representing Others: White Views of Indigenous Peoples*, ed. Mick Gidley (Exeter, 1992).

[2] Kingsley, *Travels in West Africa*, abridged version, p. 14.

[3] Tim Youngs, *Travellers in Africa. British Travelogues, 1850-1900* (Manchester, 1994), p. 209.

her frequently noted[1] inconsistencies clustering around questions of sexual identity, as in the following passage:

> The African's want of making it clear in his language whether he is referring to an animate or an inanimate thing, has landed me in many a dilemma, and his foolishness in not having a male and female gender in his languages amounts to a nuisance, and has nearly, at one fell swoop, turned my hairs gray, and brought them in sorrow to the grave. For example, I am a most lady-like person and yet get constantly called 'Sir'. I hasten to assure you I never even wear a masculine collar and tie, and as for encasing the more earthward extremities of my anatomy in – you know what I mean – well, I would rather perish on a public scaffold.

Kingsley then narrates an anecdote about a trader who, when she sends him a message asking him for a change of clothes, is told by a native servant that "White man live for come from X", and who consequently, in a note headed "Dear Old Man", offers her his shirts and trousers:

> Had there been any smelling salts or sal volatile in this subdivision of the Ethiopian region I should have forthwith fainted on reading this, but I well knew there was not, so I blushed until the steam from my soaking clothes (for I truly was 'in a deuce of a mess') went up in a cloud ...[2]

In her skittish avoidance of the terms "legs" and "trousers" – which, like the un-ladylike "deuce of a mess", only enter her text as quotations from the trader's note – Kingsley clearly plays to reader expectations; even so, her deliberate exploitation of sexual/textual ambiguities reflects the fact that Kingsley travels as an individual who is marginalised in her own society by her gender, but in Africa belongs to a supposedly superior "race".

However, these ambiguities also result from the genderedness of the genre which Kingsley had adopted, the travelogue, especially as developed by famous late eighteenth- and nineteenth-century explorers in Africa such as Mungo Park, David Livingstone, Henry Morton Stanley, or Richard Burton. As Mary Louise Pratt has argued in her controversial study *Imperial Eyes. Travel Writing and Transculturation*[3], the typical stance of the explorer is that of the "Monarch of all I survey": the white explorer usually

---

[1] For example by Shirley Foster, *Across New Worlds: Nineteenth-Century Women Travellers and Their Writing* (Hemel Hempstead, 1990).

[2] Kingsley, *Travels in West Africa*, abridged version, pp. 205-206.

[3] Mary Louise Pratt, *Imperial Eyes. Travel Writing and Transculturation* (London, 1992), particularly pp. 201-227; see also Sara Mills, *Discourses of Difference. An Analysis of Women's Travel Writing and Colonialism* (London, 1991); Karen R. Lawrence, *Penelope Voyages. Women and Travel in the British Literary Tradition* (Ithaca, 1994).

positions himself on a hill, with a virginal land spread out before him in all its unspoiled beauty, and awaiting his civilising touch. Another, related form of self-representation in these male-authored travel narratives is that of the big-game hunter. In both scenarios, the position of authority which the traveller assumes vis-à-vis the African landscape and its inhabitants (non-human as well as human) is translated into the relationship between the travel writer and his readers.

In *Travels in West Africa*, Kingsley repeatedly expresses her admiration of her male predecessors, and follows in their footsteps; thus, when she has climbed Mungo Lah Lobeh, she remarks that Richard Burton has been there before her, but has reached the summit by a different route. At the same time, she is clearly aware of the difficulties which beset her appropriation of their genre; on the surface of her text, this awareness manifests itself in stylistic inconsistencies, often self-parodic in nature, as when, in the following passage, she is stuck in a swamp which she suspects to be tidal:

> No need for an old coaster like me to look at that sort of thing twice to know what it meant, and feeling it was a situation more suited to Mr Stanley than myself, I attempted to emulate his methods and addressed my men. 'Boys', said I, 'this beastly hole is tidal, and the tide is coming in. As it took us two hours to get to this sainted swamp, it's time we started out, one time, and the nearest way [...]'. The boys took the hint.[1]

The two tropes of the "Monarch of all I survey" and of the big-game hunter are similarly subjected to a self-ironic treatment. In Kingsley's text, no great panoramas ever reveal themselves to the delighted eyes of the traveller: mostly, she crosses swamps, invariably highlighting those situations in which her boat capsizes so that she is not even at eye-level with her African landscapes (let alone capable of viewing them from above), but quite literally disappears into them. When she is on terra firma, she tends to focus on her spectacular falls, for example into pits dug by native hunters. Finally, on the one occasion on which she does gain higher ground, on the Mungo Lah Lobeh, she is blinded by an impenetrable fog; she adds a few rocks to a cairn built by her predecessors, and puts her card among them, "merely as a civility to Mungo, a civility his majesty will soon turn into pulp. Not that it matters – what is done is done."[2]

Whereas it may just be possible to ascribe Kingsley's comparatively restricted perspective to the accidentals of her journey – her route, or the

---

[1] Kingsley, *Travels in West Africa*, abridged version, p. 127.
[2] Ibid., p. 254.

weather – her refusal to model herself after a big-game hunter is rather more deliberate – "I am habitually kind to animals, and besides I do not think it is ladylike to go shooting things with a gun" – though again not unhedged with ambiguities. One night, she is awoken by a commotion outside her tent, and when she rushes out to investigate, she discovers a leopard, on which she "fires" two native stools, followed by an earthen watercooler, thus converting domestic articles to non-domestic use: "Do not mistake this for a sporting adventure. I no more thought it was a leopard than that it was a lotus when I joined the fight."[1] At the same time, and throughout *Travels in West Africa*, Kingsley herself employs the language of big-game hunting, and quite unselfconsciously assumes the position of authority on which it is predicated, as when she "stalk[s] the wild West African idea", "net[s] one reason for the advantage of possessing a white man's eyeball", and cautions that "if you go hunting the African idea with the flag of your own religion or opinions floating ostentatiously over you, you will similarly get a very poor bag."[2]

If in *Travels in West Africa* the relationship of mastery between the seer and the seen is compromised by the seer's gender, the same applies to the relationship between the travel writer and her readers. In a period in which the discipline of ethnography is undergoing rapid re-orientation, Kingsley stresses the advantages of modern fieldwork over the methods of traditional, more speculative – "armchair" – anthropology. At the same time, her insistence on the validity of her own research is undercut by her self-representation: not only as a traveller, but also as a fieldworker Kingsley quite literally "stumbles" across her discoveries, and her readers "happen" upon them, equally inadvertently, in the middle of comic interludes. Again, as in the relationship between the seer and the seen, the instabilities of the travel writer/reader relationship are reflected on the stylistic level of her text: on the one hand, Kingsley's African is invariably male, as are the animals which she encounters; for Kingsley, as for the male ethnographers and zoologists of her period, the male specimen of a genus constitutes the norm, so that, for example, the British missionary Mary Slessor becomes an instance of "what one white can do [...]. Only the sort of man Mary Slessor represents is rare."[3] On the other hand, Kingsley employs a number of strategies which, in Lakoff's early, and admittedly problematic study of "language and woman's place"[4], are classified as characteristically femi-

---

[1] Ibid., pp. 228-229.
[2] Ibid., pp. 161-164; for a discussion of these aspects of Kingsley's texts see Mills, *Discourses of Difference*, pp. 158-162, and Lawrence, *Penelope Voyages*, pp. 130-153.
[3] Kingsley, *Travels in West Africa*, abridged version, p. 19.
[4] Robin Lakoff, *Language and Woman's Place* (New York, 1975).

nine: she repeatedly uses terms like "nice" or "charming", and she draws upon a highly differentiated repertoire of terms denoting colours, and fabrics. Kingsley's meadows are studded with "bright blue flannelly-looking flowers", her forests have "heavily-lichened-tasselled" fringes, and she distinguishes between a "white, gauze-like" and a "wool-blanket" mist.

Ethnographic fieldwork, as Mary Louise Pratt, among others, has noted[1], produces an authority which is anchored in subjective experience; but the text to result from this experience must conform to the norms of a scientific discourse which is characterised by the effacement of the experiencing subject. Kingsley tries to solve this dilemma by splitting, as it were, her West African narrative into the more subjective *Travels in West Africa* and the more scientific *West African Studies*. In both texts, and particularly in the former, her attempts to mediate between the two discourses are rendered ineffectual, as has already been suggested, by the expectations of her Victorian readers, who grant Victorian women writers a position of authority only if they *do not* appear to efface the experiencing subject – a subject, furthermore, whose field of expertise is the domestic; cannibalism, violence, and unusual sexual practices, the stuff travel narratives about Africa are made of, are by definition excluded from this field.[2]

As may by now have become evident, however, it is not only personal and scientific discourses which intersect in *Travels in West Africa*, but also two discourses of alterity, the Africanist and the patriarchal. The two coalesce, in a powerful conjunction of the savage and the feminine, in the image of Africa as a virgin land, to be penetrated by the (male) explorer.[3] Again, Kingsley's appropriation of this image is fraught with sexual/textual ambiguities: she does portray Africa as a woman – specifically, as John Keats's "La Belle Dame Sans Merci" – but, in the process, she subtly transforms the relationship of power between the conqueror and the (about to be) conquered into one between equals:

> I succumbed to the charm of the Coast as soon as I left Sierra Leone on my first voyage out, and I saw more than enough during that voyage to make me recognise that there was any amount of work for me doing down there. So I warned the Coast I was coming back again and the Coast did not believe me; and on my re-

---

[1] Mary Louise Pratt, "Fieldwork in Common Places", in: *Writing Culture. The Poetics and Politics of Ethnography*, eds. James Clifford and George E. Marcus (Berkeley, 1986), pp. 27-50; see also, in the same volume, James Clifford, "On Ethnographic Allegory", pp. 98-121.

[2] See Lawrence, *Penelope Voyages*, "Introduction" and Ch. 3, particularly pp. 125-130; see also Stevenson, *Victorian Women Travel Writers in Africa*, p. 147.

[3] See Louis Montrose, "The Work of Gender in the Discourse of Discovery", in *New World Encounters*, ed. Stephen Greenblatt (Berkeley, 1993), pp. 177-217.

turn to it a second time displayed a genuine surprise, and formed an even higher opinion of my folly than it had formed on my first acquaintance, which is saying a good deal.[1]

If this passage indicates an awareness on Kingsley's part of the way in which constructions of gender and race are based upon difference, with the woman and/or "the African" both perceived as deviating from the cultural norms of white masculinity, one might expect that it is, in particular, in the depiction of the African (male or female) Other that *Travels in West Africa* explore these analogies. The following, and concluding, sections of this paper will be dedicated to this aspect of Kingsley's text.

One ethnic group to which Kingsley pays particular attention, and for which she develops what might almost be called fellow feeling, are the Fang, or "Fans", as she calls them[2], who were marginalised in their West African environment because of their supposed cannibalism. Even before Kingsley's own sojourn among them, the Fang had become a favourite topic of ethnographic speculation because they were regarded as comparatively untouched by Western civilisation.[3] Kingsley writes:

> The cannibalism of the Fans, although a prevalent habit, is no danger, I think, to white people, except as regards the bother it gives one in preventing one's black companions from getting eaten. The Fan is not a cannibal from sacrificial motives like the Negro. He does it in his common sense way. Man's flesh, he says, is good to eat, very good, and he wishes you would try it. Oh dear no, he never eats it himself, but the next door town does. He is always very much abused for eating his relations, but he really does not do this. He will eat his next door neighbour's relations and sell his own deceased to his next door neighbour in return, but he does not buy slaves and fatten them up for his table as some of the Middle Congo tribes I know of do.[4]

---

[1] Mary Kingsley, *Travels in West Africa. Congo Français, Corisco and Cameroons*, ed. John E. Flint (London, ³1965), pp. 11-12.

[2] The Fang, collectively: as has already been noted, Kingsley does not show any particular interest in female, as opposed to male, Africans, and if she describes the latter at all, she does so in the same terms as her male contemporaries: "dark, but comely" (borrowing from the Song of Solomon, of course).

[3] See Frank, *A Voyager Out*, 165.

[4] Kingsley, *Travels in West Africa*, abridged version, p. 145; the chapter in which this passage occurs is entitled, tellingly, "Pursuits and Pastimes of my Friends the Fans." The question of anthropophagy cannot be addressed adequately in this context; what Kingsley's passage shows, though, is that accusing one's neighbour of cannibalism is, primarily, a way of marking the difference between one's own "civilization" (indeed, perhaps, humanity), and the neighbour's lack of it.

Kingsley's sympathies with the Fang, as with other West African ethnic groups, seem to be called forth by the very social practices which, in the literature on Africa of her time, were considered as crying out for Western intervention in "the black continent": cannibalism, polygamy, slavery, and fetishism. Even the ritual killing of twins, to the eradication of which practice Mary Slessor's missionary work is devoted, is for Kingsley embedded in a specific culture, and has its specific functions in it. In speculating upon the motives behind these and other African "abominations", Kingsley displays an enormous capacity for change of cultural perspective; she demands the same cultural relativism from her readers when she argues, for example, that in some West African societies the missionaries' endeavours to dissuade the dependents of a dead chief from providing him with a retinue for the underworld in the form of his wives and slaves are misguided:

> Try and imagine yourself how abhorrent it must be to send down a dear and honoured relative to the danger of his being returned shortly as a slave.[1]

While African customs, Kingsley suggests, may seem strange, even abhorrent, to Western eyes, they serve their – clearly delineated – purpose in their respective societies. Christianisation, according to her, alienates Africans from their own cultures without fully replacing the African system of social norms and values which it has destabilised; as the example of Sierra Leone, with its long history of Christianisation, indicates, the result is, in Kingsley's term, "degeneration".

Kingsley also repeatedly rejects the contemporary "philanthropist" attitude towards "the African" as, phylogenetically speaking, on a lower rung of the evolutionary ladder. However, her own "racist"[2] view of the place of "the African" in the evolutionary scheme strikes a modern reader as even less palatable: for her, "the coloured races" do not represent a less advanced version of the same human species, but belong to another species altogether:

> The difficulties that have arisen from their teaching have come primarily from the failure of the missionary to recognise the difference between the African and themselves as being a difference not of degree but of kind. I am aware that they are supported in this idea by several eminent ethnologists; but still there are a large number of anatomical facts that point the other way, and a far larger number still

---

[1] Kingsley, *Travels in West Africa*, abridged version, p. 198.

[2] The terms "philanthropist" and "racist" are taken from the contemporary (that is, Victorian and Edwardian) debate on race; see Helen Callaway, *Gender, Culture and Empire. European Women in Colonial Nigeria* (Champaign, 1987), p. 31.

relating to the mental attributes, and I feel certain that a black man is no more an undeveloped white man than a rabbit is an undeveloped hare ...[1]

It is for this reason that Western attempts at civilising "the African" are doomed to failure. The passage, however, continues:

... and the mental difference between the two races is very similar to that between men and women among ourselves. A great woman, either mentally or physically, will excel an indifferent man, but no woman ever equals a really great man.

In patriarchal discourses of alterity, there are two methods of accounting for the Otherness of women, the quantitative and the qualitative: women can either be perceived as lesser men, in which case it might be possible, as British feminists of the seventeenth and eighteenth centuries such as Mary Astell, Catherine Macaulay, or Mary Wollstonecraft asserted, to educate them up to the level of men. Alternatively, and this is the culturally dominant construction of gender difference in Victorian Britain, women and men can be seen as different in kind, not in degree, so that female and male qualities complement one another; women, therefore, cannot, indeed should not, be educated like men – just as Africans cannot, indeed, should not, be educated up to the level of the whites. Kingsley, then, is aware of the nexus between gender and race: as the (male) African is "not keen on mountaineering in the civilisation range", he will never be able to follow the white woman up to her summit – although that, like Kingsley's own Mungo Lah Lobeh, may well be shrouded in fog.

The passages just quoted occur in the middle of a chapter entitled "Trade and Labour in West Africa", and primarily dedicated to the economic aspects of colonisation, specifically to the role of the British traders in West

---

[1] Kingsley, *Travels in West Africa. Congo Français, Corisco and Cameroons.* ed. Flint, p. 659; see also p. 680: "I do not believe that the white race will ever drag the black up to their own particular summit in the mountain range of civilisation. Both polygamy and slavery are, for divers reasons, essential to the well-being of Africa – at any rate for those vast regions of it that are agricultural, and these two institutions will necessitate the African having a summit to himself. Only – alas! for the energetic reformer – the African is not keen on mountaineering in the civilisation range. He prefers remaining down below and being comfortable. He is not conceited about this; he admires the higher culture very much, and the people who inconvenience themselves by going for it – but do it himself? NO. And if he is dragged up into the higher regions of a self-abnegatory religion, six times in ten he falls back damaged, a morally maimed man, into his old swampy country fashion valley."

Africa, and to their import of alcoholic beverages to West Africa.[1] That trade, in particular, was condemned by British missionaries, who also complained that West Africans educated in missionary schools were discriminated against by the traders, who saw them as potential competitors. On both issues – issues on which the missionaries were increasingly successful in converting local administrators in the colonies as well as public opinion in Britain to their point of view – Kingsley takes the position of the traders: she denies that the import of alcohol has a damaging effect on African societies, and she considers the missionaries' – and, for that matter, the colonial administrators' – activities to be both misdirected and, ultimately, futile. For Kingsley, the traders are a marginalised – and much maligned – group, a group, furthermore, which, during her time in West Africa, treated her as an equal, not least because Kingsley supported herself on her journeys partly by trading. Apparently – and, in the light of the economic imbalance of power between British traders and their West African counterparts, somewhat naively – Kingsley regards the area of trade as one in which diverse ethnic groups can interact non-hierarchically on the basis of their mutual interests.

However, Kingsley claims, in the West African market-place it is not only diverse ethnic groups but also men and women who can barter as equals: *trade English*, the language in which Kingsley communicates with her African partners, is, of course, the very language which generates the gender ambiguities of "White man live for come from X" described above.

From this perspective, Kingsley would have enjoyed the tribute paid to her after her death by Sir George Goldie, and elaborated upon gallantly by one of her biographers, Cecil Howard:

> 'She had the brain of a man and the heart of a woman.' In these words Sir George Goldie summed up the qualities of one who challenges comparison with England's greatest men in judgement, courage, and breadth of understanding, but who yet possessed the sympathy and the tenderness of a woman.[2]

---

[1] On the role of the traders in what might be called the "economy" of *Travels in West Africa* see John E. Flint, "Mary Kingsley: A Reassessment", *Journal of African History*, 4 (1963), 95-104.

[2] Cecil Howard, *Mary Kingsley* (London, 1957), p. 225.